Reform Catholicism and the International Suppression of the Jesuits, 1554-1791

CATHOLIC HISTORICAL REVIEW

CATHOLIC HISTORICAL REVIEW

REFORM CATHOLICISM AND THE INTERNATIONAL SUPPRESSION OF THE JESUITS, 1554-1791

Dale K. Van Kley

Yale
UNIVERSITY
PRESS
New Haven & London

Published with assistance from the Annie Burr Lewis Fund.

Copyright © 2018 by Yale University.
All rights reserved.
This book may not be reproduced, in whole or in part, including illustrations,
in any form (beyond that copying permitted by Sections 107 and 108 of the U.S.
Copyright Law and except by reviewers for the public press),
without written permission from the publishers.

Yale University Press books may be purchased in quantity for educational,
business, or promotional use. For information, please e-mail sales.press@yale.edu
(U.S. office) or sales@yaleup.co.uk (U.K. office).
Set in PostScript Electra type by Westchester Publishing Services,
Danbury, Connecticut.
Printed in the United States of America.

Library of Congress Control Number: 2017951821
ISBN 978-0-300-22846-5 (hardcover: alk. paper)

A catalogue record for this book is available from the British Library.

This paper meets the requirements of ANSI/NISO Z39.48-1992
(Permanence of Paper).

10   9   8   7   6   5   4   3   2   1

*For Sandra
and
our children,
Annique, Erik, and Kristen*

CONTENTS

PART III REFORM CATHOLICISM AND THE ULTRAMONTANIST INTERNATIONAL

PREFACE

This book is largely an accident. The subject of what in it is called "Reform Catholicism" and its agency in the international suppression of the Society of Jesus between Portugal's expulsion of its Jesuits in 1759 and the papal suppression of the Society in 1773 was supposed to be a chapter in another book on the trajectory of Reform Catholicism from the mid-eighteenth century until the end of the French Revolution, when Napoleon Bonaparte's concordat with the papacy in 1801 gave this cause the coup de grâce. The intended trajectory of that book is sketched out in an essay entitled "Catholic Conciliar Reform in an Age of Anti-Catholic Revolution, 1758–1801," published in 2001 in a book of essays entitled *Religion and Politics in Enlightenment Europe,* edited by James E. Bradley and myself. Although fragments and spinoffs from that book project have steadily appeared in two coedited books and extended essays here and there, the book itself—alas—remains unfinished in manuscript and may or may not yet happen, depending on health and—as I write—the possibility of tranquillity of political conscience.

I fancied that writing a chapter on Reform Catholicism and the international suppression of the Jesuits would be easy because the thesis of my first book on Jansenism and the suppression of the Society in France seemed to have survived without too many cuts and bruises. Although the international turn of my post-2000 research had obliged me to think of Jansenism as a component of a European-wide Reform Catholicism after 1750, I had already tried to factor that adjustment into an entry on the international suppression for Timothy Tackett and Stewart Brown's *Cambridge History of Christianity* for the early modern period in 2003. Research in contiguous areas in the course of previous book projects had meanwhile turned up additional bits and fragments of corroborative evidence, all of it raw material for such a chapter.

As things turned out, however, I did not know what I thought I knew and needed to know about the long-term fabrication of Catholic anti-Jesuitism—an essential component of the chapter I contemplated—nor was I any longer abreast of the literature on the Portuguese and Spanish expulsions, which had exploded in both languages as well as in Italian since 2003. Filling the first lacuna eventually took on the dimensions of a stand-alone essay, while my getting up to speed on the recent literature on the Portuguese and Spanish cases was not speedy at all, in good part because these Iberian languages are the last and most precarious of the additions to my linguistic capacities. Along the way, the work of sketching out accounts of the "events" of the suppression in France and the expulsions in Portugal, Spain, and the two Bourbon Italian states wooed me into a interim project of trying my hand at a small book hitching the long history of the largely French ideology of Catholic anti-Jesuitism to the events in which it visibly played a part.

But by the time the narrative reached the papal dissolution of the Society in 1773, this short book had grown so long that it seemed best to treat anti-Jesuitism as the negative agenda of Reform Catholicism and, by bookending the whole with chapters on Reform Catholicism before and after the suppression of the Jesuits, fulfill the original intention of the still unwritten chapter while propounding many if not all the theses of a hopelessly interrupted book. Far too many years later, and for whatever its worth, this book is the accidental result.

Let this story be a cautionary tale for those historians who suppose that at an advanced stage of their lives and careers they can enlarge what had hitherto been their chronological and geographical "field" of specialization and launch out in international directions, especially if doing so entails archival research and additional languages. At the very least, they should think twice. Still, the comparative dimension is enlightening, and it proved valuable for undergraduate courses in early modern European history, but most especially for graduate education at Ohio State University, where only half of the doctoral dissertations with which I had to do confined themselves within the parameters of French history. Although I never taught them at Ohio State, even courses on French history in particular would benefit from a more comparative dimension, in that it is impossible to single out the culturally or politically salient without comparison with the states and cultures surrounding France.

Further, a book on the international suppression of the Society of Jesus is sorely needed. Making retrospective contact with the sixteenth-century Reformations and prospective contact with the French Revolution, the international suppression of the Jesuits is arguably the most important event in European Christianity—perhaps European history *tout court*—between them. And yet in English we have only national histories except for books of essays such as Jeffrey Burson and Jonathan Wright's recent *The Jesuit Suppression in Global Context*. Translated into English though it is, Ludwig Pastor's always indispensable *History of the Popes* includes all the other matters demanding papal attention in an account that he stretches through three volumes, while José Antonio Ferrer Benimeli's summary *Expulsión y extinción de los jesuitas* slights France, and Christine Vogel's stunning and inexhaustible *Der Untergang der Gesellschaft Jesu als Europäisches Medienereignis (1758–1773)* focuses laser-like on publicity and the role of the anti-Jesuit press.

As a very thesis-oriented book about the actions and ideology of the Jesuits' enemies and suppressors, this book perforce neglects all the misfortunes and miseries suffered by the Jesuit victims of persecution, for which recent studies by Niccolò Guasti and Immaculada Arriaga as well as Ferrer Benimeli's are indispensable. Even as a thesis-oriented book about the expellers, however, a consequence of its largely accidental and incidental origin is that it does not directly draw on archival sources in Rome, and in the best of worlds I would have not only looked at the relevant reports of papal nuncios with my own eyes but also undertaken a thorough examination of the correspondence of the Vatican librarian Giovanni Gaetano Bottari in Rome's Bibliotheca dell'Accademia Nationale dei Lincei e Corsiniana with the question of his anti-Jesuit salon or Archetto's role in the international suppression in mind. Fortunately, however, the historians Sidorio Pinedo and Mar García Arenas have largely done for Spain and Portugal what I have been able to do for France, making it possible to put the various pieces of a quasi-conspiratorial puzzle together. Historians are exceptionally averse to conspiracy theories, and this one is no exception. Something strongly conspiratorial nonetheless haunts the story of the international suppression of the Jesuits; it is hard to dismiss out of hand the unhappy Jesuit general Lorenzo Ricci's pointing at a *cabala giansenista* as its final if not always efficient cause. I have every confidence that further research there would only strengthen the more nuanced argument here.

That a lot of the funded research if not time for another book went into the making of this one means that I must profusely acknowledge the support I received from Oxford University's All Souls College for a Michaelmas term's stay in 2001, from the National Endowment of the Humanities for a year's research at Chicago's Newberry Library in 2002–2003, from the Fulbright Commission for five months in Paris the same year, and from the University of Madison–Wisconsin's Institute for Research in the Humanities for a Solmsen Fellowship for writing in 2005–2006. For summertime research in Utrecht and Paris during my tenure at Ohio State University from 1998 through 2013 I thank both the university and its history department for a modest but life-saving research fund.

For the process of research hither and yon I thank the unfailing assistance of the staff of the Newberry Library and the help and camaraderie of David Sorkin, Loretta Freiling, and Lee Wandel at the IRH at the University of Wisconsin–Madison. I reserve a very special word of gratitude for the help and also friendship of archivists and historians Fabien Vandemarck and Valérie Guittienne-Mürger of the Bibliothèque de Port-Royal in Paris and Huib Leeuwenberg and his wife, Froukje, of Het Utrechts Archief in Utrecht. (Huib and Froukje also extended their hospitality to the shelter of their vacant house in Vianen during the summer of 1998, for which my wife, Sandra, and I only inadequately thanked them by nursing one of their egg-laying hens back to health.) My expressions of gratitude to the staffs of the Archives nationales and des Affaires etrangères and the Bibliothèque nationale, de l'Arsenal, de Saint-Sulpice, and Mazarine, all in Paris, are of long standing; I reiterate them here.

For their collegial patience and help in reading and critiquing chapters inflicted on them by me I thank my professional colleagues James Bartholomew of Ohio State, Jeffrey Burson of Georgia Southern, Thomas Kaiser of the University of Arkansas at Little Rock, and most especially my former graduate students Daniel Watkins of the University of Northern Florida and Mircea Platon, now editor in chief of the Romanian literary journal *Convorbiri Literate*. I could not have written the chapter on Spain and Portugal without the help of my former graduate student Andrea Smit of Geneva College and above all Niccolò Guasti of the Università degli Studi di Foggia, whose magisterial book on the expulsion of the Jesuits from Spain was a lifeline for someone temporarily totally out of his depth. Nor would I ever have dared to part with the manuscript at all had it not been for the encouragement of Yale University Press's assistant editor Erica Hanson, who, now a stay-at-home mother, acted as this book's midwife by seeing in it a potential about which I labored in chronic doubt.

Last and most I thank Sandra and our now-adult children, Annique, Erik, and Kristen, for their unfailing love but equally unfailing patience with and forgiveness for the fretful inattention of a supposedly retired husband and father who persists in agonizing over all-too-numerous blank pages instead of paying more mind to them.

REFORM CATHOLICISM AND THE INTERNATIONAL SUPPRESSION OF THE JESUITS, 1554-1791

INTRODUCTION

In Paris on the Feast of the Assumption in 1535, seven men who had become friends while earning Master of Arts degrees at the University of Paris gathered in the chapel of Saint-Denis at the foot of Montmartre and, after one of their number had celebrated Mass, took a solemn vow to undertake a pilgrimage to the Holy Land and there work for the good of souls or offer to do the same for the pope elsewhere if the voyage proved impossible. But after wars and rumors of wars continued to block passage and to confine their ministries to preaching and the poor in Venice and elsewhere in Italy, these seven, joined by three other recent recipients of arts degrees, reconvened in Rome in 1539 and, having all meanwhile been ordained, these "companions of Jesus," as they had been calling themselves, resolved to seek papal authorization to form a new religious order that unlike other orders would vow to place themselves especially at the papacy's disposition for missions.

Against high odds they succeeded in persuading Pope Paul III, who instituted the new society with the bull *Regimini militantis ecclesiae* as the Society of Jesus on 27 September 1540. Thereupon they elected their original magnet, a Basque-born nobleman named Iñigo or Ignatius de Loyola, as their general and began their self-defined mission. Besides Ignatius, the other companions at that point included the fellow Spaniards Diego Laínez, Alfonso Salmerón, and Francisco Xavier, the Portuguese Nicolás Bobadilla and Simâo Rodrigues, and the Frenchmen Paschase Broët, Jean Codure, Pierre Favre, and Claude Jay.[1]

These ten "Jesuits," as they soon became known, defined their mission with the formula of furthering the "progress of souls in Christian life and doctrine and the propagation of the faith," meaning that like the Dominicans and Franciscans before them they would devote themselves to the preaching of the word, the administration of the sacraments, and the spreading of the faith by missions both in Europe and in newly discovered lands abroad. In these capacities they soon accomplished wonders. By the time Julius III reaffirmed and expanded the new Society in 1550, the support of the Portuguese king John III had enabled Xavier to establish new missionary beachheads in India, the Moluccas, and Japan and the newcomer Manuel de Nóbrega to penetrate the Brazilin hinterlands. Meanwhile, in Europe Broët had gone as a papal nuncio to Ireland; Laínez and Salmerón had advised cardinals at the Council of Trent; Jay and another recruit, Pieter de Hondt, or Canisius, had begun to take stock of the new Lutheran challenge as lecturers in Ingolstadt; and they and all the others to confess, catechize, preach, and minister to the sick and poor.

The experience of lecturing in churches and universities plus the need to give its new recruits the education all the founders had received in Paris soon lured the Society into establishing its own colleges. At first merely residences for novices and "scholastics" to pursue their studies at nearby universities, a few, such as those in Gandía in Spain and Messina in Sicily, became colleges in their own right; in a move unprecedented for a religious order, the Society also began to accept secular students free of any charge. Although the only kind of teaching envisioned by his original plan was catechetical instruction for children, in 1551 Loyola began to order the opening of such colleges for all comers wherever possible, and by the time he died in 1556 Catholic Europe and the missions already contained around thirty-five colleges manned by many of the thousand Jesuits who had joined the Society by then. For their part the colleges offered eight years of study and a strongly humanist curriculum based on Latin grammar, rhetoric, and Greek and Latin classical literature plus some theological and ethical instruction on the assumption that grace corrected and completed pagan "nature." Some even became doctoral-conferring universities, beginning with the Roman College in 1551, although more often Jesuits with the support of princes began to dominate the theological faculties of existing Catholic universities. In all cases, however—and in contrast to the colleges—they continued to hew to an Aristotelian-based and largely Thomist scholastic philosophy and theology.

As time went on, the colleges all but took the place of residences. With a chapel or church and a Marian confraternity or sodality attached, the colleges became ideal means of cultivating the good will of surrounding townspeople and the wealthy and most influential members of the nobility and bourgeoisie. With the support of local bishops, the colleges and their churches also served as bases from which the Jesuits undertook their characteristic and sometimes month-long domestic missions to the surrounding rural population that typically began with preaching, catechesis, and confessions and ended with processions, mass communions, and the founding of Marian confraternities. In parts of France and along the borderlands between the Protestant German and Catholic states plus Poland, the Jesuit educational institutions and catechetical acumen also acted as the chief antidotes to Lutheran and Calvinist religious "heresy," as Germany's "second apostle" Canisius perceived it, even as early as during Ignatius's lifetime.

Along with its privileged relation to the papacy and support of the high nobility, the Society's ethical and doctrinal prowess is what made Jesuits the royal confessors and preachers of choice for just about all the ruling Catholic dynasties by the mid-seventeenth century. During that century of religious controversy and warfare, the conspicuous presence of Jesuits in these politically influential positions was what chiefly earned the Jesuits the dubious reputation of the "shock troops" of the Catholic Counter-Reformation. But far from hindering it, that reputation only augmented the growth, influence, and power of a society that had every reason to celebrate the centennial of its founding during the bloodiest phase of the Thirty Years' War in 1640.

In good part, the secret of its success lay in the formulae left by its founder, Loyola, who gave up an intended courtly and military career after he lost an intact right leg to French artillery in 1521 only to find another career by reading the lives of Jesus and the saints while recovering in the family castle. He would now be a soldier for Jesus in his new lord's contest with Satan for the salvation of his own soul and that of others.

The first of these formulae are contained in his *Spiritual Exercises*, which in propositional directives distilled and programized his spiritual restoration after a searing and near-death ascetic experience while Ignatius was lingering at Manresa near Barcelona on his way to a pilgrimage to Jerusalem.[2] Designed to be interiorized under guidance of a director, Ignatius's spiritual manual was not an exercise in spiritual edification but rather a practical step-by-step guide toward the goal of replacing the last trace of self-love with love for God as exemplified and directed by the life, death, and resurrection of Christ. The exercitants were therefore like Christ to be poor and humble, the better to serve and teach others in obedience to God unto suffering and death, not only for the progress of their own souls but also for the salvation of others in the world and for "the greater glory of God" and Christ's kingdom, in opposition to that of Satan.

Although the dedication to advance the greater glory of God in all vocations in the world bears a certain comparison to Calvinism, the "election" to do so was for Ignatius's exercitants the result not of any preordained calling but of a deliberate choice, just as their frequent requests for divine grace does not obscure their will's paradoxical role in the decision to divest themsleves of it in favor of Christ's. Other traits distinguish the *Exercises* from the mystical tradition. While for mystics the senses and its images were a scaffolding to be discarded on their way to a state of self-negating "indifference" in total union with God, for Ignatian exercitants the senses enabled them to see "Christ in all things" while a state of "indifference" empowered a life of undistracted action in the world. The *Exercises* also differed from Cenobite and in particular Benedictine spirituality in that while praise and prayer in these orders were performed audibly in a community and for the world, in the *Exercises* both became largely individual, mental, and a constant companion of and prelude to Christ-like action in the world.

What Ignatius's spiritual manual was to the directed exercitant, the Society's future constitutions would be to the Jesuits. Although outlined in anticipation of papal approval by six of the first future Jesuits in Rome in the spring of 1539, the Society's constitutions did not receive finished form until Loyola turned to the task with secretarial help from Juan de Polanco between 1547 and 1551. In spirit and purpose the constitutions picked up where the *Exercises* left off and similarly projected the spiritual maturation of the Jesuit from his entrance into the Society until death, while making provision for differences in individual abilities and temperaments. True to the outline of 1539, the finished constitutions required a special vow of obedience to the papacy by its most senior members. To that obedience, however, they added the unquestioning obedience by all Jesuits to their superiors at every level of a hierarchy that culminated in a lifelong superior general who in turn appointed those superiors while answering only to the general assembly that had elected him. As the composition of the constitutions progressed, Ignatius emphasized the importance of obedience in proportion to distance from the center, as far-flung Jesuits in four continents threatened to escape from central control.

This itinerancy required by a Society that had come to specialize in teaching and missions translated obedience into a readiness to go anywhere at the superior's command; it also entailed discarding the hitherto characteristic monastic practices of communal chanting of the divine office, permanent residence in the same community, and both collective decision making and election of superiors by these communities meeting in chapters. In these respects the Society of Jesus differed even from the mendicant orders it otherwise most resembled. So did its graded selectivity that after a two-year novitiate divided the survivors into temporal helpers or coadjutors and eight-year students or scholastics who took "simple" vows and these in turn into spiritual coadjutors, or "professed fathers," who took final vows. At the top level, professed fathers alone swore the solemn vow of obedience to the papacy; at whatever level, no Jesuit was secure until he took final vows. Hierarchy, obedience, mobility, and selectivity— these are the qualities that came to characterize Ignatius's new Christian militia dedicated in principle to doing everything for "greater glory of God."

Animated and sustained by these living documents, a hundred years after its birth the Society numbered sixteen thousand Jesuits divided into forty provinces organized into national assistancies, while its two hundred and some colleges in Europe educated the cream of the aristocracy. Although it had lost its Japanese mission to persecution at the outset of the century, it had added missions in China, Malabar India, the Philippines, all of Spanish America, and French North America. Meanwhile both Loyola and Xavier had achieved canonization, and the Society had become all but synonymous with baroque art and architecture. The Society, moreover, continued to grow in cultural reach and numbers until midway through the eighteenth century, when it stood at twenty-two thousand members, ran about eight hundred colleges and seminaries, governed or otherwise dominated most of theological faculties in the universities in Catholic Europe outside France, shouldered most of the Catholic Church's mission work from the Americas to southeast Asia, and still provided the preachers and confessors to most of the Catholic royal courts in Europe.

Yet it was precisely in 1750 that the Society's fortunes began seriously to go south, quite literally so when Braganza Portugal expelled all the Jesuits from both the metropolis and the colonies in 1759, followed by Bourbon Spain, Naples, and Parma in 1768. Meanwhile, in Bourbon France the royal law courts, or parlements, had maneuvered a reluctant King Louis XV to suppress the Society in stages from 1761 and 1764, whereupon the other Bourbon states plus Portugal subsequently prevailed upon the same king to cooperate in putting pressure on the papacy to dissolve the whole Society, which Pope Clement XIV finally did in 1773. By the time all this dust had settled, hundreds of elite colleges and some theological faculties had to find new staff members, as many lay sodalities lost their sponsors, and Catholic mission fields around the world lay largely untended. As for the Jesuits themselves, a few like the Portuguese Jesuit Gabriel Malagrida had suffered trial and execution, many more like the general Lorenzo Ricci had spent years in prison, hundreds had died during the long voyages from the colonial missions back to Europe, thousands faced displacement from their homelands or colonial countries of adoption to the Papal States or later elsewhere, and all underwent various degrees of secularization.

More event-like than either the Protestant Reformation before it or the French Revolution soon after it, to either of which it is comparable in religious importance, the international suppression of the Society of Jesus is nonetheless not a single event but a series of discrete national expulsions and a suppression clustered during a decade-long span, and it would seem to demand more than a collection of sundry gripes and grievances to explain the apparent contagion.

In retrospect, it is clear that tensions between the Society's virtues and sundry realities on the ground indeed gave rise to sundry gripes and grievances that acquired mass and made enemies over time. It was a virtue for the Society to offer and deliver free education and, more arguably, to preach and administer the sacraments to all who came their way. But the papal privileges that entitled it to do so rode roughshod over the more historically rooted prerogatives of universities to educate and of priests to save. Common to all religious orders, the vow of poverty was a theological virtue, but the need of the Society to find donors for its colleges and engage in revenue-producing commerce to finance its missions sometimes made piety look like a pretense for avarice. The total self-abnegation of taking up Christ's cross was a similarly holy goal, but the polish and urbanity needed to cultivate the good will of powers and potentates, the better to convert their subjects, sometimes made piety look like the quest for power. Humility, like poverty, was a vow taken by Jesuits as individuals, but it did little to prevent the rise of pride in the accomplishments of the whole Society that aroused the jealously of other orders. Obedience too was a theological virtue in which the Jesuits specialized, but the unity that was supposed to be its product seemed to make the Society complicit in the aberrations of every last wayward Jesuit, whether in word or deed.

But although these faults may have made for a field ripe unto an inimical sickle, no one of them nor even all of them together offer a plausible reason for what befell the Society between 1759 and 1773. A fault held against the Jesuits before 1789, but also sometimes alleged in their favor by postrevolutionary apologists, is that their retention of a sixteenth-century humanist curriculum for college and an Aristotelian-Thomist approach to natural philosophy and theology made it difficult for them to adjust to the turn toward the vernacular and to breakthroughs in natural philosophy that went into the making of the European Enlightenment. A vice for critics before and during the expulsions and suppression, the Society's putatively outdated outlook had by the mid-eighteenth century become a virtue in the eyes of postrevolutionary "conservatives" who thought that the Enlightenment had brought on an antireligious French Revolution. So great was this conviction that postrevolutionary Catholic conservatives could think of no better way to prevent the recurrence of revolution than to restore the Society of Jesus, which Pope Pius VII did in 1814. A post hoc ergo propter hoc fallacy though it obviously is, this mode of causal reasoning seemed so conclusive to nineteenth-century Catholic conservatives and anticlerical liberals alike that throughout Catholic Europe, and at least until the Spanish Civil War of 1936–1939, "liberals" who aimed to renew the Revolution or enlarge upon its unfinished work defined themselves in part by their hostility to Jesuits.

Now, nobody among the Catholic kings, statesmen, or publicists who perpetrated this suppression had or could have had anything like the French Revolution in view. With a few French exceptions, the vast majority of them opposed it, or came to oppose as it took its course. For many of them the tragic consequence of the Revolution was to have victimized the Jesuits by the same conservative causal logic that attributed the Revolution to the suppression of the Jesuits that had preceded it. That is to say that the Revolution criminalized the cause of Catholic reform in much the same way that the Protestant Reformation had criminalized the cause of Catholic Christian humanist reform in the sixteenth century.

If Catholic reformers worked to suppress the Society of Jesus in the late eighteenth century, they did so because they saw the Society as an obstacle, not to a revolution, but to a reform or restoration of a pristine Catholicism and church as they conceived them. The formal argument in the pages that follow is that it was this Reform Catholicism that gave coherence to the accumulated but otherwise disparate gripes and grievances of those on whose toes the Jesuits had stepped, while the matter is the characteristics of that eighteenth-century reformist Catholicism and the role it played in motivating—or at least legitimizing the motives of—those who effected the national expulsions between 1759 and 1768, followed by forced papal suppression in 1773. The concept of Reform Catholicism is therefore used to show the interrelation between the various national expulsions and suppressions while telling the story of each in its own terms and as best as the existing literature now permits. Finally, this account of events takes every available occasion to highlight the crucial structural differences between the French case and the others that already pointed toward a revolutionary outcome that could not have happened anywhere else. In sum, the book is an exercise in comparative history, with one eye toward the varieties of eighteenth-century Catholicism and their interaction with the papacy and Catholic states in a century of "lights," and the other toward the origins of the revolution in France. Its originality consists in its deployment of the concept of Reform Catholicism, its international scope, and its demonstration of the interconnected tissue between the various national expulsions.

The book falls into three parts, the first about anti-Jesuitism and Reform Catholicism, the second on the expulsions and suppressions themselves, and the third on the trajectory of Reform Catholicism after the papal suppression until the French Revolution.

A first crucial and highly conceptual chapter presents anti-Jesuitism as the negative face of "Reform Catholicism" while making a case for the utility of this concept in revisionist opposition to the current one of "Catholic enlightenment." While one component of Reform Catholicism does indeed consist in those aspects of the European Enlightenment compatible with religious belief, these aspects are different from those appropriated by Jesuits, many of whom have an equal claim to have been "enlightened." The other and more obviously anti-Jesuitical elements of Reform Catholicism are the "liberties" of both the secular state and the national churches vis-à-vis the papacy known as Gallican, in combination with the morally rigorist Augustinianism known as Jansenism. Although both Gallicanism and Jansenism are largely French in origin, this chapter argues that the rest of Catholic Europe imported them in the second half of the eighteenth century with the help of diplomatic realignments that united all of Catholic Europe and opened borders to French influence. This chapter describes each of these three components in turn, makes a case for their collective coherence and self-consciousness as Reform Catholicism, and charts their European-wide diffusion after 1750.

Since Reform Catholicism inherited much of the anti-Jesuitism that became part of its agenda, the second chapter of the book's first part describes the successive stages in the long history of anti-Jesuitism from the 1550s to 1759, that is, before and until it became part of a European-wide movement for positive Catholic reform. A largely French story, its stages are Gallican and Jansenist, followed by the eighteenth-century synthesis of the two. This chapter therefore makes a case for the preponderance of the French role in the formation of Catholic anti-Jesuitism despite long forays to England, the Dutch Republic, China, and New Spain (or Mexico).

The three chapters of the second part successively describe the suppression in France from 1759 to 1764, the expulsions from Portugal in 1759 and Spain in 1767 and then from Naples and Parma, and the suppression in Rome under Bourbon pressure from 1768 to 1773. Although the Portuguese expulsion precedes the French suppression, the case of France is taken up first. The reason for this order is that, coming hard after a long-term analysis of the largely French fabrication of anti-Jesuitism, the similarly drawn out process of the suppression in France most clearly displays the successive Gallican and Jansenist cases against the Jesuits, while the plot-like correspondence with Italian Augustinians that precedes the action dramatically illustrates the transformation of the Gallican and Jansenist legacy into an international reformist Catholicism. That in

France the action came from the royal law courts against their king and that these parlements dissolved the Jesuits' Society rather than expel the Jesuits further demonstrates the uniqueness of the French case in contrast to the other states, where the initiative came from the monarchies and the action took the form of literal expulsions.

After a brief summary of these structural differences between France and the "expelling" states, the ensuing chapters on Iberian and Italian states aspire to do justice to the unique circumstances of each case: in Portugal the revolt of Tupi-Guaraní natives in the Jesuit missions in Paraguay and an attempted assassination of the king, in Spain one of the largest popular uprisings in prerevolutionary Catholic Europe, and in Naples and Parma not much more than the known wishes of the Spanish king. At the same time, these chapters also illustrate the extent to which the Jesuits found themselves framed both as scapegoats for events with far more complex causes and as guilty figures in an interpretational reformist Catholic framework that depicted their whole Society as a "despotic" international state that by definition conspired against every "national" state, whether in the papacy's interest or just its own. The commonality of the case against the Society extends to the reformist identity and international contacts of those who most influentially pressed it.

Following the the story of the diplomacy of the papal dissolution—in the last part of the fifth chapter—the single chapter of the third part of the book charts the apogee and perigee of the more positive agenda of Reform Catholicism in states that did not take any initiative against the Jesuits, especially Austria, the Austrian Netherlands (Belgium), and the grand duchy of Tuscany. This agenda included the extension of state jurisdiction at the expense of the papacy, the enhancement of the secular at the expense of the monastic clergy, and even a reformist purge of the "superstitious" aspects of popular piety. Lastly, this chapter shows how this aggressive reformist offensive provoked the rise of an opposing international "ultramontanist" and ex-Jesuit Catholicism and the polarization of Catholic Europe, as well as how in France reformist Catholicism metastasized into antimonarchical "patriotism" that, in combination with other elements, would take France in a revolutionary direction. A concluding "Afterword as Fast-Forward" briefly sketches out how that revolution would in turn scare all the reforming monarchies back into the pro-papal—and Jesuit—fold.

Part One

THE PLACE OF ANTI-JESUITISM IN REFORM CATHOLICISM

1

FROM THE CATHOLIC ENLIGHTENMENT TO REFORM CATHOLICISM, 1540-1759

The particular accusations leveled against the Jesuits in the states that expelled them varied widely from state to state. In King José I's Portugal, the Jesuits succumbed to the hostility of the newly all-powerful royal minister Sebastião José de Carvalho e Melo, who accused them of engaging in commerce, of fomenting a revolt by natives in Brazilian missions against the extension of Portuguese rule there, and above all of conspiring with members of Portugal's high nobility to assassinate the king himself on 3 September 1758. In neighboring Spain King Carlos III expelled the Jesuits eight years later in 1767 on account of their supposed planning and participation in the country's biggest popular uprising of the century in the form of the so-called Esquillace, or Hats and Capes, Riots that upended Madrid during Holy Week from 23 to 26 March 1766. That the aim of that plan was thought to be the downfall of the whole Bourbon dynasty provided a justification in turn for a preemptive strike against the Jesuits in the two Italian Bourbon satrapies of the Kingdom of the Two Sicilies, or Naples, later the same year and the Duchy of Parma and Piacenza early the next year. By then, both Spain and the two Italian Bourbon states could also derive ideological inspiration from France, where meanwhile between 1761 and 1764 the royal law courts, or parlements, led by the Parlement of Paris had used a case against a bankrupt mission in Martinique to examine the Jesuits' constitutions and find them incompatible with France's by reason of the Society's "despotic" structure and institutional immorality. Such was the accumulated variety of accusations against the Society that the French philosophe Jean Le Rond d'Alembert could mischievously observe that while some of these charges "might appear to be a little contradictory, . . . it was not a question of telling the exact truth, [but of] saying as much evil about the Jesuits as possible."[1]

REFORM CATHOLICISM AND ANTI-JESUITISM

A real compatibility nonetheless links these charges and provides a clue to a common frame enclosing the whole variety of particular charges against the Jesuits. That frame consisted in the contention that, in combination with the "blind obedience" owed by all Jesuits to their superiors and by these in turn to their general, the monarchical—even "despotic"—structure and transnational reach of this state made it incompatible not only with republics but also with other monarchies. Supplementing this "political" contention was a moral and theological one, namely, that, in combination with a Molinist, or neohumanist, theology that justified it, their Society's all too mobile moral theology made it possible for Jesuits to justify any course of action, including the fomenting of riots and assassination of kings. That structure and morality made it clear in turn that under the pious pretense of furthering the glory of God and serving the papacy the Society's real aim was its own political and temporal aggrandizement, even at the expense of the papacy itself.

But this apparent solicitude for the papacy concealed a far larger than exclusively anti-Jesuitical agenda. For behind its critique of the structure of the Society lurked the aim of reforming the structure of the Catholic Church, which since the papal approval of Loyola's society in 1540 had come to resemble that of the Jesuit society itself. The most obvious way to characterize this aspect of anti-Jesuit reformism is, as Ludwig Pastor argued, a drive to "nationalize" Catholic churches by enlarging the jurisdiction of the state to all aspects of ecclesiastical life short of the definition of doctrine itself.[2] This reform most obviously entailed the extension of secular jurisdiction at the expense of ecclesiastical courts, including the apostolic tribunals, the papal Inquisition, and the national nuncios' offices, to which certain kinds of cases as well as churchmen remained subject.

But where for Pastor the trend to transform the Catholic Church into a community of national churches represented a modern threat, for eighteenth-century reformers themselves reform meant the restoration of an antique state of affairs that included the rights not only of states but also of churches and churchmen. It was therefore with the collaboration of those clergymen most minded to exercise these rights that Catholic states also undertook the restoration of certain features of ecclesiastical polity, the loss for which they held an innovating papacy largely responsible. These included the restoration of the rights of bishops to appoint to major benefices and judge moral cases hitherto reserved to Rome, as well as the curtailment of nonpastoral benefices and the reorientation of all of them toward service to the lay faithful. Whether consciously or not on the part of the protagonists—sometimes not—the campaign against the Jesuits was also aimed at the modern power of the papacy itself.

Reform, alas, inevitably means change, even abolition. Hard as this reform-ist effort was on the many holders of nonpastoral benefices such as cathedral canons, it fell most heavily on members of the "regular," or monastic, clergy, in part because they were seen as the most ultramontanist and beholden to the papacy, but also because, as latecomers to the clergy, they were perceived as noncanonical—even parasitical—accretions to the parish clergy, draining energy and resources from its essential work of ministering to the nation's lay subjects and adding needless heat to its pastoral day. The campaign against the Jesuits therefore lay embedded in a larger reformist effort by Catholic states to restrict the obedience of regulars to foreign generals, limit the recruitment of new novices by extending the age at which they might take solemn vows, cur-tail the amount of property monastic houses and orders might own, and even surgically eliminate undercapitalized or underenrolled monastic houses or en-tire orders.

In contrast, the parish or pastoral clergy often felt gratitude for the state's en-hanced appreciation of their functions and reallocation of resources in their direction, while some bishops appreciated the efforts by Catholic states to "re-store" their premedieval rights to grant dispensations from canon law that the papacy had arguably "usurped" since then. But on no order did these efforts fall more heavily than on the Jesuits, perceived as they were as the wealthiest and most powerful of the regulars, and as ultramontanist symbols par excellence of the papacy's international reach.

All reformist goals derived inspiration from a conception of the Catholic Church as it existed in the "comely centuries" following the life and death of Christianity's founder when the councils met frequently, the bishop of Rome's writ did not extend beyond his diocese, monks were not part of the clergy, and the clergy minded its uniquely spiritual business. Because the reformist agenda aspired to restore this state of affairs as normative, part of it aimed to replace pro-papal, or ultramontanist, ecclesiastical histories with others that faithfully recounted that pristine origin along with the church's fall from it and to put them in as many clerical hands as possible. For their part, the moral and theo-logical charges against the Jesuits enlarged this reformist educational curricu-lum. These additions consisted of replacing scholastic theology with patristic works, "accommodating" Jesuit moral theologies with rigorist ones, Jesuit cate-chisms with those emphasizing divine grace, and in general any "modern" Je-suit theological literature with works that, though modern, self-consciously donned the mantle of primitive Christianity.

While most of these works concerned the education of the priesthood, the choice of catechisms already targeted the lay faithful, who found themselves the object of a wide-ranging reformist campaign intended to wean them from such "superstitious" forms of piety as the use of rosaries, the incantation of novenas, the veneration of relics and apocryphal saints, and processions to the sites of miracles past—all tolerated or even encouraged by most monks and the papacy. In lieu of these devotional practices the reformers sought to nourish lay piety with such meatier stuff as catechisms, instructional sermons, the reading of Holy Writ in the vernacular, vernacular explanations of sacramental myster- ies, and therefore also a focus on the central altar in the parish church to the exclusion of lateral altars and chapels administered by monks. Pious lay con- fraternities dedicated to particular saints fared no better in reformist opinion, which, reserving veneration to the whole Christ alone, would have preferred to transform these into charitable associations.

Given its desire to reform the church, its relation to the state, and its most sanctioned theologies and forms of popular piety, the most obvious label for this impulse is "Reform Catholicism." As for its constituent elements, the adjective "Gallican" best describes Reform Catholicism's call for the loosening of the Catholic Church's hierarchical structure and subordination of its temporal as- pects to the authority of the state; and "Augustinian" is the best candidate for designating its theological, moral, and spiritual orientation. Although with roots far deeper than the eighteenth century, both the Gallican and Augustinian tra- ditions underwent a radicalization by their interaction in the course of the Jan- senist controversy in France during that century, as well as by their encounter with the European Enlightenment.

Although secularization, as Marcel Gauchet has argued, may well be part of the genetic code of Christianity, the Enlightenment is part of that secularization, making the adjective "enlightened" indispensable for referring to the extent to which Reform Catholicism valorized discursive understanding over the emo- tive, the domain of the secular clergy at the expense of the regular, and the reach of the state over the church.[3] Eighteenth-century Europe's Catholic anti-Jesuitism is therefore the chief negative aspect of a reformist Catholicism that may be posi- tively defined as the union of a Gallican conception of the church and the state with an Augustinian theology and religious sensibility under the radicalizing in- fluence of the European Enlightenment.

Gallicanism is almost by definition French; early modern Catholic Augus- tinianism is inseparable from Jansenism, which is also largely French; and even the eighteenth-century Enlightenment tends to bring France first to mind. Thus defined, Reform Catholicism may therefore seem a hopelessly parochial concept for the purposes of designating European-wide Catholic reformism. For Catholic Europe as a whole—and in terms that will be clarified—"Augustinian" works better than Jansenist, and "Cyprianic" better than Gallican. But whether cause or consequence or both, the international Catholic campaign against the Jesuits carried with it an exportation to the rest of Catholic Europe of hitherto largely French divisions, which had long pitted Gallicans and Jansenists against Jesuits who owed their survival in France to the protection of the monarchy alone.

Already facilitated by the French language's status as Europe's literal lingua franca, Gallican, Jansenist, and "enlightened" literature found readier access to readers elsewhere in Catholic Europe after the Bourbon French and Austrian Habsburg alliance of 1756 and the Bourbon Family Pact between France and Spain in 1761 directly or indirectly united all the major Catholic states of Europe. Austrian rule encompassed the Catholic states of the Holy Roman Empire of the German Nation, while between them Habsburg and Spanish Bourbon dynasties ruled over the Italian duchies of Parma-Piacenza and Tuscany, the province of Lombardy, and the Kingdom of the Two Sicilies in the south.

Unique in enjoying the status of law in France, the "Gallican liberties" referred to the principles of the kingdom's temporal independence from the church in any form and the whole church's spiritual superiority over the papacy. But the Gallican tradition itself had always held that its only peculiarity was that France alone had retained the "liberties" and usages that once belonged to the early church and that they still remained an intrinsic part of the church's rightful constitution. That trait made Gallicanism all the more attractive during its post-1750 grand tour of Catholic Europe, where it emboldened indigenous traditions of antiecclesiastical royal jurisdictionalism as well as bishops, who with royal help hoped to emulate France by recovering their prepapal "liberties."

Jansenism for its part was a religiously reformist movement that took its name from the early seventeenth-century Flemish theologian and bishop Corneille Jansen, or Cornelius Jansenius, and its theological and moral cues from Augustine. But Jansenism put down its deepest social roots in neighboring France, where, repeatedly condemned by the papacy, it survived due to the protection of Gallican liberties while becoming identifiable as such due to the refusal of Jansenists to accept the state-enforced papal formulas of their condemnation. Yet everywhere it circulated after 1750, the distinguished Jansenist corpus of theological and moral literature found sympathetic readers among anti-Jesuit moral rigorists and philo-Augustinian churchmen. Whether as movers or apologists, such generic Jansenists played leading roles in all the national expulsions of Jesuits outside France.

While nothing—to complete this brief characterization of constituents— might seem as incompatible with Catholicism as the encyclopedic enlighten- ment of d'Alembert and his colleague Denis Diderot, their ontologically radical strain of enlightenment was not the only one, even in France. For Europe as a whole, the Enlightenment might more broadly be defined as the project for the recovery of the rights of civil society after a century and a half of religious con- flict and a valorization of the rights of critical human reason as recently vindi- cated by the spectacular discoveries in geography, natural philosophy, and the ongoing advances in knowledge of the past.

So defined, the Enlightenment often assumed a far more religious hue than in Paris, the reputed capital of the Enlightenment, some elements of which blended very well with aspects of reformist Catholicism. The reason for prefer- ring the concept "Reform Catholicism" to the more current "Catholic Enlight- enment" to describe this blending will become apparent in due course. Suffice it for now to observe that many eighteenth-century Jesuits too got their intel- lectual bearings from the century's "lights" while remaining largely content with the state of the church as they found it, whereas the "lights" chosen by re- formist Catholics tended rather to illuminate those aspects of the church in need of reformation. Useful outside France and until 1760 at the latest, the con- cept of a Catholic Enlightenment fares less well after a long-polarized France began to export its long-standing religious divisions to Catholic Europe.

The only country for which the concept of Reform Catholicism does not work well is France itself, not only because for decades Jansenists all but monopo- lized the Gallican voice, or because royal opposition prevented them from "reforming" much more than the presence of the Jesuits, but also because there the constituents of Reform Catholicism turned against the monarchy and metastasized into a "patriotic" ideology with politically revolutionary po- tential. That Reform Catholicism elsewhere might have the same potential did not dawn on the royal minds that supported it until after the French Revo- lution. But for lack of a better term, "Reform Catholicism" will have to do for France too.

The use of the concept of Reform Catholicism need not entail relabeling all Gallicans, Jansenists, or variously enlightened Catholics as Catholic reformers when the evidence clearly points in the direction of one of these identities more than others. Gallicans and Jansenists will therefore retain their identities and continue to figure as such in parts of the story that follows, all the more so because the history of anti-Jesuitism begins with the founding of the Society in the sixteenth century while, in this analysis, Reform Catholicism awaited the second half of the century of lights to make historical sense. The label of Reform Catholicism will then designate a movement that coalesced after midcentury and its diverse constituents when they acted together. But before describing that collaboration, a fuller introduction to the identity of the actors is in order.

THE GALLICAN LIBERTIES

The origin of the Gallican liberties lay in the late thirteenth and early fourteenth centuries and Philip the Fair's conflict with the papacy in the person of Boniface VIII over the French monarchy's right to tax the French clergy and to try members of it in secular courts in "royal" cases.[4] In this conflict, the French clergy sided with the monarchy in its successful attempt to defend the principle of its "liberty" from any other sovereign, including the papacy, in "temporal" matters. The target here was the late medieval papacy's claim to ultimate temporal as well as spiritual lordship over all other heads and members of medieval Christendom.

A second, more ecclesiastical set of "liberties" originated in the collaboration between the French clergy, the University of Paris, and the French monarchy in reforming the church and ending the late medieval Great Schism, which by 1415 had produced three rival claimants to the papacy. The institutional agent that finally ended the Great Schism was a "general council" representing the whole church that, meeting in "nations" in Constance in 1414–1415, deposed one pope, obtained the resignations of two other claimants, and elected a new pope who took the name Martin V. Along the way, France and such university-based French churchmen as Pierre d'Ailly and Jean Gerson had played leading roles, and the council itself had laid down the principles that the supreme spiritual authority in the church was the whole church assembled in councils, and that these councils should meet frequently in order also to reform the church "in head and members."[5] With those of Jacques Almain, John Major (or Maier), and Edmond Richer later, the works of d'Ailly and Gerson would come to make up the ecclesiology of the "École de Paris" and figure prominently in the corpus of Gallican classics.

After a second general council meeting in Basel frittered away its moral capital in the 1430s, it was again the French clergy and King Charles VII meeting in Bourges in 1438 that incorporated many of the council's decrees in a concordat, including the principle of conciliar supremacy and the right of cathedral chapters to elect candidates to the church's benefices without papal intervention. Given the hostility of the papacy and the absence of subsequent councils, the Gallican Clergy and the University initially tended to look to the monarchy to protect ecclesiastical as well as temporal "liberties." The Concordat of Bourges later became an object of Gallican nostalgia in France and a model to emulate for similarly inclined churchmen elsewhere.

The price of dependence on the monarchy became apparent in 1516 when King François I negotiated a concordat at Bologna with Pope Leo X that gave the French monarchy the lion's share of nominations to French benefices in return for relinquishing its support for general councils. This concordat sounded the death knell of episcopal elections until the French Revolution; it also gave birth to the possibility of Gallican-inspired resistance to the monarchy by the episcopacy and the Parlement of Paris, both of which vainly protested against the Concordat of Bologna.[6] Resistance to the monarchy in the name of Gallican liberties assumed a more active form during the ordeal of the French religious civil wars of the later sixteenth century. Fastening upon elective elements in the Gallican tradition as well as the medieval monarchy, both Protestant reformers and militant Catholics acted on the principle that a king's devolution into a tyrant—especially a heretical tyrant—gave the political community the right to reclaim its delegated sovereignty and to resist him, even assassinate him. Just before the Reformation, the University of Paris's Gallican theologians Almain and Major had drawn explicit analogies between the delegated and revocable nature of papal and royal authority.[7] At the outset of the wars of religion, Protestant reformers alleged their constitutional right to resist "tyranny" in justification of their seizure of cities and territories; toward the end of these wars, members of the militant Catholic League not only did the same but specialized in this justification for ridding the realm of "tyrants," especially "heretical" ones. Such justifications accompanied or followed the assassination of Henri III and repeated attempts on the life of the formerly Protestant Henri IV.[8]

The assassination of Henri IV by a zealous Catholic in 1610 plus a further Protestant revolt fourteen years later provoked the last meeting of the Estates General in 1614—and the Third Estate's proposed "absolutist" article proclaiming the unmediated divine origin of the monarchy's temporal authority and disallowing any disobedience to it even for spiritual reasons. By that time the target was not only the clergy but also the newly admitted Society of Jesus, whose members had meanwhile acquired notoriety as theoreticians of regicide and defenders of the papacy's "indirect" temporal power. Although resisted by the clergy, the Third's absolutist article gradually became a linchpin of absolutist Gallican orthodoxy, the one verity that united an increasingly fragmented tradition. The self-anointed defender of temporal independence, the Parlement of Paris—a fuller definition will follow—used the tradition not only to oppose the Jesuits and the papacy but also to whittle away at the Gallican Clergy's "spiritual" jurisdiction. Meanwhile the clergy interpreted the Gallican liberties quite differently, in defense not only of its own jurisdiction against the papacy and the regular orders but also of its liberties against secular authority as vindicated by the Parlement.[9]

The last time the monarchy successfully reconciled and controlled these ever more rival inflections of Gallican discourse is when a momentary conflict with the papacy prompted Louis XIV to cajole the Gallican Clergy into proclaiming the chief tenets of the Gallican tradition in its General Assembly in 1682.[10] But by 1693 the monarchy began to back away from the older conciliar tenets of that tradition, whereupon the Parlement of Paris became the clergy's chief champion, sometimes with, but more often in conflict with, the Gallican bishops, while also in ever more in tension with the monarchy. What remained was a very fragmented discourse, with some of the shards boomeranging back to afflict the monarchy.

The reason Louis XIV distanced the monarchy from the Gallican tradition's conciliar tenets is that he needed the spiritual authority of the papacy in its campaign against Jansenism, in which he perceived a degree of complicity in the recent uprising known as the Fronde and, more distantly, against the twin threat of both the Protestant reformers and the Catholic League.[11] Although Jansenism initially enjoyed the sympathy of many Gallican bishops, the monarchy's control over episcopal nominations eventually enabled it to purge the episcopacy of most Jansenists, while Jansenists for their part eventually sought refuge from papal condemnations behind the Gallican liberties as interpreted by the Parlement.

Essentially an eighteenth-century phenomenon, it was that alliance—to fastforward a little—that engineered the suppression of the Society of Jesus in France between 1761 and 1764. The period of that suppression also coincides with the anti-Jesuit offensive elsewhere in Catholic Europe, and with it the exportation of the influence of the classic Gallican corpus composed of the original École de Paris, Pierre Dupuy and Pierre Pithou's compilations of the Gallican liberties, Noël Alexandre and Claude Fleury's ecclesiastical histories, and Bishop Jacques-Bénigne Bossuet's recently published defense of the Gallican articles of 1682.[12] All these works, however, assumed that the monarchy might be counted upon to defend ecclesiastical liberty as well as its own against the papacy, while in France itself the alliance of dissident Jansenists and the Parlement was producing works that justified the defense of those liberties by the parlements against both the monarchy and the Gallican episcopacy. That curious turn of events calls for a preliminary word of explanation about the parlements, and a later one about Jansenism.

The realm's chief law court, the Parlement of Paris separated from the king's ambulatory council, or curia regis, when the medieval Capetian monarchy gave its trained jurists a fixed abode on the Île de la Cité in Paris.[13] In succeeding centuries the monarchy created thirteen provincial parlements, such as the Parlement of Normandy in Rouen and that of Brittany in Rennes, although the Parlement of Paris possessed by far the largest territorial jurisdiction and emerged as the final royal court of appeal. Composed of judges whose offices became purchasable and later inheritable in the course of the late fifteenth and sixteenth centuries, the parlements combined their judicial functions with important administrative ones.

But they also acquired the legislative power of "registering" royal edicts, ordinances, and declarations—that is, of inscribing them in their registers of the laws—along with the duty of calling the king's attention to cases of perceived defects in these royal initiatives. Increasingly construed as a right as well as an obligation, the remonstrance eventually opened up a space for political conflict within the monarchy, even after the monarchy became "absolute"—or rather especially after it did, because it was also the absolute monarchy that completed the process whereby the magistrates became irremovable as owners of their offices.

After this newly absolute monarchy ceased convening the more literally representative Estates General after 1615 and put many of the provincial estates on ice, the Parlement of Paris began to consider itself the successor of the Estates General, or better still that of even earlier representative assemblies founded by the Frankish kingdom. Advised by his council, the king could in principle override this resistance by means of reiterated orders culminating in his physical appearance in a *lit de justice*, or bed of justice, but the parlements eventually found ways to counter even these acts of absolute authority in the eighteenth century by staging judicial strikes supported by the barristers and appealing to "public opinion" through use of the press. Such confrontations between the parlements and a supposedly absolute monarchy punctuate the entire history of the French Old Regime except for the height of Louis XIV's reign.

That the Parlement might oppose the monarchy itself in defense of the Gallican liberties became evident as early as its opposition to the Concordat of Bologna—and to the monarchy's admission of the suspiciously pro-papal Jesuits in 1554–1563 and their readmission in 1603. At that point the Parlement still spoke for the University of Paris and at least part of the Gallican episcopacy. What finally disrupted this coalition was the Parlement's opposition to the episcopacy's official acceptance of most of the Council of Trent's decrees, which the bishops had come to favor. And what weakened all the parlements in relation to the monarchy until 1715 was their conspicuous role in the five-year Fronde against the regency government, a complicity that enabled Louis XIV to deprive them of the right of prior remonstrances in 1673.[14] Surviving the Fronde, however, was a body of published pro-parlementary theory that had justified the Parlement's oppositional role in its rightful exercise of colegislative powers held by virtue of a historical constitution rooted in the Frankish nation's past.[15]

These constitutional theories of original "national" liberty became relevant to the Gallican liberties after Louis XIV's death in 1715, when the Parlement regained its right of prior remonstrance in return for granting regency powers to the deceased king's nephew. Even earlier, Louis XIV had begun to lose control over the Parlement as well as the clergy by reason of his religious policies, which had increasingly sacrificed the traditional Gallican liberties to the papacy in return for Rome's support for a royal crusade to condemn Jansenism. As it will be elaborated later, at issue were new anti-Jansenist bulls, most especially *Unigenitus* (*Only* Begotten) in 1713. In reaction, part of the magistracy and the whole order of barristers warmed to the Jansenist cause, while Jansenist theologians in turn not only became parlementary Gallicans but also began to take a hand in reviving and radicalizing neo-Frondish parlementary political theory in potent combination with an application of the classic Gallican thesis of the church's superiority to the pope and to the nation's sovereignty vis-à-vis the monarchy.[16] As inflected by the Parlement of Paris, therefore, the Gallican liberties crossed paths with the trajectory of political or constitutional liberty.

These developments inevitably redounded on the perception of the Jesuits in France. Gallicans had long demonized their Society as not only a papal Trojan horse but also a monarchically structured harbinger of the direction of the post-Tridentine papacy. But when the Gallican tradition began to turn against the monarchy on account religious policies favored by Jesuits, the Jesuits found themselves targeted twice over again, first as responsible for the anti-Jansenist papal bulls and also as a "despotically" structured harbinger of where the monarchy seemed headed.

That said, parlementary polemicists usually maintained contact with the Gallican liberties "absolutist" article with the claim that they resisted the king's whimsical will in the name of his real, or legal, one. As part of the baggage of Gallican literature when it began to travel elsewhere in post-1750 Catholic Europe, anti-"despotic" language for the most part spared monarchs, for the good reason that, unlike France, it was monarchs and not parlements who supported the acquisition of Gallican-like liberties at the expense of Rome. Yet such was its discursive force that it occasionally bled onto temporal governance even in places that did not proceed against the Jesuits. Dependent though he was on the Empire's temporal princes for sponsoring any reformist action against the papacy, the mid-eighteenth-century auxiliary bishop of Trier so stridently denounced the papacy's degeneration into what he called a "despotic" as well as absolute "Politico-Sacral Monarchy" that at one point he openly questioned whether monarchy was indeed the best form of government even for temporal states.[17] That he had read some of the anti-Jesuit pamphlets and parlementary proceedings produced by the trial of the Society in France is evident in his treatise's references to them.[18]

THE INTERNATIONALIZATION OF GALLICANISM
IN CATHOLIC EUROPE AFTER 1750

The auxiliary bishop in question is Johann Nikolaus von Hontheim, alias Justus Febronius, and his treatise is entitled *De statu Ecclesiae et legitima potestate romani pontificis* (On the Constitution of the Church and the Legitimate Power of the Roman Pontiff). First published in 1763, this treatise is one among many indices that the international campaign against the Jesuits came accompanied by a wider internationalization of Gallican ecclesiology facilitated by the opening of diplomatic barriers between France and most of the other Catholic states after the alliances of 1756 and 1761.

Besides Hontheim's, like-minded treatises to appear between 1750 and 1770 were the Austrian canonist Paul Joseph Riegger's four-volume study of canon law, the Spanish councilor Pedro Rodríguez Campomanes's treatise on Spain's right to limit the expansion of ecclesiastical property, and the Portuguese Oratorian António Pereira de Figueiredo's similarly regalist treatise on the rights of kings over the church, followed by two more treatises on the rights of Portuguese bishops vis-à-vis the papacy. While France itself did not produce any major addition to its Gallican corpus, changes in censorship policy enabled by the marginalization or expulsion of the Jesuits in most Catholic states allowed new editions of those classics to circulate more freely.

A second index is the accession of royal ministers who either sponsored or approved of such publications—or wrote them themselves, as did Campomanes, who became an influential fiscal official under Carlos III of Spain in 1762. Other obvious examples are Manuel de Roda y Arietta, who became Carlos III's minister of grace and justice in 1765; Carvalho, who became de facto first minister under José I of Portugal in 1755; Bernardo Tanucci, who rose to the position of first minister in Naples in 1759; Léon-Guillaume Du Tillot, who assumed the powers of first minister under Felipe I in Parma in 1759; and finally Wenzel Anton Fürst von Kaunitz-Rietberg, who became imperial Austria's chancellor and minister of foreign affairs under Empress Maria Theresa in 1753. A final index is the domino-like dismissal of Jesuits as royal confessors in favor of priests or members of other religious orders, whether as advance signs of disgrace in those states that expelled them, like Spain, Portugal, and Naples in 1755, 1757, and 1767; or in advance of the papal suppression in 1773 in those states that had not, like Austria and Tuscany in 1768 and 1770. Only in France did a king reluctantly part with a Jesuit confessor when in 1764 he reluctantly formalized the actions that his parlements had taken.

Hontheim may be thought of as having acted as a public canonist for Trier's prince-bishop elector Johann Philipp von Walderdorff in a way analogous to Pereira de Figueiredo's role in relation to Carvalho in Portugal or Riegger's to Kaunitz in Austria. The pro-French elector dismissed the Jesuits from their teaching positions at the University of Trier at Hontheim's prodding on the occasion of the French suppression in 1764, while his successor, Clement Wenzeslaus von Sachsen, drew inspiration from *De statu Ecclesiae* along with his colleagues from Mainz and Cologne for their gravamina presented against the curia in their joint démarche in Koblenz in September to December 1769.[19] But unlike Carlos III or José I, neither the prince-bishop of Trier nor his colleagues were in a position to expel the Jesuits from states, much less exert much pressure on the papacy to listen to their gravamina without the unreliable support of the Holy Roman Empire. So weak and divided were even the Catholic states of the empire that Hontheim was hard pressed to borrow many of his Gallican principles from the royalist versions of them, which assumed the presence of a prince strong enough to defy the papacy.

It was therefore a largely episcopalist variant of the Gallican tradition that Hontheim adapted to German conditions. His treatise's point of departure was the papacy's gradual deprivation of the German Church's liberties over the course of twelve centuries. By "liberties" he chiefly meant the liberties of the bishops, the losses of which he regarded as tantamount to "usurpations" and therefore also "abuses."

The first and perhaps most important of these usurpations was the papal bestowal of benefices hitherto under the control of local bishops to an increasing number of candidates ordained without benefices—another abuse—first by means of ad hoc requests and eventually enshrined in formal impositions. Besides depriving bishops of control over their clergies, these devices also became a source of revenue for the curia, as did the exaction of the first year of a newly provisioned diocese's income as "annates"—a second abuse—as the price of papal confirmation of its bishop. The papacy had in turn acquired the prerogative of appointing new bishops and abbots by means of creating a category of "major" cases "reserved" for the papacy that—a third abuse—also included the deposition or transferal of bishops, the erection of new bishoprics, and even the judgment of localized controversies concerning the faith. A fourth category of usurpation and source of curial income was the papal monopoly of dispensing both clergy and lay persons from the provisions of church law, most notoriously in the case of marriages within the prohibited degrees of consanguinity. Closely related to this usurpation in Hontheims's estimation was the papacy's assertion of the right to entertain judicial appeals about anything by anybody able to afford them, a practice that grew from its infancy in the fifth century to a profligate maturity in the twelfth. A final category of abuse concerned the exemptions from episcopal jurisdiction by religious orders that, as "a sacred militia" at the service of the "Sovereign Pontiffs" within Catholic states, introduced a "great alteration in the Ecclesiastical Hierarchy."[20] In singling out this abuse Hontheim largely spared the Benedictines while bearing down on the thirteenth-century mendicant orders, and most especially the Jesuits, distinguished by their espousal of the papacy's most monarchical pretensions and "the most absolute and unlimited power of their general."[21]

While the general councils of Constance and Basel may have contained the proliferation of appeals to Rome, Hontheim maintained that even that "abuse" remained a problem in Germany and regarded all the other abuses as alive and well, even in France. Indeed, the elimination of many of them figures prominently among goals of state-sponsored reformist Catholicism everywhere. Although the hoary ancestry of Hontheim's gravamina made these chapters the most Germanic in his treatise, he freely confessed that in his calling for the restoration of the liberties of the German Church his proposals did nothing more than take a page from the book of the "most wise, such as the French," who had long learned how to preserve their liberties. Among Catholic nations, the French alone, thought Hontheim, "deserved the praise in having furnished the foundations on which other churches could also establish their liberties" while reestablishing the "ancient common law" of the early church, as the Gallican theologians had always made clear."[22]

No reason exists therefore to reify Hontheim's ecclesiastical thought as a separate Febronian "ism" distinct from Gallicanism, as though France had not thrown up enough variations on the Gallican theme to have one in stock for every ecclesiastical season.[23]

The thesis that the Catholic Church had gradually lost its original constitutional liberties to a usurping and ever more domineering papacy, or Court of Rome, presupposed an ecclesiastical history in the tragic trope of decline and fall—or rather of fall and further decline—which in Hontheim's telling took place in distinct stages, beginning in the fifth century when Leo I began to transform the bishop of Rome's occasionally solicited advice to other bishops into the prerogative to decide all "major cases." But by far the most decisive such stage for Hontheim occurred in the ninth century, when the unlettered "ignorance and superstition" of the era allowed a pseudonymous Isidore Mercator to promulgate a collection of altered or forged decretals that seemed to demonstrate the bishop of Rome's supreme power over other bishops and even over general councils prior to the fifth century. The papacy's post-Gregorian transformation of what had been a constitutional Christian republic into an absolute "politic-sacred [papal] monarchy" only built on the false decretals' foundations, as did the financial exploitation of these accumulated papal prerogatives by the Avignonese papacy and then the Great Schism's rival popes that provoked the general councils of Constance and Basel. But although they memorably—and in Hontheim's opinion infallibly—proclaimed the principles of the superiority of general councils to the papacy and the need for their frequent convocation, they neither got very far in reforming the church "in head and members" nor made much headway in fending off the Protestant schism.

Far from being unique to Hontheim, however, this version of ecclesiastical history as decline and fall attained canonical status in reformist Catholic milieux in the eighteenth century, combining elements from classic accounts of decline and fall set in the Roman Republic and Empire.[24] Not only did it subtend much of the anticurial and antimonastic legislation by Catholic states, it also provoked pro-curial ecclesiastical histories, such as Cardinal Giuseppe Agostino Orsi's *Storia ecclesiastica*, published in time for Hontheim to have taken note of it.[25] Most influential in establishing this trope was a corpus of Gallican ecclesiastical histories on which Hontheim himself heavily depended, above all Fleury's short *Discours* and twenty-volume *Histoire ecclésiastique*, Alexandre's *Histoire ecclésiastique* in twenty volumes, the Oratorian Louis Thomassin's *Ancienne et nouvelle discipline de l'église*, and the history contained in works in canon law, including Bossuet's recently published defense of the Declaration of 1682.[26] The only secondary German authorities consistently cited by Hontheim are his contemporaries Johann Caspar Barthel and Gregor Zallwein, professors of canon law at the universities of Würzburg and Salzburg, respectively.[27]

Since the trope of decline presupposed the normative character of the early church's laws and practice, and because bishops in the early church had wielded far more independent power in relation to Rome than in the "modern" Catholic Church, the gap between eighteenth-century reality and Hontheim's exalted view of the bishop's office was all but immensurable. At the heart of Hontheim's vision of the church as it ought to be lay a collegial conception of the Catholic Church's "unity" that, ultimately indebted to the third-century bishop Saint

Cyprian of Carthage, endowed all the bishops with an undivided and universal authority that they nonetheless exercised as though by one, just as had the apostles after the ascension of Christ.[28] Although Hontheim conceded that the church's expansion had made it necessary to divide the exercise of that authority into dioceses, he held that each bishop's jurisdiction was in principle as universal as the spiritual power conferred on him by ordination, and that under certain circumstances any might concern himself with the business of all.

This universal conception of the episcopate even allowed each bishop to take the pope to task, as Cyprian had Pope Stephen I. Rather than as referring to the Apostle Peter and his successors exclusively—the standard papal interpretation—Hontheim followed Augustine, Cyprian, and other church fathers in interpreting the "rock" in the person of Peter to whom Christ had vouchsafed the "keys" of the kingdom of heaven in Matthew 16:16–19 as referring to Peter's profession of faith or Christ himself, but above all to the unity of the church for which Peter stood as a symbol for all the apostles and their successors. To Peter and his successors in the Holy See Hontheim granted a "primacy" by divine right that gave the pope the task of inspection and direction over all parts of the church with a view toward maintaining rather than curtailing their pre-Isidorian liberty, while denying the pope any direct jurisdiction outside his own diocese, much less a universal one over the whole church.

The obedience owed to the pope by bishops was in Hontheim's opinion limited by the canons and therefore "reasonable" rather than "blind" obedience. Well before Hontheim wrote, this phrase had become one of the watchwords of Reform Catholicism, as had his statement of the goal of papal primacy as presiding over a church defined in turn as a "communion of saints . . . sustained by humility, piety, and charity, and not by the force of empire wielded by the kings of nations." This characterization of the governance of the church obliquely refers to Christ's contrast between his kingdom and that of the Gentiles in Matthew 20:25–28, just as the phrase "reasonable obedience" is taken from Paul's letter to the Romans 12:1.

In elaborating this vision of what he considered to be the pristine and still normative constitution of the church, Hontheim had recourse to a different corpus of works in canon and civil law. Besides to the erudition of Barthel and Zallwein and the Flemish canonist Zeger Bernard van Espen, under whom he had studied at the University of Louvain in the early 1720s, Hontheim owed his most massive indebtedness to the battery of Gallican classics, among them Pithou and Dupuy's compilations, Pierre de Marca's treatise on the harmony of church and empire, Fleury's dissertation on canon law—and even the notoriously radical Sorbonne syndic Edmond Richer's defense of Jean Gerson and the supremacy of the church and general councils in relation to the papacy.[29] It was from Richer as well as Louis Ellies du Pin that he gained access to the major works of late medieval Gallican conciliarists and the "most celebrated theologians of France" such as Gerson and d'Ailly, who along with Almain and Major were Hontheim's guides in the defense of the decrees of the councils of Constance and Basel.[30] The only German works Hontheim often cited were Nicolaus Cusanus's on Catholic concord and Hermann von der Hardt's commentary on the Council of Constance.

If in Hontheim's opinion papal primacy did not include the infallibility apparently promised to Peter in Matthew 16:17–19, for a Catholic it had to lie in some ecclesiastical body rather than Scripture, and for Hontheim it resided in the whole church as assembled in general councils.[31] "The unique and only total rule of faith of the Catholic faith," he laid down, ". . . is the divine revelation delivered to the prophets and the apostles [and] proposed by the universal church, either by a general council or by the general observation of that same church."[32] Had infallibility initially been an appanage of papal primacy, it would have been pointless, Hontheim argued, for bishops to assemble in so many councils just to hear what had already been decided by the bishop of Rome. Far from popes having convened them during the first five or six crucial centuries, it was Roman emperors who had. That since late antiquity such general councils that had met had usually done so on the initiative and direction of the papacy obliged Hontheim to concede that convening and presiding over general councils had become a papal prerogative. Hence the pains he took to establish the self-validating decrees proclaiming the ultimate superiority of general councils and the need of their frequent convocation by the late medieval councils convened by the Empire against the will of popes.

That in his own century ultramontanist theologians such Orsi and Prospero Fagnani could still be "abandoning the spouse of Jesus Christ to the darkness of a dispute so many times rehashed about the superiority of the pope or council" was for Hontheim a "scandal" that helped perpetuate the ongoing Protestant schism.[33] Among the most passionately written pages of the treatise, the very end of Hontheim's sixth section on general councils culminated in a call for a new council, or in the case of a refusal a "subtraction of obedience" to the papacy on the model of what states had done to force the convocation of the Council of Constance, whether by the "German nation" alone or in alliance with others, beginning with France.

But what Catholic German prince was to take such an initiative in the religiously and politically divided Holy Roman Empire if not the emperor himself? Although the classically Gallican justification for such a "recourse to the prince" and his power as "outside bishop" to see to the enforcement of the Catholic Church's own canons was far from absent from *De statu Ecclesiae*, neither Maria Theresa or, much less, her successor Joseph II indicated the remotest interest in such a project.[34] Nor for that matter did either the empire or any other state correspond to the "German nation" to which Hontheim rhetorically appealed.

In contrast to Hontheim's reticence, the "recourse to the prince" is either spelled out or the elephant in the room in all of works of the Oratorian António Pereira de Figuereido, Portugal's counterpart to Hontheim. While in Hontheim's treatise the Society of Jesus appears only in passing as the most "despotic" caricature of the absolute monarchy that the papacy had become, the Jesuits haunted the pages of all of Pereira's treatises. That was so because in contrast to the "withdrawal of obedience" to the papacy that Hontheim called for, José I and Carvalho had actually executed such a withdrawal, having broken all diplomatic ties with the papacy over the issue of the Jesuits, whom they had expelled from Portugal and its colonies in 1759. It was this rupture that prompted Carvalho to turn to Pereira to complete and formalize the gallicanization of Portugal's hitherto more limited regal jurisdictionalism.[35]

Given these contexts, it is hardly surprising that Pereira's first treatise "on the supremacy of the monarchy and the power of bishops" set out to do what Hontheim's did not, and that is fully to domesticate the first, or royal, tenet, the Gallican liberties. It therefore laid it down that the clergy's power was "purely spiritual" and admonitory and possessed no indirect, much less direct, power over temporal rulers, whose power came as directly from God as the clergy's and whose concern was civil society's "happiness and tranquillity."[36] Least of all did the church have the right to allege its subjects' spiritual welfare as a reason to authorize attempts on a king's life, as Carvalho accused Portuguese Jesuits of doing in 1758. Having shrunk ecclesiastical authority to the ethereally spiritual, Pereira filled the vacated space with the state's temporal jurisdiction over the clergy, which he expanded over not only all civil and criminal misdeeds but also violations of the church's own canon law or even of "natural equity." For all so victimized, the empowered state afforded a judicial "recourse to the prince" against ecclesiastical censures. It also followed from these premises that the clergy held its existing legal and fiscal exemptions and property by regal pleasure alone, which the "prince" could revoke at will.

But given the relative institutional weakness of the Portuguese clergy, what may be more surprising is the extent to which Pereira followed Hontheim in empowering Portuguese bishops in relation to the papacy as much as Hontheim did for the far more independent German bishops. That turn of the argument became apparent with the publication of his second and far more famous treatise, his *Tentativa theological*, which appeared in 1766.[37] The occasion for its publication was the duration of Portugal's rupture with the papacy, which created the problem of obtaining dispensations from canon law for subjects marrying within degrees of kinship prohibited by canon law. Such dispensations figured among the papacy's "reserved cases," while Portugal's high and highly ingrown nobility routinely needed them in order to endure. To defy the royal rupture and opt to obey the pope was not an option for Pereira, because while the French parlements were subtly subjecting the royalist strand in the Gallican tradition to a "national" interpretation, the Portuguese Oratorian stuck to the letter of that tradition's insistence on absolute obedience to kings as "God's image on earth, even—or most especially—in conflicts with the papacy."[38] It followed for Pereira that Portuguese bishops had an obligation to obey their king in granting marital dispensations from canon law, even if to do so meant to disobey the pope.[39] Unlike the pope's, the monarch's demand for obedience was a "reasonable" one in that, far from asking the bishops to do anything in violation of divine, natural, or even canon law, their king was only asking them to reclaim an imprescriptible right that had never been within their power to forfeit.

Pereira's argument therefore rested on as high and Cyprianic a conception of the Catholic episcopacy as Hontheim's did, including the collective possession of the Petrine keys, the superiority of the general council, and an ecclesiastical history read as a degeneration from its pristine origins into the ever more Jesuit-like "despotism" on display in his own day.[40] In buttressing these theses, Pereira put on a better show of "nationalizing" a generically Gallican ecclesiology than did Hontheim of his, seeing that the era from the Council of Constance to the Council of Trent had produced no few Spanish and Portuguese allies of the French in defending a similarly high view of the episcopacy and a scaled-down conception of papal primacy.[41] But quite like Hontheim, Pereira freely admitted to having leaned on only the "most circumspect" theologians, such as the French, above all those of "the Faculty of the University of Paris," beginning with d'Ailly and Gerson.[42] As in Hontheim's case as well, the vast mass of Pereira's support came from the same set of Gallican canonists, theologians, and ecclesiastical historians, such as Alexandre, Fleury, and Thomassin.

In his *Tentativa*, Pereira made so bold as favorably to cite not only the Jansenist theologian Arnauld but also the abbé de Saint-Cyran, even mentioning that he had been Jansen's friend.[43] In 1769 he also signed a letter to the archbishop of the archdiocese of Utrecht, thereby signifying his communion with a clergy that had adhered to the French Jansenist appeal to a general council and had sustained excommunication by the papacy in part for this reason.[44] Rather than identifying with the Jansenist cause in either of these ways, Hontheim had explicitly distanced himself from that appeal in the second volume of his *De statu Ecclesiae*. This distancing might explain his rather tortured argument that in some cases the universal church's tacit consent to a papal decision might suffice in lieu of convening a general council.[45] In the same breath, however, Hontheim's admission that any such consent would have to include the "witness" of priests and even "lay faithful" bears witness to a certain Jansenist influence.[46] Whether he was aware of it or not, Hontheim's ecclesiology reflected some of the radicalization—even democratization—undergone by post-1713 Gallican thought in Jansenist hands.

JANSENISM

No sketch of Reform Catholicism can hope to get further without introducing a second major and theological element, namely, Jansenism and the Jansenist controversy. It is this controversy that lay at the source of the fragmentation and politicization of Gallican discourse. Jansenism also added a moral and theological layer to Reform Catholicism's anti-Jesuitism, one that cast the Jesuits as the persecutors not only of Protestants but of Catholics too.[47]

Although the term "Jansenism" is named for the Flemish theologian Cornelius Jansen, its true homeland was not to be in Flanders but in France, where by the 1630s an indigenous—and decidedly non-Jesuit—Catholic Reformation had produced a kind of proto-Jansenism within new religious orders, such as Pierre de Bérulle's Oratory, parts of the secular clergy, and in the University of Paris. Known as the "school of French spirituality," this reformation had effected what one of its historians, Henri Bremond, called a Christocentric "Copernican revolution" in its emphasis on the nothingness of humanity without God as incarnated in Christ, the agent of man's redemption, whose "grandeurs" Bérulle memorably celebrated.[48] More than Jansen, it was his lifelong French friend Duvergier de Hauranne, better known by the name of his abbacy of Saint-Cyran, who represented this French school of spiritual sensibility. At the heart of this reform movement was an awesome regard for Christ's ongoing incarnation in the sacrament of the Eucharist and a heightened view of the vocation of the priest who administered it. Jansenism's original stake in the Gallican liberties, this view of the sacerdotal vocation of the secular clergy already stood in tension with Jesuits as members of the regular clergy; inspired by the theology of Augustine and the practice of the early church, the view of penance and the Eucharist as the unique points of contract between "fallen" humanity and a transcendent God stood in contrast with the Jesuits' neohumanistic optimism about the capacities of fallen human nature and the facility of devotion.[49]

Although supported by the monarchy, the Jesuits were getting the worst of a war of words with the University and the episcopacy on these issues when Jansen's summation of Augustine's theology of grace appeared posthumously under the title of *Augustinus* in 1640.[50] Jansen's systematic restatement of that theology laid bare some possible theological underpinnings of Saint-Cyran's penitential theology and practice: in order for "good works" and penitence to find favor with God, they had to be undertaken out of "charity," or a love for God, that could not be summoned up at will but depended on God, who gave it to some but not all, and then only sometimes. But just as for Calvinists the doctrine of divine predestination functioned as a fence around that of justification by faith—a doctrine quite foreign to Jansenism—so for Jansenists did it function as a fence around a penitential theology in which the sinner worked out his or her salvation with a fear and trembling in ways that neither Jesuits nor Calvinists were called on to do. The connection between Jansenists and Calvinists ran through Augustine, but Jansen's Augustine was a decidedly Catholic Augustine, one for whom human "merit" mattered.[51]

While the Gallican tradition had existed long before the Society of Jesus, the Jesuits had celebrated their centennial anniversary when "Jansenists" came on the scene. So Jansenists defined themselves against Jesuits from the outset, while Jesuits returned the compliment, inventing the term "Jansenists" to categorize these new enemies as a sect.[52] Both sides agreed that fallen humanity needed divine help or grace for redemption or salvation. But while Jesuits held that an always "sufficient" grace became "efficacious" only after penitents chose to use it, Jansenists held that this grace was efficacious by itself, bending an otherwise irredeemably self-interested, or "concupiscent," will toward charity for those to whom God gave it.

The issue of divine predestination versus mere foresight would have arisen sooner or later, since the Society of Jesus had already staked out its own position with the work of the Spanish Jesuit Luis de Molina, who in 1588 had sketched out a scenario whereby God foresaw how every person would benefit from or resist grace, having from all eternity vouchsafed to each person a "sufficient" amount of it to resist sin in every possible situation should he or she choose to accept it.[53] Jansen's book was already directed against this theology, as had been the work of Michel de Baye, or Baius, Jansen's predecessor at Louvain. But when the meteor of Jansen's hard formulations descended on the lush landscape of the French Catholic Reformation, it produced fissures that divided not only Jansenist from Jesuit but also Saint-Cyran and his associates from some of

Bérulle's other spiritual descendants, such as Jean-Jacques Olier's Suplician priests and Vincent de Paul's Lazarists.[54] Like the ultraclear distinctions between extended matter and immaterial thought injected into the intellectual scene by Descartes's philosophy, with which Jansenists developed a kinship, the distinctions imposed by *Augustinus* were clear to the point of mutual exclusion: between the innocent and fallen states, concupiscence and charity, grace and free will, and the purity of the early church and the corruption of it in the contemporary "refuse of the centuries."

Though Catholic in intent, Jansen's summa resembled Calvinism in the mold of the Synod of Dordrecht sufficiently to enable the Jesuits to counterattack with the charge of "rewarmed Calvinism," both in Louvain from their college there and in Paris from the pulpit in sermons by Notre Dame's capitulary theologian, behind whom already lurked the figure of Louis XIII's first minister, Armand-Jean du Plessis, cardinal de Richelieu. In Paris the most obvious target was Jansenism's first stronghold in the formerly Cistercian but now independent convent of Port-Royal. There, Saint-Cyran had become the spiritual director, the influential Arnauld family had contributed its abbess and another sister, and numbers of illustrious friends and "solitaries" had taken residence in its rustic abode outside Paris and begun to hold "little schools" for the children of the abbey's friends. That these Arnauld sisters were also daughters of the famously Gallican and anti-Jesuit barrister Antoine Arnauld did little to recommend this community to Jesuits. Other targeted groups included Jansenism's first enclaves within the University of Paris, the Parisian parish clergy, and the Parlement of Paris's sprawling judicial community, which tended to be Gallican and anti-Jesuit by inheritance. The judges and parish clergy were both bridges to lay worlds; what distinguished French from Flemish and all later Jansenisms was the importance and extent of its lay constituencies.

Just released from prison and too infirm to act, Jansen's friend Saint-Cyran turned for help to his younger friend and acolyte Antoine Arnauld, the youngest son of the Arnauld family and now newly famous in his own right as a Sorbonne theologian and the author of *De la fréquente communion* (*On Frequent Communion*), a treatise on proto-Jansenism's originally chosen terrain of criticism of the Jesuits' reputed practice of frequent and facile Communion.[55] Arnauld thereupon took up his cudgels in defense of Jansen, then of Saint-Cyran, and then of the sisters of Port-Royal, and so on until, joined by his Oratorian friend Pierre Nicole, he finished his long life as the full-time, anti-Jesuit "syllogistic Gatling gun," as Bremond uncharitably characterized him.[56] As early as at the time of the publication of *De la fréquente communion*, French

Jesuits such as Jacques Sirmond had joined the fray, and the century-and-a-half-long Jansenist controversy was under way.[57]

Not even at the outset was it probable that Jansenists would prevail in the ensuing set-to. The Jesuits, having ensconced themselves at the royal Bourbon court as living proof of the sincerity of Henri IV's conversion, had since obtained royal permission to teach in Paris and found college after college in the provinces. As early as 1638 Cardinal Richelieu had imprisoned Saint-Cyran, in part because his rigorous, or "contritionist," insistence on the prerequisite of love in the sacrament of penance recalled the "devout" or neo-Leaguish opposition to Richelieu's rise as first minister. For its part, the post-Tridentine papacy had already distanced itself from hardline interpretations of Augustine's theology of grace, having already condemned seventy-nine such propositions by Jansen's predecessor, de Baye, in 1567 and 1579. Meanwhile the Jesuits had become all but indispensable to the Counter-Reformation papacy in education, missions, and in attempts to influence policy in the royal councils of Catholic Europe. For these and other reasons, the Jesuits enjoyed privileged access to the corridors of the powers and principalities in Paris as in Rome. Jansenists did not.

The weakness of the regency government during the Fronde gave Jansenists a brief stay of retribution, just as it did the Huguenots. But in the end that reprieve did them more harm than good, since one of Port-Royal's chief protectors, Jean-François de Gondi, not only put himself at the head of the Parisian Fronde but also continued to protect Jansenists when he became the archbishop of Paris and later Cardinal de Retz, even after escaping prison and fleeing to Rome in 1652. The Jansenists in question were Parisian parish priests who began to associate under his titular authority, both in defense of his authority and against the Jesuits and the first condemnations of Jansenism.[58] To the government of the queen mother, the boy king Louis XIV, and the cardinal-minister Jules Mazarin, it was as though the Jansenists represented at once the threats of reboiled Calvinism and the ultra-Catholic League, which had similarly drawn much of its strength from the Parisian priesthood.[59] Further, the eldest and most courtly of the Arnauld sons, Robert Arnauld d'Andilly, penned a couple of Frondish pamphlets against Cardinal Mazarin, who had recently taken Richelieu's place as first minister and was to prove as anti-Jansenist as Richelieu would have been.[60]

The sad saga of Jansenism's losing battle is relevant to the analysis of anti-Jesuitism by way of background and to the extent that Jesuits might plausibly have been blamed for it. At no point did Jesuits occupy the foreground. It was again Notre Dame's theologian, now a bishop, joined by most of his colleagues, who denounced the propositions from *Augustinus* for possible condemnation by the papacy. It was again not the Jesuits but the regency regime of Anne of Austria and Mazarin that put decisive pressure on Innocent X to condemn these propositions as heretical in the bull *Cum occasione*—"on the occasion" of the book *Augustinus*—in 1653, as it was the Sorbonne packed with mendicant monks that expelled Arnauld from the faculty in 1653.[61] When, led by Arnauld, most Jansenists tried to evade this papal condemnation by arguing that the condemned propositions could not be found in *Augustinus* and distorted its meaning, it was again Mazarin and anti-Jansenist bishops who successfully pressed the papacy to attribute them to *Augustinus* rightly understood, first in a brief in 1654 and then in a bull in 1656. Nor was it the Jesuits but rather the clergy's General Assembly, pressed by Mazarin, that first imposed an obligatory "Formulary" of acceptance of papal condemnation in this rigorous sense on the entire clergy in 1655. Since the regular clergy included the sisters of Port-Royal, it was with this community in mind that Louis XIV made the Formulary into a law of state and, with the help of a new archbishop of Paris, used it to disperse its solitaries and schools and begin closing down the convent 1661.

An arrangement called the "peace of the church" negotiated by philo-Jansenist Gallican bishops gave the community a decade-long reprieve after 1668.[62] But the death of Port-Royal's leading Bourbon protectress and the end of Louis XIV's Dutch War in 1679 spelled the end of the Peace of Clement IX, allowing the king to resume his policy of persecution. That policy culminated in the flight of Jansenism's leaders to the Habsburg Netherlands or the Dutch Republic, the final dispersion of Port-Royal's remaining sisters, and the physical destruction of the abbey in 1711. By that date the Sun King had literally persecuted Jansenism into the ground, having seen to the disinterment of the tombs at Port-Royal-des-Champs. For all anybody would have been able to predict in 1712, Jansenism would soon be just a memory.

Had Jansenism disappeared with Port-Royal, collective memory might have retained much that would go into the making of Reform Catholicism. Besides a mythicized memory of Port-Royal, these legacies would have included the cult of Christian antiquity, a preference for patristic to scholastic theology, a deepened sense of human debility and dependence on divine grace, a rigorous and antiprobabilistic moral theology, an exaltation of the secular relative to the regular clergy, an insistence on the laity's access to the sources of Christian revelation in vernacular languages, and a new method for teaching ancient languages in French.[63] Among "classic" works conveying these legacies were Arnauld's *La fréquente communion*, Arnauld and Nicole's quite Cartesian *Logique* and defense of the Eucharist against Protestants, Nicole's *Essais de morale* (*Ethical*

Essays), Le Maître de Sacy's French Bible, and Blaise Pascal's *Pensées* (*Thoughts*) in defense of the Christian religion.[64]

Prominent among these classics, however, stands Pascal's *Lettres provinciales* (*Provincial Letters*) against lax casuistic ethics and confessional standards, culminating with the last three, addressed to the Sun King's Jesuit confessor, François Annat.[65] One fixed constant in an otherwise variable Jansenist phenomenon is therefore the polemic against Jesuits. Developments could hardly have fallen out otherwise, since for Jansenists there was no one else they could publicly blame. It is not as though they could have attacked Louis XIV, his lay councilors, the Gallican Clergy, or even the papacy while hoping to advance their cause. Although Jesuits could not have carried the day on their own authority, they never stood far behind the papal, episcopal, or royal protagonists, beginning with Louis XIV's three successive confessors, Annat, François d'Aix de la Chaise, and most especially Michel Le Tellier. Jansenists could therefore bequeath an image of their Jesuit foes as conspiring in the shadows and as more dangerous in proportion to their obscurity.

But if seventeenth-century Jansenists added theological and moral layers to the Gallican case against the Jesuits, their own case had been only partially and sporadically Gallican. The only consistency in their commitment to the Gallican liberties was their defense of the secular clergy, especially against regulars. But with time even that preference tended to tilt toward the parish clergy away from the bishops to the degree that bishops nominated by Louis XIV sided against them. Even less classically Gallican was most Jansenists' provisional acceptance of the principle of papal infallibility where decontextualized doctrine was concerned. The Gallican qualms of the Parlement repeatedly blunted the full effect of papal condemnations against Jansenism, while Jansenism's lay constituency drew disproportionately from the judicial milieu.[66] But no Gallican-minded Parlement could have made the Jansenist cause totally its own so long as Jansenist priests stood for the spiritual independence of the clergy in relation to temporal authority in ways displayed by their associations during the final phase of the Fronde.

All that changed in the eighteenth century after Louis XIV ironically revived the dying embers of Jansenism in the very attempt to extinguish them by soliciting yet more papal bulls against it.[67] In effect, Jansenism minus Port-Royal had never lost a constituency within the Parisian parish clergy and some of the University's colleges, and acquired a newer one within the Parlement in reaction to the monarchy's pro-papal drift during the last two decades of Louis XIV's reign. Clement XI's bull *Unigenitus* of 1713 put a torch to this tinder.[68] Directed against Pasquier Quesnel's *Réflections morales sur le Nouveau testament* (*Moral*

Reflections on the New Testament), this bull condemned 101 propositions incontestably drawn from Quesnel's book, leaving Jansenists no choice but to take on papal infallibility directly.[69] Pressed by a setting Sun King to promulgate the bull, the pope took the occasion to include some Gallican propositions among those condemned while insisting on nothing less than "pure and simple" acceptance of it, leaving the Parlement and part of the Gallican Clergy little choice except to join Jansenists in contesting the bull on Gallican grounds as well.

A period of drift under his nephew's regency after the death of Louis XIV in 1715 allowed just enough time for the Jansenist and parlementary opposition to coalesce, while the monarchy's eventual decision to resume the policy of enforcing the bull put it once and for all in an all too un-French position in relation to the Gallican tradition. Since with the monarchy's support anti-Jansenist bishops appointed for that reason began to discipline Jansenist priests and their parishioners, these turned to the lay courts for redress, converting Jansenists to the parlementary version of the Gallican liberties that curtailed ecclesiastical "independence." The same realignments also produced a Gallican episcopacy ever less able to recognize episcopal Gallicanism in the Gallican tradition thus interpreted, by mid-century producing a "party" of bishops more papal than some popes.[70]

Most decisive was the decade of 1717–1727, during which three-fourths of the Parisian clergy led by four bishops formally appealed *Unigenitus* to a general council, the Parlement supported the appeal, the regency government eventually sided against it, and Jansenism acquired a popular lay Parisian constituency and cultivated public opinion as never before by launching a clandestine weekly news sheet entitled *Nouvelles ecclésiastiques* (*Ecclesiastical News*) in 1728 that thumbed its nose at church and state alike.[71] Jansenism itself changed in ways corresponding to its popularization. Although still standing for the original Augustinian "truths," the movement developed a new "figuratist" theology that interpreted the Hebrew Testament as prefiguring Christ's alliance of grace in the New, and both in turn as prefiguring the apostasy of the post-Jesuitized Gentile church. Under figuratist inspiration, and around the tomb of a deceased appellant, Jansenism produced miracles and bodily "convulsions" interpreted as vindicating or acting out Augustinian "truths."[72] With help from the works of Edmond Richer, Jansenist canonists also radicalized Gallican "liberty" by locating the church's infallibility in the "assembly of all the faithful." The same canonists began to apply that ecclesiology to the state, translating conciliar supremacy in the church into the principle of national consent as the ultimate basis of the Parlement's right to resist the royal will.[73]

After 1730, the monarchy and the pro-*Unigenitus* episcopacy reacted with purges of the priesthood, the Sorbonne, the seminaries and university colleges, and many religious orders, and also with a hail of lettres de cachet, or extrajudicial warrants of arrest, that made those accused of Jansenism into the largest category of prisoners in the Bastille.[74] The biggest single religious conflict in the century of lights, this ultimate phase of the Jansenist controversy also provoked major political crises between the monarchy and the Parlement of Paris that punctuated the century, as in 1730–1732, 1753–1754, and 1757–1758, even in some sense in 1770–74. The most damaging of these dominated the decade of the 1750s when the Parlement and others intervened in defense of Jansenists— and against the monarchy—after pro-*Unigenitus* bishops led by the archbishop of Paris systematized a policy to deny the last sacraments to priests and parishioners suspected of Jansenism.[75] By the trial of the Jesuits, French Jansenism had begun to take the form of a patriotic opposition that bears comparison to Anglo-Saxon patriotic protests in contemporaneous England and its American colonies.

No more than in the seventeenth century did Jesuits occupy the official foreground of this anti-Jansenist offensive, except in their role as Lenten preachers in parish churches and leaders of domestic missions in the provinces. The Parisian Jesuits even shut down their shop of "scriptores librorum," or writers of anti-Jansenist tracts, preferring to polemicize by proxy.[76] Yet they resembled their predecessors in never being far in the background either, whether as cardinals' consultants, court preachers, royal confessors, or the writers of episcopal mandamuses and pastoral letters. As in the seventeenth century, however, this background role served only to make the Jesuits seem more sinister, further darkening their reputation as troublemakers and persecutors by definition.

JANSENISM OUTSIDE FRANCE

It was in the company of neo-Gallican ecclesiology that Jansenism contributed to the articulation of Reform Catholicism when it spread elsewhere in eighteenth-century Europe. That Italian and Roman Augustinians did not think that *Unigenitus* had outlawed Augustine's theology of grace hardly disqualified then as "friends" of the "good cause" that French and Dutch Jansenists deemed them to be. It was not until toward the end of the century that the pontificate of Pius VI, in Mario Rosa's words, turned many philo-Jansenist "reformers" into radical neo-Jansenist "rebels."[77] What makes it difficult to separate "Jansenism" from its larger reformist matrix is that outside France and the Netherlands the formal acceptance of either the Formulary of Alexander VII or

Unigenitus never became a requirement for an ecclesiastical benefice, and with it the capacity to act as a touchstone by which to distinguish between "hard" Augustinians and Jansenists. While with one breath the Kingdom of the Two Sicilies' rabidly anti-ultramontanist first minister Tanucci hoped that Jansenists would not emerge triumphant in the wake of the expulsion of the Jesuits, with another he also professed to be a believer in the doctrines of *grazia effiace* and *predestinazione*.[78] So, was Tanucci a Jansenist or not? We have no more than his say-so as contrary evidence.

The problem is best illustrated by reformist Catholics' attitudes toward the Dutch archdiocese of Utrecht, where a Catholic clergy beached in a Protestant Republic by the Reformation trying to reconstitute itself as an "ordinary" hierarchy ran into chronic resistance from Rome. While the papacy regarded any formerly Catholic state as missionary territory, Jesuit missionaries there thumbed their noses at this clergy.[79] After 1660, a shared rigorous penitential theology as well as common enemies brought that clergy into a spiritual communion with some Parisian priests and the convent of Port-Royal, where Utrecht's archbishop Johannes van Neercassel visited and preached and whence French Jansenists fled to Utrecht when royal persecution resumed in France after 1779. Besides the subject of Jesuit high-handedness, chronic tensions between this clergy and Rome about the issues of whether the head of this clergy was a de facto archbishop or an "apostolic vicar" and whether Rome or Utrecht had the right to appoint him came to a head in 1702, when Pope Clement XI interdicted Utrecht's apostolic vicar Petrus Codde on suspicions of Jansenism and neither the Dutch Republic nor Utrecht's clergy accepted Rome's replacement. The standoff between Rome and a bishopless Utrecht starved of new ordinations went on until part of Utrecht's clergy adhered to the French appeal of *Unigenitus* to a general council and then elected and consecrated its own archbishop in 1723–24. The author of *Unigenitus*, Clement XI, responded to these provocations with anathemas, making this clergy into a reluctantly separated Catholic Church.

Subsequent attempts by this church in the course of the century to reestablish communion with Rome on something like its own terms went nowhere and attracted little attention until its clergy took advantage of Catholic Europe's mid-century anti-Jesuit turn to stage a provincial council in Utrecht in September 1763. That council made a case for its orthodoxy by condemning the Jesuits' doctrinal deviations along with those of a Protestantizing French Jansenist, whereupon that clergy's French theological consultants arranged to publish its *Actes* and send them to every corner of Catholic Europe, including the papacy.[80] The response from Catholic members of the clergy and even laymen in the form of individual or collective "letters by communion" to the

archbishop of Utrecht was impressive—about 650 signatures in 1764–1765 alone—
and conveniently spells out much about the composition and nature of reformist Catholicism from the 1760s through the French Revolution.[81]

The vast bulk of such letters over the century emanated from France, above
all from such Jansenist strongholds as Auxerre, Châlons-sur-Marne, Troyes, the
Norman Vexin, and Paris itself. Together they may be taken as representing
the Jansenist and doctrinally Augustinian component of the reformist mix.
Thus in 1765, to take a few examples at random, Troyes's archdeacon and cathedral canon Jean-Baptiste d'Aguesseau congratulated the archbishop of Utrecht
for his church's fidelity to the truths that *Unigenitus* had condemned, while
one Defays, a prior-priest of the church of Saint-Jean in Evreux, compared the
Council of Utrecht to the sixth-century Council of Orange in point of defending "the [same] dogmas that Saint Augustine had defended against the enemies
of the grace of our Savior."[82] But this priest's reference to a late antique council
is evidence that for many the mere sight of the convocation of a nonpapal deliberative council elicited the "hope"—wrote Charles Bardon, a canon in the collegial church of Leuze in Hainaut—that this "council, so [carefully] fashioned
on the model of those we most admire in antiquity, might serve as a model for
all who will follow it."[83]

To these encomia the law faculty of the University of Paris added its endorsement of this council's "wise distinction" between the canonically constrained
"primacy of the papacy . . . and the power to order other bishops despotically
around," as well as its care in recognizing the obedience due to temporal authority as an article of faith"—in effect, the first of the Gallican articles—even
in a Protestant Republic.[84] What most impressed reformist Catholics looking for
contemporary inspiration from Utrecht's example was the spectacle of a small
minority of Catholics trying to reconstitute a "national" hierarchy in a confes-
sionally heretical republic in the face of an "unjust" papal excommunication,
and forced for that reason to maintain indirect communion with the Holy See
by means of letters with other bishops, as Cyprian had done in a still pagan
Roman Empire.[85]

If in these letters the ecclesiological element tended to prevail over the
doctrinal has in part to do with Utrecht's *Actes* themselves, which soft-peddled
the theological aspect of its appeal against *Unigenitus* in 1719 in favor of the
ecclesiastical one. Unlike the French appeal in 1717, this appeal had been
double, directed not only against the bull's supposed condemnation of Augustinian truths but also against Rome's refusal to recognize this church's
continuity with the pre-Reformation Catholic hierarchy and jurisdictional
right to elect and consecrate its own bishops.

What held for French epistolary responses to Utrecht's *Actes* therefore holds in greater measure for German, Italian, and Iberian parts of Catholic Europe where a largely unenforced *Unigenitus* had produced no appellants and Jansenism shaded off into a rhetorical preference for patristic theology to propositional scholasticism, a "soft" Augustinian opposition to Molinist theology, a "harder" rigorist opposition to the Jesuits' probabilist moral theology, plus a positive admiration of the literature of Port-Royal. In view of Utrecht's larger symbolic significance as an alternatively structured Catholic Church—and despite Hontheim's rejection of the specifically Jansenist appeal of *Unigenitus*—the archbishop of Utrecht's French advocate and amanuensis, Gabriel Dupac de Bellegarde, only stretched the truth a little when he used some sympathetic comments about its council's *Actes* in the second French edition of *De statu Ecclesiae* to include Hontheim in his published list of those who had publicly "witnessed" to the Catholicity of the Utrecht church.[86]

Hontheim's oblique "testimony" in 1765 to Utrecht's Catholicity corresponds not only to the height of epistolary support for this church's provincial council as well as for the international offensive against the Jesuits—but also to the dramatic internationalization of the Gallican and Augustinian mix that has so far gone into this anatomy of Reform Catholicism. That expansion is evident in the ever more international provenance of the letters of communion themselves. First appearing in significant numbers in the mid-1760s, the number of signatures from beyond France began to compete with French ones by the end of that decade, only often outnumbering them from the 1770s onward. The numbers are small, but the trend is clear: from about ten "foreign" signatures to about fifty French ones in 1769 to nineteen foreign ones to a mere two in 1775, after which the foreigners never again lost the lead to French correspondents except in 1784 and 1787, when a Jansenist contingent from Auxerre wrote collectively and in force for the last time.[87] The letters came from Austria, the imperial principalities, Portugal, and Spain—even Ireland—but above all from the various states in the Italian Peninsula, which outdistanced all the others combined by more than a hundred to thirty, culminating in 1801, when they prevailed by seventeen to only one from France.[88]

To be sure, names of those outside France who may be described as theologically Jansenist occur in increasing numbers in Utrecht's list of epistolary communicants as the new century approached and traversed the French Revolution. The signatures encompass seminary superiors such Giuseppe Simioli in Naples, bishops such as Scipione de' Ricci in Pistoia, priests such as Marx Anton Wittola in Schörfling, and theologians such as Vincenzo Palmieri in Genoa—even royal councilors such as the physician Anton de Haen in Vienna and Miguel López in Zaragoza.[89] Among them, three also figure importantly as protagonists in the expulsions of the Jesuits, namely, Pereira de Figuereido in Portugal, the royal minister Manuel de Roda in Spain, and the Spanish but Rome-based general of the Augustinian Order Francisco Vázquez.[90]

More illuminating by Jansenist criteria are such Roman theologians as the Augustinians' procurator-general Augustino Georgi and the Scolopian theologian and cardinal Mario Marefoschi.[91] While their lack of Gallican-like animus against the principle of papal infallibility made them less than ideally Jansenist by French standards, their hard-edged Augustinian bias against Molinism and probabilism is probably what stood behind their letters of communion. But it is the opposite combination of a flexible Augustinianism with a willingness to look to the temporal powers to help transform the Catholic Church into a more collegial and locally empowered polity that inspired the letters of communion by the majority of bishops who sent them. Some such combination stood behind Hontheim's sympathy for that church, as it did behind the support of numerous others as diverse as Hieronymus Joseph Franz de Paula Graf von Colloredo of Salzburg, José de Arellano of Burgos in Spain, Paolo Caissotti of Asti in Piedmont, and a nest of no fewer than eight Neapolitan bishops, among them Filippo Sanseverino of Alife and Tomasso Taglialatela of Sora.[92]

But by far the most important of Utrecht's Italian epistolary communicants for his role in the suppression of the Jesuits was the Vatican's librarian Giovanni Gaetano Bottari. Better known as a Florentine man of letters and connoisseur of Roman antiquities, and for his description of the art works in the Vatican Palace, he was also and not least of all an ardent philo-Jansenist Augustinian and despiser of Jesuits.[93] As such he had come to preside over a group of like-minded prelates and theologians known as the Archetto that, meeting in the Corsini Palace with the blessing of the clan's two cardinals, also included Cardinal Domenici Silvio Passionei among many others, some of whom, like Bottari, wrote letters of communion to Utrecht.[94]

The role of Utrecht's quest for letters of communion in the growing cohesion and momentum of Reform Catholicism in the era of the campaign against the Jesuits came into clear focus in 1767 when Utrecht's clergy sought advice from its cadre of "friends in Vienna" about the wisdom of undertaking a new "peace" initiative toward restoring direct communion with Rome. At that point these "friends" had begun to gather in an *Abendgesellschaft*, or "evening society," grouped around the empress's quite Jansenist confessor Ignaz Müller and physician de Haen, and their advice to Utrecht was to bide its time until the next pontificate while gaining more support from Catholic princes by means of epistolary communion with their ministers and bishops. But they also warned

Utrecht to stand prepared to resign their sees and humor Roman pretensions if the next papacy insisted on reconstituting this church as though from scratch. So confident, however, that "times had so changed" in their favor that while agreeing that Utrecht should continue its quest for signs of communion, its Parisian friends counseled it to ignore Vienna's suggested concessions because the whole Catholic world now stood disabused of "ultramontanist fables," such as that the pope was a universal bishop and the bishops only his vicars, and that churches became missionary territory as soon as their sovereigns ceased to be Catholic.[95]

Exemplified by this exchange between Utrecht, Vienna, and Paris, it was this literal republic of letters uniting "friends of the Truth" on behalf of the "good cause" that held Reform Catholicism together and gave it its consistency as a movement conscious of itself as such. Largely the work of the French appellant abbé Jean-Charles Augustin Clément du Tremblay, who began to exchange letters with "friends" of that cause in Rome in the 1750s before meeting them there in 1759, that correspondence acquired many more adherents after Utrecht's theological consultant and secretarial assistant Dupac de Bellegarde similarly traveled to the Catholic capital in 1774 and on his way there and back established personal contacts with all such friends in the Catholic German states, including the Viennese Abendgesellschaft, as well as in Rome, Lombardy, and Tuscany. Although the active non-French correspondents at no time numbered more than about a hundred, many of them enjoyed direct or indirect contact with all the major movers and shakers in the campaign against the Jesuits, including Carvalho, Roda, Tanucci, and Pacciaudi in Parma. They in turn exploited that epistolary network as both a source of information and a means of disseminating their own accounts of events.

But besides the end of the Jesuits and a papal "peace" for appellants and the Catholic Church of Utrecht, this reformist republic of letters also aimed to propagate "good doctrine" and to reform the church in head and members, and to that end it distributed "good books" on "solid doctrine," canon law, and church history hither and yon. Aided by their considerable familial wealth and a Jansenist war chest known as the Boîte à Perette, Dupac did so by way of the postal director J. Gelders in Maseyck in Limburg and Girolamo Astorri in Rome, while both he and the abbé Clément had massive recourse to the services of the Jansenist booksellers Madams Desaint and Mequignon and a postal agent named Besson in Paris.[96] Typical of the inaugural exchanges between Dupac and each of his new correspondents was a request for books. Thus, for example, in 1775 Brünn's new seminary director Mechor Blarer began his correspondence with a plea for Sacy's Bible and Bonaventure Racine's short ecclesiastical history, while in 1778 the Livornian priest Antonio Baldovinetti in Tuscany began his with a request for Duguet's *Institutions catholiques* and Mésgenguy's *Exposition*, followed in subsequent letters by demands for many of the Port-Royal classics.[97] By 1789 Dupac alone had engineered an avalanche of such books down the southern slopes of the Alps into northern Italy, where in Pistoia the bishop Scipione de' Ricci published many of them in Italian translation in a series entitled "works of importance for religion."

All also asked for issues of the weekly *Nouvelles ecclésiastiques*, which, like the books, they shared or passed around to the like-minded. Although it is not possible in the present state of research to gauge the increase in the periodical's international distribution, it is impossible not to notice the vertiginous rise in its coverage of events and publications in Catholic Europe outside France during the second half of the century. A back-of-the-envelope sounding of that coverage in five years of samples from 1750 to 1785 reveals that the typically four-page, two-column weekly's international coverage rose from nothing in 1750 to 6 percent of its available space in 1755, to 12 percent in 1760, and to about 20 percent from 1765 to 1775, before peaking at 44 percent, or nearly half the total space, in 1780.[98] These percentages rose in obvious tandem with the high points of the anti-Jesuit campaign in southern Europe in the 1760s and early 1770s, followed by the reformist legislation in Lombardy, Tuscany, and the Flemish and German Habsburg possessions in the 1780s. Besides the "constants" of Rome and Utrecht, the chief beneficiaries of this increase were Portugal, Spain, and Naples, followed in time by Austria, the Austrian Netherlands, and the Rhenish prince-bishoprics. As time went on, the provenance of the information also grew in precision, as "Italy" gave way to Florence or Pavia; "Portugal" to Madrid or Evora; "Germany" to Vienna or Mainz; the "Austrian Netherlands" to Brussels and Louvain; and so on.

For its informants on the ground in these diverse places, the *Nouvelles* not surprisingly relied on the newly non-French correspondents in the reformist republic of letters. In some cases these informants can be identified with a high degree of certainly, as in the case of Bottari for Rome, Bishop Ricci and Bartomoleo Follini for Tuscany, Mark Anton Wittola and Johann de Terme for Vienna, and the governor Patrice von Neny and the canonist Josse Le Plat for the Austrian Netherlands.[99] In other cases these identities are much more conjectural, although Pereira and Roda had to have been involved in Portugal and Spain. Such was the volume of news from outside France by the 1780s that it overwhelmed the capacities of the *Nouvelles*, spawning diverse national offshoots, such as the *Annali ecclesiastici* in Florence, the *Wienerische Kirchenzeitung* in Vienna, and the *Mainzer Monatschriften* in Mainz.[100]

REFORM CATHOLICISM OR CATHOLIC
ENLIGHTENMENT?

Was Reform Catholicism also "enlightened"? If such massive recourse to a print-oriented public sphere on the part of a self-conscious republic of letters is thought to be inseparable from the Enlightenment, then Reform Catholicism would seem to merit the title. But if so, this question poses the further one of why the concept of Reform Catholicism should be preferred to the far more current conceptual coinage of a Catholic Enlightenment, which may be briefly defined as eighteenth-century Catholicism's positive rather than reactionary engagement with the European Enlightenment.

This concept originated with the early twentieth-century German Catholic historian Sebastian Merkle's defense of a prerevolutionary "enlightened" Catholicism against still ongoing accusations of the complicity of any such thing in the French revolutionary maelstrom that followed it. After a long hiatus this concept has enjoyed a robust revival since Vatican II's ecumenical opening inspired Bernard Plongeron and others to put it back on the historiographical map in the 1960s. The most distinguished historians of the Catholic Enlightenment currently include Jeffrey Burson, Harm Kleuting, Ulrich Lehner, and Michael Printy in their ranks.[101] But since many of the works on this subject also use the terms "Catholic Enlightenment" and "Reform Catholicism" interchangeably even though not all "enlightened" Catholics thought the church in need of reform, it may be heuristically helpful to distinguish between these concepts and state why "Reform Catholicism" seems preferable for the era during and after the suppression of the Jesuits.[102]

As characterized by Plongeron in a paradigmatic essay, the Catholic Enlightenment elaborated a new "religious anthropology" that vindicated the rights of reason within the bounds of revelation in contrast to Immanuel Kant's proposal to confine religion within the bounds of reason alone. It similarly endorsed the century's rehabilitation of human nature within the bounds of its revealed fallen condition and hence held out the prospect of temporal progress within the bounds of tradition.[103] Like the Enlightenment's as a whole, to some degree this progress took the form of picking up and advancing from where Renaissance Christian humanism left off; this form included an erudite recovery of the rhetorical style of patristic theology to scholastic theology's logical and prepositional form, a preference for more irenic and evidentially scrupulous ecclesiastical histories to the Tridentine era's polemical anti-Protestant ones, and a sympathy with Erasmian textual criticism and vernacular translations of Holy Writ to uncritical reliance on the Vulgate. At its most radical, this enlightenment called for a biblically based purification of Catholic devotion to replace leftover medieval "superstitions," such as the veneration of the apocryphal saints.

Yet the philosophically humanist side of the Catholic Enlightenment also enabled it to embrace the side of the moderns against the ancients in its acceptance of post-Copernican natural philosophy as well as both the mathematical and the observational methodologies that had enabled them. By the end of the century that openness had come to include the new human sciences, above all political economy. Strongest during the mid-century pontificate of Benedict XIV in the Italian states, Spain, and Portugal, the Catholic Enlightenment had its most emblematic exemplars in the priest Ludovico António Muratori in the Duchy of Modena and the Benedictine Benito Feijóo y Montenegro in Spain.

The most obvious difficulty with translating the concept of "Catholic Enlightenment" into the "enlightened" component in Reform Catholicism is that, however characterized, enlightened Catholicism has to include the many Jesuits who contributed significantly to it, while nothing negatively characterized "Reform Catholicism" quite so much as did its hostility to Jesuits. Which is to say that the late eighteenth-century polarization of Catholic Europe into anti- and pro-Jesuit camps makes it difficult to sustain a notion such as "Catholic Enlightenment" that connotes a self-conscious movement, presupposing in turn a modicum of consensus encapsulated by Ludovico Muratori's advice in 1740 to the Florentine publicist Giovanni Lami to "get to work, for the wind is blowing in our direction."[104] Confined as it may be to the century of lights, it nonetheless seems an atemporal procedure to identify everything "enlightened" in this Catholicism, deposit it all into a container corresponding to that century, and call the accumulated contents the "Catholic Enlightenment."

To be precise, the straws in the wind to which Muratori referred were the scholarly debunking of mythical saints, an emphasis on charity instead of "ecstasies, miracles, and the gift of tears," refocusing of the laity's piety on the mystery of the Mass instead of peripheral devotions, and even reconceptualizing the hierarchical church as "the body of the faithful united to Jesus Christ"—all of these trends seemingly favored by Benedict XIV and the new archbishop of Florence. At that point, however, Muratori thought generally well of the Jesuits, while the Jesuits for their part oversaw the Bollandist scholarly enterprise at Antwerp that was busily and controversially rectifying the record of all the saints whose lives had become objects of veneration in Catholic breviaries and feast days. To Robert R. Palmer's classic sketch of French Jesuits in particular as meeting philosophes as far as the doctrine of original sin would allow in the reasonable enterprise of rehabilitating human nature, more recent scholarship has added demonstrations of their belief in possibility of universal salvation without revelation and their receptivity to John Locke's empirical epistemology and Newtonian physics.[105] Variously "enlightened" Jesuits also people the pages of Lehner's recent synthetic work on the Catholic Enlightenment, especially their contribution toward a positive appreciation of non-Christian religious cultures, from the most highly "civilized" ones of China and India to the more or less "primitive" ones of Brazil and North America.[106]

But just as the Enlightenment spectrum can be broken up into many quite different lights, the Catholic Enlightenment yields more than one variety of engagement with the Enlightenment.[107] What is peculiar about the Jesuit take on the Enlightenment is its dependence on a sense-based empirical epistemology that, although distantly indebted to the scholastic dictum that "nothing resided in the intellect that was not previously in the senses," was ultimately to prove open to Locke's purely perceptual and nonessentialist version of empiricism. That relative openness in turn had to do with the Jesuit or Molinist view of humanity's Fall from created innocence. For if in that view the first human couple's disobedience to God resulted in humanity's loss of the "supernatural" gift of the immediate vision of God, a fading memory of the original revelation plus a dependence on sense perception left the will largely intact, and with it the natural capacity to use knowledge of created things to climb back toward a knowledge of an uncreated creator and the moral obligations of natural law.[108]

Hence in part the orientation of the Jesuits toward natural philosophy's new findings about creation, their generous view of postlapsarian human nature, confidence in the unaided human capacity to divine and follow the moral dictates of natural law—perhaps even the need for a divine redeemer fully to meet them.[109] It was the confidence given to them by these premises that inspired the Jesuit missionaries in their search for the most fertile soil within "pagan" religions into which to transplant revealed Christian "truth" and justified their provisional toleration of such cultic practices as China's Confucian and India's Brahman Malabar rites. Religious "toleration" being a notoriously "enlightened" virtue, the relative espousal and practice of it qualifies eighteenth-century Jesuits as meriting a secure place under the Enlightenment's sun.

This enterprise did not sit well with otherwise "enlightened" reformist Catholics who preferred antique martyrs to modern Mandarin missionaries. Nor did they appreciate domestic Jesuit missionaries' capacity to tolerate what they regarded as the "superstitious" idolatry of popular religion's quite "horizontal" veneration of saints and their relics, processions to sites of their miracle-working prowess, and earthly dependence on such "material" helps to piety as sacred images, novenas, rosaries, repetitive Marian invocations, and even bodily-bound Christocentric devotions, such as to the Sacred Heart of Jesus.[110] That the capacity of the Jesuits to "tolerate"—even aid and abet—such material ladders leading toward more abstract truths also has much to do with their partially "enlightened" sensate-oriented epistemology goes without saying.

Bound to a special vow of obedience to the papacy and and their reputation as Rome's anti-Protestant and Jansenist janissaries, professed Jesuits were not expected to find favor among those late eighteenth-century Catholics who set out to reform the structure of the Catholic Church by diminishing the power of the papacy to the benefit of states, bishops, and general councils. Jesuits qua Jesuits could not defend themselves without also defending the papacy that had authorized their Society, and with it the exercise of papal jurisdiction in all the ways that neo-Gallican ecclesiology found objectionable—annates, the Inquisition, ipso facto excommunications, territorial claims, and governance. But quite apart from these institutional considerations and even faith in divine providence, the religious sensibility of the Society of which its theology and sensate epistemology were only two outcroppings inclined it to regard the basic pyramidal structure of the church as a product of eighteen centuries worth of collective human "experience" and therefore an example of "progress" in respect to the primitive church. This view was not very different from the way David Hume, António Genovesi, and their student Voltaire regarded contemporary commercial monarchies as examples of civilizational "progress" in respect to ancient warrior republics.

Quite different was Reform Catholicism's positive engagement with the Enlightenment, one that grew into a chasm after the spread of Jansenized Gallicanism accompanying the campaign against the Jesuits ripped apart whatever consensual fabric might have underlain a self-conscious Catholic Enlightenment.[111] As in the case of the Jesuits and their like-minded allies, these differences begin at the basic epistemological level, in that to a man—and even to a woman—the Jansenist component remained unrepentantly Cartesian in the sense of positing and even feeling a radical dichotomy between the world of mind and soul on the one side and material "extension" on the other. While neither Jansenist nor Cartesian writ ran unproblematically into Catholic Europe outside France, in the Catholic German states the formidable staying power of the philosophy of Gottfried Leibniz as conveyed by Christian Wolff set limits to the influence of Lockean empiricism that held for Catholic as well as Protestant Pietist reformism.[112] That philosophy in turn found religious footing in Lutheran Augustinianism's accent on the inner as opposed to the outer man as well as on the invisible rather than visible church, reinforced at the end of the century by the Kantian standoff between human understanding and raw experience. While Wolffian Leibnizianism was not Cartesianism, the rationalist biases were akin to it, as were the sharp differences between the inner and the outer, or between the certainty of the intuitive truths of reason as opposed to the contingency of those of experience. And while Iberian and Italian Catholic Europe was more eclectic, the Gallican-Augustinian component of Reform Catholicism carried a certain Cartesian bias with it wherever it went.

What attracted Jansenists to Cartesian duality of soul and body was Augustine of Hippo's similarly Platonic dichotomy between the concupiscent senses and the directive superiority of the soul. Although vastly less systematic and more autobiographical, Augustine's procedure for "finding" God was similar to Descartes's a priori proofs in that it found him not in sense-based information or even in the soul's emotions or memories but in the seat of the soul itself, or rather in a moment of divine illumination when the soul realized that neither the truths of which it was certain nor its awareness of the author of Truth could have originated in the changing self, much less in the fickle senses, but had to have come from an immutable God "who is not offered to the corporeal senses and transcends even the mind."[113] Further, the rigid Cartesian distinction between extended matter and mind as two incommensurate substances seemed to act as a proof for the independent existence of the soul that became important to the degree that advances in eighteenth-century biological sciences made the soul an object of radical enlightened doubt.

As in the case of the Jesuits, this Augustinian Jansenist epistemology had to do with a view of humanity's Fall that in contrast to the Jesuits' view made the will the Fall's chief victim. This it did by helplessly entangling the will in the grip of the concupiscent senses and rendering it unable to heed the admonitions of a reason that retained a fragile access to truth. While for Jesuits the senses acted as a ladder toward God, for Jansenists it was only by discarding that ladder and using undistracted reason to go inward that, like Augustine, they could hope to encounter God. It was that encounter that for Jansenists revealed their unworthiness of God, brought home their dependence on divine grace, and induced receptivity to the doctrinal truths of efficacious grace and divine predestination that distinguished their theology. Although outside and even within France reformist Catholicism gradually took the sharp edges off these "truths" by putting them back in the rhetorical context of Augustine's thought, these dogmas nonetheless made for an apparently unenlightened view of postlapsarian human nature as well as so stingy a view of salvation as to diminish their estimate of "natural religion" and capacity for "enlightened" religious toleration.

Yet the same antischolastic spirit that softened Augustinian doctrines when placed in a rhetorical rather than propositional form also led Reform Catholicism on an erudite quest to rediscover antique Christendom that produced the ecclesiastical histories of Alexandre, Fleury, Thomassin, and Louis-Sébastien Le Nain de Tillemont—all of them authorities cited by Hontheim—that qualifies this aspect of Reform Catholicism as part of the enlightenment of ecclesiastical erudition identified by J. G. A. Pocock as that of Edward Gibbon, even if Protestant counterparts tended to be Arminian rather than Augustinian.[114] As translated into institutional form, that antischolastic erudition also led to a similar reformist attempt to soften the contemporary Catholic Church's hierarchical rigidity into a more supple collegial polity as well as to restore the rights of both the secular clergy and the state, as that erudition revealed those rights to have once been theirs. As Jotham Parsons reminds us, erudition had long become Gallicanism's second name.[115]

In areas where Reform Catholicism came to enjoy the protection of the "secular sword," its Augustinian bias in favor of "reason" eventually sent it on a bookish campaign literally to "enlighten" popular piety by means of catechisms, doctrinal explanations of the sacraments, and translations of both Scripture and the Mass into the vernacular. This negative side to the militant Muratorian project toward a better "regulated devotion" entailed the redistribution of monastic wealth to parish priests, the closing of chapels to the benefit of parish churches, the abolition of side altars to highlight the parish-wide Mass, the transformation of saint-orientated confraternities into companies of charity, and the abolition of images, relics, and processions in favor of instructional edification conveyed by sermons and books. Although "enlightened" in its way, this discursive attempt to address the understanding had its origin in the doctrinal conviction that, being one of the chief consequences of the Fall, ignorance was itself a sin that could not excuse any others. This typographically oriented religious sensibility stood in salient contrast to the Jesuits' toleration of popular devotional practices so long as these implied an "implicit" faith in orthodox doctrine via belief in the infallibility of the church's decisions and the efficacy of its sacraments.

Far from any belief in ecclesiastical "progress," its erudite cult of antique Christianity's pristine purity and desire to restore it gave Reform Catholicism "enlightened" company by way of eighteenth-century civic humanism, in which a similar if more secular cult of antique simplicity and denigration of decadent modernity is evident.[116] Obvious examples of civic humanist works in eighteenth-century France are the histories of Gabriel Bonnot de Mably and a certain side of the thought of Jean-Jacques Rousseau.[117] Although civic humanist thought valorized the human will where Reform Catholicism did not, its lament over the loss of ancient republican liberty and the virtues that once sustained it bear comparison to Reform Catholicism's lament over the loss of the liberties of the early church and the grace that once sustained them. In both cases liberty figures as the victim of the rise of despotism and its associated vices, in the one case in the state and in the other in the church, and in some cases both.[118] Although civic humanism's antimodernism makes it the least assimilable to any single characterization of "the Enlightenment," it nonetheless belongs in the eighteenth century with other "enlightenments," if only by virtue of its relative valuation of the *civitas terrena* and its secular well-being in relation to eternity.

While in France both Jansenism and civic humanism entered the "patriotic" lists against the monarchy's "despotic [constitutional] revolution" against the parlements in 1770–74, Reform Catholicism elsewhere in Catholic Europe limited its contestation within the church in alliance with absolute monarchies unencumbered by parlements. This pattern of alignments is entirely different from that in France, where royal policy had badgered Jansenism into a patriotic posture. Yet patriotism's antidespotic rhetoric accompanied Reform Catholicism in its baggage wherever it went, always already susceptible of antidespotic deviations toward targets other than Jesuits. Hontheim's treatise rings with denunciations of the Court of Rome, for which the Jesuits stand as shorthand, against which the appeal for action is less to the emperor than to the German "nation." In ducal Tuscany a decade and a half later, the Jansenist bishop Scipione de' Ricci of Prata and Pistois used some inherited Machiavelli papers to publish a new edition of his works featuring a preface by his equally Jansenist collaborator interpreting *The Prince* as a satire on tyranny and thinly disguised defense of republican virtue.[119] Providing theological justification for these proto-republican straws in the wind was is a slow evolution in eighteenth-century Jansenism's politial thought that made room for a civic "virtue" or "love of country" that, falling short though it did of extraterrestrial "charity," nonetheless made for its "happy preparation."[120] The phrases are those of the Jansenist theologian Jacques-Joseph Duguet, whose influential *Institution d'un prince* (*The Education of a Prince*) at Ricci's urging became one of the Tuscan duke Pietro Leopoldo's bedstand manuals.[121]

Spanning all the "enlightenments" with which Reform Catholicism made contact, however, was its willingness to use the concepts of natural law to enlarge the purview of the secular state over the church. While the Jesuits and like-minded Catholics also amply helped themselves to the concepts of nature and natural law, they did so to rehabilitate "fallen" humanity and its ability to perceive and act on the moral natural law without the church, whereas reformist Catholics wielded the concept to justify the secular state and its increasing intervention in the governance of a fallen church. That increase in the state purview had of course long been the stock-in-trade of the Gallican liberties as interpreted by the parlements, which could argue that French king's sacral identities as the "Lord's anointed," the "eldest son of the church," or "outside bishop" made him the quasi-episcopal head of the church, and that as such both he and his judges possessed the right to enforce the Gallican Church's observation of its own canon laws. But during the fraught controversy over the clergy's public refusal of the sacraments to Jansenists, Gallican magistrates instructed by Jansenist canonists, such as Claude Mey and Gabriel-Nicolas Maultrot, had increasing recourse to the king's identity as generic "political magistrate" that entitled even non-Christian potentates, such as the pagan Roman emperors, to discipline churches and their clergies in the interests of the public good.[122]

One key to this development is the growing authority of the Flemish Jansenist Zeger-Bernhard van Espen, whose various works on canon law came out in a complete edition entitled *Jus ecclesiasticum universum* in 1753 and in other editions and translations in the years following. As Michael Printy helpfully explains, van Espen's work increasing subjected various canon laws to "universal ecclesiastical laws," including those that regulated relations between church and state and made these in turn a branch of "universal law" derived from natural law accessible to human reason.[123] In the hands of jurists such as Mey and Maultrot minded to expand the state's reach over the domain of the church, the result was conceptually to embolden the interpretation of canon law, even in Gallican France, where canonists had already gone far in that direction.

A particularly flagrant example is the barrister François Richer's *De l'autorité du clergé et du magistère politique*, which, published in 1766, factored the clergy's "purely spiritual" authority as that of the weaker partner into a contract with a "sovereign" within a larger contract between it and the "nation" based on natural law.[124] This contract in turn made the "conservation and agreements of terrestrial life" of its subjects the sovereign's only concern, reducing the church to a purely voluntary association, the "exterior" and public aspects of which were subject to sovereign inspection and approval. At once enlightened and radically Gallican, Richer's treatise found both the canon laws of clerical celibacy and the indissolubility of marriage to be incompatible with the public interest.[125] The treatise is quite representative of Reform Catholicism's components in that it was also Jansenist enough in its opposition to public refusals of sacraments and belief in the divine origin of parish priests as successors of the seventy-two disciples sent out by Christ.

One measure of the impact of Richer's two-volume work is that only a year after its appearance it became the subject of a set-to in Habsburg Austria's censorship commission between Empress Maria Theresa's philo-Jansenist advisers and an ever more conservative archbishop of Vienna.[126] By that time, however, the same natural law tradition radicalizing Richer's Gallicanism had by way of another route radicalized an indigenous school of political thought in the Holy Roman Empire that similarly subordinated church to state and acquired official status the same year when the state transferred the teaching of canon law from the University of Vienna's theological faculty to the law faculty under the new rubric of public law.[127] The indigenous tradition in question was the "science" of state welfare known as Cameralism, which, Protestant in origin, had enlarged the ruler's already preponderant role as secular head, or "summus episcopus," of the empire's established churches to one that entitled the state to regulate all the "external" features surrounding inner, or "sacred," activity—things said to be "circa sacram"—by virtue of public law based on natural law. Quite apart from any divine revelation—and also like Richer's procedure—human "reason" in this scheme of things quickly discerned the need for associations endowed with collective force in view of procuring protection and material happiness. The natural need for "spiritual" associations in view of extraterrestrial happiness arose within the more basic political contract and employed the arms of persuasion rather than physical force, with the further consequence that the external form it assumed could not contradict the laws of the more basic association or state.

That this external form included Roman Catholic canon law went without saying. It was nonetheless repeatedly spelled out in the legal works of Riegger, Karl Anton Martini, Joseph Valentin Eybel, and still others, all of whom taught law in the University of Vienna. Among these others is Riegger's student Josef Johann Nepomuk Pehem, whose *Praelectionum in jus ecclesiasticum universum* showed up as a mandated textbook in canon law in the state-regulated "general seminaries" with which Emperor Joseph II replaced all episcopal and monastic seminaries in all Habsburg territories in 1787. In these works Joseph II found all the justifications he needed for his root-and-branch "Josephist" reform of every "external" form of the Catholic Church during his rule from 1780 to 1790. That the Catholic Church might use some "external" force of its own in resisting these reforms became evident in the Flemish reaction to the emperor's establishment of a general assembly in Louvain in 1787. It was also in the name of the state's rights circa sacram that Joseph II similarly launched his campaign to purify popular piety.

But what Reform Catholicism could not tolerate in popular religion the many remaining ex-Jesuits and their numerous allies in the secular as well as regular clergy not only could tolerate but also actively—even violently—defended against all comers, public officials not excepted. Lest it be supposed, however, that after the mid-century fracturing of an "enlightened" Catholic consensus the virtue of religious toleration became a Jesuit monopoly, it must not be forgotten that the same Joseph II who waged war against popular "superstition," or *Aberglaube*, was also the author of prerevolutionary Catholic Europe's only measure granting full civil toleration to both Protestants and Jews. While the inspiration of his *Toleranz Patent* of 1781 undoubtedly came from the influence of natural law and its capacity to tolerate the presence of non-"established" religions that did not run counter to the common good, this measure also enjoyed wide support by reformist Catholics, including Jansenists. Veterans of persecution themselves, since the mid 1750s French Jansenists in particular had begun to distinguish the civil from the sacramental aspects of marriage in view of legitimizing the marriages and children of French Protestants to whom Louis XIV had denied a legal existence in France in 1685. So it was also Joseph II who in 1783 followed his *Toleranz Patent* with another edict in 1783 that redefined marriage a civil contract, leaving Catholics and Protestants alike to solemnize marriages as they wished.

Nor did Joseph II's policies of religious toleration lack for Jansenist allies in his own domains, including Habsburg Lombardy, where under the pseudonym of their student "Taddeo von Trautmansdorf" (Thaddeus von Trautmannsdorff) two theologians produced the boldest statement in defense of civil toleration to appear under Catholic auspices in the prerevolutionary eighteenth century. The theologians were Pietro Tamburini and Giuseppe Zola of the University of Pavia, and their treatise concerned "ecclesiastical and civil toleration."[128] Starting with a conception of the church founded by Christ as "purely spiritual" and of the state as endowed by natural law with coactive force, these two Pavian defenders of efficacious grace and divine predestination not only limited the church's means against heretics to those of "sweetness, patience and persuasion" but also praised Joseph II by name for respecting the "rights" of heretics as citizens in the interests of Muratorian "public tranquillity" and "terrestrial felicity."[129] In Tamburini's and Zola's as in others' hands, Jansenism's contacts with the Enlightenment included a dramatic vindication—indeed, sanctification— of secular public authority in relation to the church.[130] Thus, in sum, the two sides of late eighteenth-century Catholic polarization employed the concepts of nature and natural law to divide up the work of "toleration," the Jesuits tolerating devotional and religious "deviations" in their domestic and foreign missions while reformist Catholics tolerated Protestants and Jews in Europe.

The reverse side of the concept of natural law is that of natural rights, and although Reform Catholicism did not typically extend such "imprescriptible" rights to presocietal individuals as such, it did indeed attribute them in those terms to corporate groups, such as the episcopacy versus the papacy, the parish priesthood versus the bishops, and in France the "nation" versus the monarchy. Although Hontheim's first instinct was to defend the "ecclesiastical liberty" of the German episcopacy on the basis of the "indubitable oracles of Jesus Christ and the usages of the first centuries," in a pinch he showed himself willing to appeal to the natural "law of nations" as well.[131] For their part French and Italian Jansenists alike willingly extended natural rights to Protestants by virtue of the right to marry without sacramental solemnization.[132] The appeal to the natural and therefore imprescriptible rights on behalf of the nation against the monarchy by patriotic French Jansenists from 1771 forward is too notorious to belabor.[133]

CONCLUSION

Reform Catholicism's combination of theological, ecclesiastical, and enlightened parts and parcels produced a vision of a best state of affairs that, though never realized in practice, gave direction to many of Catholic Europe's political makers and shapers and scored its most spectacular success with the international expulsions and suppression of the Jesuits. In this ideal Catholic Christendom, a church based on an image of the early church's "comely centuries" minded its purely spiritual business of preaching the Gospel, administering the sacraments, and tending to the poor while remaining obedient to secular authority. This polity, moreover, provided for no benefices except for priests or bishops who served parishioners in these capacities, nor did it contain many monks.

In contrast to secular authority, the polity's superiors made no decisions without consulting their whole communities, while as pope the bishop of Rome enjoyed no other "divine" authority over the whole church than that of canonical oversight. In Rome and in all other dioceses, the bishop rose to his office via election by clergy and people, although each also derived his "spiritual" authority from Christ. Each "national" church also possessed all it needed to govern itself, free to follow its own liturgical usages in languages accessible to all. In periods of peace, each church also sent either its bishop or priests to provincial and general councils, where Rome's delegates exercised no more authority than others. In the absence of councils bishops corresponded with each other, each assuming responsibility for the whole as much as Rome did.

As imagined, this Catholic polity was compatible with anti-Pelagian Augustinian theology and rigorous penitential ethics in that it was easy to think of divine grace as reaching more communicants than after the Christianization of the Roman Empire brought in chaff in greater proportion to the wheat. In a state of grace more often than not, Christians might then take Communion daily, as Arnauld imagined they once did and hoped they might again. Although its only salvific means were persuasion, this imagined community might still excommunicate sinners, as all knew the early church had done after communicants apostatized in times of persecution. That in contemporary Catholic states excommunication would entail civil consequences did not always diminish the nostalgia for the early church, although Reform Catholics softened the rigor by rejecting Rome's ipso facto excommunications and regarded excommunications as just only when accompanied by the entire congregation's presumed consent.

Although Catholic potentates did not share the affection Reform Catholicism had for deliberative councils, they perceived their temporal interest in its vindication of secular authority and call for the recovery of the authority lost during the medieval "centuries of ignorance." At its most radical, this recovery distinguished between the secular and sacramental aspects of marriage and the civic and religious identities of Protestants in view of asserting state control over marriage in the one case and the right to tolerate religious dissident in the other. While ultramontanist Catholic theologians thought that the state's acceptance of Christianity had limited its jurisdiction to what was strictly temporal, reformist Catholics thought it had enhanced the Christian ruler's authority by extending it to areas around if not within the sacred. Nor did aversion to councils prevent princes or their councilors from using conciliar theory as a means to oppose the papacy as a competitive monarchy, especially as defended by the Jesuits.

In these as in many other ways, Reform Catholicism encountered its mirror opposite in the Society of Jesus. In contrast to the collegiality of reformist Catholics stood the monarchy of the Society, to their deliberations its blind obedience, to their localisms its unity, to their diversity its uniformity. These differences reformist Catholics morally magnified through the lenses of their ethical and doctrinal differences and experience of defeat. So to their intuitive understanding corresponded the Jesuits' externality of idolatry; to their quest for the pristine, its cult of contemporary decadence; to their principled disobedience, its blind obedience; to their spirit of truth, its desire of domination; and to their work of persuasion, its shortcut by persecution. In a few words, reformist Catholics styled themselves as standing for liberty against despotism, candor against conspiracy, light against darkness—in sum, virtue against vice.

2

THE GENESIS AND TRAJECTORY
OF ANTI-JESUITISM, 1554-1761

Late eighteenth-century Reform Catholicism defined itself negatively by its opposition to the Society of Jesus. Yet that opposition was inherited from its largely Catholic progenitors, anti-Jesuitism having preceded it by two hundred years. Necessary to a full understanding of the justifications of the international suppression of the Society, the long history of anti-Jesuitism features a succession of protagonists, none of whom took part in a reformist Catholic movement until such a movement took shape on an international scale in the mid-eighteenth century. Until that point, the genesis of anti-Jesuitism is a largely French story.

THE JESUITS AS AN ULTRAMONTANIST THREAT
TO THE RENAISSANCE STATE

It goes without saying that the fledgling Society's unique fourth vow of obedience to the papal vicar of Christ made it immediately anathema to the newly Protestant territorial or city-states of Europe, quite apart from the reputation for anti-Protestant prowess—as the shock troops of the Counter-Reformation—that the Society later acquired in education, polemical theology, the direction of royal consciences, and complicity in plots to assassinate Protestant princes. Whether they acknowledged it or not, later Catholic polemicists drew generously from a copious Protestant production. Still other features raised Catholic hackles everywhere, not only in France. Combined with the papal fourth vow, for example, its highly monarchical structure,, culminating in the authority of its general, made the Society more international than other Catholic socieites and therefore put it at variance not only with republics such as Venice but also in potential competition with royal authority in emerging proto-national "new monarchies" such as France and Spain. Nor did the papacy's conferral of exemptions from "ordinary" episcopal, parochial, and even secular authorities endear the Society to priests, bishops, or judges, however Catholic they might be. That France emerged as the leader in the formation of Catholic anti-Jesuitism does not mean that the French polemicized alone.

No less a Catholic stronghold than seventeenth-century Poland—and no less a Jesuit than the former father Hieronim Zahorowski—contributed the famous *Monita privata Societatis Jesu*, better known as *Monita secreta*, which in seventeen chapters pretended to reveal the "secret" of Jesuit instructions in contrast to the Society's official constitutions composed by Loyola and perfected by Diego Laínez.[1] Machiavellian in tone and perhaps in imitation, the treatise supposedly laid bare the methods by which members of the Society were to acquire influence, property, and power, as well as how to keep them. Although the *Monita secreta* saw almost simultaneous republication in Italy and France during the suppressions and expulsions of the mid-eighteenth century, it was as an appendix in a four-volume book in France that its influence was most telling.[2] The Jesuits' homeland, Spain itself, gave birth to one of the classics in the anti-Jesuit genre, the *Teatro Jesuítico*, attributed to the Dominican Juan de Ribas y Carrasquillas, who taught in Cordova.[3] If, however, this censured and almost inaccessible polemic continued to find readers, it was because the French Jansenists Antoine Arnauld and Sébastien-Joseph du Cambout de Pontchâteau translated and reprinted portions of it in 1669 in the first volume of what would be the multivolume *La morale pratique des jésuites* (*The Moral Practice of the Jesuits*).[4]

Spain nonetheless largely escaped such concentrated doses of anti-Jesuitism, in part because of the Society's largely Spanish origin, and in part because it aligned itself with the anti-Protestant foreign policy of the Habsburg king Felipe II, who in 1580–1582 added adjacent Portugal—and with it, Portuguese Jesuits—to his dominions. For Spain was also the metropolitan center of an empire secure enough to absorb them and even use them as its agents. The Spanish sixteenth century produced only two critics of the Jesuits to whose authority later enemies of the Society would ritually appeal: Benito Arias Montano, a celebrated Hebraist and one of the authors of Cardinal Francisco Ximenès de Cisnero's famous polyglot Bible, and Melchor Cano, a Dominican theologian, professor, and bishop and the author of the highly respected *De locis theologicis* (*Theological Topics*), published in 1563.

Of the two, Arias Montano's anti-Jesuitism most closely anticipates the politicized anti-Jesuitism of the mid-eighteenth century. For he accused the Society of nothing less than using the enormous influence it had acquired over princes to undermine the integrity of their states by its real aim of erecting its own "monarchical dominion" from within them. But these warnings to King Felipe II lay mainly unread in manuscript until recently unearthed.[5] Arias Montano's public utterances in contrast amounted to little more than complaints about the "impenetrable and mysterious secrecy of the way [the Jesuits] conduct their affairs" and a warning to the Prudent King in 1571 not to employ them as confessors or preachers in the Low Countries. If Arias Montano's name figured so prominently in later cases against the Jesuits, it is again because in 1701 the "great" Arnauld appealed to it as evidence of precocious opposition to the Society in one of his many anti-Jesuit publications.[6]

Scattered throughout his published works and letters, the objections Cano made against the Jesuits run parallel to those of many other early Catholic critics, particularly those in France. As a Catholic, Cano objected to the exclusive appropriation of the name of Jesus; as a Dominican, to the Jesuits' uncloistered style and dispensation from fasting and liturgical hours; as a bishop, to their papal privileges exempting them from episcopal authority; and as someone with an ex-officio interest in the stable parish ministry, to what he perceived as a lax confessional practice and permissive penitential theology.[7] At his most radical, in his opposition to the Society's papal privileges he verged on a critique of the post-Tridentine growth of papal power.[8] All these critiques were destined for a robust future in the ideology of anti-Jesuitism, and to that degree it was with good reason that later enemies of the Jesuits appealed to Cano as a predecessor and prophet.

But at the heart of Cano's hostility lay a theological concern specific to Spain that would later be all but forgotten, even in Spain. In the new Society's neglect of traditional monastic routines and in Ignatian spirituality's emphasis on mental prayer, Cano's scholastic theological antennae sensed something akin to the mystical self-abandoning indifference and neglect of the means of grace characteristic of the heresy of the "alumbrados," or truly "enlightened" ones, who had attracted inquisitorial attention in sixteenth-century Castile.[9] But in perceiving *alumbradismo* in Jesuit spirituality, Cano was barking up a dying tree. So far was Ignatian inner devotion from any neglect of the sacramental means of grace that Jesuit spirituality's insistence on frequent Communion would later get the Society into equal but opposite trouble. While a certain school of early seventeenth-century French Jesuits would be attracted to a more mystical spirituality than that bequeathed to them by Loyola, the rather methodical character of their own devotional style remained impervious to mystical deviations. And although many of his Catholic contemporaries shared the umbrage Cano took at the Society's structural departures from the monastic mold, the source of his most serious concerns lay in theological preoccupations unique to sixteenth-century Mediterranean Europe that would not survive as parts of the case developed against the Society in later centuries. As in the case of Arias Montano, something anachronistic adheres to later appeals to Cano's authority against the Jesuits, an authority cited either to nationalize or inflate the number of authorities.

Arias Montano and Cano did not an anti-Jesuit school of opinion make. When anti-Jesuitism took firmer form in the Spanish Habsburg world, it did so on the periphery of the empire: as an expression of anti-Spanish feeling in the Dutch and Flemish provinces in the sixteenth century, as the revenge of "ordinary" episcopal against "regular" authority in Mexico and other American colonies in the seventeenth century, or as the resentment of rival Spanish missionaries in the Far East in the seventeenth and eighteenth centuries. Juan de Ribas's *Teatro*, for example, is best situated in this emerging quarrel between his Dominican Order and the Jesuits, doubled in his case by the threat to his authority as a bishop. It was as a state trying to recover from the burdens of empire that Spain or at least its relatively new Bourbon monarchy and its ministers finally turned against the Jesuits in the mid-eighteenth century. Even then anti-Jesuitism did not run very deeply in the Spanish population.

The contrast with France could not have been starker. There, the Valois dynasty's almost constant conflict with the Spanish Habsburgs had produced no little anti-Spanish feeling, while the clergy's support of the monarchy in its late medieval conflict with the papacy combined with monarchy's support of the clergy in its effort to use general councils to reform the church during the Great Schism had produced the body of ecclesiastical theory and legal maxims known as the "Gallican liberties." Although the English, German, and Iberian clergies had also concurred in the Council of Constance's decree attributing the Catholic Church's infallibility to general councils instead of the papacy, France alone retained it and enshrined it in law, making the kingdom inhospitable even to the ultramontanist bias of the ecclesiastical decrees of the Council of Trent.[10] Last but not least, the Protestant Reformation by way of Geneva had made serious inroads into France by 1559, and the thirty years of civil religious wars between Huguenots and Catholics that began three years later would not only put the monarchy in the crossfire but also eventually threaten the unity of a realm that the monarchy had pieced together since the tenth century. In the last of the sixteenth-century wars, the Spain of Felipe II intervened on the side of the ultra-Catholic League or Holy Union against the still Protestant claimant, Henri of Navarre, thus reinforcing the association between the Jesuits, Spain, and the threat to the identity and even existence of the French realm.

At no point during these religious civil wars did the French monarchy really side with the Protestants, in part because the concordat negotiated by King François I with the papacy on the eve of the Reformation gave the monarchy close to total control over nominations to major benefices within the Gallican Church in return for the monarchy's abandonment of elections of bishops and of its support for general councils. That entente in part accounts for why that monarchy could and did support the Jesuits when they first sought admission in France. But that entente did nothing to reconcile the clergy, the University of Paris, and the French parlements. Since all of these institutions remained loyal to the older aspects of the Gallican tradition, they in turn functioned as so many additional reasons to resent the Jesuits. As in the case of the Concordat of Bologna itself in 1516, the admission of the Jesuits in France would provoke resistance by these bodies in the name of liberties in some sense more Gallican, or at least differently Gallican, than the liberty of temporal independence dear to the king.

It was therefore the French monarchy in the person of Henri II that first sponsored the admission of the Jesuits in France with royal letters patent in 1554. Henri II died from a wound incurred in a joust in 1559 before being able to make good on the royal resolve, but royal support survived his death and continued throughout the long and tumultuous regency of Catherine de Medici and the reign of her sons Charles IX and Henri III—indeed, all the way to the mid-eighteenth century. In addition to the support of the monarchy, the first French Jesuits enjoyed the support of some bishops from the high nobility—another future source of support—most notably Charles de Guise, archbishop of Reims and cardinal de Lorraine, and Guillaume du Prat (or Duprat), bishop of Clermont, who would establish the first French Jesuit college, in Billom in Auvergne, and provide the locale for the Jesuits' college in Paris in the Hôtel de Clermont in the rue de la Harpe. Along with Eustache du Bellay, bishop of Paris, these churchmen had come to appreciate the anti-Protestant potential of the Jesuits while participating as France's delegates in the Council of Trent in spite of their quite Gallican objection to the strident stand of the Jesuits' general Diego Laínez in favor of the supremacy of the pope over the whole church and its general councils in 1562–1563. For in addition to its already notorious ultramontanism, the new Society bristled with papal privileges not only exempting Jesuits from the tithe but also entitling them to preach and administer the sacraments without the permission of the "ordinary" clergy, whether bishops or curés. None of these features was likely to endear it to the rest of the Gallican Clergy, not to mention the parlements and the University of Paris. Even with the backing of the monarchy, the struggle for the Society's admission in France was an uphill one from the outset.

Thus it was that, initially seconded by Du Bellay and the dean and theological faculty of the University of Paris, the Parlement of Paris led a rearguard resistance against the registration of royal letters patent intended to give the Jesuits a legal existence in the Hôtel de Clermont, their first foothold in Paris. Of most concern to the Parlement was the Society's needless newness and array of papal privileges, including an exemption from the tithe, to Du Bellay on behalf of the clergy its arrogation of the name of Jesus and immunity from the jurisdiction of clerical "ordinaries," and to the University of Paris its secular-like deviations from the monastic model that threatened to enable its members to escape the University's curricular restrictions on its affiliated monastic orders and become a pedagogical rival. But these features of the new Society disturbed all its critics, not only in France but elsewhere as well, as did its many papal exemptions and privileges, including one that allowed it to acquire benefices despite the vow of poverty it shared with other regular orders.[11]

What was different about the lay of the land in France was the banner of the Gallican liberties, to which opponents of the Jesuits could appeal to mount a more principled resistance than elsewhere. It was likewise the existence of these principles that accounts in good part for the comparatively large anti-Jesuit literature that the conflict began to produce there. In the Parlement and the newly established General Assembly of the Gallican Clergy, moreover, these liberties had two fiscally indispensable and regularly meeting institutions diversely determined to defend them. A third institution with a stake in these liberties was the University of Paris, which in a judgment that would resound through the centuries concluded that the new Society would be "dangerous for the faith, apt to trouble the peace of the church and overturn the monastic order, and more likely to destroy than to edify."[12] But while the University had contributed illustriously to the conciliar tenets of the Gallican tradition, it was also the weakest of the three and had the most immediately to lose to a society defined by learning and teaching.

It was in view of that threat that the University again objected to the Society's hermaphroditic character in a suit against it ten years later, in February 1565. "Are you seculars, regulars, or monks?" the rector of the University asked of the Jesuits representing their society. We are "tales quales," or "such as we are," was the unsettling answer, one that also went into the making of the image of the Jesuit as a slippery presence. By this date the University's worst fears had materialized, and its rector was trying to get the Jesuits to admit that they were regulars or monks in order to fend off the Society's first attempt to obtain formal incorporation. For meanwhile, in 1561, the Parlement of Paris had finally registered royal letters patent accepting the Society's presence in Paris, but only as a "society," or "college," and not as a new religious order. Duly recorded by the Sorbonne at the time, these restrictions on the Society's admission had been the price paid to obtain the consent of the bishop of Paris, who also insisted that the Society not be able to take the name of Jesus or be allowed to interpret Scripture without the University's authorization. Still, it had taken nothing less than the threat of Protestantism to obtain the endorsement of the Gallican Clergy at the Colloquy of Poissy, and this endorsement in turn for the royal court to overcome the resistance of the Parlement of Paris, which finally registered the royal letters patent in 1562. Registering the restrictions of the bishop of Paris as well as those of the colloquy, the Parlement therefore authorized the presence of the Jesuits in Paris only as the "College of Clermont," with the additional provisos that they renounce all papal privileges, undertake nothing contrary to the rights of curés, parishes, chapters, universities, or secular powers, and accept the supervision of the bishop.[13] Last but not least, the Parlement made the presence of the Jesuits as a "college" provisional on the fulfillment of these terms.

That as early as 1564 the Jesuits opened classes in a newly purchased edifice called the "College of the Society of the Name Jesus" became evidence for their enemies that they were not men of their word. Challenged by the University, the Jesuits appealed to it for official affiliation; when instead the University charged that the Jesuits were indeed acting as both Jesuits and "regulars" and had violated the conditions of their provisional acceptance, the Jesuits appealed their case to the Parlement of Paris. With the bishops of Paris and Beauvais, Parisian curés, the University, the affiliated mendicant orders, and the city government all arrayed as plaintiffs against them, the Jesuits would hardly have prevailed against an already hostile Parlement had not the queen mother and Charles IX intervened in their favor. The case therefore ended in something of a draw, with the Jesuits able to continue teaching but without incorporation into the University. For its part the Parlement never judged the substance of the case but instead "appointed," or postponed, it sine die.

But before it was over, both the Parlement's *avocat général*, Charles Du Moulin, and the University's advocate, Étienne Pasquier, produced classics in the growing genre of anti-Jesuit literature.[14] While Du Moulin emphasized the ultramontanist and "foreign" threat posed by the Society's special vow of obedience to the papacy, Pasquier dwelt on its distinction between the "small" and "great" membership—between simple and solemn vows, that is—which in his opinion enabled Jesuits to have it both ways. As novices they might inherit money from their families, while as fuller-fledged members they would bequeath it to the Society in a manner that would belie their vows of poverty. If they were to be tolerated, he concluded, "there is no prince or potentate able to secure his state against their attacks."[15] So far, in sum, the French case against the Jesuits depicted them as avaricious, duplicitous, enterprising, liminal, and above all as subversive as a Trojan horse for papal pretensions in Gallican France.

By the time Du Moulin and Pasquier had emptied their inkwells and unloaded their lungs against the Jesuits, France's bloody civil wars of religion were under way, having begun with the duc de Guise's massacre of Huguenots at Vassy in 1561 and the Protestant seizure of town governments in 1762. So long as it was the Protestants who were on the offensive, French Jesuits remained a peripheral target; Protestants themselves benefited from this situation by casting themselves as allies against that common enemy. In the ensuing melee, no one except Protestants thought to blame the Jesuits for the assassination of Admiral Gaspard de Coligny or the massacre of the Huguenot nobility on Saint Bartholomew's Day in 1572. But it was otherwise after the Catholic League seized power in Paris at the expense of the king in May 1588, and even more so after the assassination of Henri III in 1589 made his distant Protestant relative Henri of Navarre his successor by virtue of the Salic Law. For five or six years the forces of the League held out against the army of Henri of Navarre in a number of cities, including Paris, where in 1593 the League convoked an assembly of the Estates General with an eye toward finding a dynastically plausible substitute for the Bourbon heir apparent.

Since the Jesuits did not then populate Paris or France in force, they could hardly have been the most numerous of the League's clerical supporters. Far more influential were the famous "leaguer" curés of Paris and the various offshoots of the mendicant orders, especially on the Franciscan side. Further, French Jesuits constituted far from a unified force in France during the religious civil wars. Exemplifying this inconsistency is Edmond Auger, the Society's most famous preacher in France, who at first took the side of the ultra-Catholic Guise family against King Charles IX, only later to support Henri III and his attempt to chart a middle course between the Protestants and the League. Most consistently militant on the ultra-Catholic side was the provincial of France, Claude Mathieu, who, known as the "courier of the League," helped organize the League in 1584 and favored Spanish armed intervention in France against Henri III in 1788. Somewhere in between was the Paris provincial Odon Pigenat, whose letters to the general Claudio Acquaviva suggest a state of real stress at the need to make such political choices.[16]

But the Jesuits were new and few enough to attract disproportionate attention; fine distinctions between them got lost in the contemporary shuffle. What got retained in Gallican memory was that Auger had preached incendiary sermons in the wake of St. Bartholomew's Day in Paris, that Claude Mathieu was more loyal to Felipe II than to any of the kings of France, and that Odon Pigenat had acted as the secretary for Paris's insurrectionary government known as the Sixteen. For subsequent anti-Jesuit polemicists, the distance between such reasonably well established facts to assigning central causal roles to Jesuits in these and other cases was an irresistible one. While the origin of most mendicant orders was no more French than that of the Jesuits, the Society's Spanish origin, dedication to the papacy, novel organization, and brash attempts to gain official affiliation with the University made its members renewed targets of royalist and Gallican ire.

Symptomatic of their vulnerability is the numbers of pamphlets that singled out the Jesuits as agents of Spain, even as early as during the League's reign in Paris. Published in 1592—and probably written by Antoine Arnauld—the full title of the pamphlet *Anti-espagnol* (*Anti-Spaniard*), for example, denounced the "doings and ruses of the Jesuits with the Inquisition and Castilian slavery." This and other pamphlets renewed suspicions that any and all gatherings of Jesuits acted as so many "Spanish colonies" that had used the appearance of piety to foment conspiracy, employed the confessional to enlist recruits of the League, and had changed French liberties into disloyalty and rebellion.[17] Among the liberties in question were of course the liberties of the Gallican Church.

Already depicted as foreign and pro-papal by 1593, the Jesuits were the most obvious suspects in the attempts to assassinate Henry of Navarre after his less than universally convincing conversion to Catholicism and his assumption of the title of Henri IV. To be sure, no evidence linked Jesuits to the assassination of Henri III at Saint-Cloud on 1 August 1589—the work of Jacques Clément, a Dominican monk. But when a boatman turned League-side soldier named Pierre Barrière intent upon stabbing the king stumbled into a manhunt for him in Melun in August 1593, his contacts with other monks and the curé of Saint-André-des-Arts did nothing to prevent Pasquier from highlighting Barrière's denunciation of the Jesuit Amboise Varade as his encouraging confessor. In his *Histoire prodigieuse* (*Extraordinary History*) of the event published the following year, Pasquier interpreted the entire episode as a plot by the "Jesuit sect" and the "Spanish party"—and the fulfillment of his own direst prophesies as the University's advocate against the Jesuits thirty years earlier.[18]

Nor for that matter did that confession prevent the Jesuit preacher Jacques Commolot from actually calling for an "Ehud" (the biblical assassin of the king of Moab) to assassinate Henri IV in the winter of 1594.[19] Meanwhile, news of contacts between Jesuits and William the Silent's assassin, Balthazar Gérard, in 1584 as well as Jesuit involvement in plots against Queen Elizabeth for the benefit of either Felipe II or Mary Stuart of Scotland began to add to the regicidal image of Jesuits in Catholic France. While assassination attempts against "heretical" princes may have seemed beside the point in Catholic France before 1585, they took on a more sinister aspect after France's own heir by Salic Law was a Protestant, even after his conversion in 1593.[20]

So when after Henri IV's reentry into Paris the University's new rector, Jacques Amboise, reopened the still "appointed" case of 1564, this time with the request that the Jesuits be "exterminated" from both the niversity and all of France, it was with far heavier ammunition than in 1564. To be sure, the University's advocate in the case before the Parlement, Antoine Arnauld père, did not fail to retrace the terrain already traversed: the Society's offer to teach for nothing was a means of luring children away from parents and into its nets, the Society's nonreciprocal simple vows a means of inheriting property while having its poverty too, its confessions a means of knowing the secrets of families while adding to its wealth, and so on.[21] But Arnauld's essential case was quite new and consisted in the charge that, in contrast to the "frank and free" French, the Jesuits were the "spies of Castile" and the killers of kings. If, in their "boutiques of Satan," the Jesuits were also corrupters of the youth they taught, it was because their only real precept was "to kill, massacre, hang, and torture."[22]

Still, the University's case against the Jesuits would probably have failed had not a young law student named Jean Chastel lunged at Henri IV with a knife near the Louvre in late December 1594, succeeding only in cutting a lip and breaking a tooth. Although Chastel refused to inculpate any Jesuits, his interrogation revealed that he had studied at their college until seven months earlier under one Jean Gueret. A search of the college also turned up in the possession of the librarian some compromising although undated writings against Henri IV and in justification of tyranicide.[23] This evidence was enough for the Parlement to exile Gueret and hang the librarian—and to decide the University's ongoing case against the Jesuits, expelling them from France in January 1595.[24] Although Henri IV would disculpate the Jesuits in this and other cases and readmit them despite the Parlement's resistance a mere seven years later, their association with Pierre Barrière and Jean Chastel would remain forever fixed in historical memory.

At that point, in 1794–1795, the Gallican case against the Jesuits could point to regicidal actions and rhetoric but to little by way of theory. A substantial body of Christian philosophical and theological casuistry defining different types of "tyrants" and stating when and under what circumstance his subjects might revolt or an individual might assassinate him had slowly accumulated since late antiquity, from Saint Augustine to Thomas Aquinas. With the coming of the Reformations and the wars of religion, theologians on both sides of the religious divide expanded these conditions, especially when the tyrant endangered the spiritual destiny of his subjects as a heretic.

What distinguished Catholic casuistry was the role reserved for papal excommunication in designating a ruler as a heretic, and in the emphasis on individual action. Thus, the papacy had excommunicated both Henri III and Henry of Navarre, to say nothing of Queen Elizabeth or William of Orange, and individuals had plotted and acted against all (with success against Henri III and William of Orange). But Jesuits had so far contributed very little to this body of casuistry. As of 1594, the only such utterance by a Jesuit that might have come to Arnauld's attention was the Portuguese Jesuit Emmanuel Sà's *Aphorismi confessiorum* (*Aphorisms of Confessors*), which, published in 1590, gave anyone the right to dispatch a "tyrant" who had legitimately come to the throne so long as a public judgment or sentence preceded his or her action.[25] Similar pronouncements by the English Jesuits Robert Parson and John Bridgewater did not appear until 1593.[26] Yet neither Arnauld nor Pasquier had built a case on any of them.

Far different was the case in 1603 when Henri IV sought successfully to restore the Society in France, and the Parlement again led the resistance.[27] Predictably recalling the Jesuits' connections to the assassination attempts by Barrière and Chastel and their role in the League, the remonstrances of the first president, Achille de Harlay, on 24 December 1603 lost no time in connecting these events to the Society's oath of obedience to the papacy and adherence to the Spanish-like maxims.[28] But these remonstrances did little more than summarize one of the classics of anti-Jesuitism to emerge from this controversy over the reestablishment, namely, Antoine Arnauld's *Le franc et véritable discours au roi, sur le rétablissement qui lui est demandé pour les jésuites* (*Frank and True Address to the King on the Subject of the Requested Reestablishment of the Jesuits*).[29]

Published the previous year, Arnauld's treatise named names, among them Emmanuel Sá. But by this time the Italian Jesuit Roberto Bellarmino had also gone on record with his theory of the papacy's "indirect" temporal power to permit subjects to disobey and even to change their rulers by reason of his direct spiritual power to judge and excommunicate impenitent rulers. By this time as well, the French Jesuit Louis Richéome had done Arnauld the favor of restating this theory in his anonymous reply to his *Plaidoyer*.[30] Not only did Arnauld argue that the Jesuits' vow of obedience made the Society responsible for every such utterance, he also held that theory had always already preceded practice, making the Jesuits the "true fathers of the League" in theory as well as in practice. For Arnauld, that putative consistency in turn explained the inconsistency and duplicity of all Jesuit denials or claims to the contrary—in short, the fact that, unlike the "bon François," they "did not speak French." If there was any language the Jesuits spoke—the final association—it was Spanish, "showing themselves to be perfectly committed to the King of Spain."[31]

The theory of tyrannicide also enabled Étienne Pasquier to complete the indictment of the Jesuits that he had begun in 1564 with his *Catéchisme des jésuites (The Jesuits' Catechism)*, an anti-Jesuit *Summa* published in 1603. Villainy, dupery, duplicity, trickery, heresy, hypocrisy, charlatanry, impiety, and what Pasquier called "papalardy"—there was nothing in this indictment of which the novel "sect" of the Jesuits was not guilty. As in 1564, Pasquier continued to hold the Society's part-secular, part-regular "hermaphrodite" character against it. In perhaps the *Catéchisme's* best-known scene, Pasquier staged a celestial procession in which Ignatius and his Ignatians tried in vain to take their places in the column headed by Saint Peter, who refused to recognize them as bishops or priests; by Saint Anthony, who refused to hail them as hermits; by Saint Benedict, who did not see them as cenobites; and even by Jean Gerson, the fifteenth-century chancellor of the University of Paris, who refused to accept them as scholars.[32]

The author of the *Catéchisme* remained just as concerned as he was in 1564 with the Society's vow of obedience to the papacy and papal privileges, incompatible as they were with "the Majesty of our Kings and the liberties of our Gallican Church."[33] But in now perceiving the Jesuits' "blind obedience" to their general as nothing less than a usurpation of the power of the papacy as well, Pasquier turned this ultramontanist society into an apparent threat to the ultramontanist cause itself and formulated an argument destined to have a devastating future. He similarly construed the principle of blind obedience as the real source of the Society's theory and practice of tyrannicide. As for what constituted the "soul" of the Society, Pasquier parted paths with Arnauld, who still thought it was Spanish and opted instead for the "commodity of its own affairs."[34] Far from being a society devoted to Jesus or even the pope, it had become an "absolute power" unto itself, a "tyranny" with no purpose but its own.

Pasquier's *Catéchisme* and Arnauld's *Franc et véritable discours* mark the crest of France's first and mainly Gallican wave of anti-Jesuitism. In sheer force and violence, it is equal to anything produced by the rest of the seventeenth and the eighteenth centuries. Yet having postured themselves as the defenders of Henri's accession and absolute royal authority against the Jesuits and the Catholic League, good Gallicans and former "politiques" found themselves defenseless when, in need of papal support, the first Bourbon king decided to use his newly reinforced absolute authority to recall the Jesuits and legitimize their position in France in 1603. Not even the assassination of Henri IV by François Ravaillac in 1610 in the wake of the publication of a recklessly regicidal treatise by yet another Spanish Jesuit enabled the Parlement of Paris to reverse the gains made by the Jesuits under Henri IV. For the regency government of Marie de Medici lost no time in emphatically reaffirming the monarchy's support for the Society.

To be sure, the regency government allowed the Parlement to condemn Juan de Mariana's *De rege et regis institutione* (*Of the King and Kingship*)—the treatise at issue—but did not permit it to use this condemnation to indict the Jesuits, and it was even more resistant to the Parlement's attempt to condemn a succession of other such treatises, among them Bellarmino's *Tractatus de postestate summi pontificicis in rebus temporalibus* (*Treatise on the Power of the Pope in Temporal Matters*).[35] The most the Parlement and the University of Paris could accomplish was to prevent the Jesuits' College of Clermont in Paris from obtaining official affiliation with the University in 1609–1610, although not from reopening its doors to students with royal permission in 1618.

Apart from fixing the image of the Jesuit as theoreticians and practitioners of royal assassination, what these controversies accomplished was to maintain the Jesuit as a symbol of foreign interference and sinister servility in the Gallican ideology of the bon françois. A prolongation of the politique ideology of the last stages of the wars of religion, the bon françois ideology defined itself in opposition to the pro-papal and Spanish turn of the French foreign policy of the regency government. It therefore also squared off against the influence of what contemporaries called the pro-Jesuit *parti dévot*, or devout party, that, headed by the queen mother and the guardian of the royal seals, Michel de Marillac, was itself an outgrowth of the Catholic League. In the view of the bon françois, the Jesuit remained an inassimilable presence in France due to his vow of "blind obedience" to another prince, who, whether the pope or the king of Spain, made that vow incompatible with the "Royalty of France . . . , with the doctrine of the Gallican Church and the University, and with being subjects of the State, in view of the unique obedience owed by them . . . to their prince."[36] If choose he had to between the Jesuit and the Huguenot, the bon françois would prefer the Huguenot, "who had at least never renounced his patrie."[37]

Yet the condemnation by the bon François of the Jesuit's refusal to acknowledge the king's absolute authority sat uneasily with his conviction that this authority had to be exercised in conformity with "justice" as represented by the advice of the Parlement of Paris and the Estates General, without which that authority would degenerate into "tyranny"—the very pretext for Jesuit disobedience.[38] That balancing act did not survive the rise to power of Armand-Jean du

Plessis, cardinal de Richelieu, and his combination of a "good French" policy against the Habsburg threat of a universal Catholic monarchy abroad with a continuing devout-like campaign against Huguenots and support for Jesuits at home.

THE JESUITS AS IMMORAL SUBJECTS

With the absolute monarchy's unwavering support of the Jesuits, Richelieu's embrace of an anti-Habsburg and anti-dévot foreign policy in the Thirty Years' War pulled the justificatory rug out from under the anti-Jesuitism of the party of the bon françois, and therefore also from an aspect of parlementary Gallicanism. The result was a long eclipse of the ideology of the bon françois from the mid-seventeenth until well into the eighteenth century, when it reappeared in combination with newer elements in the form of "patriotism." Since it made ever less sense to regard the Jesuits as a threat to a French monarchy that continued to favor them, nothing remained for the bon françois except to accept them as legitimate subjects of that monarchical state. But subjects were not necessarily good ones, opening the door for their enemies to depict the Jesuits as immoral subjects. Even if they no longer posed an immediate threat to the life of the state as incarnated in its king, the Jesuits might very well corrupt the good faith and morals of its subjects and, through them, the whole society on which the state rested. Richelieu's triumph over the parti dévot in the Day of Dupes of 1630 therefore marks the end of one phase of anti-Jesuitism and the beginning of another that was to last until the second quarter of the eighteenth century.

Meanwhile in both France and elsewhere the Jesuits fell afoul of Catholics in other ways that added new layers to the image of the Jesuit. Although condemning the Protestant doctrine of justification by faith alone, the Council of Trent's torturous decree on justification left the precise relations between divine grace and free will in salvation unresolved. As Pasquier had already argued, just as the Jesuits opposed the Protestant denial of papal primacy by dedicating their society to magnifying the power of the papacy to excess, they likewise tended to answer the Calvinist denial of human free will by enlarging its agency in salvation to excess. The first site of inter-Catholic controversy on the subject was the Flemish city of Louvain, where the theologian Michel de Baye, or Baius, of the University of Louvain, laid down a "hard" version of the Augustinian doctrines of divine predestination and efficacious grace that incurred papal censure in 1567. But Louvain soon hosted a Jesuit college, and two decades later, in 1586–1587, the Jesuits Leonard Lessius and Jean Hamelius promulgated a series of theses there that gave so little weight to divine grace and so much to human free will that they provoked severe censures by the universities of Louvain and nearby Douai.[39]

As it happened, the next year witnessed the publication of the Spanish Jesuit Luis Molina's signature treatise on free will and divine grace, which, setting out to reconcile the two, did so by redefining "predestination" as God's "middle knowledge" about how humans would choose to use or not to use a divine grace that, predestined to be available to each and all for every possible occasion, would enable those who chose it to resist sin on every such occasion. It was the choice that made the grace "sufficient" to the temptation. The theology argu-ably made salvation contingent on human free will, enlarged its role well be-yond the limits set by Thomas Aquinas—to say nothing of Augustine—and provoked a controversy with Spanish Dominicans, who rushed to defend the Thomist position. Although it is possible to identify a few anti-Molinist Jesuits, the Society sufficiently identified with Molina's book and theology to defend both at close quarters.

In an effort to assert control over an embarrassing debate, the papacy tried to silence both parties and moved the debate to Rome, leading to a battle under papal auspices between Jesuits and Dominican theologians known as the *De auxilliis* controversy, which spanned the turn of the century and the pontificates of Clement VIII and Paul V.[40] The Dominicans won the battle but lost the war because Paul V's need for Jesuit help in his quarrel with the Republic of Venice caused him to postpone sine die the promulgation of a bull condemning Mo-lina.[41] While the Jesuits emerged from the set-to with some new enemies and the label of modern Pelagians or Molinists, the debate did them little further damage, confined as it was to the realm of technical theology, with few reper-cussions in the wider culture.

Among the countries least affected by the debate was a France still in the throes of the civil wars of religion. If Jesuits haunted the Gallican and Protes-tant imagination in these wars, it was not in their capacity as Pelagians. But when in 1626 one of the future founders of Jansenism, the abbé de Saint-Cyran, turned to the task of refuting the Jesuit François Garasse's *Somme théologique des vérités capitales de la religion chrétienne* (A *Theological Summa of the Prin-cipal Truths of the Christian Religion*), the proximity to the Pelagian heresy was the charge that dropped most readily from his pen. Like many others, Saint-Cyran lingered less than lovingly over this summa's many mistakes and pro-miscuously mixed metaphors.[42] But far more serious in Saint-Cyran's eyes was Garasse's misuse of the authority of Augustine to assert that virtuous pagans, such as Virgil and Epictetus, might have found their way to salvation by means of the light of natural reason, and in general Garasse's tendency to soften the stark contrasts in Augustinian theology between human nature before and after the Fall. Nothing was more offensive in Saint-Cyran's view than Garasse's suppositions that God might have created a creature in his image for whom death would have been natural, or that living a virtuous life after the Fall was easier than living a wicked one.[43]

At the same time, Garasse figured as a minor protagonist in the last and most protracted of the political crises apropos of Jesuit treatises allowing for a papal deposition of heretical rulers and the legitimacy of tyrannicide. What provoked this crisis was the Italian Jesuit Antonius Sanctarellus's *Tratatus de haeresi . . . et potestate summi pontificis* (*Treatise on Heresy . . . and the Power of the Supreme Pontiff*), which had just appeared. As before, the conflict pitted the University supported by the Parlement, both determined to condemn the book, against the Jesuits supported by a royal court still under the influence of the parti dévot and reluctant to offend Rome at a time of pro-Protestant alliances against the Catholic Habsburgs. As before as well, the French Jesuits found themselves obliged to "equivocate," telling the Parlement that although they condemned their Italian colleague's doctrine as Frenchmen, in Rome they would have done as the Romans did. But the objects of the equivocations were about to change. One sort of anti-Jesuitism was about to give way to another.

On yet another front, the Jesuits acquired more Catholic enemies within residual Catholic clergies in such states as England, Scotland, and the Dutch Republic. Having embraced the Protestant Reformation during the sixteenth century, these states had disestablished the Catholic ecclesiastical hierarchy and secularized its property. In reaction, the papacy chose to regard these states as missionary territories in a category with lands formerly Christian, like the Ottoman Empire, fit for the efforts of missionaries under the titular authority of bishops in "unfaithful regions" or of apostolic vicars answerable only to papacy. But as the Jesuits surpassed the Dominicans and Franciscans as the Catholic Church's chief missionaries, and also came armed with papal privileges exempting them from local authorities, they tended use their privileges and make short shrift of the authority of any resident clergy minded to oppose them. As recounted earlier, it was exactly this sort of conflict with a would-be Catholic clergy in the Dutch Republic that merged with the Jansenist conflict and culminated in the schism that produced the independent Church of Utrecht in 1723.

Although it ended in no schism in England, a similar conflict in that recently Protestant realm went into the making of the Jansenist conflict in France itself after Pope Urban VIII's newly appointed apostolic vicar, one Richard Smith, came into conflict with Jesuits, among other missionary regulars, upon arriving in that country in 1625. To be sure, the broad interpretation by Smith of his jurisdictional powers as an "ordinary" made enemies aplenty, including the members of a segment of the Recusant Catholic laity, afraid that exercise of his powers would expose them to the ire of an established Protestant church, the government of King Charles I, which issued a warrant for his arrest, and the papacy itself, which publicly disavowed Smith's interpretations of his powers and accepted his resignation in 1631 after his retreat from England to the safety of Richelieu's France.[44] But it was the attempt by Smith to rein in the regulars by limiting their right to administer the sacraments without his permission that provoked a controversy with the Jesuits that ricocheted widely around Catholic Europe and later earned him a martyr's halo in Reformist Catholic memory. The public set-to began when Rudescind Barlow, head of the English Benedictine Congregation, published a critique of Smith's interpretation of episcopal powers, whereupon one Matthew Kellison, the president of the English College in Douai, came to Smith's defense with A *Treatise of the Hierarchie and Divers Orders of the Church*, which awkwardly tried to draw Gallican episcopalist corollaries from ultramontanist premises. In response, the Jesuits fell upon the inconsistencies in Kellison's treatise with a hail of pamphlets that did not spare Smith himself.[45]

Not only did Smith then enter the lists directly, he also mobilized his English episcopalist allies in France, who enlisted in turn the power of the theological faculty of the University of Paris and numerous Gallican bishops resident in Paris, who in February 1631 condemned a number of propositions extracted from these pamphlets.[46] The objectionable propositions laid down that regulars were an integral part of the ecclesiastical hierarchy, that their vows made their ministry more perfect than the bishops', that in times of persecution whole churches might do better without bishops, and that the Catholic Church needed only enough bishops to ordain priests. Since bishops alone might administer the sacrament of confirmation, these English Jesuits also downplayed the importance of this sacrament, holding that the strengthening of virtue consequent upon persecution might take its place or that the papacy possessed the power to delegate mere priests to administer it.[47] The episcopal censors numbered not only thirty-four bishops but also the archbishop of Paris in a separate judgment. Together with the theological faculty, these censors found the propositions not only offensive to Gallican ears but some of them also no less than "heretical."[48]

This controversy also has the dubious distinction of provoking future Jansenists into entering the field, among them Jansen's friend Saint-Cyran and his nephew Martin de Barcos, who picked up the Jesuit gauntlet with a spirited defense of the episcopal hierarchy under the pseudonym Petrus Aurelius. The defense targeted the entire Society of Jesus and moreover employed the accusations of "Molinists" and "Pelagians."[49] When in the midst of these converging controversies the Jesuits again went to the royal court in 1643 with yet another request to force the University to incorporate Clermont as one of its colleges, the University drew heavily on the evidence of these controversies to interpret this request as but the first step in the Society's aim to incorporate the whole University into their college, much as the Jesuits aspired to substitute themselves for the entire episcopacy everywhere.

As in the controversy over Molina, the behavior of the Society readily lent itself to the perception that it would always rally around the cause of any controversial member, and that its corporate honor would always take precedence over the honor of God. At this point, the sin perceived as most typical of what the University's defender called the Jesuit "Colossus" was its "spirit" of corporate pride and "vanity," the sources in turn of "error" and even "heresy." This defender, Godefroy Hermant, was perhaps the first to accuse the Jesuits of the "spirit of domination"—"so true is it," he charged, "that everything is capable of offending [the Jesuits] and that their domination can brook no rival, usurping every kind of sovereignty." While still appealing to the "bon François" in defense of the Jesuits' threat to monarchs, he echoed Pasquier's newer concern in discerning its source in the interest of the Jesuits' own monarchy, a threat to the popes as well.[50]

As for error and heresy, they too had become part of the University's case against the Jesuits by 1643. The rapid multiplication of their colleges and the chapels that went with them—from just a handful to thirty between 1603 and 1643—combined with their activity as confessors in Europe and in their missions drew attention to their moral theology and practice. That attention grew all the more intense in that, as preachers and confessors, the Jesuits trod on the holy ground that defined the mission of the secular clerical hierarchy. Indeed, while the controversy over the English case raged, numbers of ugly conflicts erupted in France itself between Jesuits and bishops unwilling to allow them to preach or to hear confessions in their dioceses without episcopal permission.

Where moral theology was concerned, at issue was the difference between a facile penitence dispensed by a mobile regular clergy and a more severe form of spiritual direction that only a long-term relation between priest and parishioner could sustain. Thus, the same years that witnessed the Smith-related set-to between the Jesuits and the bishops allied with the University also saw the publication of a number of moral treatises by Jesuits—Pierre Le Moyne's *Dévotion aisée* (*Devotion Made Easy*) was the most telling title—that shocked the moral sensibilities of Gallican Catholics and became an issue in its own right. By breaking down "sin" into so many sins, Jesuit moral theology seemed to find reasons to absolve them all. When the Sorbonne's Louis-Gorin de Saint-Amour argued the University's case against the admission of the Jesuits, prominent among his reasons was the University's ability to demonstrate that "there were no articles in our religion that the Jesuits have not corrupted and still daily corrupt . . . by means of their erroneous novelties." Crucial to his demonstration was the corporate "amour propre" that led the Society to defend the deviations of each Jesuit, with the result that it had become an accomplice in transforming "Christian morality into a body of problematic opinions" in order to "accommodate the more delicate sensibilities of the century."[51]

It was as a culmination of this controversy and a pivot to another that the classic treatise bearing the title *De la fréquente communion* appeared in 1643. The youngest son of the anti-Jesuit barrister Antoine Arnaud, its author was none other than the future "great" Arnauld of the same name and already famous as a theologian. His treatise was a culmination in that it was the best if not the last word in the anti-Jesuit contention that the penitential "route to heaven" was not "all covered with flowers" and that after a mortal sin had forfeited baptismal innocence, the penitential restoration of grace presupposed a "laborious baptism" consisting in a detestation of sin and a genuine love for God, until which point it might be better to defer Communion. Arnauld's model was the theology and practice of the early church, while his target was clearly Jesuit confessors accused of contenting themselves with only the servile fear in lieu of real contrition, the better to woo unrepentant "penitents." But the treatise was also pivotal in that, more than others in its genre, it laid bare the premise that the contrition demanded for renewed access to Communion presupposed the prior grace to attain that state, and that this grace was God's alone to give rather than the product of "frequent communion."[52]

The Jesuits as regulars against the secular hierarchy, as educators against the universities, as accommodating confessors against rigorous spiritual physicians, as Molinist theologians against Dominican defenders of Thomas Aquinas and Augustine—all these conflicts converged at the mid-seventeenth century and would seem to have pointed toward a second expulsion of the Jesuits. But Arnauld, alas, was not only the son of the barrister Antoine Arnauld père—for the Jesuits, a problematic pedigree—but also the acolyte of Saint-Cyran, whose penitential practice as spiritual director of the reformed convent of Port-Royal had attracted adverse notice and whom Cardinal Richelieu had just released from prison at Vincennes, in part for maintaining a similarly contritionist view of penitence. Saint-Cyran was in turn the friend and collaborator of Cornelius Jansenius, or Jansen, the recently deceased bishop of Ypres in Spanish Flanders, whose treatise on Augustine's theology of grace had appeared posthumously just three years earlier, in 1640. Like Arnauld's *De la fréquente communion*, Jansenius's *Augustinus* was directed against the Jesuits, in this case their Molinist theology that Jansenius saw as an updated version of the heretical theology of Pelagius combated by Augustine in the fifth century.

Although by far the least intelligible, the controversy pitting the defenders of Augustine against Molina over the doctrine of grace proved to be the long fuse that ignited every other conflict. Just as surprising, perhaps, is that the theological issue inflamed the others against protagonists whom Jesuits would soon be calling "Jansenists." For it is this issue that enabled the Jesuits to accuse their deadliest enemies of a denial of human free will tantamount to "reboiled Calvinism," a charge that for the royal court, a good part of the clergy, and even much of Parisian popular opinion was a far more potent accusation than neo-Pelagianism.

With the post-Renaissance cultural winds at their back, and with strong support by the monarchy, which in turn put pressure on the papacy, the Jesuits won the war for the soul of Catholicism, both in the short run and in the longer one. The Jansenist controversy enabled the Jesuits to reverse their partial setback in the *De auxilliis* controversy by obtaining papal condemnations of Jansen's book in 1642, 1653, 1656, and 1661. Back in the mid-seventeenth century, Jansenists even lost the battle in their home territory of the Sorbonne when, employing a technique already used to avoid the condemnation of Sanctarellus, the Jesuits' allies used royal backing to pack the assembly with deputies from the four mendicant orders, who on this occasion—even the Dominicans—voted to expel Arnauld from their ranks.

Along the way, however, the Jansenist cause drew lasting blood when, in 1656 and with Arnauld and Pierre Nicole's help, the great mathematician Blaise Pascal counterattacked with the clandestine publication of the series of *Lettres provinciales* (*Provincial Letters*). The genius of the Pascalian riposte was to reposition the battle from the rarefied theological plane and back to the more palpable penitential and moral planes. Published singly and anonymously from January 1656 to March 1757, the letters failed in their immediate object of saving Arnauld from expulsion from the Sorbonne. Nor did Pascal's first three letters even succeed in their aim of winning the support of the Sorbonne's Dominican doctors, whose Thomist theology of grace was closer to Jansen's position than to Molina's.

But in a series of fictive interviews between a Parisian "friend" of a provincial and a conceited but naïve Jesuit father, Pascal pilloried the concepts by which Jesuits justified their less than rigorous ethical decisions.[53] Among these, the first to be targeted was the principle that no act could be considered a sin if the person who performed it was fully conscious that it was, a principle—later known as "invincible ignorance"—that seemed to yield the consequence, in Pascal's words, that more people are "justified by this ignorance and forgetfulness of God than by grace or the sacraments." Pascal's second target was the principle of "probability," later called "probabilism," which allowed a confessor to condone an action on the sole condition that at least one "grave doctor," preferably a Jesuit, had judged it to be sinless, even if the opinion was less probable than other casuists who had thought the contrary. Third in Pascal's order of opprobrium came the method of "directing the attention," by which a confessor might excuse whole such sins as slander, theft, and even murder by the device of directing the attention of the "penitent" not to the sin itself but to some commendable end to which the sin was a means.[54] But just in case these devices failed to transform mortal into venial sins, the Jesuit in the tenth letter unveiled his society's ultimate elixir: that the sacrament of penitence required no more of the penitent than that he or she fear the material consequences of sin and not hate God. As depicted by Pascal, the sum total of the Gospel for "his" Jesuit seemed to be that God had so loved the world that he gave his only begotten son so that Christians, unlike Jews, might not have to keep the first commandment to love him above all else.

What the tactical return toward the Jesuits' moral theology and practice enabled the Jansenists to do was to put moral flesh onto the skeleton of theological abstractions. As the Jansenist deacon Pavie de Fourquevaux put it many decades later, the innovations of the Jesuits in matters moral were far "more evident and striking" than those in their theology of grace "in that they concerned behavior, and turned the duties of man upside down."[55] Although not always clearly related to these moral matters, the background of fundamental theological opposition between Jansenism's "hard" reading of Augustine and the Jesuits' Molinism also became more salient than before. While for Pascal humanity's disposition was so totally self-centered that even the most indifferent acts offended the gaze of God unless motivated by charity, for Pascal's Jesuit confessors humankind was not totally corrupt and "sins" were therefore individual acts susceptible of being isolated and neutralized one by one by means of casuistry in the confessional.

Showing how the Jesuits' "lax" casuistic principles flowed from their principle that "natural" loves might legitimately take the place of "supernatural" love for God—and citing Molina along with other new casuists—is about as far as Jansenists went in the seventeenth century in drawing clear lines between the moral case against the Jesuits and Molinist theology's naturalization of the fallen state. But given Louis XIV's unwavering support of the Jesuits and hostility to anything that smacked of Calvinism or political opposition, additional rhetorical weaponry would have availed the Jansenists little. At least in Paris and other northern cities, the case against the Jesuits took attention away from the Jansenists' own ascetic, heroic, and largely unattainable insistence that every action proceed from charity. When, as it eventually did, anti-Jesuitism traveled elsewhere in Catholic Europe, it similarly rode on the energy of antiprobabilism. In mid-eighteenth-century Italy, one of the chief agents of hostility to Jesuits was a Dominican priest named Daniele Concina, who devoted his entire career to a campaign against confessional probabilism and in defense of the position— probabiliorism, as it is known—that confessors were always bound to follow the more probable of two moral options.[56]

For what Arnauld and Pascal's counterattack against the Society's very vulnerable confessional and ethical flanks accomplished was a successful appeal above—or below—the level of the faculty of the Sorbonne and the royal court to Parisian public opinion. In the wake of his *Lettres provinciales*, Pascal repeated his moral case against the Jesuits in the form of factums or briefs to the General Gssembly of the Gallican Clergy on behalf of and in the name of the curés of Paris. Annoyed at the capacity of the Jesuits to attract penitents from their parishes to their own chapels, these curés for their part had shed their erstwhile loyalties to the ultramontanist ideology of the Catholic League and completed their migration into the camp of a Gallican defense of their corporate rights against the royal court and its support of a Spanish-born society of regulars. Although Jansenism's liaison with the Parisian judicial nobility and bourgeoisie would wait until the end of the century for completion, there too Pascal's appeal to the upright ethics of the *honnête homme* against the moral deviation of the Jesuit helped the process of assimilation along.

By the time royal and episcopal persecution of Jansenists began in good earnest with the personal reign of Louis XIV and the first dispersion of the sisters and solitaries of Port-Royal in 1660, Jansenism had already acquired social constituencies well beyond the elite milieu of the sisters and solitaries in and around the reformed Cistercian monastery in the valley of Les Chevreuses. And with Louis XIV's removal of the royal court from Paris to Versailles—and with it, the royal preachers and confessors—the elements of a remaking of a Parisian civic identity and something like the proto-patriotic ideology of the bon françois with Jansenism as a glue were in place. The enemy against which this ideology would crystallize would be the Jesuit.

But for the duration of Louis Quatorzian absolutism's apogee, the ground gained by the tactical turn toward the Jesuits' moral theology came at the

expense of the political as well as the ecclesiastical tenets of the Gallican gravamen against the Jesuits. When in 1664 Arnauld and Nicole tried to revive
Gallican nightmares by pointing out that the Jesuits' defense of the papacy's
claim to infallibly in matters of fact would fortify papal claims to temporal power
and with it the right to depose kings, their pamphlet elicited no reaction by the
Parlement of Paris.[57] And when one Titus Oates's denunciation of a popish plot
to assassinate King Charles II of England resulted in the execution of five Jesuits on 20 June 1679, the event passed all but unnoticed in France.[58]

Nor could Jansenists very plausibly pose as champions of the general councils against papal infallibility when their own factual challenge to the papacy's
condemnation of the five Jansenist propositions presupposed the principle of
papal infallibility in point of doctrine. It was not even easy for Jansenists to stand
for the rights of bishops against regulars or the papacy when most French bishops endorsed the condemnations of Jansenism along with just about all bishops
elsewhere in Catholic Europe. Although Arnauld assented to the Gallican liberties when proclaimed by the Gallican Clergy's General Assembly in 1685, the
use he made of them was to write a pamphlet in defense of absolute royal authority against William and Mary's usurpation of the English throne in 1688.

To be sure, Arnauld and Pontchâteau devoted a few volumes of their *Morale
pratique* to the case of saintly bishops persecuted by the Jesuits who were supposed to serve them.[59] In this eight-volume work written in the 1680s and early
1690s, Arnauld and Pontchâteau set out to complement Pascal's *Provincial Letters* by showing that the Jesuits were as corrupt as their word, that there was
"nothing they permitted to others against the word of God and the principles of
the Gospel that they did not practice themselves in pursuit of their greed and
the glory and aggrandizement of their Society." That the Jesuits tended to challenge or ignore hierarchical authority whenever it got in their way best exemplified this practical morality, at least in Arnauld and Pontchâteau's analysis.[60]

Yet the episcopal authority that got in the way of Jesuits in theses volumes
tended to be safely away from Gallican France in colonial or genuinely mission territory where episcopal authority was bound to be weak and missionaries had to cut some corners. Where Europe itself was concerned—the stuff of the
first and last volumes—the evildoing of Jesuits assumed by now a familiar aspect:
the vainglorious self-portrait in the *Imago primi saeculi Societatis Iesu* (*Image of
the First Century of the Society of Jesus*), the many Benedictine and Cistercian
abbeys and priories annexed by Jesuit colleges in the Empire, the use of the confessional by Jesuits to get their hands on the inheritances of their penitents, their
activities as merchants and usurers everywhere, and their tendency to make enemies of anyone who did not bow the knee before the society's Baal.[61]

THE JESUITS AS IMMORAL MISSIONARIES
AND PELAGIAN PAGANS

Symptomatic of the paucity of genuinely Gallican grist for his anti-Jesuit mill was the need Arnauld had to go to the strongholds of the Jesuits in far-flung foreign mission fields to find cases of episcopal authority to defend against them—examples such as Hernando Guerrero in the Philippines, Bernardo de Cardenas in Paraguay, and Juan de Palafox in New Spain. This foray into the mission fields in quest of Gallican issues also turned into a flanking movement in the ongoing campaign to depict the Jesuits as immoral, even irreligious. By linking the Jansenist theological case against the Jesuits as neo-Pelagians to apparent examples of literal idolatry, this campaign further concretized the abstract doctrinal issues of grace and free will. By the time it reached China, the campaign had really come to feature the Jesuits as complicit in the worship of pagan gods—if not Baal, then the city gods of walls and moats.

Among Arnauld and Pontchâteau's instructive examples of conflicts between the Jesuits and episcopal authority on the mission field, the one that delivered the most punch—and to which Arnauld and Pontchâteau devoted an entire volume—concerned the trials and tribulations of Juan de Palafox y Mendoza, who fell afoul of the Jesuits as bishop of Puebla de Los Angeles in the late 1640s. An Aragonese nobleman who had cut a figure in the Council of the Indies before entering the church, Palafox had come to Mexico in 1640 not only as a bishop but also as King Felipe IV of Spain's visitor-general empowered to audit the administrations of the two previous viceroys, even briefly acting as viceroy himself after taking a hand in the recall of the existing one.[62]

Palafox's quarrel with the Jesuits began soon after his arrival in New Spain when he challenged the Society's exemption from the tithe to his diocese. A classic conflict between secular versus regular clergy though it was, it carried stakes higher than in the metropolis because the Society's exemption from tithe on its ever-growing territorial holdings in Mexico spelled the impoverishment of Palafox's diocese and the secular clergy in general. Having obtained a legal ruling obliging the Jesuits to pay the tithe on newly acquired property, Palafox renewed the conflict in 1647 when he forbade the Jesuits the right to preach or administer any sacraments without his permission. The stakes were again high because in challenging the right of the Jesuits to exercise these functions, Palofox was striking at a power that added spiritual to economic domination over the native labor force on their extensive holdings.

As in the case of the tithes, the Jesuits appealed to their papal exemptions while also alleging the existence of permissions by previous bishops in the matter of the sacraments. In reply, however, to the episcopal vicar-general's order to produce these privileges and permissions, they invoked a papal privilege exempting them from the obligation to show either. When, further, they persisted in acting as parish priests in defiance of the ordinance Palafox had issued, his vicar-general threatened them with excommunication. But this threat's only effect was to provoke the Society into designating two Dominicans to act as a tribunal of "judge-conservators" to adjudicate disputes between ecclesiastical authorities. Since Palafox had earlier alienated both Franciscans and Dominicans by attempting to replace them with secular priests in the parishes, these Dominican "judges" not surprisingly ruled in favor of the Jesuits. Push came to shove when Palafox excommunicated the judges and the judges returned the favor, excommunicating both Palafox and his vicar-general.

That this impromptu tribunal was able to act with impunity was due to the support of the new viceroy and his ally the archbishop of Mexico, who had really created this tribunal. Adamantly opposed to Palafox's ongoing efforts to reform secular governance as a royal visitor-general, the viceroy unsurprisingly allied himself with Palafox's Jesuit enemies on the ecclesiastical front, going so far as to dispatch royal troops for use by the tribunal while blocking all attempts by Palafox to take his cause to the royal courts. Having begun as part of a conflict between the secular and regular clergy, the quarrel now took on the proportions of a showdown between secular and ecclesiastical authorities.[63] By the time this set-to had settled, Palafox would have fled into hiding in the wilds of Chiapas, a number of his officials and members of the chapter would have gone to prison or in exile, and a purged chapter and new episcopal government installed by the tribunal would have overturned all of Palafox's ordinances.[64] In letters to Innocent X and Philip IV, Palafox set out a case that projected a self-image of a Saint Athanasius or Chrysostom, obliged like them to flee his diocese in the interests of peace while waiting for justice.

In the end, the battle ended in barely disguised defeat for Palafox. Although both Felipe IV and Pope Innocent X eventually intervened in defense of episcopal authority and Palafox was able to return to his cathedral in 1649, he never really obtained justice from the Jesuits as he saw it, and in 1650 he returned to Spain, where he lived out his career in semidisgrace as the bishop of the small see of Osma. Yet the whole affair did no little damage to the reputation of the Jesuits as members of a society set on self-aggrandizement to the exclusion of every other consideration. Palafox's letters to Innocent X and Felipe IV became public in short order. In these, Palafox himself cited the case of Bishop Guerrero of Manila, thus fitting his own episode into a larger pattern of the Jesuits' disrespect for episcopal authority.

What these letters also made apparent was the vast extent of the Jesuits' hold-ings in land, livestock, sugar refineries, silver mines, and native labor, enabling the Society to add still more to its resources by engaging in both local and in-ternational commerce in all these commodities.[65] On display as well in Palafox's letters was the willingness of the Jesuits to flout papal authority when it suited them, as they did in 1649 when they appealed to the Council of the Indies to rescind its acceptance of a papal order to respect Palofox's episcopal authority. As would be the case in China, the spectacle of Jesuit defiance of papal author-ity seemed to vindicate Pasquier's claim that the Society posed a threat to the papacy itself.

That act of defiance at variance with their famous fourth vow of obedience to the papacy became public because it prompted Palafox to write his third and longest letter to Innocent X. After recounting his flight to Chiapas, this missive concluded with a global indictment of the Jesuits and call for their reform into either a clearly monastic order or a society of secular auxiliaries.[66] "So formi-dable" in the bishop's opinion was the Jesuits' "power in the universal church today, so great their riches, so extraordinary their credit, and so absolute the deference they command, that they tower above all dignitaries, laws, councils, and apostolic constitutions," with the result that unless the Society were re-formed, "the bishops would have to resign themselves either to die or succumb in defending their dignity or cravenly to take their orders in all things from [the Jesuits]."[67]

Interested in the Catholic mission to China and later the author of a history of the recent Manchu Conquest, Palafox concluded his third letter with the charge that as missionaries in China the Jesuits preached a Christ without the cross and had christened converts still wedded to forms of pagan idolatry. By happenstance, the relatively new papal Congregation of the Propagation of the Faith had just issued a first still tentative condemnation of certain forms of cul-tural accommodation practiced by Jesuit missionaries regarding their converts in Confucian China. By the time it was over, the controversy over "Chinese rites" would do as much damage to the reputation of the Jesuits as did Pascal's pillorying of Jesuit casuistry in his *Provincial Letters.*

In contrast with their presence in Mexico, the Jesuits had no bishops to con-tend with in China. Under the titular authority of the bishop of the offshore Portuguese outpost of Macao and the more distant authority of the archbishop of Goa in India, the Chinese missionary church did not see a semblance of epis-copal authority on the mainland until the end of the seventeenth century. Al-though in New Spain the Jesuits commanded the support of the Dominicans and Franciscans against Palafox, in China their chief rivals turned out to be

Dominicans and Franciscans, who allied themselves with bishops when episcopal authority finally became a factor. It was a Dominican, Juan Baptista de Morales, who was Palafox's principal source on the subject of the Jesuits' tactics as well as the chief informant behind the papacy's condemnation in 1645. And while the Jesuits obtained the aid of a viceroy's secular authority against their rivals in the conquered and forcibly Catholicized New Spain, neither the Jesuits nor their Catholic rivals could assume the support of the indistinguishably secular and religious authorities in the independent, long "civilized," but quite "pagan" empire that was Confucian China.

It was in an effort to obtain the good will of those Mandarin authorities, culminating in that of the emperor and his court in Beijing, that the Jesuits made their eventually controversial concessions to Confucian and other rites and beliefs. As in India and Japan, the Jesuits here cut a more sympathetic figure because, in further contrast to their situation in New Spain, they wielded only arms of persuasion and constantly courted the danger of persecution. Indeed, they sustained periods of real persecution in 1618–1623 and again in 1664–1668.

The rites in question consisted in the veneration of familial ancestors, the honors paid to the sixth- and early fifth-century BCE sage Confucius, the sacrifices accorded to the city deities of walls and moats, the respects paid to the emperor himself, and—at the very highest level—participation in the emperor's annual sacrifices to heaven and earth and other apparently divinized aspects of "nature." By far the most basic and pervasive of these were the household rites involving the presence of "tablets" inscribed with the names of familial ancestors along with periodic presents or offerings of food and wine, as though the ancestral souls were present and in a position to reward these attentions.

The other rites mainly concerned the learned Mandarin magistrates whose official duties obliged them to engage in or lead these ceremonies. But since the entire missionary enterprise depended on the good will of some of these literati, and since converts among them could not refuse to participate in these rites without endangering their positions, a disproportionate emphasis fell on such acts of apparently pagan worship as the bimonthly veneration of Confucius and the city gods of walls and moats. Other related ritual matters that became problematic concerned the place of the cross in the presentation of Christianity, the propriety of paying taxes to support the official rites in cities, and the applicability of the gamut of Catholic fasting and feast days to Chinese converts and of baptismal rites, to Chinese women in particular.

From their first encounters with Mandarin officials in early 1580s, the Jesuit pioneers Michele Ruggieri and Matteo Ricci and their companions shied away from head-on confrontation and sought to soften the incompatibilities and build bridges between Christianity and the Confucian tradition. Ranging from the adoption of Mandarin dress to the interpretation of ancestor veneration as an extension of the Mosaic commandment to "honor thy parents," the Jesuits put to use their famous tactic of redeeming exterior actions by "directing" the intention behind them. The hardest such nut to crack was the bimonthly offerings to the city gods of walls and moats. While the Jesuits may not have tried to "redeem" this ceremony by allowing Mandarin converts to direct their directions toward a cross hidden among the bouquets of flowers used in these ceremonies— this became one of many accusations against them—the Jesuit Giulio Aleni incontestably argued that converts might be allowed to carry on by regarding these deities as guardian angels of the sort believed in by Christianized nobles under the late Roman Empire.[68] When, later in the century, the Jesuits had securely established themselves at the imperial court in Beijing and had won the support of the new Manchu rulers, they also allowed for the presence of inscriptions wishing the emperor a life of ten thousand years and a tablet enjoining reverence for "heaven"—"Jing Tian"—in their churches.[69]

Terms such as Tian, or heaven, were also problematical because along with the Jesuits' partial accommodation of Chinese "rites" ran a terminological accommodation that, pioneered again by Ricci, used certain Chinese words to convey key Christian concepts. Impressed by the rectitude of Confucian ethics after a decade devoted to assimilating the Chinese language and Confucian canon, Ricci and Ruggieri took the humanist tack of trying to bypass the Buddhist and Taoist religious layers and even the body of neo-Confucian commentary in favor of the original wisdom of Confucius himself, as well as the still more ancient wisdom that Confucius had sought to recover.

At the bottom of this quest lay the conviction that, all people having descended from Adam and Eve and therefore indirectly from the "children of Israel," each people must have retained some residue of an original revelation including knowledge of a creator god separate from creation, the idea of souls as distinct from bodies, and the need for a redeemer from sin. But in choosing such terms as Tian for a spiritual heaven, "Shangdi," or "sovereign on high," for God, and the word "linghum" for souls, these Jesuits ran the risk of confusing the Christian message with the neo-Confucian cosmological freight that these terms carried, and that designated either the material sky, an ethereal but still material air, or deities strictly subordinate to an ultimate but material principle.

As early as 1618 a Jesuit veteran of the Japanese mission, João Rodrigues, warned his confreres in China about the idolatrous connotations of this terminology, reservations that the late Ricci's companion Niccolò Longobardi had come to share. While confined to Macao during the persecution of 1618–1621, the Jesuits debated these issues among themselves, as they did again at their visitor André Palmeiro's bidding in Jaiding in 1627. By that date if not before, the Jesuits decided to cut their losses with the terms "Shangdi" and "Tian" themselves in favor of "Tianzhu," or "lord of heaven," although that term was not without its problems either. By that date too the Jesuits had decided upon a policy of mitigated accommodation of the related practice of Chinese rites in connection with both Confucius and familial ancestors.

When the Jesuits next debated these issues, it was in Canton during the enforced leisure of the persecution of 1664–1668. At that point, however, the debate included not only Jesuits but also some Spanish Dominicans and Franciscans, among them the Franciscan Antonio de Santa Maria Caballero. For meanwhile, in the early 1630s, a few Franciscans but mainly Spanish Dominican missionaries had established a presence in Fujian province, arriving there from Taiwan and ultimately from the Spanish Philippines, where they had learned Chinese in an attempt to make inroads into a Chinese merchant enclave there. Making contact in Fujian with the Chinese literati previously converted by the Jesuits, they found themselves appalled by the degree of license given to them by the Jesuits to continue to officiate in ancestral and Confucian rites. In a report that would ricochet from one polemical writing to another, Caballero described a lineage-level ancestral rite that he and the Dominican Juan Batista de Morales witnessed in the town of Muyun near Fu'an in 1635.

To them, the rite seemed "religious" in the sense that the officiants, including some Chinese Christian converts, offered prayers and sacrifices in return for material benefits.[70] It was Morales who eventually took his concerns in person to Rome after his request for an explanation from the Jesuits' vice provincial went unanswered. It was Morales too who obtained the first condemnation of some of the "Chinese rites" allowed by the Jesuits, at least as described by himself. Promulgated by the Congregation for the Propagation of the Faith in 1645, this decree condemned most of the "accommodations" of indigenous practices allowed by the Jesuits without naming them.[71]

When it finally came to their attention in China, the Jesuits paid little attention to a decree couched as provisional. In any case, the papacy just as provisionally reversed its position in 1656 after the Jesuit Martino Martini made it to Rome and managed to persuade Pope Alexander VII that the ancestral and Confucian rites and ceremonies at issue were primarily civic, political, and at most honorific rather than religious in nature.[72] But while practice may have remained largely unchanged on the Chinese ground, this missionary "monks' quarrel" over tactics in China had already begun to metastasize into something more virulent in Europe, as Morales's "doubts" made their way into Palafox's public letter to Innocent X in 1649 and later into Juan de Ribas's *Teatro Jesuítico* in 1654.

More ominous still, Palafox's letter figured among the references in the Parisian curés' letters against the Jesuits' moral casuistry in the wake of Pascal's *Provincial Letters*. In China, Jesuits, Franciscans, and Dominicans nonetheless remained on sufficiently good terms for members of the three orders, including the Dominican Fernández Domingo Navarrete, to try to coordinate their missionary strategies during their enforced exile in Canton in the mid-1660s. But where ancestral and Confucian rites were concerned, that good will was not enough to convince Navarrete, who, after his return to Europe, dropped a bomb in 1676 in the form of his *Tratados historicos, politicos, ethicos, y religiosos de la monachia de China (Historical, Political, Ethical, and Religious Treatises on the Chinese Monarchy)*.[73] That treatise also contained Ricci's companion Longobardi's hitherto unpublished reservations that Navarette had obtained while conferring with Jesuits in China.[74]

With the publication of Navarrete's *Tratados*, the Chinese rites controversy ceased to be an argument between Jesuits and Dominicans and began to assume an anti-Jesuitical life of its own. By 1690 Arnauld was using Navarrete's treatise to add two fresh volumes—the sixth and seventh—to his ongoing *Morale pratique*, comparing the Jesuit missionaries in China to the Galatians described in Saint Paul's epistles, for whom "the desire to make many conversions got the better of the care that they ought to have taken to make only good ones."[75] Arnauld also took the occasion to reiterate Pascal's and his own charges of the Jesuits' versatile morality—and his own view of the papacy's factual fallibility—by arguing that the papal decree of 1656 was beside the point. in that it was based on Martini's deliberately deceptive interpretation of the ancestral and Confucian rites. By happenstance the pope in question, Alexander VII, was the same pontiff who had decreed that Jansen's five infamous propositions were to found in his *Augustinus*.

The whole controversy was tailor-made to become part of the Jansenist controversy because the most basic assumption on which the Jesuits had predicated their missionary efforts in China was the fundamental integrity of human nature, even after the biblical Fall, and therefore also the partial validity of pagan cults as imperfect recognitions of God's existence.[76] Nothing could have been more opposed to the Augustinian view of the fundamental corruption of human nature after the Fall and therefore also the idolatrous character of any cult uninformed by knowledge communicated by means of revelation vouchsafed by grace. In reply to the charge of conniving at idolatry, Jesuit apologists hardly helped their cause by arguing that present-day neo-Confucian

Mandarins who practiced theses rites could not be idolatrous, because they adhered to a purely materialistic and hence atheistic cosmology, and that, while civic for them, the rites were only idolatrous as understood and practiced by common people. For Jesuits the result was to make themselves vulnerable to the charge of complicity with atheism as well as with idolatry, and of arguing, as did Pierre Bayle, that atheistic societies could be civilized and virtuous too.[77] The controversy reinforced a widespread conviction that for the Jesuit, being all things to all men meant doing whatever it took to gain power and lord it over others.

In France, the controversy also ended badly for the Jesuits in 1700 when the still heavily Augustinian Sorbonne censured an assertion in the French Jesuit Louis Le Comte's book that the Chinese had preserved knowledge of the true God since Confucius and had worshipped him all that while.[78] In the rites fight, things went no better for the Jesuits in Rome, where Pope Clement XI, bowing to adverse judgments by the Sorbonne, the Propaganda Fide, and the Inquisition, reversed Alexander VII's provisional approval of 1656 and condemned the rites as well as the Jing Tian inscriptions in the Jesuits' churches in China. Entitled *Cum Deus Optimus* and issued in 1704, this papal brief preceded a more solemn condemnation by the same pope in the bull *Ex illa die* in 1715.

In acting as he did, Clement XI was responding not only to the condemnation by the Sorbonne but also to the situation in China, where events were no kinder to the Jesuits than in Europe. There, in the 1680s his predecessors had established a new ecclesiastical division in China that put the vast vice province under the immediate authority of a number of apostolic vicars. The intent in imposing a kind of episcopal authority over the Chinese Church was in part to reign in the power of the regulars, in particular that of the Jesuits, and in part to dismantle the remaining influence of a declining Portugal that had long exerted power over the Chinese and Indian churches via the bishops of Macao and Goa and by virtue of the *padroado* granted the Chinese Church by the papacy in 1497.

It was one such apostolic vicar, Charles Maigrot in Fujian province, who issued a decree in 1693 that forbade the use of the terms "Shangdi" and "Tian" and therefore also the display of the Jing Tian tablets in churches. His decree also forbade any participation in the Confucian and ancestral rites, going so far as to regulate such tablets used in private homes.[79] In forbidding the term "Shangdi," Maigrot was pushing on an open door, as the Jesuits had long abandoned that term, along with Tian by itself. But the decree against all Jing Tian inscriptions was an insult to the emperor, who had had them put there, while the prohibition of all participation in ancestral and Confucian rites and attempt to regulate even private ones would make life difficult for some and all but impossible for others. Perhaps forgetting that Christianity had arisen from within the Roman Empire as opposed to being imported from without, Maigrot and others did not see why more blood from martyrs should not nourish Christianity in China, as it had in imperial Rome.

The reaction of the Jesuits to the decree by Maigrot was to contest his authority and to ignore the decree, thereby adding to their reputation as a society that flouted episcopal authority and made the law up as it went. But it was harder to ignore papal authority when it came to China in the form of the papal legate and bishop Carlo Tomasso Maillard de Tournon, who arrived in China bearing Clement XI's barely dry brief confirming the tenor of Maigrot's decree. Received with all the pomp and circumstance due a papal emissary by the Manchu emperor Kangxi in Beijing in 1705, Tournon rapidly wore out his welcome by persisting in his opposition to Ricci's construal of the Confucian tradition as compatible with Christianity.[80] The end of Tournon's disastrous visit to China also spelled the beginning of the end of the first Catholic mission in China. The result in Europe was that the Jesuits were widely perceived as having preferred the Chinese emperor's authority to the pope's and to have all but tortured Tournon to death as a prisoner of the Portuguese in Macao.

What finally did in the Jesuit mission in China was the papacy and the reassertion of its authority. As the irony of history would have it, the same pope that condemned the Jesuits' practice in China—Clement XI—was also the pope who sided body and soul with the Jesuits in the Jansenist controversy, the author of not one but two bulls against the Jansenist cause, the second being the lethal *Unigenitus* that condemned Pasquier Quesnel's *Réflexions morales (Moral Reflections)* at the behest of Louis XIV in 1713. Another factor in the demise of the Jesuits' Chinese mission was Louis XIV's decision to send his "own" French Jesuits to Beijing, causing a partial split in the Jesuit presence there. Louis also nurtured the recently established French Congregation of Foreign Missions as a stable for apostolic vicars to the Far East, among them Charles Maigrot.[81]

Although the Sun King's purpose was to hasten the demise of Portugal's remaining ecclesiastical power, the irony of history again had it that Louis XIV was the same king who oversaw the rise of the Jesuits to the pinnacle of their power in France, as well as aiding and abetting his Jesuit confessor Michel Le Tellier in the role of midwife to *Unigenitus*. But by indirectly contributing to the demise of the Jesuit mission in China, Louis XIV provided no end of munitions for the anti-Jesuit arsenal. Nor could anything have been worse for the Jesuit cause in Gallican France at the time than to have Jesuits as notorious as Le Tellier defending their Chinese mission, which he did in a two-volume work against Arnauld completed in 1690.[82]

THE JESUITS AS DESPOTIC CONSPIRATORS
AGAINST THE *PATRIE*

Yet the Chinese rites controversy would not have done the damage it eventually did to the Society had it not been for the rekindling of the Jansenist controversy in France, and with it the revival of the Gallican tradition as inflected by Jansenism. That rekindling was in turn the work of the two new anti-Jansenist papal bulls for which Le Tellier as well as Louis XIV had beseeched the papacy, namely, *Veniam Domini* in 1709 and of course *Unigenitus* in 1713. By the first, Pope Clement XI again disallowed the distinction between propositions condemned and the fact of their presence in *Augustinus*, thereby officially ending the so-called Peace of Clement IX whereby nineteen Gallican bishops had brokered an agreement with Clement to allow Jansenists to sign the Formula in that way. Although Louis XIV had already ended that "peace" by 1679, this bull gave him a mandate to destroy the abbey of Port-Royal-des-Champs and disperse the remaining sisters there.

By the second bull, the same pope condemned 101 propositions that in this case came word for word from Quesnel's book. That precision left Jansenists no alternative but to contest the principle of papal infallibility and to take cover under the Gallican liberty that located infallibility in general councils. And because neither Clement XI nor Louis XIV allowed the Gallican bishops to amend the bull by explaining the sense in which it condemned some Gallican-sounding as well as Jansenist propositions, the bull had the effect of reviving Gallican sentiment within the episcopacy and the Parlement, confounding while magnifying Gallican and Jansenist causes. Particularly disturbing was the condemnation of the ninety-first proposition that an "unjust excommunication should not deter us from fulfilling our obligations," recalling as it did the all but forgotten memory of subjects being mandated to resist excommunicated rulers as tyrannical.

At that point what remained of its bon françois sensibilities spurred the Parlement to resist registering this bull, even against Louis XIV, and then obtained the restoration of its right of prior remonstrance from the regency government after his death. With these advances, all the constituent elements of the old Gallican, or bon françois, alliance—the Sorbonne, the curés, and the Parlement—began to snap back into realignment, this time held in place by a religious cohesive stronger than "old" Gallican Catholicism. Whereas after the wars of religion this constellation of elements could not but orient itself around absolute monarchy, it now found itself in explicit conflict with a monarchy that the Jansenist conflict had driven into closer alliance with the papacy. But at the center of a royal court now aloof from Paris still stood the Jesuit, the hated symbol of all of these developments. The fulmination of *Unigenitus* therefore introduced a final phase in the trajectory of anti-Jesuitism that might be characterized as patriotic. By the time it reached its apogee in the mid-eighteenth century, the Jesuits remained immoral subjects, but less of France than of a foreign general who ruled "despotically" over a would-be universal and transnational empire that aimed to turn French citizens into slaves and their king into a subservient "despot."

No sooner did the bull against Quesnel's book appear than from their exile in the Dutch Republic Quesnel and Nicolas Petitpied revived an old Gallican charge against the Jesuits. Seizing the occasion of the French Jesuit Joseph Jouvency's history of his society, they published a collection of documents apropos of its supposed endorsement of tyrannicide, including the interrogation of Jean Chastel and excepts from the works of Mariana, Bellarmino, and others.[83] Along the way—a crucial connection—this collection elided the earlier Gallican charge of Jesuit "equivocation" in the face of Gallican maxims and Pascal's anatomy of probabilism and pointed them all in a regicidal direction.[84] Hard upon this collection came the defense by Quesnel of the orthodoxy of the propositions condemned by *Unigenitus* in his *Hexaples*, including a chapter on the ninety-first proposition and the history of regicidal casuistry as exemplified in the works of Jesuits.[85] (That by resisting *Unigenitus* Quesnel was also resisting his king did not seem to occur to him.) It must also have been during these years that Quesnel went to work on a history of the Jesuits posthumously published in 1741, the fourth volume of which dwelt on the Jesuits' role in France's sixteenth-century civil wars of religion.[86]

But Jesuits would not forever do as stand-ins for the Gallican tradition's ecclesiastical—and antipapalist—tenets. So when in 1717 four bishops formally registered their appeal of *Unigenitus* to a future general council at the Sorbonne and an astonishing three-fourths of the Parisian clergy adhered to it, Jansenists, among others, became Gallican "appellants." On one level the appeal was impractical; no council ever met. But for the abbé Jean-Baptiste Le Sesne de Ménille d'Etemare and other masterminds of the "figuratist" turn in Jansenist theology, this appeal's actual function was publically to "witness" to the truths condemned by *Unigenitus* in a time of "obscurity" and magisterial apostasy and therefore was ongoing evidence that Christ remained faithful to his promise never to abandon his church by maintaining the visibility of its "Truth" for those with eyes of faith to see it, even if upheld by only a small minority. [87]

Thus interpreted, the appeal to a general council at last enabled Jansenist theologians to cast Jesuits in the role of plotters against the truth comparable to the role assigned to Jansenists in the Jesuit version of a plot to destroy Catholicism that, known as the Bourgfontaine plot, owed its origin to Jean Filleau in 1654 and saw updated republications in the eighteenth century. The theologians in question were d'Etemare and Pavie de Fourquevaux, who in 1729 published a *Catéchisme historique et dogmatique sur les contestations qui divisent maintenant l'église (Historical and Dogmatic Catechism about the Conflicts Now Dividing the Church).*[88] In the place reserved for Jansen, Saint-Cyran, and Arnauld in 1621 in the Bourgfontaine plot, the *Catéchisme* featured Loyola's successor, Diego Laínez, whose plan of studies committed Loyola's society to the project of substituting the Pelagian heresy for Augustinian orthodoxy in order to rehabilitate "nature" and make "sin" more natural and the sacraments more forgiving, all with a view to attracting penitents to the Society's churches and confessionals.[89] Because this theological revolution needed a strong papacy to effect it, Laínez and his successors set out to exalt the papacy while secretly directing its power at the expense of all other ecclesiastical and doctrinal authorities—even to the temporal detriment of both Catholic and Protestant princes should they stand in the way.[90]

What d'Etemare and Fourquevaux's plot did was to bring together all the successive cases against the Jesuits and relate them as chapters in a continuous conspiratorial history. A serial still being written, that story so far told included episodes about the Society's initial battles against the universities and clergies, its fight against the Gallican liberties in France, the revolt against royal authority in the name of the papacy's spiritual authority, the set-to with Dominicans in defense of Molina's book, its open defiance of episcopal authority in Europe and on the mission field, the casuistic assault against the canons of morality, and the manipulation of papal authority into repeatedly condemning an imagined Jansenist heresy.

In d'Etemare and Fourquevaux's telling of this Jesuit plot, political power still functioned as a means to theological and spiritual power. That this relation of means and ends might be reversed is evident in an almost simultaneously published pamphlet, the Jansenist Jérôme Besoigne's *Mémoire pour MM. les plénipotentiaires du Congrès de Soissons (Memoir for the Honorable Plenipotentiaries [Gathered] at the Congress of Soissons,* reprinted in 1755 and 1761 as a *Juste idée que l'on doit se former des jésuites (Duty to Acquire an Accurate Picture of the Jesuits),* which laid it down that the "desire to dominate" was the Society's sole purpose transmitted by its founders to all their successors in all its diverse enterprises, including its theological and missionary ones.[91] On the one hand, the pamphlet's insistence on the overriding importance of the Jesuits' political agenda recalled the pristine Gallican case as articulated by Arnauld père and

Pasquier. Indeed, the years following saw republication of Arnauld père's *Franc et véritable discours* as well as *Anti-Coton*, which had fingered the Jesuits as the authors of the assassination of Henri IV in 1610.[92] On the other hand, Besoigne's crediting the Jesuits with the aim of erecting a "universal monarchy" structured as an "absolute and Despotic authority" anticipated the novelist feature of the case against the Jesuits by 1759.[93]

These publications came out during the political crisis of 1728–1732 and represent a high-water mark of post-*Unigenitus* Jansenism as well as its first series of setbacks due to the monarchy's renewed attempt to suppress it. On the expansive side stood the florescence of figuratist theology, the "Jansenization" of the Parisian magistracy and priesthood, the popularization of the movement via an outbreak of pro-Jansenist miracles, and the proliferation of a Jansenist press led by the clandestine Jansenist weekly *Nouvelles ecclésiastiques* (*Ecclesiastical News*) that began to appear in 1728; while on the suppressive side stood the deposition of the Jansenist bishop by provincial council, a new archbishop of Paris's purge of the Parisian priesthood, the forced registration of a royal declaration making *Unigenitus* a law of state, and the exile of the Parlement in reaction to this and related royal measures. That none of these setbacks could be pinned exclusively on the hidden influence of the Jesuits did not prevent *Nouvelles ecclésiastiques* from doing so with considerable effect. In this periodical France had an organ possessed by no other Catholic state: one that regularly devoted nearly half its space to the vilification of Jesuits.[94] So detested had the Jesuits become in Paris by 1730 that when the Jansenist barrister Jacques Aubry described the "details of their political and monarchical government" on the winning side of a case involving the claim by the Jesuits to valuable paintings bequeathed to them in a will, it was "not possible," according to a police observer, "to express the joys of the public, particularly those who heard the reading of the sentence."[95]

A yet more spectacular public display of popular hostility against the Jesuits in support of Jansenism as a politicized cause accompanied a judicial case between one Catherine Cadière and her Jesuit confessor Jean-Baptiste Girard when it came up for trial in the Parlement of Provence two years later. At issue was who had done the seducing, Cadière by means of her seductive claims to sanctity or the Jesuit by means of the libidinous application of the Quietist principle that union with God consisted in an attitude of utter indifference even to sin. That Cadière was in no sense a Jansenist and that the Jesuits had combated the Quietist doctrines of Spanish mystic Miguel de Molinos in 1680s did not prevent some of that parlement's pro-Cadière barristers and advocates from tarring the Society with the Quietist heresy or making the affair part of the Jansenist controversy by picturing all Jesuits as persecutors of innocents, pred-atory confessors, lax moralists, apologists for each other's crimes, and of course ultramontanist enemies of the Gallican liberties and threats to temporal author-ity.[96] The press massively followed suit, spilling well beyond the *Nouvelles ecclésiastiques* and into more ribald forms of printed and sung clandestinity.[97]

Although the Quietist accusation would seem to have recalled Melchor Ca-no's concerns about Ignatian spirituality's proximity to that of the heretical "alumbrados," in the 1730s memories went no further back than to the 1690s and the Society's associations with François de Salignac de La Mothe-Fénelon, bishop of Cambrai, whose defense of a Quietist-like tract by one Madame Jeanne-Marie Guyon incurred papal condemnation in 1699. But the Quietist accusation did not stick, and in the longer run the affair's longer-term effect was to conflate it under the classic Jansenist indictments of too frequent commu-nion based on accommodating penitential theology and confessional laxity and put literal flesh on these issues in an unprecedentedly prurient "affair." Besides the rhetorical appeal to and street-level mobilization of public opinion as dis-played in the burning of Girard in effigy in Toulon after the trial ended in a hung parlement, what the Cadière affair added to anti-Jesuitism was a social dimension implied by Society's threat to the realm as mirrored in the family exemplified by the destruction of the Cadière family during and after its ordeal with the Society. That destruction was in good measure the work of Provence's intendant and parlementary first president, Cardin Le Bret, who blamed his par-lement's refusal to exonerate Girard on a miniature Bourgfontaine-like Jan-senist plot and pursued all the imagined plotters with malice armed by sealed letters of arrest.[98]

That is the only reference to a plot that the case threw up, however. Coincid-ing as it did with the end of the political crisis of 1728–1732 and followed by the wars of the Polish and Austrian Succession, the Girard-Cadière affair gave way to a two-decade-long period of relative inattention to the "political" in the Jan-senist press despite the cardinal minister André-Hercule de Fleury's ongoing anti-Jansenist purge of the University of Paris, the clergy, and the religious orders. In *Nouvelles ecclésiastiques*, this inattention translated into a decline in references to Jesuit ultramontanist opposition to the ecclesiastical, much less political, tenets of the Gallican tradition accompanied by a two-decade return to Jansenism's originally moral and theological gravamen against the Jesuits. Taking Girard's place as bête noire in the Jansenists' press was the Jesuit Jean Pichon, who decided to observe the anniversary of Arnauld's *La fréquente com-munion* with a refutation entitled *L'esprit de Jésus Christ et de l'église sur la fréquente communion* (*The Mind of Jesus Christ and of the Church on Frequent*

Communion), which appeared in 1745.[99] In it, Pichon quite simply substituted auricular confession for any evidence of contrition in the sacrament of penance, reducing contrition itself to simple fear of punishment and making one Communion the best preparation for another in lieu of the "charity" required by Arnauld's theology of a "laborious baptism." In reaction, the Jansenist cup of indignation ran over, flooding the journal's pages until the end of the decade. These pages also gave Jansenists another opportunity to restate and solidify the connection between what they regarded as penitential laxity and the "heretical" Molinism that lowered the moral bar to which sinners were held. Most adversely affected by this lowering in Jansenist opinion was the obligation of charity, or love, for which the Jesuits stood accused of substituting self-interested fear.

To be sure, Pope Benedict XIV's final condemnation of the Chinese rites in the bull *Ex quo singulari* in 1742 gave *Nouvelles ecclésiastiques* ammunition for another of its targets, this one Jesuit missionaries as aiders and abettors of pagan idolatry, as did the same pope's bull *Omnium sollicitudinum* by also condemning comparable accommodations to Brahmin Malabar rites two years later.[100] In this affair, the belated counterpart to Navarrete in the Chinese rights controversy was the Capuchin Père Norbert de Bar-Le-Duc, also known as the abbé Platel, and Pierre Parisot, who in 1744 went to press with some *Mémoires historiques* against the Jesuit Roberto Nobili and his successors' syncretistic accommodation to aspects of Brahman Hinduism.[101] But the related subject of the Society's domestic missions in France itself never failed to bring the Jansenist journal back to the subject of Jesuits' Molinist laxity, characterized in its judgment by facile conversions effected by the offer of effortless grace conveyed by homiletic histrionics and spectacular processions followed by meaningless mass Communions and sustained by "little [devotional] practices." Recounting a mission in Lyon in 1734 in very few words, it could think of no better ones than "fables and little stories peddled, confessions hurriedly said, plus collective communions no less inclusive than the processions [that preceded them]."[102]

Second only to the substitution of fear for love, another sin on which Jansenist attention fastened during these decades was the inculcation of doctrinal ignorance as the best guarantee of blind obedience to ecclesiastical authority as embodied in such decisions as *Unigenitus*. It was with the purest outrage, for example, that in 1737 the Jansenist journal caught a rector in Toulouse in the flagrant act of publicly opining that "it was more advantageous for well-being in this life to be ignorant rather than learned."[103] The chief casualty of the Society's glorification of obedient ignorance, in the Jansenist view, was the Holy

Scriptures translated into the vernacular, for which the Society substituted devotional practices and helps. As the 1740s gave way to the 50s, *Nouvelles ecclésiastiques* devoted an entire New Year's editorial to the Society's politics of popular ignorance, locating the raison d'être of the Society in its design to insinuate its "new corpus" of Molinist ethics and religion into the French Catholic bloodstream by recruiting the mentally lazy into its churches and confessionals. Thus by degrees did the two-decade retreat to the moral begin to return to 1730-vintage politics and the plot.

What brought the plot and the overtly political back to the fore of the anti-Jesuit agenda was the controversy over refusal of sacraments that had already begun by the time this editorial appeared and provoked another *Unigenitus*-related political crisis more virulent than in 1728–1732. Although as the young Louis XV's first minister Cardinal Fleury had perpetrated a purge of Jansenists from every institution except the largely immune judiciary, he had also kept pro-*Unigenitus* zealots among the bishops on a tight leash, lest the whole episcopacy feel obliged to support these zealots against a pro-Jansenist Parlement and leave the monarchy in the crossfire. That is precisely what happened during the 1750s after Fleury died in 1743 and an irresolute Louis XV tried to govern by himself.

Beginning in the provinces, a practice of publicly refusing the last rites to dying appellants by some zealously anti-Jansenist bishops made its way to Paris, where the new archbishop, Christophe de Beaumont, began doing so in 1749. After the king failed to heed the Parlement's entreaties to stop the practice, the Parlement intervened on Gallican grounds on behalf of the appellants and their legal rights as Catholics to public access to the sacraments. The result was a slugfest between the episcopacy initially supported by the monarchy on one side and some of the parlements and members of the lower clergy on the other. While the century's previous wars had distracted attention from the religious conflict, the disastrous Seven Years' War did nothing of the sort, only increasing the fiscal leverage of the parlements vis-à-vis the monarchy. Before it died down, the conflict produced two major exiles at the hands of the Parlement of Paris and several crises with provincial parlements, two minor exiles of the archbishop and several provincial bishops, and yet another shower of lettres de cachet imprisoning Jansenists.

A vacillating king caught between a conflict between Jansenists and an ultra-zealous clergy during a war aligning France with a Catholic Habsburg power against Protestant states—all of this was too reminiscent of the League-dominated stages of the sixteenth-century religious civil wars not to go unnoticed by contemporaries. Although this conflict drew no blood and produced no massacres, it amounted to a very intense war of words and warrants for arrest. And while Jesuits and their allies had long identified Jansenists as re-boiled Calvinists, those on the parlementary and Jansenist side now began to perceive their enemies in the role of an ultramontanist Catholic League. By 1752 even non-Jansenist observers such as the marquis d'Argenson detected the "onset of the League" and feared as much as Jansenists that any attempt to find a middle way between "what are called Jansenists these days" and pro-*Unigenitus* bishops might make the scepter every bit as precarious as that wielded by Henri III.[104]

If a Catholic League had returned, circumstances were right for Jansenists to complete the recovery of the language and ideology of the bon françois that had all but disappeared during the era of Richelieu and Louis XIII. And indeed, the phrase "tout bon françois" ("every good Frenchman") began to resound every-where in parlementary and Jansenist lungs. Except that with Spain now safely in Bourbon hands, Rome or perhaps even the Jesuit himself would have to take its place. As an editorial of 1752 concluded, the Jesuits were always already "more ultramontanist than French, but even more Jesuit than ultramontanist," their goal being not only "to use the bull to enslave us to the yoke of the Court of Rome, but even more to enslave us to their own."[105] Yet the language might better be characterized as "patriotic," seeing that an appeal to the Gallican *patrie*, or nation, was never too far from the textual vicinity. But while the original ideology of the bon françois did not survive the rise of Bourbon abso-lutism, the ideology's revival as patriotism in the mid-eighteenth century came to direct itself against royal absolutism in alliance with the Parlement and therefore with all the more reason against the Jesuit as its symbol.

It goes without saying that to the extent that the ideology opposed the mon-archy, it did so in the name of the monarchy—in the name, that is, of a judicial monarchy constrained within the bounds of "fundamental laws" and a certain conception of a historic "constitution" that, however traditional in intent, be-came ever more radical in the 1750s by its appeal to the "nation" as its ultimate support. Deployed by the parlements against the ministry on a variety of fronts, that constitutionalism was largely the work of Jansenist barristers and canon lawyers, who in turn adopted it from the Fronde and—ironically—from sources on both sides of the sixteenth-century wars of religion.

That France had an "ancient" constitution with roots in the customs of the Franks and institutions of the Merovingian and Carolingian dynasties, that this constitution vested the making of the laws with the entire Frankish people later represented in the Estates General, that it was the duty of magistrates to autho-rize resistance to kings when they became "tyrants"—all these tenets became constitutional commonplaces in both Huguenot and later Leaguish justifications for active resistance, with the difference that the League's political thought factored in an important role for papal intervention. After fading and then reappearing in attenuated form during the Fronde of 1648–1653, this constitutionalism went into a long dormancy during the apogee of Louis Quatorzian absolutism, only to reappear after the Parlement of Paris regained its right of prior remonstrance in 1715 and in the thick of the century's first peak in the Jansenist controversy in 1728–1732. Secure in the magistracy and in the order of barristers from the turn of the century, Jansenist barristers and canon lawyers continued to radicalize this constitutionalism while tailoring it to fit the Parlement as the representative of the nation, which took the place of the Estates General in this kind of constitutional thought after they had ceased to meet after 1615.

This sort of constitutionalism left the Jesuits undisturbed until the very end of the sixteenth-century wars of religion, when Pasquier objected to the "absolute" and monarchical power of the Jesuits' general. If he did so, however, it was not only by reason of the danger this power posed to the Gallican liberties of the church but also because he saw it as incompatible with his own king's absolute authority, to which he did not object. For its part the Fronde's constitutionalism also left the Jesuits largely alone. But French constitutional thought began to take an anti-Jesuit turn during the crisis of 1728–1732, which produced the first Jansenist reworking of a Fronde-vintage pamphlet entitled *Judicium Francorum*, as well as the first Jansenist accusations of "despotism" against the structure of the Society, quite apart from whether it was competitive with the king's or not. And in this case, the general's "despotic" power was condemned synonymously with his "absolute" power—that is, with what was still the orthodox adjective to describe royal power.[106]

By pitting the Parlement against a weakened but still "absolute" monarchy perceived to have taken the Jesuits' side in a period of intense politico-religious divisions, the conflict over refusal of sacraments at once consummated the antidespotic turn in its own constitutionalism and also the scapegoating of the Jesuits as the authors of these divisions. Inquiring into the cause of those divisions in 1752, the inaugural editorial of *Nouvelles ecclésiastiques* already thought it unlikely that anyone could be "so little clairvoyant as to fail to discern the common interests of the Court of Rome and the [Jesuit] Society beneath the troubles that now agitate us."[107] By 1758 the same journal was ready to spare the "Court of Rome" and single out "a species of querulous . . . men spread out in all places [while] yet singular in them all" as solely responsible for the religious divisions among Frenchmen. Reviewing in turn all the possible perpetrators and benefactors of the policy of refusing the Viaticum and Extreme Unction to those who had never been denied them in their lifetimes, the editorial concluded by process of elimination that, "yes, the Jesuits alone desire this schism" in order to divide and conquer; and that this "progeny of Ishmael" wished to do so not only in the interests of its "new corps of religion" but as a "faction" exclusively devoted to the "interests of the Society that is its Idol."[108] The Jansenist journal thereby designated the Jesuits as the not so hidden authors of French divisions, and marked them out as the scapegoats whose ouster alone would end this perceived renewal of France's Reformation-era religious civil conflict.

To be effective, in any case, the strategy of casting the Jesuits as the authors of France's religious troubles in the language of patriotic rhetoric entailed an effort to denaturalize as well as hereticate the Jesuits' doctrinal orientations while further nationalizing the Gallican liberties themselves.

Reviewing the Parlement of Aix's advocate general's indictment of several ultramontanist theses defended by Jesuits in Marseilles in 1754, the editor argued that misdirected zeal for *Unigenitus* snuffs out the "just attachment that every good Frenchman ought to have for the liberties of the [Gallican] Church."[109] And reacting in 1756 to a Jesuit professor's reported conviction that the Gallican Declaration of 1682 was "contrary to . . . Catholic unity as centered [in] . . . the Chair of Saint Peter," *Nouvelles ecclésiastiques* invoked the "nation" as having an interest in maintaining this "monument of the Maxims of the Church of France."[110] Later the same year it was the vigilance of "all the good Citizens" of France that the *Nouvelles* alerted in faulting the Jesuits for failing to teach their students the history of "their *Patrie*," including not only the liberties of the Gallican Church but also the "veritable constitution of the State, the Public Law of the Monarchy, and the obligations it imposes on each member of the Nation."[111]

Which is to say that a renewed attention to a "constitutionalized" version of the royalist side of the Gallican tradition kept pace with the ecclesiological side. Renewed efforts in Rome in the 1750s to beatify Cardinal Bellarmino gave the *Nouvelles* occasion to explain Bellarmino's theory of the indirect power of the papacy to intervene in the temporal governance of kings as well as its putative role in the assassination of Henri III and IV—and to attribute the papal efforts, the "horrible maxims" of the theory, and its practice to the Jesuits.[112] The year 1755 witnessed the republication of the *Juste idée que l'on doit se former des jésuites* first published in 1728 as a *Mémoire pour MM. les plénipotentiaires*, this time accompanied by Quesnel and Petitpied's 1713 collection of documents about the Jesuits' first expulsion from France "for having taught and put into practice [the doctrine] that it is permissible to kill kings."[113] While in 1729 the *Nouvelles* gave this pamphlet little more than a notice, in 1755 it fell and fastened upon it. And in 1756—more on this later—the revolt of natives in the Jesuit missions in Paraguay against the Treaty of Madrid's reassignment of some of these missions to Portuguese rule first impinged on French Jansenist attention as proof positive that the Jesuits, already guilty of idolatry in their missions, were also capable of using them as staging grounds for revolts against their temporal sovereigns.[114]

The remaining barriers to the renewed stigmatization of Jesuits as regicides gave way entirely in the year 1757, which began with a knife attack on Louis XV as he was entering his carriage at Versailles by an unemployed lackey named Robert-François Damiens. Detained on the spot, Damiens made no attempt to escape, as his self-professed purpose was to convey a message that in essence advised the king to heed the remonstrances of the Parlement of Paris and part paths with the archbishop of Paris and his like-minded colleagues. What had politicized this eccentric and barely literate domestic servant was the ongoing conflict over the refusal of sacraments to appellants in which he had clearly taken sides against the bishops and Jesuits and for the Parlement's magistrates, some of whom he had served.

That this motivational evidence was inconvenient for the magistracy and Jansenists is the understatement of a trial that took place amid a political crisis in which the mass of magistrates had submitted their resignations in protest to forcibly registered royal edicts related to the *Unigenitus* and the conflict over refusal of sacraments. In an atmosphere of suspicion and mistrust, the trial therefore took place in a Parlement composed of the realm's specially convened princes and peers and the few magistrates who had not resigned. In it, Le Paige's patron—and the king's cousin—Louis-François de Bourbon, prince de Conti, did everything he could with Le Paige's help to direct the prosecution's search for conspirators away from parlementary and Jansenist quarters and toward the Jesuits. But what the investigation turned up consisted in literally little more than that Damiens had served as a busboy and part-time lackey in two separate stints for the students at the college of Louis-le-Grand twenty years earlier and circumstantially little more than that the death of the king would have brought the far more pro-Jesuit dauphin to the throne. The trial's official conclusion that Damiens had acted alone convinced virtually no one except those who had conducted the trial and the Jesuits.[115]

Yet to a remarkable degree the Jansenist press turned the tables on the evidence and convinced the Parisian "public" to which it explicitly appealed that Damiens had intended to kill the king and had acted as the agent of Jesuits and some allied bishops. Taking advantage of the almost universal assumption that no one as lowly as a lackey could independently have formed political ideas, much acted them out, this press effectively argued that Damiens's self-professed motives were only a theatrical "mask" he wore in order to incriminate the Parlement and that the only "body" of people in France with the capacity to perpetrate such an act was, as the symptomatically entitled *Lettre d'un patriote* put it, "a body of men that from its birth exhibited the irrevocable aim of seizing Sovereign authority in the Church and all the States."[116] While rehashing what had become common wisdom on Jesuit complicity in the sixteenth-century assassination attempts, this and like pamphlets amplified Jansenism's patriotic take on the Gallican tradition by explicitly appealing to the Gallic "patriot," to "every good Frenchman" as well as to the "nation" against this rootless "race of men" who had spread everywhere on the earth.[117]

Nor did it help the Jesuits' cause that an apparently new edition of the German Jesuit Hermann Busembaum's casuistic *Medulla theologiae moralis* (*The Marrow of Moral Theology*) came to the attention of the Parlement of Toulouse and to that of the Jansenist press in 1757.[118] Originally published in 1645 in Münster, it came out in a new edition expanded by Claude La Croix in Cologne in 1729 and repeatedly thereafter.[119] While the Jansenist journal had barely mentioned that edition, it more than made up for its earlier inattention by pouncing on a supposedly new edition in 1757, noting its assertions of the pope's ultimate suzerainty over even temporal authorities and justifications for the assassination of kings proscribed or excommunicated by the papacy, even by anybody in self-defense.[120] It did not advance the Jesuit cause any further when it became apparent that the Jesuits' *Journal de Trévoux* had recommended the book when it first appeared with La Croix's additions in Cologne in 1729, or that the Italian Jesuit Francesco Antonio Zaccaria published an apology of it in 1758.[121] As for the Jesuits' disavowal of the book's "maxims," the Jansenist press dismissed them as meaningless in the light of the Jesuits' casuistry, reinforcing the connection previously made between regicide and the moral casuistry of probabilism.[122]

Not only did the year 1758 maintain the momentum of the anti-Jesuit torrent, but after 3 September amply added to it with its coverage of an attempt on the life of José I, king of Portugal, followed by the use of it by the all-powerful first minister, Sebastião José de Carvalho e Melo's—later the marqués de Pombal—to frame the Portuguese Jesuits and literally expel them from the metropolis and colonies alike the very next year. Reserved for its proper place, that story is out of place here. Suffice it to say that in jointly framing the Jesuits as being among the architects of this event Carvalho generously availed himself of the Damiens affair's revival of the Society's regicidal reputation, while the French Jansenist press feasted on Carvalho's interpretation of events in Portugal in order to further that reputation in France.

Meanwhile, the publication of the second part of the Jesuit Isaac-Joseph Berruyer's *Histoire du peuple de Dieu* on the Gospels in 1753 brought French Jansenist attention back to the subject of Molinism—the matter, that is, for the form of Jansenism's theological quarrel with the Jesuits in its infancy.[123] As in his previously published volumes of his novelized version of the Old Testament, Berruyer freely embroidered his account of the biblical action and put words in the mouths of his dramatis personae, above all Jesus himself.

Part of Berruyer's purpose in paraphrasing rather than translating Holy Writ was undoubtedly to lend a semblance of scriptural support for the principle of papal infallibility as well as such signature Jesuit doctrines as divine prescience, merely "sufficient" grace, free human agency in salvation, and the practice of frequent Communion. But in his attempt to give these doctrines and practices a semblance of scriptural basis. Berruyer wandered into the minefield of the mystery of the hypostatic union between God the Father and God the Son, plausibly exposing his text to charges of such Trinitarian heresies as Arianism, Nestorianism, and Socinianism while incurring real condemnations by such un-Jansenist authorities as the Sorbonne, the archbishop of Paris, and the papacy itself. Not only did the second part of his *Histoire* provide no end of copy for the Jansenist press at a time when the Society could least afford it, it also enabled that press to tar both Molinism and sacramental practice with the brush of heresy as nothing that had emanated from a Jesuit pen had ever done before.[124] Since the book soon came out in various translations and Jansenist critiques followed them everywhere, the names of Berruyer and his teacher Jean Hardouin figured in the cases of all the states from which the Society was expelled.

By 1759 something like a plot to do away with the Society of Jesus had come to exist in France. But if plot it was, part of it was to depict the Jesuits as the most dangerous of plotters, just as the Jesuits had once and still depicted Jansenists as plotters.[125] And if the depiction of a Jesuit plot were to work, it would have to recall all the many and various accusations that had accumulated against the Society over time and relate them to each other as parts of a single if multifaceted plot. Such a plot theory had been at hand since d'Etemare and Fourquevaux had sketched one out in their *Catéchisme historique et dogmatique*, according to which the Society had plotted to increase and control the power of the papacy in order to supplant Augustinian orthodoxy with Laínez's Pelagian theology. In order to be fully functional as a reason to suppress the Jesuits, however, the plot had to include what d'Etemare and Fourquevaux's version had still left aside, notably the whole pre-Jansenist political Gallican layer as well as the pagan accommodations in the mission field. But when in its New Year's issue of 1755 the *Nouvelles* recalled and revived d'Etemare and Fourquevaux's "long chain of evils" constituting a multisecular plot, events during the intervening period had likewise recalled and repristinated all of these missing links.[126]

While the Cadière-Girard, Pichon, and Berruyer affairs had refreshed the memory of the Jansenists' confessional, penitential, and doctrinal indictments of the Jesuits and related them to each other, all had also reminded contemporaries of the Society's policy to come to the aid of any of its erring members as well as its willingness to thumb its nose at hierarchical authority, whether it be the bishops who condemned Pichon's book or the papacy that repeatedly condemned Berruyer's. Along the way, Benedict XIV's bull *Ex quo singulari* revived memories of the Jesuits' "pagan" accommodations to Chinese rites and similar ones in India, Indochina, Japan, and Thailand; while more recently another round of *Unigenitus*-related conflicts culminating in the Damiens affair revived memory of the Jesuits' League-era theory and practice of regicide, since then fortified by that theory's association with the Society's "probabilistic" ethics. It remained for the Jansenist journal's New Year's editorial of 2 January 1759 to bring this new evidence together and fill out the missing aspects and stages of the Jesuit plot. Rather like themes seemingly left dangling in a Bach fugue only to be recalled and combined in a final crescendo, every theme ever sounded against Jesuits seemed to resonate and resound anew in the acoustics of contemporary events with the help of a little editorial orchestration and direction.

The lead theme was the two-hundred-year war between a minority of defenders of the "Truth" and its enemies, the Jesuits, who from 1588 plotted to subvert the church's "ancient doctrine" and moral law both in Europe and among its converts elsewhere, finishing with a challenge to authorities in both church and state. Responsive everywhere to the direction of an "absolute Chief," the Society had first displayed its perverse genius in matters of religion, fabricating a doctrinal "system" from the debris of every doctrinal deviation and heresy in history while inventing new ones as need arose.

Yet between the religious and political aspects of its plot and program, the political now took precedence. For the Society had modeled its "universal plan in Religion" on its political aim, which amounted to no less than to "dominate" in every sphere and to reduce all and sundry to a condition of "servitude," wrote the *Nouvelles*.[127] The main means to that end employed by the Society was to constitute itself as a "Republic unto itself with branches in . . . all States, or as a kind of Co-State with its own particular laws to which [the Society] owed preference over those in the states in which it was mixed."[128] It was in pursuit of that end that Jesuits brought conflict wherever they went as well as in France, where, as "the true authors of the troubles that agitate us," they use the "mask of Religion" with the aim of stirring up people, making them factious and even Leaguers if they could, as . . . in times past."[129] Where, then, was the "faithful Frenchman" who did not "fill with indignation" at the sight of a new edition of the Jesuit Busembaum's book in 1757 on the heels of the "execrable assassination attempt of 5 January[?]"[130] Long at home with secrecy, the Jesuits had, however, most recently committed the imprudence of coming out into the open. "Behold them unmasked!" declared the *Nouvelles*. After surveying all the recent evidence to this effect not only in France but also in Rome, South America, Portugal, and even their birthplace in Spain, the editorial did not "hesitate to place among the things most necessary for the Church and the salvation of her children the grace of being finally delivered from a Society so noxious to the one as to the other."[131]

By 1759 these were not words in the air but "speech acts." To complete the spelling out of the sort of patriotism under the banner of which latter-day Gallicans and Jansenists would array themselves against the Jesuits, the only thing lacking was the accusation of despotism against the structure of the Society, which did not differ all that much from the absolute monarchy that the ideology of the bon français had once defended against the Society's regicidal theory. That was the additional step taken by Le Paige and the abbé Christophe Coudrette in their *Histoire générale de la naissance et des origines et des progrès de la compagnie de Jésus* (A General History of the Birth, Origins, and Progress of the Company of Jesus), which appeared in 1761. The book included not only a "general history" but also a detailed analysis of the Society's constitutions, on the basis of which it concluded that the "regime of the Society is Monarchical, even Despotic," all the while equating these terms with the adjective "absolute."[132]

As the 1759 editorial in the Nouvelles could not, the book's four volumes recounted every accusation ever leveled against the Society and every set-to it had ever had with other corps in France and elsewhere. If this editorial might be compared with an anti-Jansenist summa, laying down no fewer than sixty-four propositions while refuting all the objections, it also bears comparison to an anti-Jesuit art of the fugue, extended for many more than eighteen canzone.

The pretentious inclusion of Jesus by the Society in its name; its hermaphrodite character; its accumulation of papal privileges; its devious combination of simple and solemn vows; its pretense of poverty amid ill-gotten wealth; the mysterious instability of its constitutions; its incompatibility with the rights of universities and bishops; its threat to kingship and the papacy alike; its casuistry, Molinism, idolatry, and insatiable greed in action in Europe and in the mission fields—all these themes the four volumes recalled and combined, culminating in the conclusion that "by the very nature of their Institute the Jesuits were not receivable by any civilized state."[133] Addressing only the Jesuits' educational empire while pulling out all the patriotic stops, where, asked this *Histoire*, is the "civilized state that would not be frightened by an immense University despotically governed by a foreign and ultramontanist General composed of 612 colleges, thirty thousand Jesuits, and an innumerable multitude of pupils entirely given over to these Masters, refusing to swear the essential oaths . . . while dedicating themselves to the aggrandizement of this fearful Monarchy, aspiring only to bring everything within its orbit and all animated by the same spirit, being nothing more than their chief's servile instruments and slaves disposed to sacrifice everything for his interests, obeying him blindly in all things?"[134]

As did the 1759 editorial—probably also written by Le Paige—the four volumes also subordinated all aspects of the Society's history and character to the sole goal of the greater honor and glory, not of God, but its "despotic" empire. Utterances already inseparable from action—the volumes appeared in 1761—they reached the dangerous verdict that the legal status of the Society remained irregular, as it had been granted a precarious presence in France by the Parlement in 1562 only on conditions never fulfilled. In truth the Society owed its presence to the royal will. That will was already faltering in the face of this anti-Jesuit catechism by the time this book was published, just as another royal will had already used it to expel the Jesuits from Portugal and other royal wills would do in their turn in Naples and Parma, and against the papacy in 1773.

CONCLUSION

Largely if not exclusively a French creation, by 1759 Catholic anti-Jesuitism had recovered and synthesized all of its successive phases and stages while assimilating to its corpus every other gravamen against the Society from every other corner of Europe and the European-influenced globe. Capable of national inflections and variations, it was therefore also more than ready for export and deployment elsewhere when, around the same time, the French and Dutch actors in this story began aggressively to break out of their national confines, to cultivate international contacts, and to build on the combination of Gallicanism and Jansenism toward the construction of a reformist Catholicism. Still mainly missing from this mix is any signature contribution by the European Enlightenment, which in France was far more interested in monks in general as "useless" than in Jesuits in particular as pernicious. That Enlightenment's particular contribution to the debate consisted in scattered comments by Voltaire and d'Alembert's *Sur la destruction des jésuites en France*, which in 1765 laid claim to the spoils of the Jesuit suppression for the cause of "philosophy" while wishing a pox on both the Jansenist and the Jesuit houses. Even in a uniquely polarized France, however, that pamphlet obscures a certain Gallican overlap between the "philosophical" and Jansenist camps, consisting in the excoriation of the "fanatical" and "superstitions" and the valuation of secular utility and the extension of the state's secular authority. Elsewhere in Catholic Europe, in contrast, the blurring from what passed as "Jansenist" to the "enlightened" was to be far more gradual, even imperceptible. But whatever the contours of Reform Catholicism here or there, at its center lay a case against the Society of Jesus formed in the crucible of Gallican and Jansenist opposition to it in Old Regime France.

Part Two

THE EXPULSIONS AND SUPPRESSIONS OF THE JESUITS

3

THE CASE OF FRANCE, 1758-1764

By 1757 some Roman enemies of the Jesuits, such as Cardinal Passionei, voiced concern that the Damiens affair would rebound against the Parlement in favor of the Jesuits.[1] Besides having his own salon, Passionei was part of the nest of philo-Jansenist and anti-Jesuit Italian prelates and theologians headed by Bottari known as the Archetto that met in the palace of the similarly oriented Corsini cardinals. Like Passionei, Bottari had been in correspondence with French appellants since the mid-1750s, beginning with the abbé Clément.

Another such Italian friend was the conte and abate Gaspare Cerati, director of studies at the University of Pisa, who besides admiring and corresponding with Montesquieu and other French philosophes had also revolted against a Jesuit education and fallen in with the Archetto and its members, with whom he remained in contact after settling in Pisa in 1749. As in the case of Bottari and Passionei, Certati displayed an admiration for the literature of Port-Royal, a real commitment to Augustinian theology and rigorist ethics, and genuine sympathy for the "good cause" of French appellants and the church of Utrecht, which went hand in hand with polymathic interests in antiquity, literature, and the sciences. This pattern of interests mirrored Muratori's in contrast to that of full-time Jansenists in France. Also like Bottari and Passionei, Cerati had entered into correspondence with Clément, whom he had met along with other appellants during a trip to France.

It was Clément who was the more important correspondent on the French appellant side.[2] Strategically positioned in Paris since the death of Auxerre's protective Jansenist bishop in 1754, Clément was also the brother of several equally Jansenist magistrates, including Clément de Feillet, a councilor in the

Parlement of Paris and a linchpin of the *parti janséniste* there. By the time of the French Revolution, this reformist Catholic "international" was to have outposts not only in Utrecht and Rome but also in other Italian cities, as well as in Madrid, Lisbon, Vienna, and Mainz.

PLOTS AND PLANS

Toward the end of 1757, this international's nerve center in Paris began to receive an uptick in news from Bottari, Cerati, and Passionei. The upshot of this news was that the deteriorating state of Benedict XIV's health made it imperative to make every effort to seize the moment and extract from the ailing pope's good will a pronouncement more effective than had been the recent brief *Ex omnibus*, which had opened the way to Louis XV's declaration in 1756 that the bull *Unigenitus* was not a "rule of faith." Acutely aware of the disfavor into which the Jesuits had fallen in Portugal, and of their role in publications against his recent brief in Rome, Benedict XIV, it was said, was readier than ever to do something "striking" (*strepito*) against them by way of further alleviating the situation of appellants in France. But he would do so only if he were to find himself "pushed" by the king—that is, if the initiative came from the royal court. What Bottari favored was a papal declaration that the qualification of *Unigenitus* as a rule of faith by the secret consistory of Rome in 1725 was an illicit addition to the minutes after the fact.[3] Cerati hoped for better: nothing less than a papal blessing of a project he knew existed in France that, by rejecting whatever "heresies" they could among those condemned by the papacy's anti-Jansenist bulls, appellants would by implication place the doctrines that they professed under papal protection.[4]

These hopes were not without foundation. Aside from the clouds gathering over the Society of Jesus in otherwise sunny Portugal and Spain, Benedict XIV had already condemned its position on accommodating the arguably pagan Chinese and so-called Malabar rites in India in 1742 and 1745. As these letters were being exchanged, all knew that the pope was at work on a papal brief against the second part of Berruyer's *Histoire du peuple de Dieu* on the Gospels.[5] Further, Benedict had protected the Augustinian Enrico Norris's doctrinally Augustinian *Historia Pelagiana* (*History of Pelagianism*) against the Spanish Inquisition, had made known his penchant for the Augustinian doctrine of grace, had made several if abortive overtures to the estranged diocese of Utrecht, and had most recently cooperated with Étienne-François, duc de Choiseul, at that time France's envoy to Rome, in an attempt to dampen the zeal of the pro-*Unigenitus* episcopacy in the conflict over the public refusal of sacraments to French appellants.[6]

The project to which Cerati referred and attributed to an "excellent theologian" indeed existed. Part of it consisted of a condemnation of Molinist errors
and originated in the counsels of Cardinal Antoine de Noailles, the appellant
archbishop of Paris during the first quarter of the eighteenth century, who in
1719 had used the document as the basis of an abortive attempt to reach a doctrinal "accommodation" with the papacy and pro-*Unigenitus* bishops about how
to interpret this bull and put an end to the appeal against it. That and further
attempts toward doctrinal accord during the pontificate of Benedict XIII produced additions in 1725 by the appellant theologian Laurent-François Boursier—
probably the "excellent theologian" referred to by Cerati. Meanwhile Boursier,
who died in 1749, had evidently involved the Jansenist barrister Christophe
Coudrette in his efforts, because it was Coudrette who allowed the young Le
Paige to make a copy of the project in 1725. When therefore Clément received
news from Rome that the times were more auspicious than ever for another
attempt at accommodation over *Unigenitus* with Rome, Le Paige immediately
retrieved Noailles and Boursier's project, which by then numbered twenty-
one articles. After tinkering with them himself, he also turned them over to
the bishop of Soissons's theologian Étienne Gourlin, who refined the project
further.

Known by then as the *Aspicientes* (*Regarding . . .*) after the first word of the
document, as though it were a papal brief or bull, the project indeed aspired to
be nothing less than a bull. The hope of its architects was that in some form it
would be adopted and promulgated by the papacy as a bull. No sooner did
French or Dutch appellants acquire regular Augustinian and anti-Jesuit friends
in Rome than they received repeated warnings from these friends that "the
Court of Rome's unwillingness ever to retreat (*irréculabilité*) would never permit it to abandon the bulls that have provoked such a storm in France." Yet none
of this stood in the way of an attempt, in the words of Gaspare Ceratti, the polymathic rector of the University of Pisa, to render these bulls "useless by means
of appropriate explanations and in this way indirectly sideline [them] so that
they can no longer [be used] to torment anybody."[7]

The strategy was to talk the papacy into issuing a bull that instead of condemning new errors would state clearly and positively what were the boundaries
of Augustinian and Thomistic orthodoxy in the contested matters, most of them
bearing on grace and free will. The hoped-for consequence of such a bull would
be that if, in the reported words of the Parlement's first president, Mathieu-
François Molé, those accused of Jansenism in France refused to identify with
the doctrine stated in this bull, "the evil would become manifest and proven";
but that if they could sincerely say that they professed no other doctrine, then
their innocence would become equally manifest, with the result that they could

"no longer be treated as culpable."[8] The object, in still other words, was to rectify the ambiguity of previous papal bulls of condemnation beginning with *Cum occasione* in 1653 and culminating with *Unigenitus* in 1713 by getting "'explanations" from Benedict XIV that no one had been able to obtain from his predecessors.

That someone as highly positioned as Molé had become involved is an indication that these negotiations were serious. While Clément's most direct route to the Parlement's first president lay through his brother Clément de Feillet, Le Paige's lay through Jean-François-Alexandre Murard, the president of the Parlement's third chamber of requests, and like Le Paige a highly respected Jansenist éminence grise. Although distracted by a change of domicile and his role in other controversies at the time, Le Paige showed the letters from Italy to Murard, who, convinced of their importance, in turn convinced Molé, who would have liked nothing better than a papal bull that would have helped end the Parlement's perennial standoff with the General Assembly of the Gallican Clergy over such issues as the refusal of sacraments to appellants. But Le Paige had other routes to Molé, one going though Goulin to François de Fitz-James, bishop of Soissons, who fortified Mole's convictions. Seconding Fitz-James's efforts was Malvin de Montazet, the recently elevated archbishop of Lyon, one of whose advisers was Le Paige's collaborator, the abbé Claude Mey.

Persuaded and supported on all sides, Molé approached Joachim-Pierre, the abbé de Bernis, France's recently appointed secretary for foreign affairs and one of the architects of France's recent alliance with Habsburg Austria. With Gourlin and Murard's help, Le Paige had meanwhile stitched together a new preamble for the projected bull as well as a memoir for Louis XV to persuade the king, all of which also reached the hands of Bernis via Molé, who went to confer with Bernis at Versailles on 30 April 1758. By Molé's account, Bernis professed himself "satisfied" with the plan although "frightened" by the difficulties of execution, in Rome because of the reluctance to "speak as clearly" about the papal past as desirable and in France because of the predictable opposition of "zealous bishops." Bernis nonetheless seemed to remain open to the argument that this plan was worth a try. Working on the project with Gourlin, Le Paige got all the documents in order and into the hands of Murard by the morning of 12 May. But "what," in Le Paige's expression, was Murard's unpleasant "surprise" when, delivering the documents to Molé, an extraordinary courier arrived in Versailles with the news that the pope had died nearly two weeks earlier, on 3 May.[9]

Benedict XIV's death did not immediately spell the end of this diplomatic venture, however. Although Le Paige conceded that he had never felt very hopeful about the "success of an affair that had become so difficult on account of the multiplicity and age of the engagements contracted by the two courts," the group assembled at Clément de Feillet's home on the rue Christine the following day and, having previously resolved upon sending the abbé Clément to Rome, decided to persist in this plan in view of taking the pulse of the papal curia, tracking the course of the papal conclave, and "forming liaisons in Rome that might be useful in the future." All thought that the new alliance between France and Vienna plus France's ties with both Spain and Portugal should "put France in a position effect the union of the four crowns in order to obtain a good pope." Among the electable cardinals, they deemed Corsini, Passionei, Joachín Fernández Portocarrero, Giuseppe Spinelli, and Fortunato Tamburini the most committed to the "solid doctrine," and for that reason the best. Of these, Le Paige had already written to Passionei requesting an "immediate correspondence," while Clément was already indirectly in contact with Corsini via Bottari.[10]

It was therefore as an unofficial ambassador of the Parlement of Paris, including its first president, that Clément left Paris on 17 May, arriving a month and a few days later in Rome, where he took up residence at the French embassy. No sooner was he there than he learned that events had largely passed him by, that deliberations in the conclave had already matured, and that the most potentially electable of the "pacific" cardinals, namely, Spinelli, had run into the opposition of Domenico Orsini of Naples, and had therefore rallied with Corsini and even Tamburini and the French and Austrian cardinals in favor of one Carlo Rezzonico, a Venetian and bishop of Padua. Among those deemed likely to be "good" popes by the Parisians who sent Clément, only Passionei remained opposed. By July 5—the date of Clément's second letter—Rezzonico lacked only one vote; the next day he became the new pope, taking the name of Clement XIII. Clément's first reaction could hardly have been more negative: "He has a brother and nephews who are Jesuits and another nephew who is an ultra-Jesuit; he is very ignorant, fully devoted to the Society, and given to the minutiae of piety, passing his time as bishop of Padua by scurrying from church to church and to all the evening offices in his diocese."[11]

As July turned into August, however, Clément's hosts in Rome talked him into seeing the papal glass as half full instead of half empty. The new pope did not take a Jesuit as his confessor. Nor did he back away from the condemnation of the just published third part of Berruyer's *Histoire*, disavow Cardinal Saldanha's harsh reformist decree against the Jesuits in Portugal, or strike out in the contrary direction by condemning a catechism adopted by the Jansenist bishop of Luçon, as French Jesuits were then demanding. All depended on the cardinals with whom Clement XIII chose to surround himself. While the appellant abbé worried about the influence of the pope's pro-Jesuit physician, he noted with satisfaction the papal decision to retain Alberico Archinto as secretary of state, proponent of "solid doctrine" that this cardinal was known to be. By mid-August Clément was urging his friends in Paris to continue work on the projected bull of pacification; indeed, by the end of August he was asking that the abbé Mey be sent to Rome to help him, as had been originally planned.

Yet these optimistic assessments competed for space in Clément's letters with ever more bitter complaints about the "intrigues" of the Jesuits and the Molinist cardinals Gian Francesco Albani and Henry Benedict Stuart, known as Cardinal York, who refused to stand up during the ceremony of confirmation of the newly elevated Malvin de Montazet as archbishop of Lyon and primate of France. It was with ever-greater urgency that the abbé Clément urged the Parlement to pursue the Jesuits by reason of their illicit commerce and to put pressure on the French royal court to dismiss them as confessors and preachers, as the Portuguese and Spanish courts had recently done. If, he reasoned, "this moment is missed for a spectacular [display of] discontent on the part of the entire and august house of the Bourbons, the artifices [of the Jesuits] will succeed anew, as they always have in the past."[12]

Among Clément's complaints, the vigilance of the former papal nuncio in Paris, Carlo Francesco Dorini, figured very prominently. With good reason too, for no sooner had Clément settled in at the French ambassadorial compound in Rome than he learned that the papal nuncio in France had divined his journey and its purpose and denounced him as "one of the most notorious Jansenists." Clément assured his friends in Paris that he was carefully minding his health and his own business and not indiscreetly poking his nose around Rome.[13] The nuncio's denunciations continued into the new pontificate, however, and by 9 September with what Clément called the "additional imposture, that I am an emissary of the Parlement."[14] By then, these complaints came ominously accompanied by others about the pro-Jesuit biases of the French ambassador to Rome, Jean-François de Rochechouart, bishop of Laon, who had fallen in with the French Jesuit Mathurin-Germain Le Forestier, and who in Clément's opinion did not understand his instructions and should have been replaced by someone who did.

From the outset Clément knew that the only real threat to his presence in Rome was the French royal court, and it was with naiveté that on 5 August he urged his friends in Paris to ask Bernis to put in a good word for him to the bishop of Laon. In fact, Bernis was a far more sensitive weathervane than Clément for detecting which of the many factional winds was blowing the hardest in Versailles—and in fact, it was not then blowing in anything like the Parlement's direction. Indeed, the only conceivable source for the nuncio's remarkably accurate knowledge about Clément's trip to and purpose in Rome was none other than Bernis himself.

So it was that on 11 September the French ministry of foreign affairs refused to authorize Clément's further sojourn in Rome, and the appellant "pilgrim," as the abbé Coudrette called him, was soon on his way back to Paris after a brief stay in Naples, where he had other Augustinian contacts.[15] By then Clément reported that all had "set aside any hope for a new bull, leaving us crushed beneath the enigmatic weight of the old ones."[16] Then in November, having stopped to see Ceratti in Pisa, Clément received the news that their only remaining hope, Clement XIII's secretary of state, Alberico Archinto, had just died, soon to be replaced by the unpromisingly pro-Jesuit cardinal Luigi Maria Torrigiani. At that point Clément was ready to draw the conclusion that "we can only find the resources to meet our troubles at home among ourselves."[17]

The immediate origin of the campaign against the Jesuits in France lay here. The first suggestion that the time had perhaps arrived to proceed against the Jesuits came from Bottari, who, inspired by events in Portugal, invoked the example of the late medieval order of Templars as a model of for abolition of an entire order along with the confiscation of all its wealth by princes for redistribution to indebted parishes, the secular clergy, the poor, and other such laudable causes.[18] But for two or three years Bottari had been sermonizing Clément and the editorial entourage of the *Nouvelles ecclésiastiques* for too frequently attacking the Jesuits via their doctrine and as the real authors of *Unigenitus* and other anti-Jansenist bulls, enabling the Jesuits perennially to pose in Rome as the indispensable defenders of papal authority when they were only defending themselves. So when a thoroughly discouraged Clément regained the security of his homeland, he received a barrage of advice from his Italian Augustinian correspondents to the effect that failing any immediate prospect of accomplishing anything on the doctrinal front, the time had come for him and his cohorts to keep quiet about the bull and concentrate all their fire on the Jesuits.

"It is mandatory for these truths to be understood by all your writers," wrote Bottari on 12 December, the "truths" being that the writers should "attack the Jesuits but not the Court of Rome," marveling how it happened "that the French, perspicuous though they are, have not yet divined the Jesuit strategy of having always astutely made their proper cause the same as the Court of Rome's, and always created the appearance of defending, not themselves or their errors, but rather Rome."[19] But while Bottari held out the prospect that once the Jesuits were gone or had "lost all their credit, . . . it will be possible to backtrack and remedy some of the past wrongs," the rabidly anti-Jesuit Torinese ambassador to

Naples, Count Carlo Armano di Grosso, seemed to think that the destruction of the Jesuits would save the ecclesiastical day all by itself. "Do not forget to urge [your friends] what I told you viva voce," he reminded Clément, that it is necessary to attack the Jesuits, but not to unite their cause with that of the Holy See. If only you would leave aside certain questions about which your king has imposed silence and perseveringly follow that advice, we will see the faith and Christian morality triumph and their enemies cast down."[20]

All also thought that anti-Jesuit action by France was essential to the success of the "good cause"; indeed, that without French participation the Jesuits were likely to survive their present misfortunes in Portugal and return with unparalleled vengeance. Di Gosso was convinced that "if by some misfortune their [the Jesuits'] misfortunes in Portugal should cease, we will see the return of the times of Alexander VII and Clement XI" or "even worse," he added, "without exaggerating."[21] Much therefore depended upon France's royal court, which alone, he thought, could "deliver the church from the affliction from which it groans." While Bottari at this point tended to look to the king, the Piedmontese opined that the "glory" of this action best befitted the Parlement, "the duty of which is to see to the custody of the king and to care for the advantages and tranquillity of the state," and for which, he added, he saw no reason for hope unless the Parlement undertook this "coup."[22]

Summing up with approval the Italian views of the hoped-for role of France in an analysis for his own and others' instruction, Clément reported that the Italians warned that the French "should not expect to see Rome undertake any fatal coup against the Jesuits so long as it sees them surviving in the [French] court, because however much they may be attacked in any other court, [Rome] knows that a time will come when the French court will obtain their return to the courts of Spain and Portugal."[23]

The notion that France was crucial to any campaign against the Jesuits could only have been flattering to the French appellants, and it met with little resistance on their part. So too the fear that if the Jesuits survived their misfortunes in Portugal and disgrace in Spain, they would wreak vengeance on their enemies. Before the death of Benedict XIV, Le Paige reported on a recent conversation between a member of the Academy of Sciences and Guillaume-François Berthier, editor of the Jesuit *Journal de Trévoux*, who expressed the fear that the whole Society might be "enveloped in the tempest" then raging in Portugal. Le Paige's conclusion: all the more reason to hurry and extract whatever was possible from Benedict's pontificate because "if these men ever again become the masters, they will conclude from this crisis that they must put themselves in a position so as never again to have to weather one like it, and to strike down everything contrary to their interests."[24] The same reasoning held a fortiori in favor of directly proceeding against the Jesuits under the increasingly pro-Jesuit pontificate of Clement XIII.

Far more controversial for the French, however, was the Italian argument that they should soft-pedal what had been their base line of opposition to *Unigenitus*, a tactic that threatened their very identity as appellants. Mulling matters over for himself upon his return to France in January 1759, Clément could understand the sense of the Italian point of view as interpreted by Bottari, who envisioned the possibility of revisiting the doctrinal issues "when the church could do so in liberty." In Rome, he thought, whether with good reason or not, the Jesuits were at once more visible but contained, and it was always more possible to invoke the papacy's many endorsements of Augustinian doctrine against their doctrine. But in contrast to Augustinians in Italy, the defenders of "sound doctrine" among the clergy in France were up against the obligation to sign the Formulary and to accept *Unigenitus*, as well as being excluded by a Sorbonne purged of all Jansenists and refused the sacraments by the archbishop of Paris and the "fanatical" parish clergy he had installed. So how would it serve the "good cause," Clément wondered, to extract the Jesuits from this much more pervasive mass and eliminate them.

Still, Clément saw enough wisdom in the advice of the "Romans" to urge the French appellants to act on it for now. "Good in Italy, and for the moment here"—that was his conclusion. After all, the Italians were only asking the French appellants to abide by the "law of silence" on the subject of *Unigenitus* and related issues that Louis XV had promulgated and the Parlement had registered in 1754 and reiterated in 1758.[25] Consulted on the issue, Coudrette added the proviso that if attacked in print by the pro-*Unigenitus* side, appellant writers would have to reserve the right to respond, but in such a way as to spare the papacy and target the Jesuits, a proviso by means of which Clément and Le Paige attempted to placate other appellants, such as the abbé Louis Guidi, who remained unreconciled to the law of silence.[26] It was in that spirit, and also to prepare the terrain for the offensive against the Jesuits, that Le Paige published the pamphlet entitled *La légitimité et nécessité de la loi du silence* (*The Legitimacy and the Necessity of the Law of Silence*) in 1759.[27] It was also with that offensive in mind that the *Nouvelles* trained all its guns on the Jesuits in the New Year's editorial probably penned by Le Paige in 1759.

Reasons were never lacking to hold the Jesuits responsible for what in the appellant view was the Catholic Church's entire tilt in the Molinist direction. A year earlier, even before he went to Rome, Clément noted for himself some theses defended by a Jesuit named Bertoli in their church dedicated to Saints

Ignazio and Xavier in Novare near Milan.[28] The Molinist thesis of God's "middle knowledge," the possibility of a state of "pure nature," the need to intend to do evil for an act to be a sin even if evil in itself, the sufficiency of the fear of punishment in lieu of love in order to attain justice in the sacrament of penitence—all these theses were evil and evidence enough, in Clément's opinion, that the Jesuits persisted in being as true to themselves as ever despite the revival of "good doctrine" elsewhere in Italy. But words ended up failing Clément in the face of the proposition that "fallen nature . . . lost none of its natural perfections, [and that] considered in its intrinsic qualities, it found itself no less able . . . to do what was good."

In January 1760 Clément instructed the abbé d'Etemare in Utrecht to inform that church's probably disappointed clergy of the conclusions reached in Paris on the basis of these reflections as well as the advice from their mutual friends in Rome. The "Romans," he reported, had persuaded the French to put everything besides the Jesuits on hold for the time, including the goal of Utrecht's restoration of communion with Rome on the grounds that "it is always back to the Jesuits that everything leads. So let us remedy that Society, they say, and all the rest will be easy." We can only hope, he added, that "God wills that in thus limiting his aid, we succeed, and that we will not have lost sight of other possible goals."[29]

ASPICIENTES: A DOCTRINAL PROGRAM FOR REFORM CATHOLICISM

The French historian Catherine Maire has contended that the appellants themselves scuttled the attempt at doctrinal accommodation in 1719–1720 that first produced the project of such a bull because rather than any such bull they preferred an appeal to a general council against *Unigenitus* in order to maintain a public "witness" to the "truth" during a period of apostasy.[30] If so, it should be added that this attempt at accommodation also ran aground due to the efforts of scuttlers such Cardinal Henri-Pons de Thiard de Bissy, whose intransigence was fully the equal of anybody's on the appellant side. One of the products of *Unigenitus* in France was to produce a cloud of pro-*Unigenitus* episcopal witnesses more papal than the pope who could be counted upon to get in the way of every kind of accommodation with "heresy." Also if so, no such scuttling characterizes the efforts undertaken by the appellant high command in 1758–1759, which was as above board as any negotiation so sensitive could be and remained so through the pontificate of Clement XIV, when the effort was renewed. To it, for example, the abbé Clément devoted the rest of his life and career.

It is not necessary to equate all of eighteenth-century Jansenism with theological figurism in order to hold that this Jansenism was still religious and more than a purely political phenomenon. It is therefore worth breaking the narrative for a few paragraphs to linger over what the appellant doctrinal position was at the century's noon. Since the Jansenist high command had run this document past the Roman Augustinian community and had repeatedly revised it at its behest, it is possible to extend the description of this draft bull's contents as more than Jansenist—indeed, as nothing less than the positive doctrinal program of European Reform Catholicism.

As edited and refined by Gourlin and Le Paige with a view toward sending it to Bernis for presentation in Rome in the spring of 1758, the document entitled *Aspicientes* contained twenty-one articles divided into roughly four categories.[31] Defensive in intent if not in tone, the first and most important group set out to deflect the accusation that appellants were heretical in the sense of the five propositions supposedly extracted from Jansen's *Augustinus* and condemned by the papacy in 1653. These propositions represented the most uncharitable possible reading of *Augustinus* and the most hard-line interpretation of Augustine's theology of grace. In positive terms, these propositions laid down that some of God's commandments were impossible to perform even for the justified, that the divine grace received by those justified in the "fallen" state was irresistible, and that free will in this state meant nothing more than the absence of external constraint. The last two negative propositions held that those opposed to the theology of Augustine—"semi-Pelagian" Jesuits, in other words— were heretical in that they believed that the humans might freely accept or reject divine grace, as well as because they supposed that Christ had died for all people, justified and unjustified alike.

In order to deflect these propositions, *Aspicientes* rejected the idea of commandments impossible for the just to obey and the thesis of the irresistibility of grace as both "impious" and "heretical." The document likewise dismissed out of hand the propositions that Christ had not died for all humanity and that human freedom consisted only in the absence of interior necessity or physical constraint. To the contrary, the document's third article proclaimed God's commandments to be "holy" and "just" and therefore by implication possible for the just to obey. The fifth and ninth articles similarly admitted that divine grace was offered to the merely justified as well as those who persevered in justice to election, and that it was always possible for both to resist as well as to accept this grace. So much, then, by way of disculpation.

At the same time, the first ten articles made it clear that although equally able to accept or reject grace in the state of innocence, humanity in its freedom to choose the good or reject sin sustained severe damage by its Fall into sin, and with it all its other faculties "in body and heart." The result was a "natural" law for Gentiles and a revealed law for the chosen Hebrew people that revealed the extent of sin, while by a "mysterious economy" it withheld the knowledge of the means to heal that sin, let alone the grace to do so. Although sinners remained free in principle to avail themselves of the help of the "prevenient" grace needed to choose God and the good even before the Fall, the freedom to do so was no longer equal to the penchant toward sin consisting in a disordered love of self and things.

Whence the need for the initiative of God who disposed the will to receive an "efficacious" grace procured by Christ's sacrifice on the cross. Only efficacious grace healed and reoriented the will, in mysterious cooperation with it in such a way that its recipients were far from passive and remained in principle free to reject it. Were anybody tempted to glorify himself or herself on account of this margin of freedom, however, two other articles reminded the penitent that in the last analysis the main freedom at work was that of the gift of grace.

This much might be construed to be a commentary on the Council of Trent's decree on justification. Other articles, however, made clearer the limitations of the concessions to the condemnation of the five propositions. If, for example, the ninth article conceded that actions performed before the reception of justifying grace were not necessarily sins, other articles implied that they were not sufficient for salvation either. If, again, article 9 conceded that those predestined to salvation were not the only recipients of grace, the eighth article specified that the other recipients were those temporarily justified who did not persevere to the end for reasons known to God alone. God's justice did not oblige him to have equally desired the salvation of Jacob and Esau, Saint Peter and Judas. And if article 7 conceded that Jesus Christ had died for all sinners, the same article made it clear that the benefits of his sacrifice were not equally shared or communicated. To the contrary, articles 6 and 8 proclaimed the doctrines of a grace that was efficacious by itself and a gratuitous predestination conferred without prevision of merit, both of them entailed by the "the empire of his divine majesty over the human will."

A second group of articles addressed themselves to the related issues of penitential theology and discipline that, first raised by the controversy over Saint-Cyran's practice as director at Port-Royal, had escaped papal censure until *Unigenitus* in 1713. In question was the Jansenist insistence that evidence of true contrition—in other words, love for God or the virtue of charity—rather than simple fear of punishment was necessary to motivate a penitent who had fallen into mortal sin and sought absolution in the sacrament of penitence. At stake as well was the closely related practice of postponing absolution and Communion in the absence of any evidence of contrition. That Jansenists believed that it was efficacious grace alone that conferred the virtue of charity, which tightly related their penitential theology to their theology of grace. Condemned by *Unigenitus* and also addressed by an article in *Aspicientes* was the Jansenist encouragement of the reading of the Holy Scriptures by the lay faithful in French translation. Like other issues, this had arisen in the mid-seventeenth century, in this case through Le Maître de Sacy's French translation of the Bible.

As in the case of the theology of grace and free will, *Aspicientes* attempted to blunt the main force of the critiques of excessive penitential rigor. Thus, one article conceded that mortal sin does not necessarily entail the loss of true faith, another that "salutary" fear was a useful and God-given sentiment, a third that the requisite love for God might be only the commencement of such love, a fourth that the deferral of absolution should only be used in cases of the total ignorance of the faith or flagrant impenitence, and that the reading of the Scriptures by laypeople ought to be surrounded with precautions against heretical translations and unguided interpretations.

Yet none of these concessions diminished the stout defense of a rigorous penitential theology: although faith might survive sin, charity was essential; although salutary fear was useful, contrition alone removed the source of sin; although the deferral of absolution had to be used with caution, this practice was an indispensable tool for any well-schooled confessor; and although lay access to the Scriptures was not without danger, nothing could take the place of direct exposure to the "celestial treasure of the holy books with which divine liberality of the Holy Spirit has enriched mankind." But above all and against all objections, the *Aspicientes* demanded a penitence that was a "laborious baptism" that proceeded only "by degrees," the goal of which was a state of charity in which the penitent neither "eats, drinks, eats, nor undertakes any action unless it is to the glory of God."

Last but not least, the articles about penitential theology, practice, and piety advised that excommunication be used "only rarely, and with the greatest circumspection." This article was defensive rather than offensive, appellants having been the objects of most of the Catholic Church's eighteenth-century ipso facto excommunications. It was the farthest these articles dared to go short of affirming *Unigenitus*'s ninety-first proposition condemned in Quesnel's *Réflexions morales*, namely, that the "fear of an unjust excommunication ought never to get in the way of fulfilling one's obligations."

A last group of the *Aspicientes*'s articles went decidedly on the offensive and condemned what its authors regarded as errors professed by the their Jesuit enemies. So against the Jesuits' advanced missionary soteriology that among the many people to whom the Gospel was unknown some could have been saved by virtue of obedience to natural law and a kind of implicit faith in the need for redemption, the first two articles affirmed that the grace of Jesus Christ was the only means of salvation after the Fall into sin. For those before the Advent, this grace took the form of a faith in the atonement yet to come, for those after the Advent by faith in what had already been done. The only difference between the new "alliance" and the old was that the coming of Christ made manifest what was perceived "more obscurely" until that point.

The counterpart to this document's proclamation of the law of love was similarly its resounding condemnation as a "pernicious heresy" the proposition that humanity was never obligated to love God—a proposition frequently heard in Jesuits' sermons, according to the *Nouvelles ecclésiastiques.* Two articles condemned as a "scandalous error" the supposition that a sin committed without knowledge of God or the Decalogue did not offend God or merit punishment—the so-called philosophical sin or sins committed in "invincible ignorance." A final condemnation struck the casuistry of probabilism, or the thesis that it was licit to follow the less certain of two possible moral principles.

THE SUPPRESSION OF THE SOCIETY OF JESUS IN FRANCE, 1759–1761

By 1758, however, the appellants themselves had become probabilistic in the sense that the plan behind the *Aspicientes* aspired to do little more than create a "probable" or legitimate place for Catholic Augustinianism in France. If, as they probably had, French or Dutch appellants had ever aimed to replace Molinism with their hard version of Augustinianism, by the mid-eighteenth century they had let go of that ambition in favor of the immediately more modest one of restoring what the abbé Clément called the "liberty of the [theological] schools."[32] But that restoration was never to occur with the help of any papal pronouncement, whether in 1758–1759 or in 1769–1774, when Dutch and French appellants renewed their quest during the pontificate of Clement XIV. In both cases the constructive doctrinal goal was to take a back seat to the offensive against the Jesuits, in 1759 in France and in 1769 in the entire world, by the papacy under pressure from the Bourbon powers.

The doctrinal statement therefore represents only what might have been; in both cases intended as a preliminary to doctrinal rectification, the campaign against the Jesuits is the only thing that happened. What turned out to be that campaign began in Portugal, where, however, it had origins peculiar to Portugal and where it might have also ended had French appellants, their Italian friends, and José I's first minister, Carvalho e Melo, been equally eager to exploit this event in the interests of replicating it elsewhere. Inspired though they were by the Portuguese precedent, these French appellants and their Italian friends agreed from the outset that the role of France would be far more decisive than that of Portugal in any overall campaign against the Jesuits, given the Bourbon dynasty's simultaneous presence in Spain, Naples, and Parma and France's new alliance with Habsburg Austria. Nor were they wrong in these calculations, although events played out rather differently to what they envisioned in late 1758. The French king would never be more than a reluctant participant in this campaign, nor would the papacy ever wholeheartedly be won over to its side.

Not, however, that Jansenists in or out of the Parlement of Paris and other parlements could possibly have managed the campaign without significant help from the royal ministry and royal court at Versailles. In January 1757 Carlo di Grosso expressed fear about the meaning of the "mutation" of the French court that had brought about the fall of Bernis from power and the rise of Choiseul.[33] But he need not have worried, because Choiseul was to prove a more reliable enemy of the Jesuits than Bernis ever would be.

In fact, factional intrigue at Versailles in 1760 brought to light a memoir attributed by the pro-Jesuit dauphin to one Adrien-Louis Lefebvre d'Amécourt, a councilor in the Parlement, that accused Choiseul of plotting the destruction of the Jesuits with barristers and other magistrates in the Parlement.[34] Choiseul heatedly denied these accusations, attributed them to the inventiveness of his "devout" enemies at court, and arranged for an interview with d'Amécourt in the presence of other ministers in which d'Amécourt disavowed knowledge of, much less involvement in, any such plot. Yet the memoir was nothing if not prescient, accurately predicting that the Parlement would attack the Jesuits by way of their constitutions and doctrine, that it would close the Society's colleges and prohibit new novices, that the abbé Henri-Philippe de Chauvelin would do the denouncing, that a "general history" of the Jesuits was to be written, that Le Paige would be involved, that the barrister Pierre-Olivier Piales was to translate the Portuguese propaganda—and even that the middle of April 1761 would be decisive. Now, none of these events or facts would fail to materialize if they were not already doing so at the time. Fragments of correspondence here and there also demonstrate that Choiseul was indeed in epistolary contact with Clément, Murard, and Le Paige.

That Choiseul dictated a plan to destroy the Jesuits in France is nonetheless implausible on the face of it. All that can be safely concluded from this evidence is that by 1760 Choiseul had become aware of what was brewing in the Parlement and was in contact with some of the brewers and may even have had no great distaste for the brew. As France's envoy to Rome in 1754–1756 he had taken notice of the Jesuits' opposition to his and Benedict XIV's attempt to bring calm to the troubled religious waters in France, and did not like what he saw. While Choiseul was no Jansenist, he was every inch a Gallican, and to that extent somewhat sympathetic to what Jansenist and Gallican magistrates were up to. That Pinault was translating the Portuguese first minister's justifications for expelling the Jesuits, that Le Paige and others were at work on a history of the Jesuits and an analysis of their constitutions—these were already facts on the ground discernible to anyone with a nose close enough to the ground. Responding as early as 6 February 1760 to a letter from the abbé Clément, the then still philo-Jansenist cardinal delle Lanze of Piedmont tried to dissuade the abbé from the idea of using their constitutions rather than their deeds and doctrines as an entering wedge in a case against the French Jesuits, indicating that by that date Clément and his colleagues were considering, if they had not already settled on, that tactic.[35] In the memoir postdated 17 August 1760, Choiseul would have known that the royal council had granted the Jesuits' request to appeal a verdict against them to the Parlement's Grand' Chambre, as he could have known the approximate time it would be judged. As the just-promoted Chauvelin was the only likely hatchet man in the Grand' Chambre, it is also plausible that planning might already have gone as far as to designate him as the person best positioned to widen the case in question into an examination of the Society's constitutions.

Up to this point, the plot thickened without reference to Choiseul, and at no point was he essential to it. The only place where Choiseul's role might have been crucial was in countering royal attempts to rescue the Jesuits from the Parlement once it had decided to hold a trial. But whatever Choiseul did along these lines, he could not have done it without the support of others at Versailles— Gilbert VI de Voisins and Jacques de Flesselles, for example—who were royal councilors of state quite sympathetic to the Gallican aspect of the Parlement's case. Although Choiseul might also have mobilized the titled mistress Madame de Pompadour, who was annoyed at the Jesuit confessors' refusal to grant her absolution, neither the two of them nor all of Versailles's anti-Jesuit effectives together could have prevailed against royal reluctance had it not been for Roman intransigence combined with the king's extraordinary fiscal dependence on his parlements at the end of a ruinous war. Choiseul's role would eventually be both visible and important, but only in the formation of the anti-Jesuit goal in the dynastic Bourbon Family Pact in 1767.

That much said, the suppression of the Jesuits in France was largely if not exclusively the work of the hard-core Jansenist variant of reformist Catholics and may be regarded as their most signal victory during the eighteenth century. Planning in 1759 clearly passed to action in 1760 that witnessed the publication of a pamphlet that anticipated this victory. Requested and applauded by Bottari, the pamphlet sketched out a scenario in which a particular case might open up into a general indictment of the Jesuits' constitutions and doctrines.[36] When, for example, the Parlement began the New Year with a regulatory judgment against all unauthorized congregations for lay people, it was an open secret that no congregations other than those belonging to Jesuits needed to feel threatened. Hard behind this measure came a spate of judicial reversals for the Society, any of which might have realized such a scenario had it wound up in the Parlement: the imposition of unpaid taxes by the Jesuit college of Billon to the town of that name, the Benedictine Order's successful suit to recover the revenues of two priories previously assigned to Jesuit colleges, and a successful suit by the Parisian corporation of apothecaries against the Parisian Jesuit residences engaged in making and selling certain drugs. If, as he did, Cardinal Passionei asked Marolde du Coudray, a Jansenist councilor in the Paris prevotal court, to send him a copy of his court's sentence against the Jesuits as apothecaries, it was because the cardinal was aware that this judicial reversal contained much more than what met the eye.[37] The same holds for his request for whatever judicial memoir and judgment would result from the case of worthless letters of exchange issued by a Jesuit mission in Martinique, one that Passionei thought the Jesuits had unwisely appealed from consular courts to the Parlement's Grand' Chambre.[38]

Still, no amount of plotting and planning could have arranged for this godsend of a case that began with the English seizure of a number of French ships bearing coffee, cocoa, sugar, and vinegar produced by plantations belonging to the French Jesuit mission run by Père Antoine Lavalette in Martinique.[39] The resultant bankruptcy of that mission entailed that of its chief creditors in France, the commercial house of Lioncy and Gouffre in Marseilles, setting off a landslide of defaults by its creditors and still other bearers of Lavalette's worthless bills of exchange. When the house of Lioncy and Gouffre first sought redress in the consular court of Marseilles, it obtained a favorable judgment, but only against Lavalette and the already bankrupt Martinique mission, which had nowhere near the sum of 1,552,276 livres eventually awarded to this firm.

But at a certain point—on 30 January 1760 to be precise—the consular court of Paris delivered a verdict in favor of yet another bearer of Lavalette's bills of exchange, but this time not only against Lavalette and his mission but also against his immediate superiors in the Jesuit province of France as well as the entire Society, including its general in Rome.[40] The new and winning argument was that, unlike other monastic orders or religious congregations, the Society of Jesus was so monarchically structured that no college, house, or mission was self-governing, and all held power and answered to their superiors, including those of entire provinces, such as of France.[41] It was at that point too that the case against Lavalette had come to the attention of barristers in the Parlement, including Le Paige's coreligionist Charlemagne Lalourcé, who soon took over the cause of Lioncy and Gouffre, which obtained the same dramatic results on its appeal to Paris.[42]

Against the advice of their superior general Lorenzo Ricci in Rome to find the means to satisfy their creditors and cut their moral as well as fiscal losses, the Parisian Jesuits belied their reputation of blind obedience and displayed a contrarian mind entirely their own. Even though they possessed the right of *committimus* that allowed them to appeal any civil lawsuit to the Grand Conseil—the scenario actually envisioned by the *Avis paternal*—where they might have expected more favorable treatment than in the Parlement, the Jesuits' Parisian provincial superior Mathieu-Jean Joseph Allaric took the advice of one of the Society's oracles, Claude Frey, and decided to appeal the judgments of the consular court to the Parlement.[43] Besides Ricci himself, the source of this information is Gabriel Sénac de Meihan, then the king's first physician, according to whom Frey's reasoning was that the Grand Conseil contained numbers of their enemies, which is true; that its judgments did not carry the same authority as did the Parlement, which is also true; and that their case would be judged only by the Parlement's Grand' Chambre, which contained numbers of their former students and friends, which is true as well.[44]

As it was, the Grand' Chambre's crucial decision to allow the case to be publicly pleaded rather than to accede to the Jesuit defense's request to have it discreetly "appointed" carried the day only because all the many plaintiffs other than Lioncy and Gouffre temporarily desisted from further complicating the case. Even with this help, the measure passed by only a single vote, sixteen to fifteen.[45] But the Jesuits also calculated that the Grand' Chambre would be so flattered by this display of confidence in its judgments that it would be predisposed in their favor, which turned out not to be true.[46] Nor did the Jesuits factor in the role of a hostile public, which hissed its hostility against them from Chambre's accessible galleries, just as it reportedly had in a case pleaded against the Jesuits by the barrister Aubry in 1729.[47]

Upon request of the Jesuits, the royal council duly assigned their case to the Grand' Chambre, which took it up on 31 March 1761. Taking the place of Aubry as the plaintiffs' barristers were, among others, Jean-Baptiste Legouvé and the by then renowned Jean-Baptiste Gerbier, the latter the still resentful son of a Jansenist barrister exiled from Rennes by a lettre de cachet in 1736 on account of his spirited defense of appellants there.[48] But behind the eloquence of both lurked Lalourcé, who published his massive judicial *Mémoire à consulter* (*Memoir for the Instruction*) for Jean Lioncy and others just in time for the trial. Lalourcé had in turn generously availed himself of his friends Coudrette and Le Paige's *Histoire générale*, especially its last part's analysis of the Jesuit constitutions, reading it page by page as it came off the press the same year, in return for which Le Paige corrected the proofs of the *Mémoire à consulter*.[49] With the *Histoire générale*'s obvious help, Lalourcé based his case on the peculiarly monarchical structure of the Society and the absolute power of its general, such that the debts contracted by any one house or superior were ipso facto the debts of the entire Society headed by its general.[50] Although he did not follow Le Paige in using the incendiary adjective "despotic," Lalourcé indeed described the Jesuits as their general's "slaves."[51]

That argument carried the day—8 May, to be exact—to the immense satisfaction of the Parisians crowding the galleries and the Palais de justice, but with an important proviso that exempted the property of the Jesuit colleges, residences, and missions in France on the grounds that this property really belonged to the "nation" and not to the Jesuits who had only administered it. The Jesuits were supposed to find the sum of a million and a half livres elsewhere; neither they, nor the courts, nor the "nation" ever did. Due in part to the ingenuity of the Jesuits's legal defense team, the judgment's protection of this property was also due in good part to the ineptitude of the prosecution's use of Lalourcé's argument in his *Mémoire à consulter* that Henri IV's reestablishment of the Jesuits in France in 1603 had never really rectified the defects and inobservance of the terms of the Society's original admission in France.[52] If, as the prosecution argued, the Society's existence in France was merely de facto and not legal, the Jesuits could not have legally owned any property there either.

But the purpose of that argument in Lalourcé's *Mémoire à consulter*—and in Coudrette and Le Paige's *Histoire générale*, from which Lalourcé got it—was not to serve the cause of the Jesuits' many creditors but to get rid of the Society of Jesus in France. That purpose became apparent on 17 April when the councilor-clerk Chauvelin arose and, taking advantage of the references to the Society's constitutions, called for an assembly of the Parlement's five judicial chambers—the entire Parlement, in other words—to consider the "public" question of what these never examined constitutions contained and whether they were compatible with the laws of Gallican France. Speaking, he said, not only as a magistrate

but also as a "Christian, a Citizen, a Frenchman, and the subject of the King"—
as a bon françois, in effect—Chauvelin laid out a list of concerns about the
nonreciprocal vows of the Society, the mysterious variability of its constitutions,
its justification of tyranicide, and its independence from every authority, including the pope's, that differed in few ways from the plaidoyers of a Pasquier or
Arnauld the elder.[53] What updated Chauvelin's harangue was its reference to
the Society's "idolatrous" accommodation of the Chinese rites, its quotations
from the letters of Palofox's letter of 1649, and its repeated description of the
Jesuits' "foreign" general's authority as "despotic."[54] Impressed, the assembled
chambers ordered the Jesuits to remit a copy of the 1757 Prague edition of their
constitutions to the Parlement the next day and its "king's men," or royal prosecutors, to report on them on 2 June. Much to the king's chagrin, the provincial
procurator, Antoine de Montigny, complied with the order the following day.[55]
Carefully laid since 1759, the trap clamped shut.

Unless of course the king pried it open. Without royal intervention Le Paige,
Lalourcé, and the Parlement possessed a close to airtight case against the legal
status of the Society of Jesus, although it was arguably less solid than Henri IV's
Edict of Nantes for Huguenots, which the Parlement had registered without reservations. But while in that case Louis XIV had in 1685 chosen to take back
what Henri IV had given in 1598, in this case his successor seemed minded to
maintain what Henri IV had given the Jesuits in 1603, which in "absolutist"
principle he could do by overriding his Parlement's challenge to the legality of
royal protection. Nor did a first roundabout attempt to do so tarry, coming on
30 May, when Louis XV followed the advice of his Conseil des dépêches, or
Council of Interior Affairs, and ordered his Parlement to relinquish the copy of
the Jesuits' constitutions to the king so that he might reassign the examination
of the constitutions to a hand-picked royal commission.

But the Parlement in 1761 was no longer the docile Parlement that Louis XIV
had tamed. In response, therefore, it appointed a committee that numbered Clément de Feillet among its members and contrived to circumvent the royal order
by duly surrendering its copy of the Jesuits' constitutions while arranging to replace it with another copy, just as good. The chain of panicky requests for a
second copy of the 1757 Prague edition of these constitutions went from Feillet
to the equally Jansenist councilor Guillaume Lambert, who went to the pious
Jansenist councilor Lefebvre de Saint-Hilaire, who turned to Le Paige, who
must have found a copy, since one appeared in the second chamber of inquests—
Clément de Feillet's chamber—the same day.[56] Clément de Feillet thereupon
took the copy to a scheduled meeting of the assembled chambers, which verified the new copy's conformity with the one the royal council had comman-

deered. This minor miracle enabled—or obliged—the king's men to continue to prepare their report, due on 2 June. Visibly caught off guard, they asked for and received a month's extension of this due date until 3 July.

Any attempt on the part of the king or his council to save the Society of Jesus in France was clearly up against this hard core of Jansenist magistrates and barristers in the Parlement—a parti janséniste, as those opposed to it then called it. With or without Choiseul's help, this "party" was in turn able to magnify its influence within the Parlement by using the lever of more widely shared concerns with which Jansenist ones overlapped, such as the Parlement's juris-dictional prerogatives, the Gallican liberties, and of course hatred for the Jesu-its.[57] To such well-established identities within the magistracy as Chauvelin, Clément de Feillet, Lambert, Laverdy de Nizeret, Saint-Hilaire, Murard, and Robert de Saint-Vincent, it is permissible to add the names of René-François Boutin, the councilor Duprés de Saint-Maur, and the president Antoine-Hilaire-Laurent Le Mairat, all of whom wrote letters of communion to Utrecht.[58] A sup-plementary index of adherence to the Jansenist cause, this list even includes the famous barrister—and advocate for Jean Lioncy against the Jesuits—Gerbier, whose name may be added to the far more numerous Jansenists within the Paris bar. Even those influential actors, such as Jean-Baptiste-François Durey de Meinières, who totally defy characterization as Jansenist were "patriotic" Galli-cans—in his case, even a little "philosophic"—making it possible to induct them all into a larger category with their reformist Catholic counterparts elsewhere in Europe.[59] Some if not all of these magistrates also remained on the committee originally appointed to deal the king's orders of 30 May.

The next royal attempt to save the Jesuits worked through the king's men, consisting of the chief royal prosecutor, Guillaume-François Joly de Fleury, and two "solicitors general," Guillaume's brother Jean-Omer Joly de Fleury and Michel-Étienne Le Pelletier de Saint-Fargeau. Directly appointed by the king, in ordinary civil and criminal cases the king's men brought charges and asked for sentences to which the court might or might not accede. In "public cases" such as that of the Jesuits the king's men were similarly bound to repre-sent the point of view of the Crown, although they could never afford to stomp wholesale over the sensibilities of their fellow magistrates. It was they, for ex-ample, who had presented the king's order of 30 May to surrender the Jesuits' constitutions, just as it was they who presented all royal edicts and declarations to the Parlement. And so it could have come as no great surprise when, in the name of the king's men, Jean-Omer Joly de Fleury finally delivered a *Compte rendu* on the Jesuits' constitutions on 3, 4, 5, and 7 July 1761 that confined its critique within the bounds of a classically Gallican gravamen.[60]

Echoing, as had Chauvelin, Pasquier's critique of the Society's nonreciprocal vows and the papal exemptions from secular and religious authorities, the solicitor general reserved his gravest criticism for the blind obedience sworn by members to a general whose authority he described as "monarchical" and therefore dangerous because its ultramontanist loyalties made it potentially competitive with the king's.[61] The solicitor general's proposed reforms were equally moderate. Besides a firmer and more formal subjection to the "ordinary" ecclesiastical and political authorities and more equally binding vows, the solicitor general called for papal collaboration in implementing a structural reform that would curb the general's excessive authority in France, making each Jesuit establishment self-governing and replacing the general's top-down appointment of the Society's five provincial superiors with elections by their colleagues held every three years. While this reform would have radically decentralized the governance of the Society in France, it would also have regularized its legal status in France. For—a fatal concession—the Joly de Fleury brothers granted just enough to Le Paige's and Lalourcé's demonstrations of the illegality of the Society in France to think that its presence needed further putting in order.

But the Parlement's parti janséniste did not wish to reform the Society of Jesus in France, it wished to destroy it. No sooner, therefore, had the Jean-Omer Joly de Fleury finished his report than Chauvelin rose with another discourse to deliver, this one lasting for two hours on the subject of the Jesuits' ethics and doctrines. This performance meant mobilizing the second layer of anti-Jesuitism, the theological, moral, and more or less Jansenist one, not of course excluding Pascal's *Provincial Letters,* to which Chauvelin alluded as "a Work unique and inimitable of its kind."[62] Composed with the help of others in the home of one Jean Simon, a former curé of Soleilhas in the diocese of Senez and a Jansenist refugee from its bishop in 1728, Chauvelin's denunciation excoriated the Jesuits for the casuistry of "invincible ignorance" and probabilism.[63] Classic as well as up to date, Chauvelin's citations ran from Arnauld's *Moral pratique* to the bishop of Soissons's pastoral instruction against Berruyer's *Histoire du people de Dieu.*[64] What united this discourse to the more Gallican one of 17 April was Chauvelin's fixation on the theory and practice of regicide, which his attack on Jesuit casuistry enabled him to present as the most pernicious of probable opinions that the Society might embrace and act upon when it was in its interest to do so. Chauvelin did not neglect to remind his colleagues that in his opinion it had done so as recently as against Louis XV in 1757 and José I in 1758.

The point of Chauvelin's denunciation was of course to convince his fellow magistrates in the Parlement that the Jesuits were so morally and doctrinally corrupt that that the Society was beyond reform, and that no "gallicanization" of it in France, such as suggested by the king's men, could do anything to address the rot at its core. So when, in response to Chauvelin's discourse, the attorneys and advocates general persisted in their reformist "conclusions," the Parlement contented itself with referring these conclusions along with Chauvelin's second discourse to the committee that the assembled chambers had set up on 30 May to deal with the royal demand for the Jesuits' constitutions.

The parti janséniste's second point of attack against the royal moderate report and reformist conclusions of the royal prosecutors was to challenge their tacit assumption that the Jesuits possessed a form of constitutional existence in France that was susceptible of reform. That the Society had no such status had been one of the principal points made by Coudrette and Le Paige's *Histoire générale* and Lalourcé's *Mémoire à consulter,* both of which reminded its readers that the Colloquy of Poissy and the Parlement had received the Jesuits not as a new religious society but only as a "college," with which provisions the Jesuits had never complied. Behind closed doors and in memoranda to members of the Parlement's committee, Le Paige further argued that if Henri IV's edict allowing the return of the Jesuits in 1603 had used the name "Jesuits," it did so only unavoidably by way of acknowledging their identity as "monks" in fact, but did not otherwise alter the status of the Society inherited from the terms of 1561, which had never recognized the Society's constitutions that the king' men were proposing to reform.[65] Eventually—after the fact, in fact—Le Paige went public with the same argument in the pages of *Nouvelles ecclésiastiques*: nothing could be more pernicious than to use the pretense of reform to give the Jesuits a legal status that the realm had always denied them, especially now that Chauvelin had reminded the public how immoral the Jesuits in fact were as monks.[66]

In fact as well, Le Paige and Durey de Meinières sketched out a plan of attack against the Jesuits and the royal prosecutors' attempt to reform and save them as soon as the younger Joly de Fleury had concluded the report on 8 July 1761.[67] Le Paige's plan was to strangle the Society by means of cutting off its means of recruitment. Since, he reasoned, the Parlement had accepted the Jesuits as a "college" but never as a religious society, the Parlement need not pronounce on religious vows it had never recognized but only prohibit any new vows, meanwhile allowing the Jesuits to continue to teach in colleges that would be made self-governing, each to be placed under the authority of the ordinaries, and all of them separated from the authority of their general. The Society would therefore die a slow death, as every Jesuit who died would be replaced by someone outside the Society.

But Durey de Meinières dared not leave the Society to linger for decades, and in this case his more surgical plan prevailed. "[Your plan would have] left them [the Jesuits] among us, albeit with precautions," Meinières replied. But he deemed the Jesuits so "cunning as to render our precautions quite useless."[68] His plan featured the use of the *appel comme d'abus*—or an appeal in a case of abuse—which since its inception in the fifteenth century had allowed the realm's royal courts to intervene in and overturn acts, procedures, or even judgments by churchmen that threatened secular jurisdiction or violated the Gallican Church's own canon law. This appeal would enable the Parlement to challenge the validity of the Jesuits' vows on the twin grounds that they were designed to implement constitutions at once incompatible with the laws of France and never recognized by the state as well as a doctrine and morality that were intrinsically immoral. One impediment to this plan is that it was the king's men who normally lodged such appeals in the name of the king, while the actual king's men in this case could not be expected to do so against their own recently submitted conclusions. But in extreme cases the Parlement could lodge such an appeal in their name whether they liked it or not, and that is the course of action called for by Durey de Meinières's plan. True, it was also the case that any such appeal assumed a critical lapse of time during which the appeal was supposed to be judged. But Meinières' plan proposed to surmount that obstacle to quick action by accompanying the appeal with the prohibition of new vows and the closing of Jesuit colleges as precautionary measures.

Although worried about the propriety of the Parlement's treading on the holy ground of "spiritual" vows, Le Paige allowed himself to be convinced by Meinières's argument that speed was of the essence. The more he thought about the matter, he wrote to himself, the more it appeared necessary "either to terminate everything definitively concerning the abuse of the constitutions, vows, and colleges and leave nothing provisional . . . or to keep everything in the greatest secrecy and not . . . do anything . . . that could permit a glimpse of the plan."[69] In either case, he thought, the time to strike was sometime in early November, right after the Parlement returned from its annual vacation. But these alternative courses of action did not prove to be mutually exclusive, nor was it possible entirely to conceal the party's intentions from the "other" side.

The tactical trouble on the "other" side is that it consisted of too many sides within it for them not to get in each other's way. One side consisted of the king's men who had been secretly meeting with the first president Molé, the president René-Charles de Maupeou, Choiseul, the bishop of Orléans, and Louis Phélypeaux, the comte de Saint-Florentin and then secretary of the king's household.[70] Of these, only Choiseul could have been very hostile to the Jesuits, and then only secretly so. Nor would it have served any purpose for him to have leaked the group's plans to the likes of Lambert or Clément de Feillet, because the plans misfired for reasons having nothing to do with Choiseul. Elaborated mainly by Jean-Omer Joly de Fleury, the plans consisted in stealing a march on the Society's enemies by presenting the Parlement with royal letters patent that would have reformed the Society along the lines suggested by his conclusions while—an indispensable addition—legalizing the Jesuits' right to teach in France. Although the solicitor general seems to have miscalculated the precise point of attack—the legality of the Society's constitutions—he correctly anticipated that the attack would concentrate on some vulnerable aspect of the Society's legal position in France.[71] As the younger Joly de Fleury had discovered to his consternation, the Jesuits' right to teach in France was just as precariously dependent on past royal fiat as was the status of their constitutions there.[72]

Meanwhile, this group worked under constant pressure from what the former foreign minister Marquis d'Argenson called the pro-*Unigenitus* and Jesuit parti dévot at Versailles, the heart of which consisted of the king's son and dauphin and the venerable Chancellor Guillaume de Lamoignon de Blancmesnil.[73] Exchanging sixty letters expressing their outrage at this anti-Jesuit turn of events between 1761 and 1763, both wanted to put the Parlement in its place rather than place their hopes in the plans of its more moderate members.[74] A third party trying to save the Jesuits was the special royal commission set up on 29 May to conduct its own examination of the Jesuits' constitutions had meanwhile gone to work and taken on a life of its own. At a certain point—at the end of July, to be precise—Lamoignon, who may have presided over this commission, persuaded the king that it needed more time than anticipated to conduct its examination, whereupon the king sent a declaration to the Parlement ordering the Jesuits to submit the titles of all their establishments in France to the *greffe* of the royal council and forbidding the Parlement to take any further action with regard to the Jesuits for a full year.[75] This declaration reached the hands of the chagrined king's men on 2 August, accompanied by orders to present it to the Parlement for registration the very next day.

This royal declaration totally upset the Joly de Fleury brothers' applecart. If, as Jean-Omer had hoped, the royal council had seized the initiative by presenting the Parlement with a formal edict that addressed the strongest critiques of the Society while also putting it on a firmer legal footing, its hard-core enemies in the Parlement would have been thrown off balance and reduced to remonstrating against a royal will that was visibly constructive in intent. But by clumsily evoking the case, the royal declaration frontally infringed on the Parlement's sense of jurisdictional turf; and by referring to a greffe of the royal council, it also made a claim about the council's status as a superior court that the Parlement contested. Pleas by Molé to Saint-Florentin to do something to fend off the coming confrontation elicited the lame reply that nothing could be done, because the king had left for Choisy, leaving Lamoignon at Versailles.[76]

The result was to provide the Parlement's parti janséniste with the perfect opportunity to seize the initiative. The king's men dallied until the fourth when they presented the royal declaration accompanied by a lettre de cachet, to which the Parlement responded by referring both to its shadowy commission. Planning to use the declaration as a prompt for overturning the commission entirely, Chauvelin, Clément de Feillet, Lambert, Laverdy, and Robert de Saint-Vincent convened on the afternoon of 5 August at the abbé Clément's residence, where Laverdy rehearsed a performance he intended to stage, based on the scenario drafted by Le Paige and Durey de Meinières three weeks earlier.[77] When the Parlement convened on the morning of 6 August, Laverdy persuaded his own chamber—the first of his requests—to ask for an assembly of all the chambers, which, being granted, brushed aside the reporter Joseph-Marie Terray's defense of the royal declaration and instead listened to Laverdy speak for the next hour and a half. Building on the now well belabored premises of the inadmissibility of the Society of Jesus by reason both of its constitutions and doctrine and its lack of formal acceptance in France, Laverdy proposed that the Parlement receive its royal prosecutors' appellant comme d'abus of the Jesuits' foundational acts, constitutions, and "formulas of vows."

As a "provisional" and precautionary measure until the appel comme d'abus could be judged, Laverdy also urged the Parlement to prohibit the Society from receiving new vows or novices, to dissolve its existing congregations, and to close its colleges and seminaries.[78] In response, the Parlement, in the account by *Nouvelles ecclésiastiques*, found Lavedy's proposals to be so "attractive" that it voted in favor of them by the overwhelming majority of 130 to thirteen in the form of two measures; the first received the reluctant king's men appellant comme d'abus against the Jesuits' bulls, constitutions, and formulas of vows, and the second indeed forbade the Society to receive new vows and novices. The Parlement's judgment also closed the Jesuits' lay associations and congregations and colleges, those in towns with other colleges as early as the *rentrée* in October and those in towns with no other college in April.[79] To this injury to royal intentions the Parlement added the insult of enacting these measures as "modifications" of the royal declaration, which it registered in that revised form.

Reactions to the Parlement's judgments of 6 August 1761 predictably varied according to "party." Where the dauphin saw measures so "monstrous" he could hardly believe them, Robert de Saint-Vincent discerned the hand of God in the happenstance that the date of the Parlement's judgments against the Jesuits—6

August 1761—fell on the centennial anniversary of the death of Angélique Arnauld, the renowned abbess of Port-Royal-des-Champs.[80] Long viewed as the secret architects of ecclesiastical "despotism" in Paris, the Jesuits received little consolation for their reverses there. One of the king's own *maîtres des requêtes* reported that "even the lowest sort of public" took the side of the Parlement's judgments, and that in the space of an hour "the lowest sorts of persons" had carried off every copy in the colporters' possession, obliging the Parlement's printer to lock his doors and have them guarded lest the public force entry.[81] When it came to other parts of Catholic Europe, the expulsions of the Jesuits would elicit nothing remotely similar to this public response.

VERSAILLES, ROME, AND THE PROVINCES, 1761–1764

Although Lamoignon urged the king to annul judgments so "flagrantly" disrespectful of royal authority, they proved decisive and represented the beginning of the end of the Society in France.[82] Instead of the annulment demanded by the chancellor, what emerged from a combined meeting of the special royal commission and the royal Conseil des dépêches on 29 August were simple royal letters patent that, by ordering a one-year delay in executing these judgments, seemed to recognize their legitimacy. Worse, the same group of magistrates persuaded the Parlement on 5 September to comply only partly with the new royal orders, shortening the requested delay for closing the colleges to 1 April while not altering at all the "provisional" prohibition of novices or new vows and the dissolution of congregations and associations.[83]

One reason for the royal timidity was the presence on the special royal commission and the Conseil des dépêches of former parlementary magistrates, such as Jacques de Flesselles and Gilbert VI de Voisins. Notes in Gilbert's hand of the meeting of 29 August indicate that, far from being insensitive to traditional Gallican concerns, he and others recognized a good Gallican case when they saw one. Not only was the presence of the Society of Jesus not in impeccable legal order, the case's combined emphases on the enforced unity of the Society, the inordinate power of its general, and the "pernicious [regicidal] maxims" recently reprinted in Busembaum and others made for an "attack . . . from a very dangerous angle" in France, "and the most fit to further whatever else might be undertaken against" the Society.[84] However anachronistic the fear of such "maxims" may seem in retrospect in late eighteenth-century France, the relentless inertia of the reprinting of Jesuit manuals of cases of conscience such as Busembaum's—and the inconvenient opinions of "foreign" Jesuits such as the incendiary Francesco Antonio Zaccaria—enabled the Parlement's commissioners to dredge up examples as recent as the 1740s and 1750s.[85] And who in 1760 was in a position to say that Carvalho e Melo in Portugal had made up a case for Jesuit complicity in a recent regicidal attempt in Portugal out of whole cloth?

Not unaware of the potency of these sorts of accusations, the French Jesuits lost no time in efforts at damage control, as indeed they had also done in the wake of the brouhaha created by the supposed reprinting of Busembaum's *Medula theologia moralis*. Apart from published and private defenses of the Society that began to appear in 1761, the new superior of the Jesuit province of France's, Étienne de la Croix, sent letters to the archbishop of Paris and the king on 13 and 16 August, respectively, that disavowed his province's adherence to Bellarmino's doctrine of the papacy's indirect authority in temporal governance as well as its corollary consisting of the right to resist and kill tyrants by reason of sin. In mid-October Parisian Jesuits under La Croix's authority went further, notarizing a statement that condemned the doctrine of tyrannicide, asserted the absolute independence of princes in temporal affairs, acknowledged that the authority of their general did not extend to France's laws and maxims, and renounced the use of all papal privileges in conflict with the rights of the bishops, priests, universities, and other religious orders. But the nec plus ultra of Jesuit concessions came on 19 December 1761, when, pressed by the royal commission, La Croix signed a formal adherence to the four Gallican articles of 1682, including in principle an adherence to the Council of Constance's assertion of the superiority of the whole church assembled in a general council over the papacy.[86]

By that time, however, such concessions were less than spontaneous because the special commission deemed them necessary if the royal attempt to save the Society in France were to succeed. Nor were even these concessions entirely satisfactory. Entrusted by the commission to negotiate with the Jesuits at hand, Jacques de Flesselles insisted on an acceptance of two statements, the first a condemnation of the doctrine of tyrannicide by the Jesuits' general, the second the précis of the Gallican articles by the French Jesuits.[87] Yet La Croix and his council objected to the use of the Latin verb "to feel" (sentire) in the draft condemnation of tyrannicide, on the grounds that the Society's general had no right over his subordinates' interior "thoughts," as well as to the French verb "to hold" (tenir) as applied to the Jesuits' acceptance of the Gallican articles. "To hold," he held, was the same as "to think," while he and his colleagues regarded them as "opinions" that were "free and voluntary."[88]

An acceptance of the first and most recent of the Gallican articles—that proclaiming the absolute independence of the Crown in matters temporal— had long distinguished French Jesuits from those in Habsburg Austria, post-

Habsburg Spain, and Braganza Portugal, where this antipapal tenet of absolute monarchy cannot be said to have attained the status of state "orthodoxy" until rather recently. But it is highly unlikely even in 1761 that very many French Jesuits genuinely accepted the thesis of the general council's superior spiritual authority over the papacy as an article of indisputable faith.

Under the current dire circumstances, these reservations took the breath away from Flesselles, to whom they seemed all too redolent of proverbially Jesuitical "equivocations," "directions of attention," and "mental reservations," causing him to tell La Croix that these verbal quibbles tended "to confirm his suspicious about their way of thinking."[89] Yet these semantic distinctions and refinements did the French Jesuits no more good in Rome than in France, and it was with astonishment that Flesselles received word from La Croix toward the end of November that Clement XIII had reproached the general Ricci for the profession of Gallican faith that the French Jesuits had submitted to the royal commission. The disappointment could only have been greater in that, as Flesselles had to know, both the pope and Ricci had meanwhile been plying the king, the queen, the dauphin, and the dauphine—and even Choiseul—with letters pleading for help against the Parlement's judgments.[90] What Flesselles did not know, but would only have added to his ire if he had, is that the French Jesuits "equivocated" not only to placate Ricci but also under intense pressure by Torrigiani via the nuncio Pietro Pamphili Colonna, both of whom opposed the signatures already penned. [91]

Yet not even that knowledge would have lessened Flesselle's shock in reaction to the news received at the end of December that Ricci had refused to sign the commission's statement against the doctrine of tyrannicide. Arguing that the French commission's version of the decree contained a veiled condemnation of Bellarmino's doctrine of indirect papal power, Ricci felt unauthorized to do anything more than reiterate Claudio Acquaviva's ambiguous decree dating from 1614.[92] Upon receiving this news from La Croix, Flesselles could only observe that he owed the truth to the king, and this truth was likely to be "disastrous" for the Jesuits.[93] At the king's instigation, however, Lamoignon met with the several bishops then at court, including Jarente La Bruyère of Orléans, who as benefice-dispenser was always there.[94] Like Lamoignon, the bishops were of the opinion that it was no easier for the general to sign off on the proposed decree against tyrannicide than to ratify the French Jesuits' acceptance of the Gallican articles.

But the royal commission would have none of the chancellor's mini "council," as Le Paige derisively called it.[95] In a second combined meeting with the Conseil des dépêches, this one on 4 January 1762, Flesselles therefore urged the king to tell the Jesuits that if their general had not complied with the commission's demands within a month of the meeting, "the only favor he could grant the Society [would be] to permit the parlements to decide their fate." According to Flesselles, whose account of these events survives in the Jesuit archives of France, Choiseul added that the Jesuits "might become whatever they may wish," but "they are unworthy of the favors of His Majesty."[96]

It was only in that meeting of 4 January 1762, it seems, that Choiseul learned about the commission's difficulties in obtaining concessions from either Ricci or the pope that might render the Society more acceptable in Gallican opinion. That Choiseul was in indirect contact with members of the Parlement's parti janséniste is evident in Le Paige's correspondence at the time, which contains a letter from President Murard about the best go-between "to convey the news about Ricci's refusal to approve the decree against regicide to Choiseul."[97] Yet Choiseul did not need secret sources in order to find out about Ricci's refusals; the joint meeting of the royal commission and the Conseil des dépêches was quite enough. For Choiseul waited only until the very next day—5 January—to tell the French envoy in Rome, Rochechouart, how badly advised he thought the pope was to oppose the French Jesuits' Gallican declaration while avoiding the subject of the general's refusal to sign the statement against regicide.

Both subjects were off the diplomatic table by reason of the nonnegotiability of the Gallican liberties, and the policy of silence was not Choiseul's alone.[98] The point is to outline the limits of the "influence" of Choiseul. On the one hand, the Parlement's parti janséniste was undoubtedly in contact with Choiseul and knew him to be sympathetic to the offensive against the Jesuits; on the other, Choiseul seems to have done no more at this stage than a Gilbert or a Flesselles would have done. For its part, the parti janséniste needed to do no more than to let the Society of Jesus shoot itself in its ultramontanist foot.

Lest it be thought that Ricci did not try to meet the royal commission halfway, he indeed sent a statement to the king assuring him that "all my subjects detest and reject . . . any doctrine [proposed by] any author of any State or nation . . . who would authorize the least attack against the Sacred person of Kings."[99] But this statement would have fallen well short of the desired mark in the commission's estimate because it failed to address the case of a king who in the theory of indirect papal power might have ceased to be deemed a king by reason of his descent into tyranny.

After the rejection by Ricci of the commission's proposed revision of his predecessor Acquaviva's decree against tyrannicide, it was hardly to be expected that he would consent to a major restructuring of his Society of the sort originally proposed by the conclusions of the king's men. Yet it is such a project that next occupied the royal commissioners—with this major difference, that instead of replacing the general's authority with that of triennially elected provincial superiors, it would be replaced by that of a French vicar-general appointed by the general with the approval of the king.

The reasoning was that no general of a religious order ought to exercise more authority over French subjects than the Gallican maxims accorded the pope himself, whose writ did not extend to France without the consent of the church and the king. Another justification was that the appointment of a single vicar-general who answered for the Society to the king would bring its status into greater conformity with that envisioned by its restoration in 1603, which had assigned a similar role to the royal confessor.[100] Concerted as it was with the first president Molé as well as with the Joly de Fleury brothers, the commission's project also followed their proposals by eliminating the Society's initial provisional vows, subjecting the Jesuits to the authority of all the ordinary ecclesiastical authorities, requiring conformity to the Gallican maxims, and guaranteeing the local administration and ownership of each Jesuit property.[101] This plan received royal approval during a combined meeting of the royal commission and Conseil des dépêches in mid-January 1762.[102]

Neither the king nor his commissioners lacked for warnings that no reform of the Society of Jesus altering the authority of its general or its distinction between provisional and solemn vows would meet with any more success in Rome than had the statement of adherence to the Gallican liberties or even the condemnation of the doctrine of tyrannicide. A letter from Louis XV's Jesuit confessor Philippe-Onuphre Desmarets to his royal charge on 5 December 1661 and several paragraphs in Frey's written and eventually published defense of his Society—these were just two of the signs that while this particular road to reform might lead to Rome, it would not bear the weight of Roman refusals in the return journey to Paris.[103] Nor was it likely that the removal of the reform of the Jesuits' vows—apparently by Lamoignon—would make the baggage much lighter.

The moment of truth arrived at the end of January 1762, when, after receiving the proposed reform on 26 January with instructions to present it to Ricci as soon as possible, France's envoy, Rochechouart, received a *non possumus* from both Ricci and Clement XIII, as did Louis XV by courier.[104] Neither Ricci nor Clement XIII thought he had the authority to change the institute in such a fundamental way, Ricci because he could not do so without the authority of the pope, and the pope because he could not do so without the authority of his predecessors.[105] To accord a vicar-general to France would in Ricci's opinion only encourage all the Catholic states to do likewise, resulting in the total dissolution of the Society without mollifying the parlements. Clement XIII added that the only people ever threatened by the general's power had been "enemies of religion and refractories," whom the "most Christian King of France" had similarly and solemnly vowed to oppose.[106]

The Roman rejection of the royal commission's proposal would seem to have ended the king's attempt to rescue the French Jesuits. In response, either the French Jesuits themselves or their protector Torrigiani exacted a certain revenge by leaking the French proposal to another pro-Jesuit cardinal, Giovanni Francesco Albani, who soon had all of Rome talking, much to even Rochechouart's chagrin. Still, Choiseul's missive to Rochechouart specified that the royal council might well proceed with its reform without the general's approval. And this is in fact the form of forward retreat that the royal commission and council executed—a forward maneuver because the council sent its reform under the ensign of an edict into a phalanx of certain resistance by the Parlement, and a retreat in that without the backing of either the papacy or the Jesuits, no fallback position existed short of a rout.

The only major adjustment that the council and commission made to the project was to scrap the proposed vicar-general in favor of the general's delegation of authority to five elected provincial superiors—in other words, the Joly de Fleury brothers' original proposal—as though Ricci and Clement XIII would have preferred a further dispersion of the general's authority to one that preserved the façade of unity. This maneuver's only conceivable rationale was a purely political one in view of creating the perception of having tried to save the Jesuits while placating an adamant chancellor, but without making the only adjustments in the project that would have obtained Roman approval. It was with evident sarcasm that on 17 February the chancellor reported to the dauphin about the council's new "means of conciliation" and the unlikeliness of its success.[107]

That Lamoignon was on his own, that he did not enjoy the king's confidence—all this had become apparent enough in the previous year when Louis XV transferred the function of keeper of the seals from the chancellor's office with which it was usually conjoined to René-Nicolas Berryer, the rather pro-Jansenist former lieutenant de police. Rumor had it that the king thought it necessary to let the old warrior charge once more, sure that he "would dismount with the chagrin of seeing his work rejected."[108] If ever there was an edict "in the air," as Le Paige put it, it was that of 8 March 1762, the day the king's men presented it to the Parlement.[109]

Aware that this edict was in the making, but with its hands tied until the expiration of the delay stipulated by its registration of the royal letters patent of 29

August 1761, the Parlement looked to the thirteen provincial parlements and two superior councils for help.[110] No immediate help was forthcoming from the only two parlements that had so far imitated Paris in demanding the delivery of the Jesuits' constitutions—those of Rennes and Toulouse—for they had also followed Paris's example by adopting only provisional measures while allowing time for the appels comme d'abus to be judged. But the situation was otherwise with the nearby and amenable Parlement of Normandy in Rouen, where the grand nephew of the Port-Royal solitary by the same name, Thomas du Fossé, maintained a regular correspondence with Le Paige. Suddenly striking on 19 November 1761, the Parlement of Rouen demanded the deposition of the Society's constitutions, whereupon it bypassed its notoriously pro-*Unigenitus* and conveniently sick general prosecutor, entrusting the examination of the constitutions to his "substitute" Jean-Gaspard-Benoît Charles.

Charles obligingly delivered a report and set of predictably damning conclusions in five forced marches between 16 and 23 January 1762. What followed was even more drastic. In consultation with Le Paige via Du Fossé, the Parlement of Normandy dispensed with provisional measures entirely, judging the appel comme d'abus definitively and on the spot on 12 February 1762. "That is what is called going directly to the target," admiringly wrote Le Paige.[111] So hasty was this judgment that the first editions of it had this parlement annulling the Jesuits' solemn "vows" to God instead of the "formulas" of their vows to the constitutions of the Society, lending credence to accusations that this parlement was acting as a "spiritual" power. The judgment otherwise ordered all Jesuits within its jurisdiction to abandon their residences before 1 July while requiring those Jesuits who wished to stay to swear allegiance to the four Gallican articles and forswear both the doctrine and the constitutions of the Society.

The Parlement of Normandy thereby presented Versailles and the royal council with a resounding fait accompli. Although the royal council considered several draft decrees of annulment, it never directly responded to that parlement's judgment of 12 February. Instead it sent the Edict of Reform of 8 March 1762 to the Parlement of Paris as well as to all the other parlements, not excluding that of Rouen. But the only thing the edict accomplished was to set the stage for a spectacular display of parlementary disobedience in the costumes of obedience. After several days of deliberation, the Parlement of Paris followed Laverdy's advice to decree that it had nothing to deliberate about, on the twin grounds that its own appel comme d'abus was still pending until 1 April and that the edict's own fifteenth article, which seemed to promise the presentation of reformed Jesuit constitutions, made it impossible to act on the edict until these constitutions materialized. As all already knew that no such constitutions would ever obtain either the Jesuit general's or the papacy's approval, the decision "not to deliberate" was in effect a decision to postpone any consideration of the edict until the Greek calends.

Meanwhile, the Parlement of Normandy interred the edict for the reason that it lacked any application there, the Jesuits having ceased to exist in that province. Except for the parlements of Brittany and Toulouse, which had already begun to act, the effect of the edict elsewhere was ironically to spur the remaining parlements into action, including some that might have otherwise held aloof. The result was a March awakening of hitherto inactive parlements; those of Aix, Bordeaux, Metz, Besançon, and Grenoble and the superior councils of Roussillon all sprang into action.

Since amid all this action only Versailles remained inactive, it was hard not to conclude that the king had decided to leave the Jesuits to the mercy of his parlements. Among various straws in contrary winds, the one closest to the mark was a reputed letter from Madame de Pompadour to the archbishop of Paris urging him to stop importuning her on the subject of the Jesuits, and to "leave the king in peace."[112] It was tellingly without incident that the Parlement closed the Jesuit colleges within its vast jurisdiction on the scheduled date of 1 April and took inventory of the Society's property three weeks later, with a view to providing pensions for "sometime" Jesuits and replacing them as teachers. And it was without royal answer that Lamoignon penned one final plea to the king in favor of the Society on 1 May 1762.[113]

The Parlement's only real answer to the stillborn edict of March 8 was the publication of the *Extraits des assertions dangéreuses et pernicieuses . . . que les soi-disans jésuites ont, dans tous les temps et persévéramment soutenues, enseignées et publiées dans leurs livres (Extracts from the Dangerous and Pernicious Assertions . . . That the Self-Styled Jesuits . . . Have Consistently and Perseveringly Espoused, Taught, and Published in Their Books)*.[114] Ordered by the Parlement on 5 March as a preemptive reply to the coming Edict of Reform, this collection of "dangerous and pernicious statements" originated with Chauvelin's denunciation of the Jesuits' doctrine and ethics on 8 July 1761. In this embryonic form, this collection in the making again came to the aid of the Parlement when on 31 August it sent a sampling of these "assertions" with its first president Molé to Versailles, in an unsuccessful attempt to persuade the king that the danger represented by the Society was too pressing to obey his order to delay action against the Jesuits for an entire year.

The completion of this compilation took on greater urgency in November when the Conseil des dépêches voted to convoke an informal assembly of bishops in the Parisian vicinity in order to consult them on the Jesuits' utility and

doctrines as well as on the power of their general. Besides observing the nice-
ties of consulting members of the "spiritual" power on a partly spiritual subject, the king's purpose of this meeting was to head off the otherwise certain
publication of incendiary episcopal mandamuses and pastoral instructions
against the Parlement, such as those specialized in by the archbishop of
Paris.[115] With the exception of a few notorious naysayers, such as Fitz-James
of Soissons, this consultation produced a resounding endorsement of the Society's behavior and doctrine, and even the monarchical authority of its general, which the bishops went so far as to describe as the "masterpiece of the
wisdom of this institute's founder."[116] That in this instance what remained by
way of Gallican sentiment among Gallican bishops took the form of a show
of independence from the "temporal power" in parlementary form in defense of an ultramontanist religious order, and on behalf of a similarly beleaguered king, says volumes about the transformation of the Gallican tradition
in its homeland, in contrast to the attitude of docility in the face of anti-Jesuit
royal power taken by most recently gallicanized bishops in other expelling
states.

To be sure, the bishops insisted on the subjection of the Jesuits to their authority and the obligation to teach the four Gallican articles as part of their
courses in theology. But given both Rome's and the Jesuits' refusal to sign any
declaration of Gallican faith put before them, that profession of Gallican orthodoxy was of no real use to the king, and even less to the Parlement.[117] To refute
the episcopal endorsement of the Society of Jesus therefore became yet another
of the many tasks assigned to the collection of assertions. So the same judgment
of 5 March that ordered that this printed compilation be presented to the king
also instructed the general prosecutor to send the soon-to-be-printed copies to
each bishop in the realm.

The decision to print these extracts most definitely arose in reaction to the
consultation of bishops and were the product of a meeting by the usual suspects:
the barristers Maultrot, Mey, Lalourcé, Le Paige, Jacques-Joseph Texier, and the
president Murard, meeting at Texier's residence, also in the rue Christine.[118]
Besides these barristers, those who did the work of compilation and collation
are equally familiar actors: Chauvelin, Lambert, Laverdy, Murard, Robert de
Saint-Vincent, and—a new name—Roussel de la Tour, officially meeting under
the unenthusiastic tutelage of the abbé Joseph-Marie Terray. That these magistrates in turn availed themselves of the expertise of a Jansenist team working
under the direction of Dom Charles Clémencet of the Benedictine abbey of the
Blancs Manteaux in Paris is an accusation leveled after the Revolution by the
abbé Michel-Joseph Picot that is not without plausibility.[119]

By the time it left the Parlement's printer, this compilation had come to comprise four volumes of more than four hundred pages each, with the original Latin on the left side of the page and the French translation on the right. The entire first volume documented the ethics of probabilism and philosophical sin, and the second covered the "idolatry" of the Chinese and Malabar rites and the "irreligion" of denying knowledge of and love for God as a prerequisite for access to the sacraments. Occupying pride of place among these "pernicious maxims" were the political sins of homicide and regicide, taking up a good part of the third and the whole of the fourth volume. For good measure, another part of the second volume threw in the subjects of astrology, blasphemy, impudicity, sacrilege, and simony, while the introductory chapter on the "unity" of Jesuit doctrine plus the inclusion of very recent authors drove home the point that the opinion of any of the authors in the extracts had always been and remained the opinion of the Society.

As good as its word, the Parlement sent this compilation to all of France's 130-some bishops. And among the many hostile episcopal reactions it provoked, none was more dangerous for the Parlement than Christophe de Beaumont's accusation that the Parlement was infringing on the church's uniquely spiritual prerogative of judging doctrine.[120] As it was, voices both in Rome and at the more regular meeting of the General Assembly of the Gallican Clergy in 1762 were already accusing the Parlement of usurping the church's spiritual rights by judging the Society of Jesus as "impious" and annulling its members' religious vows.[121]

The first line of defense put up by the Parlement against this accusation was to maintain that it was only calling attention to doctrines and ethical principles that the church had already condemned. But it was in part to strengthen its defenses against this accusation that many of the same Jansenist canonists and barristers who put together this printed compilation—Le Paige, Mey, and Texier, most notably—also arranged for the dissident Catholic Church of Utrecht to use the *Extraits* as the basis for condemning the same doctrines and casuistic ethics when it convened a provincial council in Utrecht in September of the next year. Published by the Parlement's printer, P.-G. Simon, via the good offices of the abbé Clément and his brother Clément de Feillet in 1764, the official *Actes* of the Provincial Council of Utrecht in 1763 lent sorely needed ecclesiastical authority to the Parlement's condemnation of the Jesuit "assertions," especially in view of the archbishop of Paris's frontal assault on this violation of ecclesiastical authority in 1763 followed by another more formal one by the General Assembly of the Gallican Clergy in 1765.[122]

But no number of episcopal remonstrances could have prevented the demise of the Jesuits in France. The only factor that held up royal acquiescence in the parlements' dismantling of the Society in France was the division between a small minority and the majority of parlements and even within some of the parlements. From the mid-1750s the Parlement of Paris had adopted Le Paige's theory that France's various parlements constituted the "classes" of a single Parlement with Paris as its Court of Peers, and some of the provincial parlements had followed suit. But although the parlementary practice never conformed more closely to theory than in the offensive against the Jesuits, the Parlement of Douai in Flanders and the superior council of Colmar in Alsace never acted at all, while a deeply divided Parlement of Besancon ended by remonstrating against the royal edict of 1764 that put the royal seal on what the parlements had done. But among parlements where the attempt to follow Paris's lead encountered strong internal resistance, none found themselves more deeply and evenly divided than the Parlement of Provence, where the division replicated the one created by the Jesuit-related Cadière-Girard affair in 1729–1730. It was not until Louis XV decided on 23 December 1762 in favor of the anti-Jesuit coalition against Boyer d'Eguilles and his pro-Jesuit faction that this royal green light prompted most of the remaining parlements into further and more decisive action.

When in early February the king sent his parlements an edict and letters patent providing for pensions for ex-Jesuits and the administration of their former colleges, all could read the handwriting on the wall.[123] While bringing uniformity to the variety of parlementary actions or inactions, the final royal edict of 1764 limited that action to the suppression of the Society of Jesus in France rather than an expulsion of Jesuits from France. By virtue of the Edict of November 1764 France was more generous toward its Jesuits than Portugal had been or than Spain, Naples, and Parma would be in 1767–1768 because it permitted ex-Jesuits to stay in France as "particulars." But whether Louis XV wanted it to be or not, this edict was more radical than anti-Jesuit action elsewhere because it legitimated the dissolution of an entire religious order in France.[124]

Because the most obvious "necessity" at hand was the Parlement of Paris's help in persuading provincial parlements to register royal declarations for additional taxes to finance the disastrous and disastrously costly Seven Years' War, the king's fiscal dependence on his parlements is the easiest answer to the question of why a king who never showed the slightest sympathy with their actions allowed the parlements to have their way with the Jesuits. The war years from 1756 to 1763 witnessed the addition of two *vingtième*, or twentieth, taxes on all property owners to the original one of 1749, a doubling—even tripling—of the poll tax similarly paid by the nobility, a forced "gift," or *don gratuit*, from the principal cities and towns of the realm, a tax on annuities and venal offices that affected the magistrates directly, an addition of a *sol* for every six *livres* in indirect taxes collected by the farmers general, plus the abolition of numerous exemptions from the *taille*. It was the royal need for a modicum of parlementary cooperation on fiscal policy to which Pompadour undoubtedly alluded when, approached by the queen's father, Stanislaus Leczinska, on behalf of the Jesuits, she reportedly replied that while she believed the Jesuits to be "good men, it is . . . not possible for the king to sacrifice his Parlement for their sake, especially at a time when it is so very necessary to him."[125]

Compelling as this reason is—and it is a reason common to all the major Catholic states under pressure to tap ecclesiastical property to finance participation or even neutrality in the Seven Years' War—more pertinent to the argument here is the policy of intransigence pursued by the Rome of Clement XIII and Torrigiani. Not the least paradox of the international campaign against the Jesuits is that, alone among expelling states, it was Gallican France that seriously negotiated with their general and the papacy yet emerged empty handed from the effort. Apropos to this point is a deleted sentence in a draft of the royal edict of 1764 that lays the responsibility for the king's passivity squarely at the door of the refusal by the "Holy Father" to countenance the "smallest change in the rules of the said Society," lest it "so disfigure the [its] essence and substance" that "it would be preferable for [the Jesuits] no longer to exist at all than to do so in a manner different from the one under which they had formed their engagements."[126]

Although this clause rightly points to the refusal of Clement XIII and Ricci to concur in the royal effort to make the Society more acceptable to Gallican sensibilities, that refusal is only the most pertinent instance in a pattern of papal comportment calculated to irritate those sensibilities. It made a difference who the pope was, and in 1759 Clément and his Roman friends were not wrong in thinking that Rezzonico's choice of Torrigiani to replace Archinto as his secretary of state spelled the shipwreck of Catholic reformist hopes. In conversations with Torrigiani, the far from anti-Jesuit French envoy came away with the impression that the secretary had defined his main mission as "inspiring the pope to pick up . . . the keys of Saint Peter that Benedict and his ministry had allowed to fall," most notably in the diplomatic pliability displayed by Benedict's secretary of state, Cardinal Silvio Valenti Gonzaga.[127] Most clearly in view were Valenti's negotiation of the papal brief *Ex omnibus* with Choiseul in 1756 and the decision to empower Cardinal Saldanha to reform the Jesuits in Portugal at Carvalho's insistence in 1758. But behind these complaints lay the resentment at what Torrigiani regarded as the excessively generous concordats negotiated by Benedict XIV with the Catholic monarchies, beginning with Fernando VI's Spain in 1753.

Torrigiani's conviction that Clement XIII's predecessor had allowed the papacy to be unduly pushed around by the Catholic courts translated into a policy of strenuous resistance and tight secrecy that produced its most provocative product in Clement XIII's condemnation of the Neapolitan edition of the French Jansenist François-Philippe Mésenguy's *Exposition de la doctrine chrétienne* (*Exposition of the Christian Doctrine*) on 14 June 1761.[128] Although Italian allies such as the conte di Grosso thought that Choiseul would have been far more effective as the French envoy than the bishop of Laon was, Rochechouart did not neglect to convey to Clement XIII that the last thing France needed under the circumstances was yet another papal condemnation of a French Jansenist book that could not fail to roil the religious waters, even one published in Naples in Italian translation.[126] Seeing that it had become apparent to Rochechouart that Clement XIII did not think that the book merited the qualification of "heretical" or even "erroneous," the French envoy thought that it sufficed to place the book on the Index of forbidden books along with the original French edition, which had been there since 1757.[130] No need for the Holy Office's "secrecy" therefore justified the papal brief's appearance in French opinion, all the more so after it became apparent that the congregation of cardinals had split their votes—six and six—on the need for a condemnation, and that it was the pope himself who had cast the deciding vote.[131] (Indeed, Clement XIII had forced the notoriously anti-Jesuit Cardinal Passionei to sign the condemnation in his capacity as secretary of papal briefs, whereupon he succumbed to an attack of "apoplexy" that contemporaries were unanimous in attributing to the forced signing.)[132]

At Murard's behest, Le Paige dashed off a memoir destined for the king via Molé and Choiseul warning that the Jesuits intended this brief to be but the prelude to a condemnation of the doctrine of the Augustinians and Thomists far more precise than *Unigenitus* had been.[133] But the ministry hardly needed parlementary prodding. When the new keeper of the seals, Berryer, told Rochechouart that the king had instructed him to express His Majesty's "surprise" to Torrigiani at the fulmination of this brief, the diplomatic language pushed the limits of politeness in the eighteenth century.[134]

Worse, the brief came accompanied by a papal circular letter warmly recommending the Roman Catechism, as though an orthodox substitute for Mésenguy's book and in the explicit interests of Catholic uniformity.[135] Dated the same day as the brief, this circular made its way to the papal nuncio in Paris, with recommendations to address it to all the Gallican bishops if he saw no "inconvenience," which he did not. So it was with ill-disguised displeasure that Rochechouart explained to Torrigiani on 29 July that no papal pronouncement might ever go to a nuncio in France and from him to the Gallican bishops without the prior authorization of the French king; and that while the cate-chism's doctrine differed in no way from France's, this catechism contained disciplinary articles incompatible with "our liberties." Nor did it improve French diplomatic disposition toward the Jesuits that Clement XIII penned a personal plea to Louis XV to intervene on behalf of the Society in France at about the same time that just about every French voice in Rome attributed the papal con-demnation of Mésenguy to the Jesuits.[136] Last but not least, the papacy of Clem-ent XIII and Torrigiani seemed purposely to drag its feet on the promotion of the French nominees to the College of Cardinals, a deeply resented insult that affected Rochechouart of Laon himself. Under these circumstances, Rochech-ouart needed no prodding by Choiesul to inform the papacy "with force how much the king has reason to feel slighted by so flagrant a lapse in regard to what is due to His Majesty."[137]

It was under all of these circumstances that Rochechouart received word from Jacques de Flesselles at Versailles that he in turn had just learned from the Jesuit superior La Croix in Paris that the pope had severely reprimanded Ricci for "permitting his charges in France to make a [Gallican] declaration that . . . would have abandoned all the rights of the Holy See."[138] Asked to learn what he could, Rochechouart could only reply that he would not be surprised if the ru-mor turned out to be true, given that the "little enlightened three-quarters [of the inhabitants] in this land make it an article of religion to be opposed to our liberties and our maxims, while the remaining and more clairvoyant quarter make [this opposition] into a point of politics."[139] Of course, Clement XIII and Ricci's non possumus turned out not only to be true but also to concern the re-vised decree against the doctrine of tyrannicide as well. These "present circumstances"—the French diplomatic euphemism for the Jesuits' desperate situation—made the papacy's insensitivity to Gallican sensibilities seem all the more astonishing to French ears.

As events played out, these insensitivities affected the Spanish branch of the Bourbon dynasty as well. For the same papal foot-dragging that held up the promotion of the French nominations to the cardinalate also slowed down that of a Spanish nominee, Bonaventura de Córdoba Espínola de la Cerda, who eight years later would play a decisive role in the selection of the pope who dissolved the Society of Jesus. Further, the papal nuncio's publication of the papal brief against the Neapolitan edition of Mésenguy's *Exposition* without royal per-mission threw King Carlos III into a rage, causing him to impose a Gallican-like *regium exequatur*, or law requiring royal authorization for the publication of any and every papal utterance in Spain. As it happened, Clement XIII's condemna-tion of Mésenguy's *Exposition*, or *Spegazione*, made for a spat between Rome and

Naples even feistier than the one between Rome and France, and as of 1738 the Kingdom of Naples had become another Bourbon satrapy. Carlos III had been king of Naples before he replaced Fernando VI as king of Spain. The new king of Naples, Ferdinando IV, was Carlos III's son, and Ferdinando's chief and all-powerful minister, Bernardo Tanucci, had been and remained one of Carlos's chief advisers.

THE FRENCH EXCEPTION

Not the first Catholic state to act against the Jesuits, France most glaringly displays the feature of Archetto-centered plotting and planning that was present in diverse degrees in all the suppressing states. In other respects, the contrasts overwhelm the commonalities. The contrast that first leaps to view is that while everywhere else it was the Catholic kings and their ministers who led the offensive against the Jesuits, in France that offensive came from "below" by parlements that took advantage of the monarchy's fiscal distress to impose a suppression of the Society on a reluctant Louis XV. That structural difference accounts in turn for the long-drawn-out and highly contingent and eventful character of the suppression in France as opposed to the "terrible swift sword" of the expulsions elsewhere. At any point in a process involving the push and shove among a bewildering multiplicity of institutions, ministries, factions, and competing "takes" on the Catholic faith and church, to say nothing of Rome and its own divisions, events might have derailed the plot-like scenario. So surprised was Le Paige himself by his own success in this scenario that by April 1762 he no longer felt sure whether he was "awake . . . or dreaming at the sight of what is happening."[140]

The open-ended nature of the offensive against the Jesuits in France points to another structural contrast, and that is the comparatively open—even contentious—political culture in France as opposed to the tight control exercised over the interpretation of events in the other expelling states. The French suppression of the Jesuits amply illustrates Keith Baker's contention that by the 1750s, if not earlier, French political culture "broke out of the absolutist mold."[141] Attesting to the breakdown of absolutist ability to shape what can already be called "public opinion" is not only the parlements' open defiance of royal authority but also the publication of hundreds of pamphlets for as well as against the Jesuits, including some by French Jesuits themselves. Although the Jesuits eschewed all invitations by parlements to defend themselves in court, numbers of them pleaded their Society's case in public with such pamphlets as Jean-Antoine Joachim Cerutti's *Apologie générale de l'institut des jésuites* (*General*

Defense of the Jesuit Society).[142] While in France Jesuits published these defenses with relative impunity, in Spain the mere possession by Jesuits of one of these French defenses was accounted a crime of *lesa magestad*.

The expression of public opinion on the score of the Jesuits in France did not remain confined to printed pamphlets of the periodical *Nouvelles ecclésiastiques* but took the form of popular hissing and rejoicing in the Palais de justice and elsewhere, attesting to the deep implantation of gallicanized Jansenism in parts of France. In contrast, popular Jansenism and anti-Jesuitism found few if any echoes in the other expelling Catholic monarchies or duchies; to the contrary, widespread hostility to the antipapal ecclesiastical legislation including the expulsion of the Jesuits in ducal Parma and Piacenza was a factor in the fall from power of the hitherto all-powerful first minister, Guillaume du Tillot, in 1772. At a higher social level, the strong presence of Jansenism in France found expression in the identity of the main perpetrators of the Jesuit suppression: namely, the canonists in the Order of Barristers and a cadre of magistrates in the Parlement of Paris, both of whom had long functioned as refuges for Jansenists ineligible for ecclesiastical benefices on account of their refusal to sign the Formulary or accept *Unigenitus*.

The Jansenist mobilization of the Gallican tradition against the king, the monarchy's loss of control over discourse about the monarchy, the open defiance of royal authority in the public sphere, popular hostility toward religious symbols of royal authority—all of these stood in contrast to the situation elsewhere in Catholic Europe and pointed distantly toward a revolutionary denouement. So did the paradoxical presence in Gallican France of a militantly pro-Jesuit and ultramontanist segment of the episcopacy that would reappear in reaction to the Civil Constitution of the Clergy. Likewise anticipatory of the Revolution on the proto-"patriotic" side was the precedent of a wholesale dissolution of a religious institution rather than an expulsion of its members. By the end of 1790, the Revolution would have dissolved just about all the religious congregations and orders—but also all the parlements of France.

4

PORTUGAL AND SPAIN, 1754-1767

The role of France in the demise of the Society of Jesus turned out to be as pivotal as the Italian Augustinians hoped it would be. But it was also pivotal in the sense of lying at the center of a train of events that began as well as ended, not in France, but in the Iberian-Italic world. The plotting and planning began in Rome after Clément's visit there in 1758–1759. Regretting that the Damiens affair in France had not led to a general assault against the Jesuits, Bottari suggested as early as 5 March 1760 that in order to extinguish the Society without recourse to the papacy, it would "suffice if other important princes such as the King of France or Spain would slay them in his realm," in which case other states might follow suit.[1] But at that point Bottari found inspiration in the example of Portugal, and it is there that the process began.

CARVALHO E MELO AND THE EXPULSION
OF THE JESUITS FROM PORTUGAL

At first glance, the expulsion of the Jesuits from Portugal and its overseas possessions would seem to be sui generis and to have little in common with the case of France. If, as in France, the action took place under the cover of royal authority, in Portugal royal authority found personification in a single all-powerful royal minister, Sebastião José de Carvalho e Melo, better known by his final title as the marqués de Pombal. Far more powerful than Choiseul, Carvalho wielded his power with the full confidence of King José I, who acceded to Portugal's throne and made Carvalho one of three secretaries of state in 1750. In this laboratory of enlightened absolutism, Carvalho had no Cortes or organized episcopacy to resist him but no parlements to help him either; in this centerpiece of counterreform Catholicism, he similarly had only Jesuits and a few bishops and nobles to resist him but few home-grown Jansenists to help him either. But while the only real plotter in the case of Portugal was Carvalho himself, his campaign against the Jesuits found indispensable aiders and abettors in his younger brother Francisco Xavier de Mendonça Furtado, his friend and bishop Dom Miguel de Bulhões, and his cousin Almeida e Mendonça. The brother was the colonial governor of Maranhão in Brazil, his friend the bishop of Para in Brazil, and his cousin the Portuguese envoy to the curia.[2]

Still, the Jesuits were a formidable presence in Portugal. Nowhere did they seem more securely ensconced than in this Iberian cradle of their society, where, welcomed in the person of Saint Francisco Xavier and his companion Simon Rodríguez de Azevedo as early as 1540, they had become the royal confessors and preachers, the mainstays of the missions in Goa, Macao, and South America, the administrators of the University in Evora and ten colleges elsewhere, as well as the sole professors of the gate-keeping faculty of arts at the University of Coímbra. Although in the mid-eighteenth century the Portuguese monarchy obtained the right to name candidates to most secular benefices, the papacy retained control over the mission fields by means of the regular orders, above all the Jesuits.[3] In Portuguese high society, the hold the Jesuits had on higher education enhanced their credit within the court nobility, while the Italian Jesuit royal confessor Giovanni Battista Carbone helped retain the good will of the monarchy until King João V's death in 1750. Even after the accession of José I and the rise of Carvalho, the Jesuits remained invulnerable at the court until the death of the protective queen mother, Mariana of Austria, who died four years later.

By then, however, Carvalho was on his way to becoming the most powerful of the royal secretaries—and the most implacable enemy of the Jesuits.[4] By the eve of the expulsion, he had taken umbrage at the Jesuits for a great variety of offenses bookended by two sermons, the first in 1756 by a certain Gabriel Malagrida interpreting the disastrous earthquake in Lisbon in 1755 as a display of God's wrath at Portugal's many sins, and the second in 1757, critical of Carvalho's new state-sponsored monopolistic companies. This second sermon Carvalho regarded as the cause of a popular uprising in 1757 in Oporto against his reorganization of the port-wine export industry in the Alto Douro region.

But it was less the creation by Carvalho of such companies in metropolitan Portugal than his imposition of the Company of Grão Pará and Maranháo and a Junta de Comércio on the production and sale of South American colonial products that brought him into conflict with the Jesuit missions or "reductions," which also harvested and sold such products as tea and wild cacao.[5] In order to "free" the mainly Guaraní tribesmen from Jesuit domination—and to make their labor available to the company—the Portuguese state officially replaced the Jesuits' temporal tutorship with military "directors" and transformed the Jesuits themselves into secular priests under the authority of "ordinaries," such as the bishop of Pará. The trade engaged in by the missions gave Carvalho raw material for the highly charged accusation of illicit commerce at a time when Lavalette's activities in Martinique were coming to European notice. At the same time, the Jesuits' temporal tutorship in the missions lent credence to the charge of "despotism" just as that particular label was acquiring currency.[6]

Even more damaging to the Jesuits was the accusation that they fomented the armed resistance by Guaraní (or Tupi-Guaraní, or Karib) natives against Portugal when the state asserted control over areas allotted to it by the new demarcation of Portuguese and Spanish colonial boundaries drawn up by the Treaty of Madrid in 1750.[7] Two areas were at issue: in the south, seven missions or reductions in Paraguay, or the present Brazilian province of Rio Grande de Sul; and in the north some missions in the southern Amazon basin in the captaincies of Pará and Maranháo. What is incontestably true in Carvalho's suspicions is that the Jesuits had trained native militias to resist Portuguese settlers, that most Jesuits on the ground were less than euphoric about the new demarcations, and that Spanish and Portuguese forces encountered armed if ultimately unsuccessful resistance by native militias. As in cases of commerce, one of the main sources of information Carvalho drew on were the reports from his younger brother Francisco Xavier Mendonça Furtado, governor of Maranhão, supplemented by those of the Dominican bishop of Pará. In Paraguay the main source was Gomes Freire de Andrade, governor of southern and western Brazil. The limited and unsuccessful native resistance provided additional lyrics to the contemporary theme song that the Jesuits aspired to empire or at least independence from all temporal authority. Mendonça Furtado also took it amiss that the Jesuits communicated with the Guaraní in their own languages.[8]

Until 1758, these charges constituted the sum total of Carvalho's quarrel with the Jesuits. It was on these grounds that Carvalho brought three Jesuits from Brazil to Portugal to face charges as early as in 1755, followed by ever more such arrests in the three years following. Meanwhile all the Jesuit confessors of the royal family at court found themselves dismissed and confined to their residences on 19 September 1757. It was on no other basis either that the Portuguese ambassador in Rome obtained a papal commission in 1758 from the dying Benedict XIV empowering the recently elevated cardinal Francisco Saldanha, soon to be patriarch archbishop of Lisbon, to investigate the charges against the

Jesuits and to reform the Society in Portugal in consequence. Entirely Carvalho's creature, Saldanha found the Jesuits guilty of both commerce and usurpation of Portuguese authority, and on 15 May he issued an edict of reform to this effect only a week after a visit to their residence of São Roque in Lisbon. The existing patriarch of Lisbon, José Manuel de Camera, thereupon disbarred the Jesuits from all spiritual functions, while the Portuguese state closed all the Jesuit colleges, including the university at Evora. The authority by which the state issued these edicts originated in a more general papal delegation by Benedict XIV to the Portuguese monarchy to undertake the reform of Portugal's overpopulated and underfunded regular orders in the aftershock of the Lisbon earthquake of 1755.

Kept at bay by force of this reform and in the dark about proof of Jesuit misdeeds in particular, the papal nuncio Filippo Acciaiuoli was already executing a rearguard defense of the papacy's shrinking authority in Portugal when an attempted assassination of King José I on 3 September 1758 gave his first minister an ideal opportunity to have done with the Jesuits entirely. The attempt was real enough: gunshots wounded José while he was returning from a nocturnal visit to his mistress, the wife of Luis Bernardo de Távora, heir to the powerful Távora family. That the attempt was part of a conspiracy remains far from certain, since this verdict was the result of an investigation conducted by a royal commission of inquiry, the proceedings of which remain as inaccessible now as they were secretive then. Targeted were the entire Távora clan headed by the husband's parents plus the related José Mascarenhas, the duc d'Aveiro, with whom the supposed conspirators wished to replace the heirless José I. Yet the theory of a conspiracy by the high nobility at court is not without plausibility, as the king had alienated the blue-blooded older nobility, or *puritanos*, by the power he had given to the upstart Carvalho, whose economic policies had in turn empowered lesser nobility.[9] In any case, an equally secretive Junta de Inconfidência appointed on 4 January that included Carvalho himself found the accused guilty of conspiracy on 12 January and sentenced them to singularly brutal deaths carried out the next day, on 13 January.[10]

As it happened, the supposed conspirators also tended to be close to the Jesuits, another barrier to Carvalho's power. Indeed, the same Malagrida whose pamphlet about the Lisbon earthquake had annoyed Carvalho was also the marquese Leonor de Távora's confessor. No sooner had the investigation begun than soldiers subjected the realm's Jesuits to de facto house arrest, while the actual arrest of ten Jesuits, including Malagrida, preceded the gruesome execution of the "conspirators" by only a day. Further measures waited until 1759, when, on 19 January, the Junta de Inconfidência formalized the Society-wide house arrest and expropriated all the Jesuits' property in metropolitan Portugal.

A formal trial of churchmen by a purely secular tribunal made for a further infringement of ecclesiastical jurisdiction that gave pause even to Carvalho, whose services in defense of the monarchy had meanwhile merited a promotion to the title of conte d'Oeiras. Not content with papal permission to use the state's Council of Conscience, or Mesa de Consciência, to try some Jesuits in this case only, the king and his ambassador in Rome—and Oeiras's cousin—the conte Francisco de Almeida e Mendonça, held out for this council's right to try all such cases. When Clement XIII predictably refused this additional concession, José I cut the cord to Rome and, having already decreed that his state's procedure against the Jesuits and their property would take "administrative" rather than judicial form, allowed the Mesa de Consciência to condemn all Jesuits as guilty. In consequence, he imprisoned about 180 of them while expelling the remaining fifteen hundred from Portugal and the colonies.[11] Meanwhile, in July, the state had already loaded about 350 Jesuits onto ships bound for the Italian port of Civitavecchia.

The affair of the Jesuits finished with a literal flare as well as flair: the burning on 21 September of the strangled body of Malagrida, convicted not only for complicity in a plot against the king's life by the Mesa de Consciência but also of heresy by the Portuguese Inquisition. Ordered on 15 June by the state to leave Portugal, the nuncio Acciaiuoli took up residence in Spain before going back to Rome. Thus began Portugal's *rotura*, or diplomatic rupture, with the papacy, which lasted nine years.

On the face of events, the Portugal's offensive against the Jesuits would seem to have been an exercise in raw regalism with a social side—regalism because Carvalho's main aim was to enhance the power of the monarchical state at the expense of the papal Catholic Church as symbolized by the Jesuits; and with a social side because the Jesuits helped sanctify the position of a traditional landowning nobility that stood opposed to Carvalho's attempt to enhance the state's economic clout with the help of those nobles more open to entrepreneurial activity. The Portuguese case stands in contrast to the French one in that in France the assertion of secular state power came at the impulse of the parlements against the monarchy in the person of the king himself, while a social side pitted an office-owning nobility of the robe in alliance with a quite traditional judicial and guild-oriented bourgeoisie against a military nobility. And of course the Jansenist element, so important in France, seems alien to the future marqués de Pombal and Portugal.

Or was it?

JANSENISM AND PORTUGAL'S PUBLIC CASE
AGAINST THE JESUITS

Employed by Carvalho no less than by others, the standard eighteenth-century justification for extending royal authority at the expense of ecclesiastical and especially papal jurisdiction was that kings—and by implication the state—derived their temporal authority from God alone, putting it off limits to papal or any other kind of ecclesiastical intervention. The clear corollary was that whatever coactive jurisdiction the church had ever exercised, it had exercised only by way of temporal concessions or outright usurpation, and that by depriving the Jesuits of temporal authority over natives in Brazil or the nuncio of his jurisdiction in Portugal, the king was only "taking back" the authority that was his own alone and that temporal powers had possessed whole and entire until the priestly Middle Ages. To say this much is to say that the standard argument for the extension of secular authority was couched in quite religious terms. Which is also to say that the argument in this form was the royalist tenet of Gallican ecclesiology, an immediate product of the French wars of religion, and that its appearance in such apparently inhospitable habitats as Spain and Portugal is evidence of the importation of Gallican ideas there.

While in the seventeenth century Mariana's casuistry in defense of regicide in the case of heretical "tyrants" or Bellarmino's of the papacy's indirect temporal power caused the Jesuits no little grief in France, such theses had landed them in no trouble in Spain or Portugal, where many of their books got published but where royal absolute power in the Gallican sense was a defining dogma in either the Habsburg or the Bragança dynastic credo. That situation everywhere changed in Catholic Europe in the latter eighteenth century. And wherever in eighteenth-century Europe the Gallican tradition extended its influence, Jansenism was never far away in one form or another, both being ingredients in Reform Catholicism.

In the post-1750 but still very Catholic Portugal of José I, Carvalho could not totally justify his regalist policies with the existing body of indigenous theory, most of it dating from the restoration of Portuguese independence from Spanish suzerainty in 1640.[12] He therefore turned for conceptual help to the Oratorian priest António Pereira de Figueiredo, who increased the caliber of that theory with heavier Gallican ordnance. Of his three previously discussed publications in this vein, the *Doctrinam veteris Ecclesiae* was the first and most relevant to Carvalho's purposes, in that it defined the church's power as exclusively spiritual in contrast to the state's God-given monopoly of coercive power—the first and most recent tenet of Gallicanism.[13] Pereira's defense of the Gallican tradition's episcopal tenets in the two subsequent publications became pertinent in proportion as the prolonged rupture with Rome made it necessary for Portuguese bishops to exercise authority in cases hitherto reserved to the papacy. While his Gallican ecclesiology took Pereira halfway to Jansenism, his pedagogy, theology, and biblical translations took him the rest of the way. Having begun his pedagogical career by pioneering Port-Royal's use of the vernacular to teach Latin in Portugal, he capped it by translating the entire Bible into Portuguese—the second such translation in Portugal—beginning with the New Testament in six volumes by 1781.[14] Among the guides Pereira used in this monumental enterprise, by far the most important was Le Maître de Sacy, whose translations and literal and spiritual "explications" Pereira tended to follow at crucial Pauline junctures where the doctrines of grace and salvation were at issue.[15] He also maintained regular contact with the clergy of Utrecht, sealing his conviction of its Catholicity with a formal letter of communion to Archbishop van Nieuwenhuyzen in 1769.

So did João Batista de S. Caetano, a professor of theology at the University of Coímbra and procurator general of the Benedictine Order in Portugal, who also sponsored a catechism composed by the metamorphic abbé Parisot, who as Père Norbert first surfaced as a defrocked Capuchin critic of the Jesuits' missionary tactics in India and an acolyte of the Archetto and advocate of Utrecht in the 1740s, until Carvalho imported him to Portugal to turn out anti-Jesuit literature in 1760.[16] The face of royally favored Reform Catholicism outside France, they and other theologians like Manuel do Cenáculo Vilas Boas exercised a preponderant influence over the reorientation of Portuguese censorship policy on Carvalho's Real Mesa Censória, an entirely secular board with which Carvalho replaced the Inquisition in 1768. There, they effected a complete reversal of Spanish censorship policy, closing off the admission of all ultramontanist and overtly Molinist or probablistic publications—most especially by Jesuits—while giving free rein to the circulation of the works of Anauld, Duguet, Nicole, Pascal, Nicolas Petitpied, Sacy, and so on with few exceptions, even Jansen's *Augustinus* and anything sent their way by the Church of Utrecht.[17]

With others, Pereira also undertook the reform of the curiculum in theology, ecclesiastical history, and canon law at the University of Coímbra as well as in diocesan seminaries, giving these disciplines a durably Augustinian, Gallican, and regalist cast by means of every text cited in Pereira's own treatises. Portugal even acquired a Jansenist catechism little short of the status of a state one when in 1765 the archbishop of Evora, Don Juan-Come de Cuhna, adopted and promoted Joachim Colbert's *Catéchisme de Montpellier*.[18] The archbishop went so far as to accompany the catechism with a mandamus that defined "Jansenism" as a charge invented by the Jesuits the better to obscure their own doctrinal deviation from Augustinian "truth."[19]

But the case for the connectedness between the expulsion of the Jesuits from Portugal and Reform Catholicism does not depend uniquely on what happened in Portugal after the expulsion. To state the case in this way is to commit the fallacy of arguing from a sequential order to a causal relation. It stands to reason that quite apart from the "causes" at work the immense vacuum created by the expulsion of the Jesuits would have attracted elements of reformist Catholicism to occupy it, Jansenist ones among others.

Yet the case can be just as cogently argued retrospectively as prospectively, upstream as well as downstream. No sooner had Carvalho's cousin Almeida e Mendonça taken up residence in Rome as Portugal's envoy there in 1756 than he fell in with the philo-Jansenist Archetto consisting of Bottari, Pier Francesco Foggini, and the cardinals Passionei, Spinelli, and others who gathered in the palace of Cardinal Corsini, the cardinal-protector of Portugal—the same group that was soon to be plotting the destruction of the Jesuits in France. Among his first reports was the news that the Italian Dominican Concina had utterly refuted the Jesuit ethics of probabilism.[20] When, beginning the very next year, push came to shove in Carvalho's quarrel with the Jesuits, Almeida leveraged the influence and skills of this group into help by having all of Portugal's official acts and Carvalho's anti-Jesuit propaganda translated, printed, and distributed in Rome and throughout Catholic Europe, to compose ad hoc refutations of any and all attempts by the Jesuits to defend themselves in print, and even to exert direct face-to-face pressure on the pope.

At the height of his influence under Benedict XIV, Almeida not only used the threat of the immediate expulsion of the Jesuits from Portugal to obtain the pope's agreement to issue a brief authorizing Saldanha's investigation of their Society in Portugal, be even succeeded in having Passionei compose this brief in his presence in his ambassadorial residence in Rome. Benedict XIV's death the day before the publication of this brief in Portugal followed by that of the papal secretary of state Archinto's on 23 September 1758 diminished Almeida's influence, especially after the new pope, Clement XIII, appointed Torrigiani as Archinto's successor. But neither of these setbacks to his cause prevented Almeida from executing a rearguard action by mobilizing philo-Jansenist cardinals in such cardinalate congregations as that of the Holy Spirit and redoubling his propagandist offensive in print until papal-Portuguese relations deteriorated to the point of rupture after the attempted assassination of José I.[21]

As it happened, Almeida's arrival as Portugal's envoy in Rome took place less than two years after Bottari had established regular epistolary contact with the abbé Clément, and with it enhanced access to "books" containing, wrote Bottari, "truths of which I stand in need." These letters included reliable news about what was happening in France, for which his only other sources in Rome were such cardinals as "Passionei, Tamburini, and Corsini."[22] Since the periodical *Nouvelles ecclésiastiques* also accompanied these books, with them came a weekly diet of the systematically mixed moral, theological, and political variety of anti-Jesuitism that had taken form in France.

These sources constituted another conduit of Jansenist influence, one that is diffuse because it took discursive form. Whatever the bill of particulars that made up the matter of Carvalho's case against the Jesuits, this matter had to be given form, and the form was by then there for the taking. It is only by ignoring the European-wide and particularly French legacy of anti-Jesuitism that one can maintain the total originality of Carvalho in inventing that form. By the 1750s it was pervasive enough that as governor of the Portuguese captaincy of Maranhão Carvalho's brother Mendonça Furtado was interpreting the Jesuit missions as a "despotism" that had exploited native "slavery" in the service of an illicit "commerce" as the economic means toward an "empire" under a general whose power posed a threat to the papacy no less than the monarchy's. Mendonça even complained about the use of Molinist and probabilistic arguments by Jesuits in defense of their "independence" and against incorporating the natives into state controlled villages."[23]

In Rome, the Portuguese anti-Jesuit pamphlet that kept Almeida the busiest in having printed, translated, and distributed was Carvalho's anonymously published *Relação abreviada*.[24] First published in Madrid in 1757, this pamphlet represents the first attempt by Carvalho to justify his actions before the bar of Catholic European opinion. In predictably prejudicial fashion, this "brief account" tells the story of the Jesuits' attempts to thwart the implementation of the Treaty of Madrid, beginning with diplomatic sabotage followed by armed resistance by their Guaraní militias and culminating in ongoing disobedience— even guerrilla-like resistance—after their native forces proved unable to hold off a combined Spanish-Portuguese army. Along the way, the account mentions the first arrests of the guiltiest Jesuits, while also interspersing the narrative with supposedly textual evidence of that guilt.

At two intervals, however—just after the beginning and toward the middle—the narrative interrupts itself in order to frame its own action with a general description of the economy, society, and governance of the "powerful republic" that the Jesuits had established over the native Guaraní population in the "forests in the environs of the Paraguay and Uruguay rivers." On the "pretext of the conversion of souls" and the "principles of the Christian religion," the Jesuits are said to have translated a "reasonable subjection" into a "blind and limitless obedience" and total loss of natural "liberty," the better to reduce the natives to a condition of abject "slavery" under a "despotic" rule. In order to maintain this state of affairs, the Jesuits are also said to have trained and commanded a well-armed military force to seal the borders against the outside while limiting the means of communication within to the Guaraní language, thereby preventing all interchange between their charges and the surrounding population of Portuguese and Spanish "whites," whom the Jesuits had taught the native people to regard as dangerous by virtue of their "diabolical arts."[25] Besides the accumulation of power and de facto independence from their Portuguese and Spanish sovereigns and their representatives in the colonies, the wider purpose of the Jesuits is said to have been the systematic appropriation of their subject population's agricultural produce in order to buy and sell in "commerce" prohibited by canon law.[26]

Now, attempts by Jesuits with papal and royal help to protect the native Tupi-Guaraní people from exploitation on colonial haciendas had long provoked complaints by Portuguese colonists, even including the accusation that under the pretense of converting them the Jesuits were themselves exploiting their labor to amass riches. The closest that any of these polemics had ever come to the model of the *Relação abreviada* was a "Capítulos" by one Gabriel de Soares de Sousa that, written in 1592 but unpublished until 1942, went so far as to accuse the Jesuits of de facto "slavery" under the pretense of preventing it.[27]

But far from denouncing it as part of a "despotic" state in defense of any natural "liberty," this philippic was in part a defense of de jure slavery on the grounds of the mental incapacity of the natives to assimilate the basic concepts of Christianity.[28] The same very indirect ancestry holds for some of the anti-Jesuit polemical literature thrown up by a mid-seventeenth-century conflict of authority between the Jesuits and Bishop Cárdenas of Paraguay, which similarly combined a defense of the colonists' right of access to native labor with a charge that the Jesuits were employing that labor in amassing riches and creating an armed schismatic state. In this case, some of that literature attained public perpetuity in French translation in the fifth volume of Arnauld's *Morale pratique*.[29]

But the *Relação abreviada*'s depiction of this "state" as "despotically" ruling over "slaves" seems most directly descended from a similar description in a supposed report to Louis XIV's navy minister, Louis Phelyppeaux, in the form of an anonymous pamphlet first published in 1710.[30] Entitled *Mémoire touchant l'établissement des pères jésuites dans les Indes d'Espagne* (*Report on the Jesuit Fathers' Establishment in the Spanish Indies*), this supposed report similarly describes the Jesuits' regime in Paraguay as a combination of "despotism" and "slavery" inculcated by the precept of fearful obedience, with the aim of total independence from Spain and commercial enrichment as well as the protection of a native militia and the exclusive use of the Guaraní language.[31] The main differences are that the obedience is described as effectively internalized more than forced, and the source of the "immense riches" is said to be mines as well as crops.[32]

Although that pamphlet went through two more editions, it achieved immortality by its inclusion as an annex in the second or 1717 edition of the *Morale pratique*'s fifth volume, devoted to the case of Cárdenas.[33] It has every mark of a Jansenist anti-Jesuit publication on the eve of Pope Clement XI's condemnation of Quesnel in *Unigenitus* and on the occasion of the prospect of the Bourbon dynasty's accession to the Spanish throne in the War of Spanish Succession. Lest that similarity escape detection, the *Nouvelles ecclésiastiques* called attention to this pamphlet as the key to understanding events in Paraguay a full year before the publication of the *Relação abreviada*, while a clearly Jansenist-inspired "avertissement" to a 1758 reprinting of this and other memoirs on the subject justified this republication as cautionary evidence that if "today the whole universe witnesses an open war . . . between the Jesuits and Indians on one side, and the two kings of Spain and Portugal on the other," it was not for want of the warning contained in these reports.[34] Although this avertissement did not mention the pamphlet's earlier republication in the second edition of the *Morale pratique*, the *Nouvelles* did.

But in order to ensure the widest possible diffusion of this pamphlet in Europe, Carvalho had it translated into other languages, especially French, and in order to do so he turned to Pierre-Olivier Pinault, a Jansenist barrister and friend of Le Paige and Lalourcé—the same Pinault who figured in the memoir that denounced Choiseul's complicity.[35] For his part, the printer to whom Almeida had recourse to have the *Relação abreviada* translated and printed in Italian was Niccolò Pagliarini, who also acted as an agent of Bottari and the Archetto and sustained arrest and imprisonment in Rome for printing not only the Carvalho's pamphlet but Jansenist literature in general.[36] His imprisonment became an affair of state, figuring in the diplomatic correspondence of France as well as of Naples and Portugal. When, not long thereafter, Pagliarini fetched up in Lisbon after a brief stop in Naples, he had less the Almighty than Almeida to thank, having become Carvalho's printer and translator in Lisbon. There, Pagliarini later organized the Italian translation of Joseph de Seabra da Silva's multivolume anti-Jesuit summa, the *Deducção chronológica e analytica* (*Chronological and Analytical Demonstration*), which did for Portugal what a historiographical tradition had long done for France by blaming the Jesuits for all that had gone awry in Portugal since João III had welcomed them there in the 1540s.[37]

For good measure, Carvalho also imported the philo-Jansenist Parisot, or Platel, who, as previously noted, cranked out justifications for the execution of Malagrida and other anti-Jesuit literature on Portugal's behalf before becoming persona not grata in 1766.[38] If that were not enough, Carvalho enlisted the services of one Jean-Pierre Viou, a French Jansenist refugee from the abbé Jean d'Yse de Saléon's anti-Jansenist campaign in the post-Soanen diocese of Senez.[39] Having since found relative safety in the rue Saint-Jacques in Paris, Viou there scratched out installment upon installment of his serial *Nouvelles intéressantes* (*Interesting News*) on the subject of the attempted assassination of the king of Portugal. This "news" received further amplification via its coverage by the *Nouvelles eccléiastiques*, which Carvalho got and read. Anything but one-way, the traffic between Carvalho and these French and Italian publicists was fully reciprocal, the propagandists putting as many ideas into his head as he into theirs.[40]

Such ideas were on conspicuous display in the heavy artillery of Gallican-Jansenism's antiregicidal rhetoric that was perhaps reformist Catholicism's main contribution to Portugal's anti-Jesuit case. Coming hard after the French Jansenist campaign to implicate the Jesuits in Damiens's attack on Louis XV, the attempt on King José I's life enabled Carvalho to fit the recent Portuguese event for the ready-made bore of this artillery. It was to this ordnance that Carvalho turned in the opening salvo of his campaign with a view to the expulsion of the Jesuits in the form of a manifesto sent to all the bishops justifying the Junta da Inconfidencia's sentence of 12 January. That salvo bore the title *Erros impios e sediciosos, que os Religiosos da Companhia de Jesus insinaraõ aos reos, que foraõ justiçados* (*Impious and Seditious Errors that the Members of the Company of Jesus Have Imparted to the Recently Punished Criminals*).[41]

Published with Carvalho's connivance if not direct contrivance, this manifesto did not directly mention the Damiens affair. Yet its copious citations of the Jesuit Hermann Busembaum's *Medulla theologiae moralis* and the right this treatise vouchsafed to subjects to assassinate their their sovereigns for sundry reasons succeeded in indirectly exploiting the Damiens affair with damning effect, via the much commented upon republication of Busembaum's treatise in the midst of it.[42] The manifesto reinforced this effect by mentioning the Jesuits' reputed complicity in the attempts on Henri IV's life by Barrière and Chastel in 1593–1594 as well in Ravaillac's successful one in 1610, thus recycling the same ancient ammunition already deployed in France during and after the Damiens affair.[43]

Now, neither the typically Gallican antiregicidal nor the Jansenist moral and theological case against the Jesuits had ever figured importantly in Iberian anti-Jesuitism until the 1750s, at which point Carvalho found both as fully integrated parts of a hitherto largely French case against their Society's "universal" and "despotic" state within divinely ordained temporal states.[44] So dependent was Carvalho's manifesto on the Gallican-Jansenist template that its only point of originality was the relation it posited between the Jesuits' "lax" and "pernicious" doctrines and the putative maxims of Machiavelli. While Pasquier, who had first leveled the charge of Machiavellianism against the Jesuits, had applied it only to what he considered the dishonestly of the Society's simple and provisional vows, Carvalho followed Machiavelli in making it an affair of state because he regarded the Society as a state.[45] Supposedly Machiavellian as well, the first three "errors" that Carvalho's pamphlet imputed to the Jesuits consisted in the justification and practice of calumniating, assassinating, and prevaricating in the interests of their society. Not attributed to Machiavelli, a fourth error consisted in the "mystery" of the constitutions of the Society and the secrecy of its conventicles, by means of which it cloaked its immoral activities under the pretense of religion in pursuit of its entirely temporal interests. These temporal interests had to do with the replacement of legitimate royal authority with the Society's unique combination of "despotism" and anarchy: "despotism" in respect to the structure of the Society, and anarchy in respect to the civil and social disorder caused by its pursuit of its goals.

The pamphlet's analysis of each of the Society's four major "errors" culminated in its role in the failed "conspiracy" against José I's life. If—so ran the pamphlet's argument—the Jesuits had defamed the Portuguese king both in the colonies and in the metropolis, they did so in order to predispose opinion in favor of his assassination. If they had also just updated its casuistry of regicidal assassination, they did so for the same reason. If Portuguese Jesuits, such as Malagrida, peddled prophecies about misfortunes about to befall the kingdom and lie about their attempts to fulfill them, they did so in order to cover their tracks in this assassination attempt, both fore and aft. And if throughout the Jesuits maintained the mystery of their society, they did so because it was all but conspiratorial by definition, having been plotted with a view to political power from the beginning.

Aside from the attempted assassination of the king, however, particular Portuguese events played little role in the substance of Carvalho's indictment. In it, a derivative form overwhelmed the current content. Part of the form consisted in the moral arraignment of the Society's techniques of verbal "equivocation," mental "reservations," "directions of intention," and the rectitude of the erroneous conscience—the warp and woof of "probabilism," as the manifesto specifically named it. Thereby did it make indirect contact with such anti-Jesuit classics as Pasquier's *Catéchisme des jésuites*, Pascal's *Lettres provinciales*, and Arnauld's *Morale pratique*. The manifesto's gallery of roguish Jesuits hence featured the usual suspects, from Bellarmino to Busembaum, just as the anti-Jesuit saints it invoked numbered Cano and Palafox. But that form also subordinated the Society's theological goals to political ones as part of a long-term conspiracy, as eighteenth-century French literature gradually did, beginning in the late 1720s and culminating in the Jansenist weekly's inaugural editorial in 1759.

That his own regime was perhaps more "despotic" than any other in Europe did not deter Carvalho from adopting the emphasis on the Society's "despotism" found in the most recent "patriotic" phase of French anti-Jesuitism. Whether consciously felt or not, that risk had to be taken if the Jesuits were to be expelled rather than reformed. The case for expulsion could only be made on the grounds that the Society was irreformable, and that case in turn could only be made by arguing that its putative combination of an immoral ethics in the service of a single-mindedly "despotic" regime with branches in all states put it beyond the reformist reach of any state.

In the longer run, Carvalho's campaign pointed toward national Catholic churches within a more collegial and decentralized polity, a direction that Reform Catholicism was later and more consciously to take. In the shorter run, meanwhile, events in Portugal were only among several factors figuring into the reformist Catholic grand strategy during the same decisive year of 1759. On the one hand, Carvalho's campaign gave the French Jansenist core no end of grist for a polemical mill further fed by the Portuguese ambassador to France, who plied Choiseul with Carvalho's version of events. On the other hand, events in Portugal were also reason to fear that, badly goaded in Portugal, the Jesuits would harness the profoundly philo-Jesuit pontificate of Clement XIII, the better to charge their enemies as never before.

For neither Clement XIII nor Torrigiani was swallowing Carvalho's version of events. Ever more convinced of the Portuguese Jesuits' corporate innocence, they dug in their heels in defense of the besieged Society, braving rupture with the Portuguese court on its behalf. Nor did the parlements' anti-Jesuit offensive in France bend the papal posture. To the contrary, Clement XIII seized the occasion of this offensive to rise publicly to the defense of the maligned Society, addressing briefs to this effect to both Louis XV and the French bishops at the meeting of their General Assembly in June 1762. While the papal plea had little effect on a weak-willed king, it found a more resonant reception among Gallican bishops largely chosen for their willingness to uphold *Unigenitus*. Having already sounded off in favor of the Society when consulted on its "utility" by the monarchy in September 1761, the bishops were again to do so even more militantly in reply to Clement XIII's *Apostolicum Pascendi* in defense of the Jesuits in 1765. Against the apparent good pleasure of their king, the stance in favor of the Jesuits by the overwhelming majority of Gallican bishops is yet another structural difference between France and Iberian Europe, where, with few exceptions, the national episcopacies sided with their monarchies against Clement XIII and Torrigiani's defense of them.

As early as 1761, when Clement XIII's hand-picked congregation of cardinals condemned the Italian translation of Mésenguy's catechism, it was becoming clear that Bottari's strategy of having French Jansenists concentrate all their fire on the Jesuits in order later to persuade the papacy to revisit some of the contested doctrinal sites was boomeranging badly. Far from driving a wedge between the Jesuits and the papacy, the anti-Jesuit offensive had so far been bringing them closer together. While in France that condemnation made for another reason for Louis XV to leave the Jesuits to the mercy of his parlements, in Rome it made Bottari fear that this papal brief would become the "*Unigenitus* of Italian Augustinians," evidence that "the Jesuits were determined to use that book as they did Quesnel's in order to light the fire [of discord] in Italy."[46] And although it was indeed to make loyalty to the papacy more difficult for Italian Augustinians, it was in Spain that this brief would have its first polarizing effect.

CARLOS III AND THE TECTONIC POLITICAL AND RELIGIOUS SHIFT IN SPAIN, 1750–1766

The anti-Jesuit domino effect was thus not even to spare Spain, the birthplace of Ignatius Loyola himself, as the polarization propelled by the anti-Jesuit campaign began to work its way around Catholic Europe. As in Portugal until the eve of the expulsion, however, the Society's presence in Spain seemed defining, with the presence of around twenty-eight hundred Jesuits in metropolitan Spain who staffed 132 colleges exercising all but a monopoly on the education of the upper nobility and its promotion to the higher echelons of royal service, culminating in the Council of Castile.

Nor was the picture different in Spain's extensive colonial empire in South and Central America and the Philippines, where another twenty-six hundred or so Jesuits and about ninety colleges dominated all other regular and to some extent even secular competition.[47] Although, as in Portugal, eighteenth-century regalist ideology and its drive to extend royal jurisdiction at the expense of the papacy did not fail to make its influence felt in Spain, it did not initially bear anything like an anti-Jesuit aspect. When—far from it—in 1753 King Fernando VI negotiated a concordat with Pope Benedict XIV that gave the Bourbon Crown the right to nominate all the candidates for major and minor benefices hitherto reserved to the papacy, it in fact subjected all these nominations to the direct influence of the Spanish Jesuits because at that point the Jesuit Francisco Rávago was the king's confessor.

What explains this consequence is that ever since reign of Felipe II, the royal confessors in Spain had exercised de facto ministerial powers of patronage and preferment by means of their advice to the king in his dealings with governmental subcouncils, or *cameras*, under the Council of Castile, which busied themselves with "preferments" for these positions and benefices. And ever since the accession of the Bourbon dynasty in 1715, the Jesuits had monopolized the position of royal confessor to the exclusion of the Dominicans, who had held it under the Habsburgs. Since then too, these confessors had enjoyed privileged influence over the policies of the Spanish Inquisition, occasionally occupying the position of inquisitor-general themselves; they also controlled the Junta de Colegios, which presided over the realm's most prestigious colleges, including the Jesuits' own *colegios mayores*, distributing scholarships to students as well as designating candidates for professorial chairs.

Since graduates of the Jesuit colleges all but monopolized the higher offices within the royal administration, Jesuit confessors also indirectly influenced the composition and outlook of the royal government as a whole. Small wonder, then, that under the first Bourbons the Spanish Jesuits tended to be more regalist than ultramontanist, quite apart from the consideration that in Spain royal jurisdictionalism carried none of the conciliar or anti-infallibilist associations that the Gallican liberties did in France. Nor is it surprising that Rávago personally took a hand in negotiating the Concordat of 1753, carrying his Spanish colleagues with him.[48]

At the height of Jesuits' power under Fernando VI, Rávago and his colleagues' notorious hostility to the Augustinian school of theology even put them on the regalist side of a standoff with the papacy in the person of Benedict XIV, who was sympathetic to that school. This confrontation marks the debut of Jansenism as an issue in Spain, concerning as it did the Spanish Inquisition's decision to include Henry, or Enrico, Noris's *Historia Pelagiana* (*History of Pelagianism*) on its list of prohibited books on grounds of its "Jansenism." When, vouching for its orthodoxy, Benedict XIV asked the Spanish Inquisition to remove the title from its prohibited list, Fernando VI undertook a such spirited defense of the prohibition that at times it seriously jeopardized and surely prolonged the negotiations for the Concordat of 1753. Because the Inquisition's censors were Jesuits, and Rávago himself supported his king, the assertion of royal power at the expense of the curia ironically pitted the supposedly ultramontanist Jesuits against the papacy in an issue about Catholic orthodoxy. Along the way, Rávago and his colleagues further alienated Noris's Augustinian Order and its Spanish general, Francisco Vázquez, just as they had alienated the Dominicans and other orders. The attendant danger was that this source of strength might boomerang against them should the Jesuits ever lose their grip on the position of royal confessor, in which case they might have to abandon regalist territory to rivals and rediscover their trademark ultramontanist vocation in adversity.

As in Portugal, that seismic tilt in the Spanish segment of the Iberian Peninsula began to occur in the 1750s—in 1754, to be precise—a year that witnessed the fall from power of one of the Jesuits' chief allies in the ministry, the all-powerful secretary of finance, war, the navy, and the Indies, Zenón de Somodevilla y Bengoechea, marqués d'Ensenada, followed two years later by the dismissal of Rávago himself.[49] At issue amid the inevitable triviality of these court politics were not only the pro-French and anti-English policies of Ensenada but also, as in Portugal, the Jesuits' resistance to the full implementation of the redrawing of Spain's and Portugal's colonial American boundaries by the Treaty of Madrid. After initially supporting the terms of this treaty in deference to the king's Portuguese consort, Maria Barbara de Braganza, who favored it, both Ensenada and Rávago tried to scuttle it after the Jesuits in South America made them aware of the disruptive consequences for their missions there.[50] Among the immediate results of this resistance was the alienation of the hitherto pro-Jesuit secretary of state José de Carvajal y Lancaster, who had voiced concerns about the treaty's implications for the Jesuit missions in the first place.[51] It was in part he who with his court clientele engineered the fall of Ensenada.

Worse, Carvajal's death the same year created a space occupied by the Irish-born Ricardo Wall, who, an outright enemy of both the Jesuits and papal influence, helped bring about the fall of Rávago. Indeed, so convinced was Wall of Jesuit complicity in the Guaraní revolt that, encouraged in this opinion by Spain's royal commissioner in Buenos Aires, he instructed Spain's new provincial governor to send eleven of the most guilty Jesuits to Spain for trial and began to negotiate a new agreement with Portugal whereby all Jesuits in the Brazilian missions would be replaced by secular priests. He was prevented from doing so only by the provincial governor's conviction of the Jesuits' innocence and Carvalho's growing reluctance to have Portugal vacate all the areas designated for transfer to Spain by the Treaty of Madrid.[52] As it was, Wall had Spain's ambassador in Lisbon send him all of Carvalho's anti-Jesuit propaganda while working hand in glove with the Portuguese ambassador, Antonio Saldanha, in circulating it in Spain, with Roda and Cardinal Corsini in Rome, and with Tanucci in the Naples ruled by the soon-to-be king of Spain.[53] In the long run, therefore, Jesuit and Jesuit-inspired resistance to the Treaty of Madrid was to do almost as much damage to the Society's standing in Spain as in Portugal.

To be sure, Fernando VI's descent into debility during the last year of his reign, combined with the militantly pro-Ignatian pontificate of Clement XIII, allowed the Spanish royal court's philo-Jesuit party to recompose itself around sympathetic members of the Council of Castile led by its president, Diego Rojas Contreras, bishop of Cartagena, and the queen mother, Elisabetta Farnese. Other obvious poles of attraction were the unexiled Ensenada and his clientele as well as Rávago, who remained at large and influential. But the death of Fernando in 1759 followed by the accession of Carlo VII of Naples as Carlos III of Spain jeopardized this precarious recovery.

Half-brother of his predecessor Fernando and eldest son of Spain's first Bourbon king Felipe V and his second wife, Elisabetta Farnese, Carlos III came to Spain in 1759 with a reputation as a fiscal, juridical, and ecclesiastical reformer. Although he initially sought to reassure opinion by retaining most of Fernando VI's ministers, that policy also meant retaining the anticurial Wall as secretary of state while keeping the still ambitious Ensenada at bay by means of honorific but powerless positions. And although he entrusted the tutorship of the royal children to Jesuits, he chose a Franciscan friar, Joaquín de Eleta, as his personal confessor, whom he appointed to the bishopric of Osma as testimony to their shared veneration for Eleta's anti-Jesuit predecessor, Palafox, earlier bishop of Pueblo de Los Angeles in New Spain.

Further, the single ministerial replacement Carlos initially hazarded proved unwelcome to Spanish opinion generally and to the church and Jesuits in particular: namely, the Sicilian Leopoldo di Gregorio, the marqués de Squillace — or Esquilache, in the Spanish idiom — whom Carlos imported from Naples and put at the head of the Treasury. More ominous although hidden from view was the new king's retention of Manuel de Roda as Spain's agent of beneficial requests in Rome. While the Spanish origins of Roda's antipathy for Jesuits remain obscure, that antipathy took on ethical and theological coloration after Roda fell in with the Archetto in the persons of Bottari, Passionei, and the Augustinian Order's general Vásquez soon after his arrival in Rome in 1758.[54] Subsequent battles at close quarters against the pro-Jesuit pontificate of Clement XIII on behalf of the Duchy of Parma's attempts to restrict the accumulation of fiscally immune church property and still other causes added an ecclesiological edge.[55] No letter from Roda to Spanish friends during his Roman sojourn was devoid of some invective against the Jesuits; nor did either Jesuits or their enemies suppose that his departure from Rome for Madrid as Carlos III's new minister of minister of grace and justice in 1765 portended anything good for the Society.[56]

Little less disastrous for Spanish Jesuits was Carlos's retention of his Neapolitan first minister and former tutor Tanucci as his weekly epistolary adviser. Although Tanucci's itinerary from a councilor of Tuscan origin to Carlos's first minister bypassed the Archetto, by 1758 Tanucci corresponded with Bottari and Corsini as well as Roda and solidified his esteem for and friendship with Roda in Naples on the occasion of Carlos's accession to the Spanish throne in 1759. Although he repeatedly disavowed any Jansenist identity, his doctrinal allegiance, radical Gallican ecclesiology, and rabid anti-Jesuitism made it hard to tell him from one. Not only did Tanucci continue to correspond with Carlos as king of Spain and Roda after 1765, he may have exerted an even greater influence on both via his correspondence with the king's grand chamberlain and personal attendant, José Fernández-Miranda Ponce de León, duque de Losada.

When Wall resigned his position in 1762, Carlos replaced him as secretary of state with another Italian, the Genoese Paolo Girolamo Grimaldi y Pallavicini, better known as the marqués de Grimaldi, who as Spain's ambassador to France had negotiated the third and most lasting Bourbon Family Pact between the two countries in 1761. For Jesuits in Spain, no Spanish alliance with France could auger very well at a time when the Society was on trial by the parlements. As time went on, moreover, Carlos began to people the offices of *fiscales* (state judicial advocates) in the Council of Castile with lower-noble or upper-bourgeois *manteístas*, such as Roda, who had obtained their law degrees from schools other than the more prestigious Jesuit *colegios majores*.

The most obvious example of Carlos's promotion of manteístas is Roda himself, who rose to head the powerful Ministry of Grace and Justice in 1765. More typical were the trajectories of Pedro Rodríguez Campomanes and José Antonio Moñino, who carried social chips on their shoulders as they faced off against pro-Jesuit "collegiates," such as Lope de Sierra Cienfuegos.[57] The absence of any specifically Jansenist identity in either case did not prevent them from being anti-Molinist and very Gallican in the regalist sense of advocating the extension of state secular power at the expense of the church. Like Tanucci, Campomanes in particular combined his regalism with a rather conciliar conception of the church and established indirect contact with Ripert de Monclar, the Jansenist prosecuting attorney of the Parlement of Aix.[58]

While genuine Jansenists remained few and far between in Spain in 1759 and, as in Portugal, did not amount to a "movement" until well after the expulsion of the Jesuits, Jansenism as an issue put in a second disruptive appearance—the set-to over Noris's book was the first—early on in Carlos's reign, playing a role both in Wall's demise in 1762, the promotion of Campomanes to the Council of Castile a little earlier, and the sharpening of Roda's anti-Jesuitism as beneficial agent in Rome.[59]

The occasion was Spain's Grand Inquisitor Manuel Quintano Bonifaz's publication of Clement XIII's condemnation of the Neapolitan edition of Mésenguy's catechism in 1761.[60] Although Bonifaz himself was no great admirer of the Society of Jesus, this publication went without saying because the Spanish Inquisition had long been a Jesuit satrapy, as evident when not even the papacy could dislodge Noris's book from its Index. The difference in 1761 is that the new king had just come from Naples, where his former first minister and ongoing adviser was Tanucci, who, as it happened, had sponsored the Italian translation of Mésenguy's catechism. King Carlos was furious, obliging the inquisitor to rescind the publication and subjecting him to proffer a humiliating apology. But with Wall's encouragement he also imposed the exequatur requiring royal authorization for the publication of any and all papal briefs or bulls, while Wall found antipapal canonistic backing in Campomanes, who in turn had found it in the Flemish Jansenist van Espen's recently published *Ius ecclesiasticum universum* and Febronius's *De statu Ecclesiae*.[61]

In contrast to Noris's case, when the issue was the Spanish Inquisition's independence from Rome, at issue in this case was the principle of royal versus ecclesiastical, specifically papal, authority. True, Carlos soon rescinded this decree due to the suasion of Clement XIII exercised through his Franciscan confessor and in view of the havoc the exequatur might wreak with some of the provisions of the Concordat of 1753. It was this royal volte face that caused Wall to resign in 1762. But this Jesuit victory was a pyrrhic one because Wall's successor, Grimaldi, soon proved to be just as regalist as Wall, and the whole affair linked the cause of the Jesuits to the ultramontanist cause of Rome more tightly than ever before.

That minor favor for the Jesuits was the last that Eleta would perfom, for meanwhile he along with the king had become the targets of a whispering campaign impugning their orthodoxy that could only have emanated from Jesuit quarters. The "heresy" in question was their shared veneration of Palafox, even though the Roman Congregation of Rites had cleared the way for the process of his beatification and the Roman Inquisition had approved the publication of his complete works, which appeared in 1762. Jesuits experienced no difficulty dismissing these papal authorizations, since they represented the work of the usual suspects: Roda with the help of Cardinal Passionei while still Spain's agent in Rome. In addition to alienating Franciscans via Eleta, the Jesuits had also used the previous reign's late turn in their favor to inaugurate a campaign against the theological incompetence of Spain's mendicant religious orders, especially the Dominicans and Trinitarians. In 1758, the Spanish Jesuits' most lethal pen, that of José Francisco de Isla, mercilessly satirized the rococo sermonic cover for theological poverty of these friars in a novel about a preacher that provoked a polemical firefight spilling into Carlos's reign.[62] But Isla's rhetorical tour de force would prove another pyrrhic victory for his society, since it also alienated just about all the other regular orders in Spain.

Transparent though they seemed, these mixed ecclesiastical and religious settos acted as signposts for an array of other seemingly unrelated disputes pitting Carlos III's newly promoted and reform-minded manteísta councilors against defenders of Spain's Old Regime status quo. Among them were issues as apparently secular as Campomanes and Esquilache's successful project of liberalizing the grain trade and phasing out controlled prices—a cutting-edge "enlightened" economic policy experimented with in many parts of Catholic Europe at this time, including France. Ambiguous though they seemed, the new king's ministerial reshufflings also signaled a decisive tilt of the monarchy's choice of religious allies. Beginning with the fall of Ensenada and Rávago in the mid-1750s and ending with the promotion of Roda to the Ministry of Grace and Justice in 1765, that tilt took the monarchy away from what the current historiography describes as the "collegiate-Jesuitical" side of the divide and toward the "manteísta-tomista," or Thomist, side.[63] The collegiate-Jesuitical label designates the blue-blooded noble graduates of elite Jesuit colleges who retained a loyalty to the Society as well as its theological orientation, while the manteísta-Thomist tag refers to the lesser nobles who had completed their legal studies at non-Jesuit universities along with assimilating the broadly Thomist and anti-Molinist theological and moral orientations that they had picked up there.[64]

Besides Jesuits themselves, the newly defensive collegiate-Jesuitical side included the Ensenada faction, the highest nobility, or *grandes de España*, the royal court's "Castilian party," an episcopal party led by the deceased minister's brother Isidro Carvajal y Lancaster, and part of a provincial Aragonese party. In sum, the redistribution of power in Carlos's ministry had marginalized the highest nobility, especially in the person of the well-connected Fernando de Silva Alvarez de Toledo y Haro Huéscar, duque de Alba, as well as anybody connected with the queen mother in the so-called Castilian party. Besides the manteísta fiscals whom he had promoted, the king for his part could count on his Italian advisers, the late Carvajal's alienated clientele, plus the Augustinians and Dominicans in addition to Thomists and philo-Jansenists within the episcopacy. While the collegiate-Jesuit side retained the majority in the Inquisition, the Council of the Indies, and the Council of Castile and its subbranches, the manteísta-Thomist side had the ear of the king, who could be expected to support it if he deemed it politically seasonable to do so.

The Thomist label notwithstanding, the manteísta-Thomist side might just as well be rechristened the reformist Catholic or Gallican-Jansenist side in view of the twin tendencies of French Jansenist Augustinians to fortify the anti-Jesuit cause by conflating it with the theology of Aquinas and to make liberal use of Gallican ecclesiology as radicalized by Jansenists. Another currently employed set of binary labels is "probabilist" versus "probabiliorist" in reference to the Jesuits' putatively "accommodating" confessional ethics as opposed to more rigorist schools of confessional ethics. But in any case these labels functioned as religiously charged shorthand designating opposing sides and policies in a pattern of ever more polarizing alignments.[65]

Three such confrontations illustrate this growing polarization, ranging from issues that united the Jesuits with others to an issue that concerned them only.

The issue least obviously related to the Jesuits was the fiscal Campomanes's proposal to set limits on the amount of ecclesiastical property immune to royal taxation, for which he had prepared public opinion by means of his *Tratado de la regalia de amortizacion* (*Treatise on Royal Rights in Amortization*) in 1765.[66] This proposal rested on the premises that the king's first duty was to enhance his subjects' "public felicity," that the church held temporal property only by leave of royal authority, and that the accumulation of fiscally immune property in the hands of the church had led to the impoverishment of the Spanish peasantry. Commonplaces in a reformist Catholic agenda as they already were, the first two premises had already undergirded legislation elsewhere, in comparison to which Campomanes's proposal was modest enough: a simple prohibition of the transfer of any more lay land to the church unaccompanied by any threat to tax land bequeathed to the church against the terms of a previous concordat of 1737.

But when Campomanes seconded by his colleague Francisco Carrasco presented this proposal to the Council of Madrid on 26 June 1765, they ran into a phalanx of opposition led by the collegiate-Jesuit Lope de Sierra backed by the council's similarly educated president, Diego Rojas Contreras, who argued that in the absence of Castilian precedents no such proposal could become law without the papacy's concurrence. But the most effective counterattack mounted by Lope de Sierra was his contention that the real cause of peasant impoverishment was the extent of *mayorazgos*, or noble entailed land, thereby serving notice to a certain nobility that it too had a stake in this debate. Knowing full well that his project could not hope to succeed in taking on the Spanish nobility allied with the clergy and that the king was getting cold feet, Campomanes effected a strategic retreat, one that was to prove permanent. But not before the substance of the debates leaked into the public sphere and alarmed the nobility and clergy alike.[67]

The only hints that Campomanes's proposal might be aimed at Jesuits in particular were a few asides in his *Tratado* about illicit commerce by regulars and the manipulation of the wills of widows by their confessors—both stock-in-trade in anti-Jesuit discourse. But it was otherwise with the issue of the tithe on ecclesiastical property and the success of the Jesuits in eluding it. No sooner had Carlos III acceded to Spain's throne than he found himself besieged by complaints from cathedral chapters in Mexico about the Jesuits' exemptions from the tithe, and by requests that he rescind a sweetheart "contract" between his predecessor and the Jesuits obliging them to pay only a thirtieth on their property instead of a tenth. Although in 1501 the papacy had given the Spanish Crown the right to collect the tithe in its colonies in the interests of the clergy's services, this right had seldom trumped the Jesuits' papal privileges. The result, as Palafox had earlier complained, was that the secular clergy had lost income in proportion as the Jesuits accumulated landed property. Nor had this new contract prevented Jesuits from wringing similar reductions after 1750 from bishops in parts of Argentina or from refusing to pay the tithe on land leased to others in Chile, producing complaints by the secular clergy in both places.[68]

The new king clearly wished to change this state of affairs to the benefit of the secular clergy. But in order to do so, he had to work with the appropriate councils, those of the Indies and its subcouncil, or Hall of Justice, both of them philo-Jesuit strongholds where his initiatives got lost in a bureaucratic labyrinth of passive resistance. It was not until January 1764 that the Council of the Indies took up the case of the Mexican request, only to send it to its Hall of Justice, where it languished for months until the king ordered the whole Council of the Indies to advise him on it. Delivered in mid-July 1765, the "advice" was that the advice should come from the Hall of Justice, which was also the advice of an extraordinary junta the king convened to instruct him on a related case, about whether the Jesuits should pay the full tithe on *novales*, or recently acquired property, in Argentina. Besides alienating the Jesuits and some of their collegial allies, all the king had to show for his efforts by the spring of 1766 was a unilateral decision against the Jesuits in Chile. And aside from the common cause that the Jesuits could make with the whole clergy on the taxation of novales—one of many unpopular fiscal measures attributed to Esquilache—the Jesuits by the same token had alienated the colonial secular clergy as well as less privileged regular orders.[69]

A final issue concerned the Jesuits uniquely, highlighting the degree of their vulnerability after Portugal had expelled them and France had dissolved their institute. The issue was the status of eighty-some French Jesuits who had refused to take the oath of loyalty to their king and the Gallican liberties imposed by the various parlements, and had discreetly sought and found refuge in Spain with the permission of their general and Spanish provincial superiors—but not the secular authorities or even bishops.[70] It was a hostile bishop, Palmero y Rallo of Girona, who brought the matter to the attention of the council. The debate again pitted Campomanes against Lope de Sierra, with the philo-Jesuits arguing that Spain should accept as many French Jesuits who wished to come there, on the grounds of natural law that protected refugees persecuted for no reason other than their refusal to swear an oath that condemned an order admitted in Spain, Against Lope de Sierra, Campomanes argued that the refusal by the Jesuits to take an oath requiring them only to loyalty to only four "perfectly orthodox" Gallican liberties put them in a "state of war with their own nation" and thus in a class incompatible with citizenship in any state. Starting from a standard of "patriotism" against which Jesuits fell short, Campomanes buttressed his position by pinning on them the ethical casuistry of "probabilism" that legitimized tyrannicide, a theory implicitly condemned by the first of the Gallican articles as well as by the Council of Constance.[71]

Supported again by the president, Diego Rojas Contreras, Lope de Sierra again won the debate, although the decision of 23 August 1764 fixed the legal number of Jesuit refugees at its current level and forbade them from polemicizing against the French parlements. But the debate also revealed to what extent Campomanes had absorbed the essentials of "patriotic" Gallicanism from across the Pyrenees by that date.[72]

While by 1766, in sum, Carlos III's reforming government had targeted the Jesuits for a number of theological, ecclesiastical, political, and fiscal reasons, it had also given the Jesuits as many reasons to target it. The Jesuits were, moreover, intricately interconnected with many segments of the population whose interests were similarly threatened by the new regime's changes in social complexion and measures of reforms: with the Spanish faction of the grandes de España, such as the ducque d'Alba, displaced from the levers of power; with the Ensenada faction headed by Ensenada himself, still aspiring to reclaim Esquilache's place at the helm of the realm's finances; with the higher nobility as a whole, threatened by disamortization of entailed estates and signories; and with other regular orders, similarly menaced in their property as well as a reduction of their numbers. Nor could the secular clergy feel secure, since the proposed limitation of amortized property affected churchmen threatened by the regime's simultaneous attempt to tighten the collection of an annual parish tax known as the *excusado*.[73]

Sharing and giving voice to the grievances of all these privileged sectors though they did, the Jesuits also stood out as the group most readily expendable. In the spectacular light of the precedents in France and Portugal across Spain's borders, the Jesuits were all too obvious as scapegoats.

Except as confessors, the Spanish Jesuits shared fewer grievances with other segments of the population, such as Madrid' poorer residents, who remained ungrateful for Esquilache's many urban improvements—spacious boulevards, oil-lighted lamps—because it was they whose increased urban taxes paid for them. Conspicuously among these improvements stood the stricter policing of Madrid. By all accounts, one such measure united two of these grievances: a rigorously enforced law banning the wearing of theft-facilitating Spanish capes and wide-rimmed sombreros, to be replaced by imported French tricornered hats and redingotes. Promulgated by the unpopular "foreigner" Esquilache on 10 March, it was this law that put the spark to the tinder of the uprising in Madrid during the Holy Week of 23–26 March 1766.

THE HATS AND CAPES RIOTS AND THE EXPULSION OF THE JESUITS FROM SPAIN, 1766–1767

Known alternately as the Hats and Capes or Esquilache Riots, the uprising in Madrid set off a grassfire-like series of uprisings in ten or so other Spanish cities and even more villages that lasted well into April before burning out.[74] Most historians as well as contemporaries have attributed this outbreak of popular violence to a spike in prices in basic commodities due to a series of bad harvests culminating in that of 1765, an effect compounded by the recent elimination of fixed prices and the disorganization of public storehouses on the heels of the recent liberalization of the grain trade. Spain was therefore to be no more fortunate than France or the Italian states in the timing of this experiment in up-to-date political economy, although sabotaging by local administrators and large landowners seems to have added to the misery in Spain's case.

But, in contrast with provincial cities, Madrid was well provisioned. Yet there too an upsurge in scurrilous antigovernmental squibs and broadsides preceded, accompanied, and continued well after the violence, which for its part displayed a discipline, organization, and political direction largely absent from the

violence in other cities. After venting itself against a much hated mercenary urban police force known as the Walloon Guard and the residences of "foreign"
ministers, such as Esquilache and Grimaldi, a crowd of twenty thousand to
thirty thousand Madrileños congealed before the royal palace during the day of
24 March and put a friar up to writing down a list of demands that a frightened
Carlos III granted from the balcony in person. The news of the king's flight that
night to his residence at Aranjuez fanned suspicions of royal bad faith, resulting
in renewed violence, which did not abate until the king had confirmed and
added to his promises the next day. Written down by a well-known Franciscan
preacher, Juan de Cuenca, the demands amounted to a reduction in the prices
of bread, butter, and oil, the revocation of Esquilache's decree forbidding sombreros and capes, the destitution of the foreign ministers, and the abolition of
the Walloon Guard, to which list the crowd added the king's return to Madrid
and a general pardon after his flight to Aranjuez.

That the crowd was not wrong to distrust royal good faith became apparent
as soon as the king did not immediately return to Madrid but stayed in Aranjuez, not to return to the royal palace until the first of December. But the full
extent of the renunciation of the royal concessions did not become clear until the
promulgation on 5 May of an *auto accord*, or self-motivated decree, that annulled
all the concessions, including those reducing prices, except—provisionally—in
Madrid, while also ordering local authorities to find and punish the authors of
both the uprisings and the political squibs. In an effort to enlist the support of
local notables for the new system of free trade in grain, this decree also provided
for the periodic election of magistrates, or *alcaldes*, in local town councils. Where
Madrid was concerned, Carlos did not act until a carefully orchestrated request
by the city's 115 noble grandees, the clergy, and five major guilds petitioned the
Council of Castile to ask the king to rescind the concessions extracted by violence on 24–26 March, whereupon he did so in early June. The only exceptions
were the exile of the hated Esquilache and the general pardon for participation in
the uprising, a pardon that did not extend to acts beyond 26 March. While the
members of the Walloon Guard disappeared into their barracks, ten thousand
soldiers took their place in the streets of Madrid.

These measures figured among the results of a general governmental reorganization that began on 8 April with an enlargement of the Council of State, followed the next day by the appointment of Pedro Pablo Abarca de Bolea y
Ximénes de Urrea, the conde de Aranda, as president of the Council of Castile
in place of the pro-Jesuit Diego Rojas Contreras. By promoting a militarily
accomplished—but also Aragonese—grandee nobleman to the pinnacle of administrative power, Carlos aimed to neutralize aristocratic resentment at the

exclusion of power, while keeping the Castilian party at arm's length. The appointment also momentarily reassured the Jesuits, since Aranda had graduated from a Jesuit college, acknowledged a Jesuit half-brother, and maintained cordial relations with his tutor, Tomás Cerda, and his mother's Jesuit confessor, Isidro López. At the same time, the king detached the potentially dangerous Alba from the ranks of the Castilian opposition by finding a place for him in the Council of State. Beneath the radar of these illustrious promotions, however, Carlos augmented his policy of filling pivotal positions with reform-minded and regalistic manteístas, naming Miguel de Múzquiz and Juan Antonio de Muniaín to take the place of the fallen Esquilache as secretaries of the treasury and war respectively, while replacing the collegiate Lope de Sierra with José Moñino as a fiscal in the Council of Castile. Moñino would soon become Campomanes's anti-Jesuit comrade in arms; Sierra got "graduated" to an honorific but less influential post.

Staffed with these appointees, the centerpieces of Carlos's institutional response to the crisis consisted in the enlarged Council of State, or Junta Cortesana, composed of the five secretaries of state Grimaldi, Muniaín, Múzquiz, Roda, and the philo-Jesuit naval secretary Julián Manuel de Arriaga y Ribera; the royal confessor Eleta; the former first minister Wall; and last but not least Huéscar, duque de Alba. This council's role was to advise the king on questions put to it. Alongside it, and much more powerful, was the Council of Castile, now presided over by Aranda, who took over the task of the restoration of "order." Besides the auto accord of 5 May and its many provisions, these measures included a law rigorously enforcing the press, a closing down of ecclesiastical presses in particular, the enforcement of a law of 14 December 1762 confining clerics to their parishes, plus episcopal and eventually papal permission obtained by Aranda and Grimaldi to subject ecclesiastics to arrest and interrogation by secular authorities.

What made these measures unusually enforceable in Madrid was the arrival of ten thousand soldiers there. That they subjected the press to such rigorous censorship indicates that the production of politically sedition literature had continued unabated since the uprising. That these measures bore down so directly on the church indicates that churchmen already figured on the list of suspected authors of the uprising.[75]

For meanwhile, on 15 April 1766, the bishop of Cuenca, Don Isidro Carvajal y Lancaster, the brother of Fernando VI's late philo-Jesuit minister, had written to Eleta, attributing the riots to popular reaction to Esquilache's policies aimed at limiting and taxing church property—a clear allusion to Campomanes's proposed and still pending disamortization law. Alerted, Carlos III asked the bishop of Cuenca to spell out his concerns, whereupon the bishop followed on 23 May with a Malagrida-like indictment of the king's whole reign since 1759 that construed its every setback, culminating in the riots, as divine punishment for the persecution of the church. The king himself he called a type of Ahab, the evil Israelite king to whom the prophet Elijah had vainly preached repentance. For Cuenca, the result was a two-year-long inquiry into the substance of his charges conducted by Campomanes and Moñino in the Council of Castile that ended in a public rebuke for the bishop and enforced residence in his diocese.[76]

Aranda's initial analysis of the uprising's causes pointed to little more than the obvious: successive bad harvests, high prices, and popular discontent—troubled waters in which certain elements from the elites might have fished.[77] Nor did Campomanes think otherwise, although he laid the blame on the maladministration of the experiment in free grain trade on the intendants.[78] But causal thinking rapidly took a darker turn in reaction to the ongoing appearance of subversive pamphlets. Almost alone among ministers enjoying quotidian contact with the king, by 16 April Roda apprised Aranda of Carlos's disappointment in the Council of Castile's failure to identify the authors of the uprising; it was also at Roda's prompting that the king ordered a secret realm-wide inquest into the authors of both the revolt and the pamphlets five days later and decided to postpone his return from Aranjuez to Madrid until the investigation had distinguished the gangrenous subjects from the sound ones.[79]

A royal order establishing an Extraordinary Council, or Junta, within the Council of Castile followed soon after, on 27 April, to be composed by Aranda in collaboration with Campomanes and one Miguel María de Nava y Carreño, another tomista who had voted with Campomanes on previous issues. But it was not until 13 June that at Campomanes's request Aranda obtained a royal order to constitute this Extraordinary Council in a "particular room" outside the purview of the whole council, and to add to it two more members: Pedro Ric y Egea and Luis del Valle Salazar, both of whom had also sided with Campomanes in earlier affairs. The most notable among the last four uniformly Thomist and anti-Jesuit members to join this secret council was José Moñino, who oversaw the investigation in Carvajal y Lancaster's diocese of Cuenca.[80]

The long and short of these appointments is that the officials who actually conducted the secret investigation were all enemies of the Jesuits, although they worked as a subordinate part of the Council of Castile that despite Sierra de Lope's departure remained largely sympathetic to them. Besides Aranda, the only other link between the full council and the "particular room" was Campomanes, who sat in both the councils, and was thus able to profit from any evidence that came to light in the weekly meetings of the full council, while being free to withhold the evidence gathered by the Extraordinary Council. While Aranda formally presided over the "particular room"'s proceedings as well as meetings of the full council, he chose to direct his energies toward the restoration of order and let the Extraordinary Council's investigation take the course it did without sharing his colleagues' animus against the Jesuits.

Meanwhile, Roda not only remained abreast of the findings of the Extraordinary Junta but also furnished it with additional information from the correspondence between Spanish Jesuits on the one hand and Torrigiani, their general Ricci, and the papal nuncio Lazzaro Opizio Pallavicini on the other, all of whose exchanges he had penetrated with the help of Spain's postal director, Lázaro Fernández de Angulo. What further augmented his influence in particular was the privileged access as head of the Ministry of Grace and Justice to the royal person afforded Roda by daily two-hour meetings with Carlos III and Eleta, enabling him to channel the king's directives downward while also controlling the information that reached him above. It was through Roda, Losada assured Tanucci, "that all the dispositions relating to the uprising in Madrid passed."[81] In Spain itself, in a word, the expulsion of the Jesuits was largely to be the work of Campomanes, Roda, and Eleta; of the influence wielded by the three, the least ponderous was probably that of Eleta, whose main contribution consisted in being neither a Jesuit nor a nag of the king's scrupulous conscience, as he had been in 1762. Outside Spain two additional actors proffered their advice, Vázquez in Rome to Roda and Tanucci in Naples to the king and anybody else who would listen.[82] Although in April the Neapolitan first minister had opposed the idea of a secret search for culprits behind a perennially unruly "popolaccio," his letters to the king, Losada, and Roda's successor, Nicolas José Azara, in Rome grew ever more precise in their insinuations, pointing toward "monks and priests" by late April, toward the Jesuits by May, and toward Castile's provincial procurator, Isidro López, and the former minister Ensenada and their machinations by mid-June. By late August Tanucci's accusations lofted into a call for the expulsion of the Jesuits on the French or Portuguese model.[83]

It is pointless to try to measure the comparative force of the "influence" exerted by Tanucci and Vázquez on the consciences of Roda and Carlos III or that by Roda versus Campomanes on the action of the king. (In letters to Bottari and Roda after the expulsion, Tanucci accorded the "credit" to Roda while Roda insisted that some of it was due to Tanucci.) It suffices to note that all this influence blew in an anti-Jesuit and Catholic reformist direction while the only influence to blow in the opposite direction came from the papacy and the queen-mother. As in Portugal and France, however, the philo-Jansenist Archetto in Rome played a certain role in the funneling of this influence, in Spain's case by Vázquez on site, by Roda as emeritus in Madrid, and by Tanucci as amplifier of its message in Naples. Against the Jesuits, all three also voiced such signature reformist accusations as "despotism," probabilism, and Molinism.[84]

What is quite different about Spain in comparison to France or even Portugal is that here a seismic social event had just shaken the state in the form of a totally unprededented—since the *communeros* revolt of 1520–1522—popular uprising in Castile itself, and that a thoroughly traumatized king needed reassuring explanations. As in Portugal after the attempted assassination, however, the Jesuits found themselves the only viable candidates for collective blame as soon as the government began to reckon with the reality that members of the aristocratic and clerical strata had connived at fomenting the revolt. Although factions within the titled nobility had incontestably participated in the revolt, the government could hardly incriminate the grandes de España as a group. It therefore co-opted part of the nobility by promoting Aranda and even the partially complicit Alba, while prohibiting political meetings in aristocratic residences in Madrid and staging some cautionary examples. These included Ensenada, whom it arrested and exiled on 19 April; a certain José Luis Valázquez, marqués de Valdesflores, whom it imprisoned for writing some antigovernmental tracts; plus incarcerating a few others, such as Juan de Idiáquez, brother of the Jesuit provincial superior of Castile, all of them also related to the Jesuits in some way.[85] Most of all, the government reassured the nobility by putting any reformist action against *mayorazgos* and *señoríos* on hold for the rest of Carlos III's reign.

Nor could the government incriminate the entire clergy or even the regular clergy, even though members of both played significant roles in voicing dissatisfaction with the government, the bishop of Cuenca most spectacularly so. Complaints against such taxes as the excusado and the tithe on novales also figured prominently in many of the squibs. As in the case of the nobility, the government contented itself with a few general measures, such as the shutting down of clerical printing presses and the enforcement of the residence law of 14 December 1762, plus individual shots across the bow. These featured the humiliation of the bishop of Cuenca, the imprisonment of the poor priest who had helped shape the popular demands, and the irregular arrest and lifelong imprisonment of the talented administrator and writer Abate Miguel Antonio de la Gándara Pérez, who, connected to Rávago and Ensenada faction, had undoubtedly lent his pen to the cause of the opposition during the uprising of 23–26 March.

The contrast could not have been greater between this decision and the one that determined the outcome of the concurrent debate over the Society of Jesus's duty to tithe and the validity of Fernando VI's contract of January 1750, which obliged the Society to pay only a thirtieth. In this case Carlos III weighed in on the side of the secular clergy and in December 1766 managed to have that law annulled by a vote of the same specially constituted junta that had referred the matter back to the Council of the Indies' Hall of Justice in 1765. Enshrined in royal letters patent dated 4 December 1766, this decision let it be known that no one needed to fear the Jesuits anymore.[86] The measure isolated the Jesuits not only from most of the other regular orders, which had other recent reasons to resent them, but even more from the tithe-dependent secular clergy.

Further to ensure the anti-Jesuitical orientation of the episcopacy, Roda and Eleta had meanwhile established a Sala de Conciencia within the Extraordinary Council by means of which they obtained virtual control over nominations to major benefices. But even without the help of newly nominated bishops— and in the sharpest possible contrast with the case of France—Roda was eventually able to prevail upon more than forty of Spain's fifty-six prelates to return endorsements for the state's case for expelling the Jesuits.[87] The death of the queen mother Farnese on 11 July was yet another blow to the Society, depriving the Jesuits of a staunch defender and stronghold in the palace of El Pardo as well as of an influential agent in the royal court in the person of her Jesuit confessor, Estaban Bramieri.[88] That on 23 July 1766 the Extraordinary Council followed Campomanes's advice to deny the request by Bramieri for permission to return to his native Venetia did not bode well for the fate of his Spanish colleagues. The grounds of the decision were his presence in Brazil during the time of the Guarani revolt, his possession of Spanish secrets of state, and his involvement in the uprising of 23–26 March, the last of these activities supposedly uncovered by the ongoing secret investigation.

So what evidence, it may be asked, did the Extraordinary Council's secret investigation turn up?

Even before the king's order of 21 April for this investigation, the Council of Castile exiled Ensenada from Madrid to his estates, most probably on the grounds of the popular cries for his return to power in Esquilache's place during the last two days of the uprising in Madrid. As the investigation got under way, hearsay evidence accumulated about his frequent visits to the queen mother in El Pardo and a prediction he supposedly ventured in 1764 that his rival Esquilache would not last in power for more than two years.[89] And hardly had the Council of Castile's Extraordinary Council officially begun to exist as of 27 April 1766 than the king sent to it Bishop Carvajal y Lancaster's letter of 23 May, which revealed the full extent of ecclesiastical resentment against Carlos III's policies since 1759, along with unfavorable comparisons to the reign of his predecessor and the ministry, or Ensenada.

But besides pointing to the clergy and the Ensenada faction, these pieces of evidence seemed also to vindicate Tanucci's suspicious of the Jesuits, in that both the bishop and Ensenada were notoriously partial to the Society and that Ensenada in particular was a close friend of the Society's Castilian procurator, Isidro López, and all of them friends of the queen mother and the marqués di Valdesflores. Yet another precocious piece of evidence pointing toward the Jesuits rather than to the whole clergy was a rumor conveyed to Roda by Spain's postal director that Jesuit confessors from Madrid's Colegio Imperial were assuring hospitalized rioters that they need not confess to having participated in the uprising as a sin, and that if they died they would do so having merited a martyr's crown.[90] This was of course the same postal director who later infiltrated the correspondence of the Spanish Jesuits as well as that of the papal nuncio with the cardinal secretary of state.

What above all convinced Campomanes, Roda, and others, including the king himself, that a conspiracy of the elites was behind the Eschilache uprising was the continuing proliferation of antigovernmental pamphlets and doggerel after the restoration of order. Initial decrees banning their production and dissemination remained without effect, causing the government to add the discovery of the identity of the authors and printers to the objectives of the secret investigation. And while sheer literary skill and numerous complaints about the excusado, the tithe on novales, and the violation of ecclesiastical immunities implicated the clergy in general, some incontestably pointed to Jesuits in particular. The hardest piece of evidence was perhaps a squib entitled *Geminos de España* (*The Laments of Spain*), which, asking why the realm was shedding "such sad tears," identified the reasons as the "furious" persecution of the "dear Company [of Jesus]" and the rise of "heresy" introduced by the royal confessor, all under an "atheist and monk-like king." As though that much were not damning enough, this pasquinade went on to describe the monarch as an untalented "intruder," Eleta as "without conscience," Roda as a "tyrant," Esquilache as "avaricious," Campomanes as "cruel," and the yearly tax as "Neapolitan." If—worse still—a remedy were to be found for the regime's persecution of the church or at least some of its "branches," the lampoon suggested that to kill a tyrant for "so sacred a cause" was not only a "probable opinion" but also the "surest" and "most embraced" by qualified theologians.[91]

In so many rhymed couplets, this squib encapsulates most of the Spanish Jesuits' reasons for feeling persecuted by their new monarch: Carlos's choice of a Franciscan confessor, the veneration of both for a notoriously anti-Jesuitical bishop, the reluctance of the king to come to the aid of the Jesuits' French confreres, his choice of Italians and manteísta as his ministers, and the threat posed by Campomanes and Esquilache's plans to tax hitherto exempt Jesuit proper-ties. It also contained evidence of what the members of Carlos's Extraordinary Junta would most hold against the Jesuits: spreading popular discontent with the king's rule, disseminating their probabilistic casuistry and theories of regicide, and using them to threaten the king himself with destitution, replacement, even assassination.

This lampoon and a few like it are among the stronger pieces of evidence that the Extraordinary Junta's investigation turned up—so public that the nuncio Pallavicini sent it on to Torrigiani, and damning enough to be the one that Tanucci probably singled out as "manifestly [penned] by a Jesuit or one of [the Society's] tertiaries."[92] Less to the point but no less real was evidence open to interpretation as impinging on the crime of lesa majestad concerning Jesuit complicity in the composition, publication, dissemination, or mere possession of other forms of illicit literature. Already targeted as the author of a refutation of Campomanes's treatise on amortization, for example, one Pedro Antonio de Catalayud had also used the College of San Andres in Navarre to distribute translations of literature in defense of fellow persecuted French and Portuguese Jesuits, for which—one of the rare Jesuits to be punished individually—he paid by being forbidden to preach.[93]

In this activity he acted far from alone, since the inspection of several other Jesuit houses in Navarre included similar caches of such material, including pamphlets, translated and printed defenses of the Society of Jesus from nearby France, and unauthorized copies of Clement XIII's spirited defense of the Soci-ety in the brief *Apostolicum Pascendi* of 1765. In Navarre, where the French pro-vincial superior of Aquitaine, Charles Nectoux, had sought and obtained refuge, the secret inquest hit its richest pay dirt, uncovering scattered evidence of Jesuit encouragement of the popular risings as well as illicit publications.[94] Not only did the publications of French defenses of the Jesuits violate the con-ditions of the admission of some French Jesuits into Spain as stipulated in 1764, they also inevitably spilled over into attacks on the Bourbon dynasty regnant and allied in France and Spain alike.

Still, none of this evidence hit Carlos III directly. It was otherwise with dis-course attributed to Jesuits or to their influence against the reputation of Palafox, the king's favorite candidate for canonization. In the one case most clearly linked to Jesuits, this "discourse" took the form of meaning-laden action against Palafox's printed works when the Jesuit tutors of the king's own son, the prince of Asturias, spirited them out of the prince's library. By itself, however—and quite apart from being pinned or not on Jesuits—this discourse was dangerous because the partiality of the king and his confessor for Palofox functioned as the most clinching evidence of "heresy" in the highest places, while royal heresy was in turn the most damning of the many national "sins" widely held responsible for Spain's foreign and domestic misfortunes since Carlos III's accession in 1759. Worse—and here the reported discourse crossed the boundary into lesa majestad—heresy was the most contagious of the misdeeds that qualified a king as a "tyrant." In the casuistry of tyrannicide, tyranny notoriously justified revolt, even assassination.

Hence the incriminating implications of reports from numerous parts of the kingdom, especially Cataluña, where the canon Francisco Berga and the captain Juan Albach undertook the gathering of evidence in Girona and Barcelona, respectively.[95] From Girona came reports that before the uprising a Jesuit had predicted that "some rumble" would soon be heard against the royal court, while shortly after the uprising another Gironese Jesuit reportedly interpreted the appearance of a comet as a sign of the imminent death of the king at the hands of the "newly risen people of Madrid."[96] From Barbastro came a report that one Hermandez y Arnal, rector of the Jesuit College of Zaragoza, had opined that "God had on many occasions transferred [kingdoms] to some other prince due to the sins of the Realm and people" and that during the uprising itself he also announced an imminent "change in the scepter of the . . . House of Bourbon due to sins that he supposed." Another report used as evidence in Campomanes's Dictamen fiscal de la expulsión de los jesuitas de España had a Jesuit predicting as early as 1759 that Carlos's reign would not last longer than seven years—until 1766, to be precise. Such reports came from Dominicans, Franciscans, cathedral canons, secular officials, and even merchants; but with a geographical concentration in the provinces of Aragón and Cataluña near France.

One casualty of the investigation was a young nobleman by the name of Don Juan Francisco de Salazar Calvete Ladrón de Guevara, sentenced to a gruesome death on 28 June 1766 for a regicidal utterance that "the revolt would not die down until Bourbon blood had flowed." He had also once studied—alas— grammar and music in Murcia with the Jesuit Juan Girón, who later surfaced as a professor in the Colegio Imperial in Madrid.[97]

If the bulk of this largely hearsay evidence produced by the Extraordinary Junta's investigation incriminated the Spanish Jesuits, the reason is that this is the sort of evidence toward which Campomanes's instructions directed his informants.[98] A comparably intensive focus toward segments of the clergy and the nobility equally disaffected by Carlos III's policies might well have produced similar results, some of which surfaced along the way. If the investigation of disaffected clergymen or nobles led to relations with Jesuits, the reverse is also the case: the investigation of disaffected Jesuits led to connections to clergymen or nobles. The Extraordinary Council had eliminated the "people" as the culprit as early as 8 June. So if blame had to be located, and some privileged corporate group had to bear it, the Jesuits were clearly more expendable than either the clergy or the nobility. Last but not least, the recent examples of Portugal and France were close at hand to suggest them as expiatory victims.

The point at which the "particular room"'s investigation began to single out the Jesuits occurred sometime in June at the earliest, by which time Tanucci's letters to Roda bristled with accusations against the Jesuits, or in September at the latest, by which time decisions in the royal court and the "particular room" clearly began to outpace Tanucci's fears that "neither the King nor Signor Dom Emmanuel have arms sufficient for combating [the Jesuits and Rome]."[99] Compromising though it was, however, not even the evidence of incriminating literature discovered in the Jesuit colleges in the Basque country proved anything more than that many Spanish Jesuits had reason to be unhappy with the reign of Carlos III from its outset and had welcomed the uprisings of the Holy Week of 1766 as evidence that these events might bring about a change for the better, perhaps with a little literary encouragement by themselves. As the Spanish Jesuit superiors themselves readily conceded, some had clearly fished in troubled waters.[100]

Tanucci need not have worried, however, since by 11 September, the die had in fact been clearly cast when Campomanes submitted to the Extraordinary Junta an *alegación*, or denunciation, singling out members of a certain "religious body" as the "secret authors" of the revolt, as well as pamphlets by means of which they had attracted adherents from other parts of the church with a view to inspiring a "general aversion for the government" and its attempt to reform "abuses debilitating the state." To the alegación Campomanes added a *consulta* requesting the king to give the Extraordinary Council power to go well beyond a verdict: indeed, nothing less than the authority to override ecclesiastical privileges in view of executive action justified by a law promulgated by the Cortes of Segovia in 1390. Construed by Campomanes as a "fundamental law," that law had asserted royal authority over monks who publicly declaimed against the sovereign. Supported by a letter by Aranda delivered by way of Roda to the king, this request received royal approval in a *cédula* dated 14 September after Carlos III had had it examined by the enlarged Council of State set up in early April. Whether Aranda realized it or not, Campomanes and Roda had endowed the Extraordinary Junta with the sole power to punish as well as judge the guilty party, thereby doing an end run around the full and still philo-Jesuit Council of Castile. Not to leave anything to chance, Campomanes persuaded the king to confirm these powers by means of a royal decree, which also enlarged the Extraordinary Junta from five to eight members.[101]

An additional action by the Extraordinary Junta on 1 October delegated the task of composing a full report on the secret investigation to Campomanes, who submitted it on 31 December. Remaining in Campomanes's private archive until the historians J. Cejudo López and Teófanes Egido López published it in 1977—the archive itself did not open its doors until 1973—Campomanes's *Dictamen fiscal de espulsión de los jesuitas de España* served as the legal basis for Carlos III's expulsion of the Jesuits from Spain.[102]

REFORM CATHOLICISM SPAIN'S PUBLIC CASE AGAINST THE JESUITS

Within the magma of information turned up by the Extraordinary Junta's inquest, Campomanes discerned a pattern of persistent conspiracy by the Jesuits against a monarchy and ministry that had deprived them of all dignities, benefices, and positions of power and means of influence, beginning with that of royal confessor in 1759. Thus had the Jesuits conspired against Carlos III's reign from the outset. To that end they set out to defame the monarchy in the eyes of his pious subjects by means of rumors ranging from the attachment to heresy of the king and his confessor to the king's adulterous affair with the marquese de Esquilache, and going so far as to predict with precision the year and the season of the uprising—the Holy Week of 1766—that would unseat him, perhaps even assassinate him. Along the way, the Jesuits also plotted to block the monarchy's every reformist initiative that threatened their material means of power, whether by obligating them to pay the tithe or to limit their accumulation of privileged property—Campomanes's own pet project—by law.[103]

Like most contemporary observers, Campomanes distinguished between an initial popular and spontaneous phase of Madrid's uprising and a second and politically motivated phase following Carlos III's acceptance of a list of demands and flight to Aranjuez. But for Campomanes, not even the initial phase was wholly spontaneous, as Jesuits fanned and exploited popular discontent with high prices, foreign ministers, and the unfortunately enforced decree against capes and sombreros in order to create an uprising in which they might realize their goals. In ascending order, these consisted in the replacement of Eleta with a Jesuit confessor; the replacement of Carlos's "foreign" ministers with an Ensenada-led ministry; and the assassination and replacement of the king himself along with his dynasty, the better to reorient Spain's domestic and pro-French foreign policies.

In Spain itself, the chief actors in this conspiracy were Ensenada and the Jesuits López and Bramieri plus their allies, such as Gándara and Valdesflores; in Madrid, the chief nerve centers were the queen mother's quarters in El Pardo and the Jesuits' Colegio Imperial, which on its side was well connected to provincial strongholds in Cuenca, Cataluña, Navarre, and the Basque provinces. Jesuits not only distributed money that they claimed came from the queen mother but themselves donned secular garb and descended into the streets. Imitating the young Louis XIV's flight to Saint-Germain during the French Fronde in 1649, Carlos III's flight to Aranjuez foiled the plans of the plotters, whereupon the Jesuits responded with additional demands designed to force the king to break faith, an intensified campaign of literary vilification, and the staging of a plethora of provincial uprisings that were to culminate in another assault in Madrid the following November.

This much of Campomanes's case against the Spanish Jesuits is particular to Spain, just as the revolt of the Guaraní tribesmen or the attempted assassination of José I are particular to Portugal. Like Carvalho in Portugal, however, Campomanes had to make these particulars plausible as parts of a Jesuit conspiracy. The expansive description of the conspiracy itself constituted the first stage in the case, including events from 1759 to 1766 in all parts of Spain and even the colonial empire, and tactics ranging from polemical publications to actions in the street. The second and most crucial stage was to argue that only the Society of Jesus had the requisite organizational capacity to perpetrate such a conspiracy by means of its top-down "despotic" structure, from the unrestrained power of the general and "blindly obedient" subordinates to its international scope that made it a state within every other Catholic state, even in the capital of Catholicity, Rome. Not even the Spanish monarchy would by this logic have been capable of marshaling such force against another monarchy, deprived as it was of the totally unreasoned obedience of all of its subjects, much less of a multitude of ready and willing agents in other realms.[104]

Such was Campomanes's emphasis on the Society's combination of "despotism" and "blind obedience" between and within each rung of the hierarchical ladder that the variations of the two terms occur no fewer than sixteen times in the *Dictamen:* twelve for "despotism" or "despotic" and four for "blind obedience" or "blindly obeying." So insistent was Campomanes on this theme that when he broached the inevitable subject of the Jesuit presence in Paraguay, the emphasis fell not on the putative Jesuit complicity in the Guaraní revolt in Portugal and Spain—Campomanes allowed that the Treaty of Madrid had not been in Spain's best interests—but on the "slavery" to which the Jesuits' "despotic" regime had supposedly reduced the native population.

That his use of the adjective "absolute" as synonymous with "despotic" might have untoward implications for the "absolute" authority of the Spanish Bourbon monarchy Campomanes served escaped his attention, and it represents a quite partial reading of the Jansenized Gallican and parlementary sources on which he was partially dependent.[105] To be sure, the fiscal cited Spanish authors, such as Cano, Arias Montano, and above all Palafox, in preference to others; he also cleverly hispanized d'Etemare's and Pavie de Fourquveaux's Jesuit-plot theory by replacing the Spaniard Laínez with the Italian Claudio Acquaviva as the general who distorted Ignatius's intentions while following Le Paige in adding "despotic" constitutions to doctrinal deviations. But no more in Spain than in Portugal had the charge of "despotic" authority hitherto formed part of the case against the Jesuits.

The same is true for the charge that the final purpose of the Jesuits' international state was the political power of that state itself. Already audible in Pasquier's charge that the Society's ultimate concern was its "absolute power" and "commodity of its affairs," the accusation that the Society's signature goals of the glory of God and vindication of papal authority only imperfectly masked the real goal of "universal monarchy" had come to a crescendo by the mid-eighteenth century. Nowhere in his *Dictamen* did Campomanes even use the term "ultramontanism," even though by land Spain was separated from Rome by even more mountains than France was. The Council of Castile's fiscal was willing to allow that in most cases the Society had found it in its best interests to further the spiritual and temporal pretentions of the papacy. But more prominent in his *Dictamen* were examples of its opposition to papal authority, as in the cases of the refusal by the Spanish Jesuits to obey Benedict XIV's order to remove Noris's *Historia Pelagiana* from the Spanish Inquisition's Index or Pope Clement XI's prohibition of the "idolatrous" accommodations to Chinese rites in 1704 or even—most startlingly—their success in persuading the same pope to promulgate the bull *Unigenitus* against the papacy's own best interests.[106] In these cases as in others, Campomanes's quite Augustinian choice of doctrinal deviations to denounce indicates less a catechetical conviction than a politically seasonable tactic of accusing the Jesuits of themselves employing doctrinal denunciations as a means toward a political power apart from even the papacy's.[107] While fomenting the Jansenist and like schisms the better to profit from the resultant divisions was one such means, others named by Campomanes were the accumulation of riches, the use of defamatory and satirical publications, and the capacity to enroll lay agents via its secret congregations.[108]

Chief among these means was the moral casuistry of probabilism and its use to justify tyrannicide. The relation between probabilism and tyrannicide was a charge all the more potent for Campomanes and the Extraordinary Junta, in that by this time at least Campomanes considered the uprisings of March and April 1766 to have been an exercise in tyrannicide with the aim of ridding the realm not only of Carlos III but his dynasty as well. While acknowledging that many theologians other than Jesuits had dabbled in the casuistry of probabilism, Campomanes credited the Jesuits alone in the person Acquaviva with the originality of both adopting these ethics for his society and transforming it into a "despotism." That only some Jesuits, such as Mariana, had dabbled with the doctrine of tyrannicide made no difference in the case of the Society because its uniquely probabilistic profession of faith transformed their opinions into probable ones, and therefore licit for any "blindly obedient" Jesuit to act on under orders of his superiors. It was for this reason that in Campomanes's logic it was impossible to individuate moral responsibility for actions and opinions in the case of the Jesuits. Hence the logic of punishing the Society as a whole rather than such individuals as Bramieri, Catalayud, and López—the names that stand out in the *Dictamen*—along with conclusion that it was irreformable and fit only for expulsion.[109]

In keeping with his general policy of citation, Campomanes minimized the number of Spain's Jesuit villains and maximized the number of its anti-Jesuit saints. Thus did he replace Laínez with Acquaviva as the architect of the Society's adoption of a probabilistic morality while crediting Palafox rather than Pascal as the first to denounce it. But heretofore as foreign to Spanish as to Portuguese anti-Jesuitism, only in the early eighteenth-century combination of Gallicanism and Jansenism—of Pasquier with Pascal—was probabilism finally linked with tyrannicide in a deadly relation of means to ends, to which Le Paige and others had added despotism as the teleological structure in which it operated. However or wherever Campomanes came by it, this discourse was as porous as Spain's border with Portugal.

Campomanes needed only one more segment from that classic Gallican-Jansenist case against the Jesuits in order to frame the empirical particulars uncovered by the Extraordinary Junta's investigation and to draw the obvious programmatic conclusions from it. The frame's needed addition was the historically based contention that the "ordinary" clerical hierarchy of bishops and priests was the only divinely mandated clergy, while the regular clergy was a belated human addition to it, giving secular states the divine right to judge the utility of particular religious orders and to accept or reject them accordingly. The desired conclusion was that Carlos III had the God-given right to judge the Society of Jesus to be inadmissible by any civilized state and expel it from Spain and all its dominions.

That this expulsion was necessary was the conclusion of a reasoned *consulta* together with a formal indictment based closely on Campomanes's *Dictamen*. Submitted by him to the Extraordinary Junta along with the supporting evidence from the secret inquest on 4 January 1767, this *consulta* obtained that junta's approval on 29 January 1767, whereupon it went to the king by way of Roda on 30 January. A conscientious Carlos III sent it for further review to the enlarged Junta Cortesana established on 8 April 1766. Although that council included the pro-Jesuit Manuel de Arriaga along with all the other secretaries of state, Eleta and Roda contrived to exclude him from this meeting, and the outcome was never in doubt. The Junta Cortesana approved the Extraordinary Council's *consulta* and indictment with just a few changes, sending them back to the king, who approved the whole on 20 February.[110] In consequence, Carlos issued a royal "pragmatic sanction" together with a decree of expulsion and sent them to Aranda for execution on 27 February.[111] But the king predated these measures to the day of their execution on 2 April, keeping them under lock and key until then. The pragmatic saction itself similarly hid the "weighty reasons" for the expulsion within the king's "royal self."[112]

Given the precedents in Portugal and France, it could hardly have come as a total surprise to even Torrigiani when at the appointed time Carlos III's decree revealed that he had decided to expel all Jesuits from his domains. Aranda executed the decree with military precision, in Madrid during the night on 31 March, in the rest of Spain on 2–3 April, and in the colonies as the winds and tides permitted. Although the decree provided the exiled fathers with a pension, their fate was to be as lamentable as that of their Portuguese counterparts, seeing that Clement XIII refused to accept any more Jesuits in the Papal States and neither Genoa nor France could adequately provide for them after Spanish boats began unloading them on a Corsica even less hospitable than usual on account of a civil war that ended with French annexation. Although Louis XV had Choiseul accommodate his cousin on the Corsican solution as best he could, the local commander of the French garrison at first refused to land the Jesuits at Bastia, much to Spanish impatience, until eventually moving French troops elsewhere to make room for the Jesuits, much to Genoa's chagrin. When by virtue of the Treaty of Compiègne Corsica became a French possession later that year, the presence of the Jesuits became untenable there, and Genoa looked the other way as they disembarked and with tacit papal permission made their way via Modena to the papal legations in Italy. Those Jesuits who eventually arrived in Italy did so in somewhat fewer numbers, as death and voluntary secularizations took their toll.[113]

That Spanish Jesuits disliked Carlos III's regime and that some dabbled in opposition to it is beyond doubt. So too, however, is that the Extraordinary

Council and its secret inquest had framed the uprising of 23–26 March as a uniquely Jesuit problem in order to justify this surgical solution. Yet there is no reason to suppose that the chief perpetrators of the expulsion did not believe their own case. Such was the persuasive power of this Gallican-Jansenist frame that the king himself was totally taken in by it.[114]

On 13 April 1767, shortly after the execution of his pragmatic sanction of expulsion, Carlos III called aside the French ambassador, Pierre-Paul, marquis d'Ossun, to assure him that he had come into the possession of "certain proofs that several disguised members of the Society had figured in the midst of the revolt that took place in Madrid the previous year, animating and directing the rebels as well as distributing money on behalf of and in the name, they claimed, of the late queen mother." The king added that Esquilache's decree against capes and hats had only functioned as pretexts of the revolt in Madrid, as had the "dearness of grain or this criminal *corregidor* or that odious intendant" in the revolts in the provinces, and that the real reason was the "revolution" that the Jesuits had been planning since his accession in 1759 "on the pretense of the preservation of the faith and right doctrine that they deemed in danger of annihilation under the regnant princes in both Naples and Spain." The Society's real "project" in Ossun's account of the conversation was nothing less than "exterminating all the Bourbons in Spain."[115] So convinced of the Jesuits' guilt was this king that he was to become the driving force behind Portugal and the Bourbon dynasty's goal of forcing the papacy to dissolve the entire Society after the Bourbon family pact added this suppression to its policy goals in 1768.

Just as persuaded were the French ambassador and Choiseul. In view of the "enormity of the conduct of the Jesuits in this realm," so convinced did Ossun profess himself that he could only agree with Carlos III when the king later told him that he considered the punishment of the Society an act of royal clemency.[116] Speaking for Louis XV himself, Choiseul assured Ossun of his agreement that "the members of that Society who live under the authority of His Most Catholic King must have been very guilty to have prompted that king to take such decisive measures against them."[117] Although Louis XV was to remain less persuaded by the evidence of Jesuit misdeeds than any of his fellow dynasts, on this occasion he asked the Spanish via Choiseul to share any information resulting from their investigations that might concern France, while assuring his Spanish cousin of his support.[118]

No such information ever materialized for France. As good as his word, Carlos III indeed kept his "weighty reasons" within the secrecy of his "royal soul" as a principle of state. A display of "projection" on his part, the "revolution" he espied at the time of his accession more correctly refers to the "revolution" in intra-Catholic religious, ecclesiastical, and political direction undertaken by the monarchy since the fall of Ensenada and by his own regime, the adversarial reaction to which he interpreted in conspiratorial terms. Conspiratorial interpretations of events and developments are common enough among Carlos's eighteenth-century contemporaries, both high and low, and may by itself account for the ability of the king and his ministers alike to generalize from evidence implicating four or five Jesuits to the entire Society in Spain.[119] So hallucinatory were some of these perceptions that they cannot be taken as other than sincere. What is otherwise to be made of the Carlos's profound relief, reported in diplomatic code by the French ambassador Ossun, at the news that the unfortunate French Jesuit Antoine Lavalette of Martinique mission bankruptcy ill fame had finally been arrested in France itself—proof positive, the king thought, that he was not in South America aiding and abetting English anti-Spanish plots and plans, as he had feared?[120]

The only judicial evidence against the Jesuits to see the light of published day was the trial record of a clerk named Benito Navarro, who initially denounced a certain Don Juan de Barranchán along with Barranchán's former employer Don Joseph Michel de Flores and a priest named Don Sylvester de Palomares. Navarro denounced Barranchán for forging letters in an attempt to implicate notoriously pro-Jesuit nobles as well as of taking a hand in the composition of antiministerial pamphlets that had emanated from Jesuit or Jesuit-allied pens.[121] As for Palomares, Navarro accused him of having falsely testified that during the uprising the Jesuit Isidor López had stood at the door of the Colegio Imperial calling for Ensenada to take the place of Esquilache at the head of the royal ministry, while the Jesuit Girón had busily preached sedition in his sermons. It was perhaps not by accident that Barranchán, Flores, and Palomares were all associated with the notoriously anti-Jesuit Scolopian Congregation as well as with proponents of the beatification of Palafox.

But midway through the trial, Navarro proved unable to sustain his judicial "confrontation" with Flores, and in a dramatic turnaround accused the accused Jesuits of having put him up to his denunciations of Barranchán and the others, the better to throw the judges off the trail of López and Girón and other Jesuit authors of these acts and pamphlets, all of them associated with the Colegio Imperial. Besides writing squibs such as an "Anti-Edict" supposedly revoking the royal edict prohibiting these squibs, Navarro now also accused these same Jesuits of having seditiously grumbled about the Eschilache ministry before the uprising, cheered on the rioters while it transpired, and translated several French defenses of their society, including Cerutti's *Apologie* and the archbishop of Paris's pastoral instruction.[122] Where the Jesuits' reputation for lax morality was concerned, Navarro's most damning charge was that these Jesuits had persuaded him that his false accusation was not a sin, because it served the "greater glory of God [and] the honor of the Society," to wit, that the direction of intention toward a laudable end justified a reprehensible means.[123]

This published show trial cannot of course be taken at face value and must be interpreted with extreme caution. It nonetheless featured many of the persons, publications, and events that figured in the evidence used by Campomanes to build his case in his *Dictamen*. Since the trial record pointed toward the indictment of three or four Jesuits besides Navarro himself, it also illustrates the conspiratorial logic driving Campomanes's case: that where two or three deviant Jesuits were concerned, there was the whole Society also. For while Navarro got off with a mere four years in prison in view of his Jesuit-inculcated "blind obedience" and "invincible ignorance," every last Spanish Jesuit got expelled.

In the absence of a regicide and with only a riot as a reason, this indictment was as close to an official account as Spanish justifications for the expulsion would ever come—unless it was a published *Consulta del Consejo de Castilla* (*Consultation of the Council of Castile*) in response to Pope Clement XIII's brief of 30 April 1767 to Carlos III in person in defense of the Jesuits and in an effort to persuade the king to suspend if not rescind his measures against them.[124]

The published *Consulta* is to the *Dictamen* what the *Dictamen's* frame is to its evidence: that is, a reformist Catholic frame without the supporting evidence of complicity in the uprising and its sequels. To be sure, the *Consulta* mentioned the Jesuits' putative complicity in the uprising, but only to assure Clement XIII that, far from being the "only motive or reason for [the Society's] banishment," the other reasons weighed just as if not more heavily in the balance. The other reasons turned out to be commonplaces of the reformist Catholic case against the Jesuits, the chief being that under the pretenses of the defense of doctrinal orthodoxy and dedication to the papacy, the Society's real goal was a universal "domination" that made it incompatible with any temporal sovereignty, much less the papacy's spiritual authority.

For the *Consulta* as for the *Dictamen*, that goal dictated the means to attain it, which consisted chiefly in the society's "despotic" structure characterized by an "alienation of power in the hands of a general in violation of canon law"; the inculcation of an intellectual "slavery" of its members in violation of natural law; a system of mutual espionage among these members in violation of divine law; an internal secrecy; and an accumulation of privileges in violation of royal law. As in the *Dictamen*, in the *Consulta* the anatomy of the Jesuits' constitutions demonstrated the impossibility of partial culpability in a religious society so organized that its members acted as "mere machines" without will except as animated by the "corrupt core" at its center.[125]

A trace perhaps of Roda's hand, the *Consulta*'s chief difference from the *Dictamen* is a greater emphasis on the doctrinal case against the Jesuits. Although both the *Dictamen* and the *Consulta* mentioned the works of Hardouin and Berruyer—even the bishop of Soissons's pastoral instruction against them—the *Consulta* dared to tread where Pope Paul IV had not and to qualify the Jesuits' preference for Molinism over the theology of Augustine and Thomas Aquinas as "heretical."[126]

As in the case of Portugal, it is curious to behold a dynastic regime that had neither parlements to pester it nor Cortes to counter it from proceeding so publicly to indulge in anti-"despotic" rhetoric against a society hitherto linked so closely to the regime. But so pervasive had this rhetoric become throughout Catholic Europe by the late eighteenth century that it overrode domestic political implications that seemed quite clear in retrospect, beginning perhaps in 1770 in France, when Louis XV felt obliged to explain to his Spanish royal cousin that his antidespotic parlements had become such a challenge to his royal authority that he had to opt to go to war with them rather than on the side of Spain against England in their dispute over the Falkland Islands.

While Bourbon Spain clamped down on coverage of the riots and expulsion, the French press rushed in, led by Antoine Boudet in Paris, who produced a *Recueil des pièces concernant les jésuites d'Espagne* (*A Collection of Documents Concerning the Jesuits of Spain*), followed by ten *Suite*[s] or *Sequel*[s] in the original Spanish accompanied by French translations by 1768. Established in the rue Saint-Jacques in Paris amid a veritable row of Jansenist printers, Boudet did not specialize in the publication of Jansenist literature as did the Lottin family and numbers of others. Yet he was not devoid of Jansenist credentials, having spent time in the Bastille in 1747 for complicity in the printing of the *Nouvelles ecclésiastiques*, since when he had traveled to Spain and Portugal and established connections in both places. Nor for that matter was the *Nouvelles* inactive, covering as it did Boudet's *Recueil* and its many sequels. As for the translators, Le Paige provides a glimpse of himself in action in a small manuscript note on the defects of the first French translation of Carlos III's Pragmatic Sanction of 1767, together with all of his corrections.[127]

To firm up French Jansenist connections in Spain, the abbé Clément took to the road again in 1768, this time to Spain, with the same goal of finding support for a bull modeled on *Aspicientes* that would swing the papal pendulum back toward Augustinian and away from Molinist doctrine.[128] But Clément also hoped to influence the reform of canonical and theological education in the universities and church in Spain. Whether due to his influence or not, succeeding years witnessed a rise in the currency of Augustinian theology, rigorist ethics, and the replacement of ultramontanist with neo-Gallican canon law, which on the eve of the French Revolution found inspiration in the canons of the Synod of Pistoia in universities such as the University of Salamanca. An article in the *Courrier du Bas-Rhin* exposing him as a Jansenist in pursuit of sectarian interests persuaded Clément to cut short his stay in Spain, but not before extensive exchanges of views with Bishop José Climent in Barcelona and Miguel López in Saragossa as well as interviews with Campomanes in Madrid and Roda at the Escorial, some of whom—Roda most notably—he enlisted as epistolary communicants of the Church of Utrecht. As in Portugal, a Jansenist "movement" in Spain was more the result than the cause of the expulsion of the Jesuits.

5

NAPLES, PARMA, AND THE BOURBON
FAMILY PACT, 1767-1773

As it happened, the friends, correspondents, and relatives of the abbé Clément once again found themselves at the quasi-conspiratorial center of the penultimate stage of the campaign against the Society of Jesus. This stage aimed to force the papacy to dissolve the entire Society of Jesus by all the states that had already expelled or dissolved it, plus Spain's two Bourbon satrapies in the Kingdom of the Two Sicilies and the Duchy of Parma and Piacenza and as many other Catholic states as might be persuaded to join them. That is in turn to say that some of the same actors who worked behind the scene in 1758–1759 to obtain the suppression of the Jesuits in Portugal and France went back into action in 1767 to obtain the papal dissolution of the Society in Rome itself.

The evidence for an element of plotting is circumstantial yet strong. The idea of concerted action by Catholic powers against the Jesuits first appears in the correspondence of Bottari, who, writing to Clément in 1759, opined: "The only remedy is that France and Vienna unite with Portugal and Spain and ask the papacy for the suppression [of the Society, as was done] in the case of the Templars."[1] Since one of the purposes of Clément's epistolary network was to influence Catholic court policy, and as Bottari was in indirect contact with all of Jansenist Europe, the idea could not have failed to make the rounds, including magistrates, such as Clément's brother Clément de Feillet in the Parlement of Paris, which in 1764 became the first institution to call upon the king of France to unite with other Catholic powers with a view toward the total dissolution of the Jesuits.

Bottari returned to his project of a French-led alliance against the Jesuits in October 1765 and again on 29 April 1767 in the wake of the expulsion in Spain. If successful, such a project, he thought, "would free the church of God from one of the fiercest and most damnable persecutions she has ever endured."[2] Hard upon the delivery of this advice, the abbé Chauvelin, one of the original architects of the suppression in France, used events in Spain to persuade the Parlement of Paris to convene its assembled chambers, where he denounced even the ex-Jesuits in France as "perverse and pernicious . . . slaves" of their institute and its "despotic" general and as such incapable of "a French spirit and heart."[3]

In the course of his harangue, Chauvelin further described the complicity of Spanish Jesuits in the Esquilache Riots in Carlos III's own words as reported by Ossun in his dispatch of 13 April, indicating that Chauvelin's source was Choiseul himself.[4] Combined with the news of the Spanish expulsion, Chauvelin's harangue prompted the Parlement to follow the example of Spain and Portugal and on 9 May 1767 call for banishment all ex-Jesuits from France, thereby annulling a crucial provision of the royal edict of November 1764 that had allowed ex-Jesuits to remain in France as "particulars." More to the point, the Parlement of Paris also reiterated its call to the king in 1764 to act with the other Catholic powers to obtain the total suppression of the Society. Never far behind Paris, the Parlement of Normandy followed suit on 14 May, as did a little later the Parlement of Aix, the attorney general of which—Ripert de Monclar—would provide Clément with a letter of recommendation for his trip to Spain.[5]

THE FORMATION OF AN ANTI-JESUIT ADDITION TO THE BOURBON FAMILY PACT

Meanwhile Choiseul, who had also been suggesting such a pact in correspondence with Spain since late April, broached the idea in the Council of State in the presence of the king two days later when on 11 May he proposed that "what . . . would suit us best is if [His Majesty], the King of Spain, the Empress Queen [Maria Theresa], and the King of Portugal would unite in order to engage the Pope to dissolve the order of Jesuits entirely, so that there remains neither a general nor any members of the said Society, and all the individuals return to the common law of their birth."[6] A few days later, Guillaume Lambert, another member of the Parlement's Jansenist contingent and in contact with Choiseul, asked Clément to observe the greatest secrecy in responding to the question of whether he knew of any means, canonical or not, whereby "the court of Rome . . . [might] annul all superiority on the part of a general [as well as] extinguish or commute solemn vows"—a clear reference to a scenario in which the papacy might be persuaded to dissolve the Society of Jesus.[7] Bottari, Clément, Chauvelin, Choiseul, and Lambert, plus dates clustered from late

March to early July—all these protagonists and events seem too tightly inter-
twined and proximate for them to have been entirely coincidental.

In Choiseul's stated rationale, nothing short of the total dismantling of the
Society would render its members harmless and enable them to "free themselves from its bonds" and live happily "without fear" in the "bosom of their
families" under the "laws of their countries." Only then would "the upright men
who were [also] Jesuits enjoy the benefits of their uprightness, virtue, and the
law." Once free from the Society, in other words, Jesuits would become merely
Catholics—even French, Italian, and Spanish Catholics at that. Although without the loaded words "despotism" and "slavery," implicit here is the "patriotic"
notion that the Society was an international despotism that had deprived Jesuits
of their freedom and countries of their citizens.

Gallican but hardly a Jansenist, Choiseul was nonetheless at one with
Bottari—and even Clément—in persuading himself that if only the papacy were
"to determine to undertake this wise measure at the demand of the principal
[Catholic] Powers, the result would be a great good for Religion in bringing the
Holy See closer to them and in fortifying a unity necessary to the preservation
of good doctrine"; but that if, on the contrary, it "persisted in defending an order
reproved by the Catholic Powers, the protector would soon be confounded with
the protected and the animosity would fall as much on [it] as on the Jesuits, who
would soon exist only in Rome."[8] His hope was to liberate the papacy from the
Jesuits and the Jesuits from their order. Although without hint of Jansenism, this
program corresponds with the Gallican component of Reform Catholicism.[9]

The same obtains for Choiseul's attitude toward the papacy. If, as his remarks
to Ossun suggest, Choiseul thought that "good doctrine" would benefit from a
papal dissolution of the Jesuits, he presumably did so not by reason of predilection for Augustinian theology but because—and this much he also had in common with Jansenists—he believed that the Jesuits had used doctrinal issues in
order to maintain the "doctrine" of the papacy's temporal power.

In council, however, Louis XV reacted coolly to Choiseul's suggestion, opining that the project required "reflection." Choiseul therefore advised Ossun not
to present the plan to Grimaldi in Spain "ministerially" but only to sound out
Spanish reaction to it informally. Carlos III's initial reaction was more positive
than his Bourbon cousin's, deeming it "very desirable" and even lauding the
Parlement's ruling of 9 May, including its call for the Society's dissolution. Not
even His Catholic Majesty thought it wise to "precipitate anything," however,
while Roda thought it necessary to wait for a Torrigiani-free pontificate and
Grimaldi for the separate expulsion of the Jesuits from most of the other Catholic states.

Seven weeks later, on 4 July, Lambert again wrote excitedly to Clément about the arrival of a dispatch from Madrid "in view of establishing a correspondence between the courts of Spain and France to obtain a bull from Rome against the Jesuits."[10] That dispatch probably concerned Spain's cordial reception of a preliminary Portuguese proposal for concerted action to end the Jesuits which Spanish ministers began to consider in early May 1767 and to which Carlos III himself gave a green light in July, eventually carrying his French Bourbon cousin with him.[11] Indeed—and whether coincidentally or not—since mid-April Spain's foreign minister, Grimaldi, had been receiving reports from Spain's ambassador, Pedro de Luján y Góngora, marqués de Almodóvar de Rio, about Carvalho and his king's suggestions for cooperation between Spain and Portugal against the Jesuits, even dangling the prospect of a political entente against the English that might bring Portugal within the Bourbon Family Pact's orbit. Although in the end Portugal was never to join that pact, Carvalho's and Choiseul's initiatives were eventually to lead to an anti-Jesuit addition to its aims when it came up for reratification in 1768.

Carlos III's main reason for reacting positively to these Portuguese overtures was not only due to the prospect of wooing their Portuguese neighbors away from their long-standing English alliance but also because he well knew that Carvalho's anti-Jesuit credentials were far more reliable than Louis XV's. Nor did France's foot-dragging over letting Spain disembark its expelled Spanish Jesuits in Corsica during the summer of 1767 do anything to reassure the exasperated Spanish allies of the bona fides of Choiseul's suggestions. Choiseul's preference for a papal "secularization" of the Society would have allowed ex-Jesuits to live as mere "citizens" in their countries of birth on the model of Louis XV's Edict of 1764—the last action that either Spain or Portugal contemplated at that point.[12]

But Choiseul still prodded. To wait for a new pontificate as Roda first suggested might be tantamount in Choiseul's opinion to wait until the Greek calends with no very certain result; as time passed, he also became ever more impatient with the Spanish king's reluctance to order his son and nephew in Naples and Parma, respectively, to follow Spain's lead and expel the Jesuits from those two Italian Bourbon outposts.[13] By 19 July Louis XV himself had tentatively committed himself to joint action in response to a personal plea by his royal cousin in Madrid.[14] Meanwhile Carvalho compensated for his elusiveness about an anti-English alliance with increased adamancy about the anti-Jesuit one and, fortified by French adherence, elaborated a proposal to put Bourbon pressure on the papacy, which Spain's Portuguese ambassador submitted to Madrid in late September 1767. Considering but rejecting the means of a state-convened

general council as too unwieldy, the Portuguese plan opted for collective diplomatic pressure, ranging from the total rupture of diplomatic relations on the
Portuguese model to the use of military force against the pope as temporal
sovereign of the Papal States.

Such was the diplomatic momentum by September that Carlos decided to
submit the Portuguese proposal to his Junta Cortesana that had earlier approved
Campomanes's dictamen recommending the expulsion of the Jesuits. Except
for Arriaga, who on this occasion formally recused himself as too sympathetic to
the Jesuits, the members whose opinions Carlos solicited in advance of a formal
meeting were predictably Alba, Campomanes, Eleta, Moñino, Musquíz, Muniaín, and Roda, as well as all the others. Their opinions, or *dictámenes*, dribbled
in from November through January 1768. By this time all the consultants followed
Carvalho in deeming the goal of the total dissolution of the Jesuits to merit a
collective demand by the Catholic powers of the papacy, although none agreed
with him in thinking a military expedition an appropriate or even practicable
option in so adjacently "spiritual" an issue. In the absence of a general council,
all also called for the participation of as many Catholic states as possible, especially Maria Theresa's Austria.[15]

By 1767 the first part of Seabra de Silva's *Deducção chronológica e analytica*
had appeared, making it easier for the opinants to suppose that its "demonstration" of Jesuit complicity in all that had gone wrong in Portugal since 1540 might
well hold for Spain as well. That said, moral and theological reasons weighed
heavily in the judgment of some of them, most especially in that of Eleta and
Roda, who lingered longest over the issues of theological Molinism and moral
probabilism, the relation of these "deviations" to the theory and practice of
tyranicide, and the political purpose of these "errors" in a religious order characterized by "despotism" and "blind obedience." Both also demonstrated the
most dependence on French sources—in Eleta's case, Coudrette and Le Paige's
Histoire générale and the Parlement's collection of *Assertions dangéreuses*.[16]

Aside from Eleta's solicitude for "welfare of the Holy Mother Church, the
purity of the Christian Religion, and the greater glory of God," Eleta's and Roda's
themes received similar emphases in another and more influential dictamen
produced on 20 November 1767 by Campomanes joined by Moñino from
within the Council of Castile's still existent Extraordinary Junta—the one that
had engineered the expulsion of the Jesuits in the first place—to which the king
had also given the Portuguese proposal.[17] What most distinguished the two fiscals' joint dictamen from the others was its frank admiration for the direction of
Carvalho's Portugal, especially the steps it had taken toward a degree of independence from Rome in the domain of episcopal dispensations in reserved

cases from canon law, even hints of local consecrations of new bishops without papal confirmation, as Pereira de Figueiredo's *Demonstração theologica* was soon to propose. The goal that Campomanes and Moñino explicitly held out for Spain was nothing less than a national Catholic Church that, while not breaking with Rome as had Henry VIII in England, would give the Spanish Catholic Church more freedom from Rome than Gallican France enjoyed.

To whatever extent Campomanes's and Moñino's stated goals for demanding the papal suppression of the Jesuits had become official policy, that policy would have changed since the expulsion of the Jesuits from Spain, or even the suppression in France. For the original architects of the suppression in France, the goal had been to create the conditions for a doctrinal reorientation of the Catholic Church—and the end of the persecution of "friends of the Truth"—by ridding both France and Rome of the chief authors of that persecution. In Spain, in contrast, the perpetrators' main unstated goals went little further than to exorcise the specter of the uprisings of the spring of 1766 by finding someone to blame for them, along with removing obstacles to further reform.

In order to achieve these goals, however, persuasive reasons from the armory of Gallican anti-Jesuitism were essential, and these reasons carried with them anticurial implications beyond any set of original intentions. By 1767, the spectacle of action by Spain as well as by Portugal and France suggested further goals that made some of these implications explicit. To the extent that the anticurial aspects of these goals were less obviously in harmony with Eleta's stated concern with the "welfare of the Holy Mother Church," they tended to marginalize this concern, and with it Eleta himself. As time went on, Eleta all but dropped out of the original troika of movers and shakers in the Spanish campaign against the Jesuits to the benefit of Campomanes's fellow fiscal, José Moñino, leaving Roda as the chief conduit to the king.[18]

What these two fiscals were now proposing was to harness the stated reasons for the earlier expulsion to the further goal of obtaining greater ecclesiastical independence from Rome without shocking Catholic opinion by attacking the papacy directly.[19] To that end, their joint dictamen followed others in rejecting both the use of military force as too material and the convening of a general council as too unpredictably "spiritual." In place of a council their dictamen therefore proposed the theological and moral mobiliztion of bishops and universities, as though their theological authority was that of a national council if not of the whole "dispersed" church; while in place of the use military force it proposed collaboration with other Catholic powers in exerting pressure in the election of a pope who would take executive action on the supposed behalf of the church—that is to say, the means eventually used. Since in the meantime the Rome of Clement XIII and Torrigiani persisted in defending the Jesuits as they were, the joint dictamen enlarged the neo-Gallican reasons for expelling the Jesuits from Spain to apply to the whole Society, and in doing so also widened their application to fit the curial foot if Rome persisted in wearing the Jesuit shoe.

The first of the dictamen's five reasons was again the Society's capacity for "unified action" obtained by means of its hierchical organization that subjected all of its denationalized members to a "mechanical obedience" to the will of its general—a capacity that the Society had displayed in its campaign against the French parlements and the antiroyal uprising in Spain. A second reason was the prideful "obstinacy" of the Society, best demonstrated by its attachment to the casuistry of probabalism that transformed its fourth vow to the papacy into one to its own aggradizement at the expense of all other powers, including the papacy. After using a third and a fourth reason to advance recent factual evidence of the Society's "incorrigability," the dictamen devoted a fifth reason to point to the unique opportunity for joint action by the major Catholic states on account of the systems of alliances that united them directly or indirectly.

But while waiting for such a concert of Catholic powers to act in a next conclave, this plan impicitly called for the expulsion of the Jesuits from as many other Catholic states as possible, and the states most vulnerable to pressure to do so were the Bourbon dynasty's two Italian satrapies, the Kingdom of the Two Sicilies centered in Naples and the Duchy of Parma and Piacenza in the north. Both states had fledgling Bourbon scions as their rulers, Carlos III's son Ferdinando IV in Naples and Carlos's nephew and Louis XV's son-in-law Ferdinando I in Parma. Both princes depended on the advice and skills of reformist Catholic—and anti-Jesuit—ministers, Tanucci in Naples and Léon-Guillaume du Tillot and Paolo Maria Paciàudi in Parma.

Even as Campomanes and Moñino submitted their dictamen of 20 November 1767, the Neapolitan first minster, Tanucci, was preparing to expel the Jesuits from the Kingdom of Naples.

NAPLES, PARMA, AND THE PAPAL *MONITORIO* OF 30 JANUARY 1768

For Tanucci, the pressure to act came not only from Spain also but from an impatient Choiseul, who at one point urged that Naples and Parma take the initiative in demanding the papacy to dissolve the Society lest they follow Spain and Portugal's example by expelling their Jesuits.[20] Since Naples was by far the bigger and stronger of the two states, the pressure fell most heavily on Tanucci, who would have none of it.

To be sure, Tanucci thought no more highly of the Jesuits than any avowed Jansenist. Not only had he sponsored the publication of the Italian translation of the Jansenist Mésenguy's *Exposition de la doctrine chrétienne*, in 1765 he arranged for the Neapolitan publication of Bottari's anonymous fourth-volume addition to his series entitled the *Inquietudini de' gesuiti*.[21] In the wake of Portugal's expulsion of the Jesuits, Tanucci lowered all his state's censorial barriers to anti-Jesuit propaganda from Portugal, while blocking all the Jesuit defenses of the Society; he similarly closed Neapolitan borders to all French Jesuits during the dragged-out trial of the Society in France, while welcoming Carlo di Grosso back to Naples after his expulsion from Rome in 1762. After the Spanish uprisings of 1766, he had also played a role in directing Roda's and Carlos III's suspicions toward the Jesuits. In the Neapolitan government itself, Tanucci could count on the support of some of his ministers, especially his minister of Grace and Justice, Carlo di Marco, and the military commander Reggio e Gravina, principe di Iaci, as well as numbers of philo-Jansenist bishops or archbishops, such as Archbishops Matteo Gennaro Testa of Reggio and Sanseverino of Alife.[22] The first had sent a letter of communion to the archbishop of Utrecht in 1764, the second in 1774.[23]

Strong as these effectives might have seemed, they did not suffice in Tanucci's estimation to risk the initiative that Choiseul invited Tanucci to take. His kingdom, Tanucci reminded Choiseul, possessed no *parlemento* comparable to France's that would enable it to make the general case that France's had. Not only was he in no position to do so on his own merely ministerial authority, but the young and barely major king—and Carlos's son—Ferdinando IV who had that authority was even less inclined to take it than Tanucci was. Nor did the idea of expelling the Jesuits obviously suggest itself in the absence of any plausible excuse to do so, such as the bankruptcy of a mission, an attack on a royal body, or a popular uprising.

Ferdinando and Tanucci did not of course govern the kingdom alone but, as in the case of Spain, did so with the Council of State. But by his count the few councilors Tanucci could rely on could not match the Jesuits' many friends there any more than the Thomist-manteístas had been able to do in the Council of Castile. For his part, Carlos III remained unwilling officially or publicly to intervene in Neapolitan affairs, although he made his wishes clear enough to the vulnerable first minister. Yet the matter was pressing, as a reputedly philo-Jesuit Habsburg princess and future queen from Austria was due to arrive in

Naples at the end of the year, where and when she would surely exercise her regal right to attend meetings of the Council of State.[24]

As did Campomanes and Roda, however, Tanucci had a sympathetic royal confessor in the person of Benedetto Latilla, the bishop of Avellino—or at least he did after he had contrived to maneuver Latilla into the place of Francesco Cardel, a Jesuit whom he sent packing back to his native Bohemia.[25] It was only by means of Latilla's "spiritual" suasion aided by the Spanish minister Grimaldi's letters that Tanucci gradually brought the young king to the conviction that the Jesuits were so evil that, far from being a sin, to expel them would in fact obviate an evil.

With the king amenable, in July 1767 Tanucci finally got Carlos III to send him the veiled authorization to proceed in the form of advice in writing. The advice was that in view of the danger evident in Tanucci's description "of the present of affairs" in Naples, "nothing good can be hoped for [from inaction against the Jesuits], and every evil is to be feared," and "it is thus not only prudent but proper [to act in order] to avoid and prevent it."[26] Feeling free to circumvent the Council of State, Tanucci took pages from the Portuguese and Spanish books and constituted an extraordinary Giunta degli abusi, or Council on Abuses, on 16 September 1768. Stacked with handpicked members, it would concern itself with the Jesuits on the pretense of looking into the bona fides of a papal authorization for the Neapolitan branch of the Society to sell property in order to liquidate a debt. Besides Tanucci, the twelve members included three royal councilors and eight magistrates whose authority Tanucci supplemented after the fact with that of four bishops, including Latilla himself.[27]

What remained was the need to come up with reasons for expelling the Jesuits from Naples and Sicily. In the absence of any incriminating activity, these reasons had to be purely formal, except possibly the danger posed for a Bourbon king by members of a society estranged from that dynasty on account of its mistreatment in Bourbon France and Spain. Still, plausible reasons were indispensable, and from the available stock of them Tanucci initially chose five that displayed a certain logic: the uniformity of opinion and action in the Society; its hatred for the Bourbon dynasty; its systematic adoption of vengeance as a policy; and its lack of legal status in the kingdom.

In an attempt to explain why the Society of Jesus should not be given legal standing now, Tanucci's fifth and final reason bore down on the content of the Society's collective doctrines and practices as documented in the *arrêts* of the Parlement of Paris. These predictably included the Jesuits' "lax" ethical standards and practices and still other unspecified doctrines contrary to Catholic orthodoxy and even natural and divine law, as well as such practices as mutual espionage and correspondence across national lines that enslaved the "reason," violated confessional secrecy, and endangered the state.

After corresponding with Madrid, however, Tanucci honed the rationale into a twelve-article dictamen that, like Campomanes's, formed the basis of the Giunta's decrees.[28] To his original rationale the new dictamen by Tanucci added a crucial first article that insisted on the combination of the "absolute and despotic" power of the Jesuit general and the "blind obedience" of his subordinates in the structure of a society that put religion in the service of the "purely political" goal of forming a state within both the church and other states, superior to them all. Now demoted to the status of means to this goal, the second article replicated Tanucci's original indictment of the Society's corruption of reason and morality, including the casuistry of probabilism. The following articles drew the inevitable connection between the Society's structure and morality and espousal and practice of tyranicide, followed by a ninth in the form of the hitherto uniquely French argument that since Naples had never formally examined, much less accepted, the constitutions of the Society, it had existed illegally there. The conclusion followed ineluctably that the Jesuits were dangerous "foreigners" in the Kingdom of the Two Sicilies and ought to be expelled as such.[29]

All seemed ready for the expulsion in late October when Maria Giuseppina, King Ferdinando's betrothed Habsburg princess, suddenly succumbed to smallpox on 14 October and Mount Vesuvius performed another of its periodic eruptions on the nineteenth. Ferdinando momentarily lost his hard-won nerve, assailed as he was by letters from pious nuns construing these events as divine warnings to desist from the rumored expulsion to come. But Empress Maria Theresa and the Austrians promptly replaced Maria Giuseppina with her sister Maria Carolina, just as good, while Vesuvius calmed down just as soon. To calm Ferdinando's qualms, Latilla and Tanucci countered with the (quite Jansenist) argument that to suppose the occurrence of new revelations since Jesus Christ was a heresy and that the nuns' revelations were therefore of no account and nothing in comparison to the advice of all the Giunta's ecclesiastical as well as secular councilors. Fortunately for the postponed plans, Latilla waited until a month after the expulsion to die, whereupon Tanucci replaced him with the just as reliable Sanseverino.[30]

The decisive meeting of the Giunta took place on 25 October. Although not formally members of a purely lay Giunta, a number of bishops and archbishops signed the edict as well, including Latilla, Testa, and Sanseverino—even Cardinal Antonio Sersale, archbishop of Naples—in part to reassure Ferdinando IV's conscience.[31] Dated 31 October and 3 November 1767, Ferdinando IV's successive royal edicts of expulsion remained just as tight-lipped about the reasons for them as had been the Spanish pragmatic sanction of 2 April. The actual expulsion also followed the Spanish model. After lulling the Jesuits into a false sense of security for two weeks, Tanucci unsheathed the edicts at the same time as he implemented the expulsion with military means, in Naples on 24–25 November and in Sicily on 29 and 30 November.[32]

In order to avoid the one Spanish misstep, Tanucci also carefully circumvented an attempt to unload the Jesuits at the port of Civitavecchia by expelling them either into the Papal States on land or by sea to beachheads elsewhere. Thus did he send about seven hundred and fifty out of a possible fourteen hundred Jesuit "foreigners" packing and confiscate the property of fifty-five colleges, seven novitiates and residences, and several seminaries—the total Jesuit effectives in the Kingdom of the Two Sicilies.[33] The comparatively low percentage of expelled Jesuits was the result of an usually high number of defections and the kingdom's policy of generosity toward the infirm and aged.

As though as an afterthought, on 23 April another two score Jesuits from the island of Malta vacated a college and residence to join their Neapolitan confreres in exile by virtue of an order from Emanuel de Pinto da Fonseca, grand master of the ruling military-religious order of Saint John of Jerusalem. Although in 1530 the order had acknowledged the lordship of Spanish Sicily in the person of Felipe II, that feudal dependency had followed the dynastic changes affecting Sicily and had thus come to rest under the Bourbon Kingdom of the Two Sicilies—and hence also of Ferdinando IV, advised by Tanucci.[34]

The nature of that kingdom's relation to the papacy also gave the expulsion of the Jesuits to the Papal States the aspect of a bid for greater ecclesiastical as well as political independence from the papacy. It did so structurally because from the twelfth century forward the king of Sicily was the de jure legate of the papacy in relation to the Sicilian Church, while as king of Naples—total unification of the two kingdoms came in 1816—the same king was at once the papal legate and the feudal vassal of the Church of Rome. Since any unilateral action by the kingdom in relation to the church was a show of independence from Rome, with all the more reason was it so in regard to action against a religious order with a special vow of obedience to Rome. Whether intended or not, the expulsion of the Jesuits from the Kingdom of the Two Sicilies fell into line with the "national" direction taken by the international campaign against the Jesuits in the Iberian Peninsula in 1767.

What held for Naples and Sicily also obtained for the Duchy of Parma and Piacenza under Carlos III's young nephew Ferdinando I, under whose authority his inherited first minister, Guillaume Du Tillot, had presided over the duchy since the death of Carlos's brother Felipe—Filippo in Italian—in 1764. While the duchy was not contiguous with the Papal States as was Naples, the papacy claimed it as a fief by virtue of its origin as a detachment from the Papal States arranged by the Farnese Pope Paul III as an endowment for a son in 1545. Thereafter the duchy remained in the possession of the Farnese family until the death of its last and childless duke, whereupon it passed into the hands of the Spanish Bourbons in 1731 via the marriage between Felipe V of Spain and Elisabetta Farnese, the last member of that family. The next year, Felipe's eldest son— and future king of Spain—Carlos took possession of the duchy as Carlo I, but he soon lost it in exchange for the Kingdom of the Two Sicilies during the War of the Polish Succession—at least until the end of the next war of the Austrian Succession brought it back to the Bourbons in the person of Carlos's younger brother Felipe, or Felippo, in 1748. Although throughout these dynastic tradeoffs the European states treated Parma-Piacenza as theirs to dispose of, the papacy never relinquished its claim to neofeudal lordship over the duchy.

That Ferdinando I would follow Spain and Naples in expelling the approximately 170 Jesuits in the duchy was a forgone conclusion. At Du Tillot's request Carlos III had conveyed his Extraordinary Council's advice to his nephew on the mode of expulsion, which like Spain's and Naples's was to be military and without warning; indeed, Parma's minister of education, Paulo Paciàudi, announced its coming to a correspondent a month and a half before it took place.[35] Dated 3 February 1768, the pragmatic sanction remained under lock and key until implemented during the night of 7–8 February, when the state seized the Jesuits' seven colleges, two novitiates, and two residences and marched their occupants toward Bologna by way of the Duchy of Modena. But for both contemporaries and historians—except for the Jesuits—the fact of this expulsion all but passed unnoticed amid the verbal din raised in reaction to the papal brief *Alias ad apostolatus* of 30 January 1768, which, better known as the *Monitorio* of Parma, invoked the authority of the papal bull *In coena Domini* of 1627 to fulminate an ipso facto excommunication of the young duke and all his collaborators. The duke had clearly timed the expulsion as a riposte to the *Monitorio* itself. Unlike Tanucci and Ferdinando IV in Naples, Ferdinando I of Parma had material as well as purely formal reasons for expelling the Jesuits, since he and all the other Bourbon kings and ministers alike blamed the Jesuits for putting Clement XIII up to the *Monitorio*.

What had provoked Clement XIII's spectacularly anachronistic anathemas was the anticurial ecclesiastical legislation inspired by Ferdinando's two chief advisers, the first minister, Du Tillot, and Paolo Paciàudi, both of them inherited from his late father when Ferdinando acceded to the throne in 1764. The "enlightened" first minister, Du Tillot, stocked his personal library with the volumes of the *Encyclopédie* and wooed the Catholic philosophe and abbé Bonnot de Condillac to Parma as Ferdinando's tutor, while the Gallican and Jansenist Theatine Paciàudi came to Parma at Du Tillot's behest in 1763 to undertake the reform of the duchy's educational curriculum. Besides through Roda, who negotiated with the Rome on behalf of Parma's ecclesiastical legislation between 1759 and 1760, the inevitable influence of the Archetto in Parma's case against the Jesuits ran through Paciàudi, who actually composed the pragmatic sanction of expulsion nominally approved by Parma's Council of State. Paciàudi's conviction that the Jesuits had foisted a "new dogmatic system" on the church provided the only semblance of a religious motive behind an expulsion otherwise undertaken for "urgent and pressing reasons" in virtue of the duke's "absolute power" and "independent sovereignty" as "protector of the canons."[36] Between them, Du Tillot and Paciàudi therefore made for a perfect Catholic reformist storm and together stood behind the controversial legislation. With still others, and after years of unproductive negotiations with Rome, they also promulgated a series of aggressive jurisdictional or regalistic measures that set strict limits on the amount of property that the Catholic Church could acquire, subjected much of it to taxation, disbarred all foreigners from Parma's benefices, and even established a jurisdictional giunta to oversee the implementation of these measures.

The audacity of these reforms in a tiny and arguably papal fiefdom may be measured by comparison to Gallican France, which had never formally subjected ecclesiastical property to royal taxation, as well as to Spain, which had backed away from Campomanes's proposed mortmain legislation after the uprisings in 1766. But what caused the Torrigiani-era curia's volcanic ire to reach the point of eruption was Ferdinando's "pragmatic sanction" of 16 January 1768 that prohibited any judicial appeals to "foreign" courts, especially Roman ones, or the promulgation of any papal briefs, bulls, and decrees in Parma without ducal authorization in the form of a *regium imprimatur*.[37] Again, Ferdinando's uncle Carlos III had retreated from precisely such a measure in 1762.

Not only did Clement XIII's *Monitorio* excommunicate the young duke and all those who had collaborated in the making of this legislation, it also annulled this pragmatic sanction and all like legislation as well as prohibiting all clerics from obeying any of it on pain of the same censures. The papal tantrum was almost tantamount to an interdict. Besides the barely noticed expulsion of the Jesuits, the duke later used his newly acquired exequatur to suppress the papal *Monitorio*.[38]

Since in the course of elaborating this regalist legislation the duke of Parma and his ministers had undoubtedly consulted with Carlos III's ministers and indirectly with Choiseul, the *Monitorio* could be read as excommunicating them as well. In any case, they chose to take it that way. If in Choiseul's opinion the pope thus picked on the most fragile and vulnerable of Bourbon states, the reason was that Parma was "only the pretext for an insult . . . directed against the [whole] Bourbon house, especially against . . . the kings who had expelled the Jesuits."[39] Choiseul's was also by far the ripest of reactions to the *Monitorio*. Upon reading it, Choiseul announced to the diplomatic world that he saw it as proof positive that the present pope was a "total imbecile" and his secretary of state Torrigiani a "fool of the first order." In his opinion not only did the *Monitorio* contain measures "unjust, violent, irregular and indecent" in themselves, it also brandished vestiges of the "fanatical and murderous doctrine" of papal power that, unknown during Christianity's first ten centuries, had arisen under Gregory VII and later caused the sectarian separation of much of formerly Catholic Europe.[40]

Hard upon Choiseul's reaction came a hail of yet harsher suppressions of the *Monitorio* by the French parlements, led by Paris, followed by similar decrees in Naples, Lisbon, and Madrid, this time brandishing the death penalty for any printer who published it.[41] In fact, no Catholic state except the Papal States sanctioned its publication. The Monitorio also provoked a series of prohibitions of the annual Maundy Thursday publication of the bull *In coena Domini*, the authority of which the Monitorio had invoked in hurling its anathemas. Not even the moderate empress Maria Theresa's Austria spared this bull, at least in the Viennese-governed province of Lombardy.

In Spain, the most substantial result was the Council of Madrid's reimposition of the regium exequatur that Carlos III had first decreed, only to withdraw it under papal pressure in 1762.[42] Dated June 1768, the royal letters patent and decree all but completed the gallicanization of Spanish ecclesiastical policy to the immense satisfaction of Ossun and Choiseul, who saw in these measures the perfect means of "maintaining temporal authority [in Spain] against the enterprises of the court of Rome" and the "total vindication" of Wall and his conduct in 1762 in reaction to the papal condemnation of Mésenguy's catechism.[43] Of the major protagonists, the only person less than enthusiastic about the reimposition of the exequatur was Eleta, who had helped Clement XIII to persuade Carlos III to rescind it after its first imposition in 1762.[44]

For Choiseul, the immediate effect of the Parmesan crisis was to alter his order of priorities, pushing the need to obtain papal satisfaction for the insult to the Bourbon dynasty ahead of the project to pressure the papacy to dissolve the Jesuits, even to the point of separating the two issues. Asked by Ossun in mid-June on behalf of the Spanish where France now stood on the project of the "extinction" of the Society, Choiseul replied that "we do not believe that it is necessary to confound this affair [of the Jesuits], however important it may be, with the far more essential object concerning the [papal] brief of this past 30 January 1768."[45] Choiseul was also worried that, given the nature of this pontificate, to press it any further on the issue of the Jesuits would only provoke it into "committing the Holy See . . . to positions so extreme" that Clement XIII's successor would find them all but "impossible to disavow."[46] So for Choiseul the problem of how best to force Pope Clement XIII to revoke the *Monitorio* and recognize Ferdinando I's full sovereignty over his the duchy momentarily eclipsed the Jesuits as the center of concern and set the ministers to devising scenarios to obtain this goal.

Among these, Choiseul's plan to respond to a papal refusal by a Portuguese-style rupture in diplomatic relations—a kind of "soft" schism—ceded to Spain's preference for a military occupation of the papal territorial outposts in Avignon and the Comtat Venaissin in France and Benevento and Pontecorvo in Italy. And so when on 21 April Clement XIII predictably refused the Bourbon demands in response to a joint Bourbon démarche by the French, Neapolitan, and Spanish ambassadors on 15–16 April 1768, French troops occupied Avignon and the Comtat on 11–12 June, while Neapolitan troops did the same in Benevento and Pontecorvo.[47] Another such demarche on 19 and 21 September succeeded no better at softening the papal heart, by which time the demands had grown to include the permanent ceding of the seized papal territories to France and Naples and the exile from Rome of both Torrigiani and the beleaguered Ricci.

But by that time Carlos III had all but lost interest in the reparation of his ducal nephew's honor as a goal to be pursued for its own sake and apart from the papal suppression of the Jesuits. To be sure, Spain's reimposition of the exequatur in June to Choiseul and Ossun's delight momentarily interrupted his growing fixation on the Jesuits. But when in August Choiseul in turn asked Ossun about where the Spanish king stood on these issues, the ambassadors' reply was that Carlos had come to deem it "absolutely necessary that from now on the three crowns demand the . . . extinction of the order of Jesuits"; the king had written to Azpuru to make it clear to the Holy See that the satisfaction of this demand was the "sine qua non" for any accomodation related to the papacy's refusal to recognize the total temporal sovereignty of Parma. So secondary had this recognition become in Carlos's priorities that he now thought out loud that it might be "too hard." And if, Grimaldi added, Choiseul remained worried that if pressed too hard on this issue Clement XIII might make irrevocably outlandish pronouncements, Choiseul should be reminded that things had already come to that point in the pope's dealings with Portugal.[48] To which Choiseul could only respond that his king had ordered him to instruct d'Aubeterre to follow Azpuru's lead in Rome in all that concerned the Jesuits.[49]

The effect of the Parmesan crisis was therefore to reverse Spanish and French or at least Choiseul's order of ecclesiastical priorities. Whereas in the early summer of 1767 it was Choiseul who was the driving force behind the aim of a total papal dissolution of the Society of Jesus, dragging his reluctant king behind him, by the summer of 1768 it was Carlos III and Campomanes's Spain that had become the driving force, dragging both Choiseul and his king behind them. While in the spring of 1767 it was Choiseul who wished to press the issue right away and Grimaldi and Roda who thought it more prudent to wait for a post-Torrigiani pontificate, by the summer of 1768 it was they and their king who wished to press ahead, even against the pontificate of Clement XIII and Torrigiani. And whereas in the spring it was Choiseul who thought that a finely honed anti-Jesuit ecclesiastical policy could "liberate" the papacy from the Jesuits, by the summer he found himself forced to support a Spanish policy intent on mounting an assault against the Jesuits and papacy together, barely seeing any light between them.

But under the circumstances, it was Choiseul who was being unrealistic. For whether Bourbon papal policy sought to separate the issue of the Bourbon dynasty's insulted honor from that of the dissolution of the Jesuits, as Choiseul had first preferred, or to bind them even more tightly together, as the Spanish now wished to do, the Bourbon aims in combination with the papal *Monitorio* and its defense had made the "Court of Rome" as much the enemy as the Jesuits had ever been. Although in different ways, for both France and Spain the Parmesan crisis was the catalyst in transforming a campaign against the Jesuits into a de facto siege of papal power.

SPAIN AND THE RETURN TO THE JESUITS

Far from allowing the Parmesan crisis to distract their attention from their goal of a papal dissolution of Jesuits, Carlos III and his ministers had meanwhile concluded that the Jesuits and their ongoing domination of Rome were inseperable from the cause of the crisis and therefore the chief obstacles to resolving it. What ensured this continuity of Spanish attention was Carlos's decision to submit the Portuguese plan of September 1767 against the Jesuits to the advice of all the members of his Junta Cortesana that, as already discussed, had produced Campomanes and Moñino's dictamen of 20 November 1767 in addition to a stream of others that had dribbled in until the eve of the Parmesan crisis the following January. Quite apart from that crisis, these dictámenes demanded some kind of summary and conclusion. As it turned out, the prospect of a fuller political alliance with Portugal that had prompted Carlos's consultation with the Junta Cortesana receded steadily from view, as Carvalho proved unwilling to formalize his political ties to the Bourbon Family Pact at the risk of jeopardizing Portugal's relations with England. Indeed, by the summer of 1768 relations between the two Iberian states had so soured that Carlos commissioned Aranda to see to the preparedness of Spain's army, navy, and provisions. But like the Parmesan crisis, the effect of this Portuguese defection was eventually only to tighten the anti-Jesuit "ecclesastial point" that still united the two states.

The task of deriving a conclusion and plan of action from all the Junta Cortesana's accumulated opinions, or dictámenes, fell initially to the secretary of state, Grimaldi, who in Feburary produced a memoir deemed too impolitic for the moment by the ficsals Campomanes and Mõnino, who thereupon produced a joint dictamen similar in substance to the one they had written on 20 November the previous year.[50] Dated 11 March 1768, their new dictamen frankly admitted, as had Grimaldi's, that the most objectionable feature of the Jesuit Order was its ultramontanist principles "diametrically opposed to the interests of temporal princes." But it differed from the secretary of state's dictamen in eschewing the public mention of papal infallibility, lest the papacy perceive the attack on the Jesuits as one on itself.

The alternative tactic urged by this dictamen took a page from Choiseul's and Bottari's manuals by rhetorically separating the case of Rome from the case of the Jesuits and emphasizing the extent to which the Jesuits, unfaithful to their vow of obedience to the papacy, had actually disobeyed it in such cases such as Noris and the Chinese rites. Where temporal interests were directly concerned, this dictamen advised that this appeal to the spiritual interests of the papacy be accompanied by one to the sovereigns' own responsibility for the "tranquillity of Catholic states," threatened as these had just been by the recent popular uprisings and attempted assassinations supposdly staged by the Jesuits. By way of supplementing these reasons with means, this dictamen also contemplated the threat of a possible abolition of the nuncio's office and forms of "national" episcopal empowerment in addition to exerting pressure on the next conclave with a view toward electing a more amenable pope.

The historian Enrique Giménes López has all but set these "public" reasons in opposition to the "real" reasons for the creation of a more "national" Catholic Church. Yet these public reasons had always already implied the real reasons, which papal intransigence culminating in the *Monitorio* against Parma had brought to the conscious surface.[51] Anticipated by the dictamen of 20 November of the previous year, by far the most potent of the public reasons for the expulsion of the Jesuits was that they owed "blind obedience" to a "despotically" structured society that had perverted Christian morality and doctrine in the pusuit of a universal or transnational "domination." Yet by means of the well-worn distinction between the "Holy See" and the all too temporal "Court of Rome," the same charge could be plausibly leveled against the papacy itself, especially if it always rushed to the defense of a society that owed a unique vow of obedience to the papacy and, in the view of its critics, had taken a hand in the monarchical restructuring of the Catholic Church ever since the Council of Trent. After all, and even apart from the Jesuits, the papacy too had its obedient agents in all the Catholic countries by way of its nuncios with special jurisdictions, the Roman Inquisition and its censors, the other regular orders with their generals in Rome, and even those members of the secular clergy in the nomination of Rome.

Further, these putative real reasons made at least indirect contact with Eleta's earlier expressed concern for the "welfare of the Holy Mother Church" and the "purity of the Christian Religion" by means of the argument that by depriving the papacy of its temporal and even spiritual "pretensions" and dividing the two between temporal princes and "national" clergies, the Catholic states would indeed be restoring the "primitive purity" of the "ancient discipline" of Catholic Church. That Campomanes in particular sincerely thought so would soon become evident when he published his *Juicio imparcial (Impartial Judgment)* and Moñino had to step in and help him amend it for public consumption.

Carlos III then had Campomanes and Moñino distill the essence of their dictamen of 11 March into the form of a consulta that, formally approved by the full Extraordinary Council ten days later, would according to Giménez López set Spanish policy until 1773.[52] At that point the Extraordinary Council had come include three bishops and two archbishops who were appointed to it by Carlos the previous November and whose approval was thought to be crucial for the success of the dictamen's strategy of mobilizing the episcopacy to make a parallel case against the Jesuits' doctrine and morality.[53] After the repeated failure of the Bourbon states to obtain any form of "satisfaction" for the dishonored Ferdinando of Parma—a second such attempt failed in September 1768—Carlos reconvened the full Extraordinary Council on 30 November 1768, mainly in order to ensure unanimous assent to the plan to press for papal dissolution of the Jesuits.

By this time, this demand found itself in the company of the four unfulfilled demands having to with avenging the papal insult to the Bourbon dynasty. By this time also, however, the king had concluded that the time had come to insist "positively and absolutely" on the papal dissolution of the Jesuits as "an article separate from the affairs of Parma, and that has nothing to do with [them] or with the other articles on which an accommodation [with the papacy] might depend." He had even speculated that the abolition of the Society might turn out to be the best means of obtaining the other demands. Having all but subsumed the Bourbon demands for Parma under the single demand of the papal extinction of the Jesuits, Carlos instead asked for the council's approval of a short memoir to this effect, which the council received "with joy and admiration," finding nothing to add or subtract and seeing it as evidence of His Catholic Majesty's "high wisdom and consumate prudence."[54]

Publicly attributed to Grimaldi, the memoir came from the pen of Campomanes and bears the stamp of the case that he and Moñino thought fit for papal ears. Campomanes therefore artfully condensed the substance of Spain's real reasons for insisting that the papacy dissolve the Jesuits while substituting more neutral terms, such as the Society's moral "corruption" for the its "prohabalism," its "political and mundane system" for its "despotism," and so on. At its best the Society was said to have maintained adversarial relations with all "legitimate authorities," including the "legitimate authority of the Holy See."[55] It was in part to vindicate that papal authority itself, the memoir alleged, that Carlos III now asked Clement XIII "absolutely and totally" to extinguish the "Company called that of Jesus." From the Extraordinary Council this memoir went into the hands of Grimaldi, who in turn sent it to Azpuru for presentation to the papacy. For Carlos there remained the formality of obtaining the French king's continued acquiesence in his papal policies. Choiseul duly delivered it to Ossun on 27 December, assuring Carlos of Louis XV's "perfect conformity of principles and intentions with the [Spanish] king his cousin."[56]

The main difference between the French demand for the papal suppression of the Jesuits and the Spanish one approved by the Extraordinary Council is that the one Louis XV had Choiseul send to d'Aubeterre—the difference between France and the rest of Catholic Europe in a nutshell—made made no reference to the Jesuits' ethics or doctrines, lest the memoir, in the French king's reported terms, "revive by reference to this subject the disputes that have troubled his realm for more than a century, and of which even the tiniest spark might . . . set off a dangerous conflagration."[57]

The three Bourbon powers of Spain, Naples, and France finally concerted a démarche to confront the papacy with their demands for the dissolution of the Society of Jesus during the week of 16–24 January 1769. Excommunicated in the person of its duke, Parma let the other Bourbon powers speak on its behalf, as it had ever since the papal *Monitorio.* Clement XIII predictably rejected the demands out of hand.[58] A few weeks later, on 2 February 1769, Clement died, perhaps the first of two papal martyrs to the cause of the Jesuits.

In conclusion, the most salient feature of this first and largely Italian phase of the Bourbon Family Pact's international campaign against the Jesuits was the triumph of Spain's policy of pressing the papacy for the total abolition of the Society of Jesus over the more flexible French policy of a softer landing for the Jesuits. By March 1768, Choiseul himself had conceded that so long as Jesuits existed they would remain Jesuits rather than becoming "citizens" as he had hoped. As for the Spanish fiscals, they had by then concluded, in Ossun's words, that "the principal motor of this whole [Parmesan] affair resided in the spirit of the Society . . . and its partisans in the . . . Court of Rome, where they flatter themselves that by . . . confounding their cause with the pretensions of that court," they will derail the intended effect of Bourbon states' measures against "so dangerous" a society.[59] To the extent that this analysis was true, the Jesuits would succeed all too well in confounding their cause with that of Rome, although not in staving off their coming dissolution. Although the issue of these rival policies would seem to have been settled by time of Clement XIII's death in February 1769, it would continue to be on display during the papal conclave that followed it and bedevil negotiations to end the Jesuits with Clement XIII's successor until 1773.

But a second, less visible but more paradoxical feature of this Italian chapter is the contrast between the moderation—almost irenicism—of the Gallican traditions and of anti-Jesuitism, as represented by those statesmen like Choiseul in their birthplace and cradle in France, and the uncompromising militancy of these same traditions as articulated by such royal servants as Campomanes in states that had only recently adopted them, especially Spain and Portugal.

Not that Choiseul's Gallican credo was in any respects wanting, and the Parmesan crisis gave him ample opportunity to reaffirm both its spiritual and temporal tenets in his diplomatic dispatches. But as a right with an ancient national pedigree, Choiseul's was a Gallicanism that could be alternately condescending, as when congratulating Spain for Carlos III's reimposition of the exequatur in 1768; or moderate, as when dismissing as Protestant and sectarian a Rhenish episcopal plea for support in an attempt to reclaim the German Church's liberties from the papacy in 1770; or even generous to an ultramontanist adversary, as when advising Spain against pressing the pope too hard or entertaining the fantasy that the papacy might be grateful for its liberation from the Jesuits or the Jesuits for deliverance from their "despotic" yoke.

It is not that Gallican France was suffering from any lack of anticurial Gallican rage comparable to Campomanes's—far from it—but there the rage came not from the royal ministry, much less the episcopacy, but from "below" in the still somewhat Jansenist parlements, such as those of Paris and Rouen, and even in the Parisian streets. The contrast could not have been greater than between

France and Bourbon Spain, where that rage remained confined to a reformist monarchy and ministry intent on catching up and perhaps surpassing Gallican France, and where even the king could be heard complaining about the "ignorance" and "superstition" of the Spanish populace. For lack of anything like them, Campomanes, Grimaldi, and Roda began to republish the texts of the French parlements' anti-Jesuit arrêts in the *Gazeta de Madrid*, anti-"despotic" rhetoric and all.[60] To the extent that the popular uprisings in the spring of 1766 bore any confessional complexion, it was pro-Jesuit rather than anti. And if by 1768 Carlos III could count on a cadre of Spanish bishops to make an ethical and theological case against the Jesuits, it was because he had created a Sala de Conciencia that picked bishops by means of criteria quite different from those of anti-Jansenism and support for the bull *Unigenitus*.

That the Gallican liberties that the Spanish monarch had domesticated concerned less the ecclesiastical than the temporal and regalist tenets is certain. Just how far Carlos III's ministry was willing to go on the record in favor of the full-blown thing, however, became apparent in Campomanes's treatise against the papal *Monitorio* entitled *Juicio imparcial* that appeared in 1769.[61] The result of Carlos's decision to submit Parma's condemned legislation to an examination by his Extraordinary Council to make sure of the justice of Parma's case, this treatise is all the more remarkable in that its neo-Gallican radicalism represents a sanitized rewriting of the unavailable first edition, which must have been more radical still.[62] As it was, the censored second edition honored the spirit if not the letter of the "School of Paris" in locating the source of the liberties not in France but in the Gospels and the biblical book of Acts and the example of the church's first and "most flourishing" centuries."[63] But it was also analogically Gallican in that it found these liberties intact in the proceedings of the Spanish kings in national councils in Spain's Visigothic antiquity and Middle Ages, both before and even after the Moorish conquest.[64] So alongside such standard Gallican authorities as Gerson, Bossuet, and Marca, the treatise also featured such Tridentine-era Spanish Gallicans as Bishop Alphonso Alvarez Guerrero, the canonist Diego de Covarrubias, and the theologian Pedro de Soto.

Given its purpose to defend Parma and its legislation against the *Monitorio*, it was to be expected that Campomanes's treatise so expanded the purview of the temporal tenet of the Gallican tradition to the detriment of the church's spiritual authority as to strip it of any intrinsic right to own property or enjoy immunities from secular jurisdiction, much less to exercise any on its own except by revocable delegation by the state. Thus did the treatise defang Clement's or any ecclesiastical censure of any civil effect. "We are sufficiently enlightened today" to entertain any doubts about the true limits of the authority of the successor of Saint Peter—so reads the treatise's most resoundingly "enlightened" utterance.[65]

What is more surprising for the Spain of 1769 was the treatise's willingness to brave the holy of holies and examine the church as a spiritual power. In the course of this examination it contrived to question the thesis of papal infallibility even in the act of renouncing any intention of raising this question; to side with the Councils of Constance and Basel in locating the church's supreme power in the assembled "universal church"; to laud the works not only of such conciliarists as Gerson and Bossuet but even of Richer and Hontheim; and with them to define the church as the "assembly of all the faithful." At one point it went so far as to acknowledge the sometime right of this "faithful" to elect or designate candidates for clerical benefices.[66]

At times, the treatise even wandered into "patriotic" territory, by finding Spanish counterparts not only to Gallican liberties but also in the radically contemporary Gallican sense of allowing an "aristocratic" notion of the church's constitution to impinge on that of a divine-right absolute monarchy. For in incautiously denouncing "despotism" and even "absolute" power on the papacy's part, the treatise also seemed to suggest that formal appeals against unjust papal decrees might be licit against laws in the state as well, and it all but asserted that no law, secular or sacred, could be regarded as obligatory until ratified by something like universal consent. It was with misty nostalgia that Campomanes viewed the Visigothic constitution and post-Moorish meetings of the Spanish "Estates General" that, though only consultative under the kings, were veritable "solemn assemblies of the nation."[67] This exercise in interested erudition is reminiscent of the way in which, evident in the case against the Jesuits in France, similar rummaging in the ruins of the putative Frankish constitution by Boulainvilliers, Le Paige, and the abbé Mably had gradually sanctified the notion of national sovereignty in France. It goes without saying that Campomanes's *Juicio imparcial* was less than impartial on the subject of the Jesuits, blaming members of the "self-styled" Society of Jesus for being the chief modern "adulators of the Court of Rome" and the authors of a doctrine that had "erected two monarchies in the heart of the state, one temporal and the other ecclesiastic, the better to subject [the state] in all and for all to the Court of Rome." Along with Torrigiani, the treatise also identified the Jesuits as the chief authors of the papal *Monitorio* against Parma.[68]

The reaction to Campomanes's treatise revealed the limits of neo-Gallican ecclesiology and ideology in Spain. So "Jansenist" in tone did the *Juicio imparcial* seem to Frédéric Masson, the editor of Cardinal de Bernis's memoirs, that he maintained that the treatise's real author was a certain abbé François de

Joubert, a quite Jansenist son of a councilor in the Cour des aides in Montpellier.[69] So distressful was the reception of the treatise in Spain itself that Carlos III submitted it for inspection by his Extraordinary Council's five bishops and archbishops, who found enough "various doctrines and propositions worthy of censure" in it for the king to withdraw the first edition and have Moñino revise it for a second.[70]

Among the bishops on Carlos III's extraordinary council, even Rodríguez de Arellano and Felipe Bertrán of Salamanca—both signatories of letters of communion to Utrecht—deemed the treatise in need of correction. But if the source of their concern was the extent that Spanish Gallicanism as represented by Campomanes's *Juicio imparcial* was tending toward granting individual bishops much less councils any real independence from the state as well as the papacy, they need not have worried. Neither Carlos III nor Campomanes would demonstrate the courage of their Gallican convictions when later that year they humored Pope Clement XIV's ire by subjecting the bishop of Barcelona's kind words about the Church of Utrecht in a pastoral instruction to the same five bishops' critical examination, or when in 1770 they had the Council of Castile impose prior censorship on all episcopal pastoral instructions in reaction to another one by the same bishop.[71] With precocity rare for any reformist Catholic in eighteenth-century Catholic Europe, the bishop in question warned the abbé Clément that, in Spain as elsewhere, regalism was as much an obstacle to the reform of the Catholic Church as ultramontanism was.[72]

That observation, too, would be on full display in the papal conclave and negotiations that followed. Inasmuch as the conciliar tenet of the Gallican tradition would ever be a danger—and it would—it was when in France it took secularized political form rather than ecclesiastical form.

THE PAPAL CONCLAVE AND THE DIPLOMATIC DENOUEMENT

The breach opened up between French and Spanish priorities by the Parmesan crisis only widened with the death of Pope Clement XIII and the politics of choosing his successor. For in order to influence the choice of his successor, the Bourbon courts needed to prioritize the qualities they hoped to find in candidates for the Tiara with a view to the demands they intended to make of the new pontificate. In doing so, it became apparent that while Choiseul's first concern was France's permanent acquisition of Avignon and the Comtat Venaissin, Carlos III's chief aim was to obtain the prompt papal dissolution of the Society of Jesus. Where Carlos thought it perfectly in canonical order to have the French, Neapolitan, and Spanish cardinals—the Bourbon "court cardinals," or the "nazionali," as they were also called—to demand that the whole conclave formalize its willingness to dissolve the Society as a condition for any candidate, Choiseul found the demand for any such prior commitment to be indecent at best and positively simoniacal at worst—that is, an exercise in obtaining a spiritual office by means of a material promise. But as the architect of both the Bourbon Family Pact and the anti-Jesuit addition to its aims, Choiseul was in no position to dismiss the Spanish king's priorities out of hand. His only alternative was to identify and help raise to the Tiara a candidate who as pope would be open to such a dissolution, and be amenable to persuasion to do so by "moderate" but firm forms of persuasion. In this endeavor he got cooperation from the Neapolitan cardinal Orsini and two of the five French cardinals able to participate in the conclave, Bernis and Paul d'Albert, cardinal de Luynes. Whether or not Choiseul liked it, the result was a papal conclave and election dominated from the beginning by the issue of the future of the Jesuits.

The obstacles were formidable because most of the Italian cardinals felt committed to the defense of the Jesuits, at the center of whose ranks stood the *zelanti* (conservative) core of the so-called palace cardinals, who, the sinews of the curia resident in or near Rome, moved in the orbits of the Albani and Rezzonico clans headed by Gian Francesco Albani and the deceased pope's nephew Carlo Rezzonico. Besides the Neapolitan cardinal, the most notable exceptions were members of the Corsini clan, whose palazzo served as the abbé Clément's refuge while in Rome.

Given Carlos III's nonnegotiable desiderata and Roda's jaundiced memories of the curia, the first Spanish ranking of the cardinal candidates not surprisingly excluded more than half of them headed by the Bourbon dynasty's rogue gallery of those allied with Torrigiani, to which Spain later added all the members of the Rezzonico and Albani clans.[73] Even the first Spanish list left only eleven cardinals as "good," the first choice of whom was Sersale, archbishop of Naples, but among whom already figured the Franciscan and eventually successful candidate, Lorenzo Ganganelli. In predictable reaction, Choiseul urged more flexibility by way of moving some of the "doubtful" cardinals into the electable category. He too, however, ranked Ganganelli as "very good," leaving only Tanucci to suspect him as too Jesuitical. The Ganganelli that the Neapolitan first minister recalled was probably the cardinal who voted against Mésenguy's catechism in the papal congregation that condemned it.[74]

Since their only hope lay in the influence of the court cardinals, the chief danger for the Bourbon courts was that resident zelanti cardinals would elect the new pope before the court cardinals arrived for the conclave. While the cardinals secluded themselves in the conclave as promptly as 15 February 1769, Bernis and Luynes did not enter the conclave until late March, and the two Spanish cardinals, Buenaventura Córdoba Espínola de la Cerda of Toledo and Francisco de Solis of Seville, not until the end of the next month. Meanwhile the Bourbon diplomatic corps, including the Spanish beneficial agent, José Nicolás Azara, were left in Rome to hold the fort. In the event of the resident zelanti trying to steal a march on the Bourbon cardinals, the Bourbon envoys, including the cardinals, occasionally brandished an ultimate weapon, namely, the threat to withdraw from Rome and refuse to recognize any nominee without Bourbon participation. This threat they often softened as a protestation that while they had no instructions to impose a candidate, they stood opposed to any effort by the conclave to elect one without their participation.[75] However stated, the threat was powerful. A hint of schism was in the air, and the Portuguese example was there. Should the conclave have forgotten that menace, Portugal's rambunctious Almeida returned to Rome at the end of April armed with the nuclear option of using an army if the court cardinals did not get their way.[76]

What the Bourbon goal and zelanti resentment against it would mean in practice is a conclave condemned to inconclusive maneuvering in which the court party refused to propose any candidates for fear of damning them by association, while the zelanti "Sanhedrin"—the Neapolitan cardinal Filippo Maria Pirelli's term—occasionally tried to carry the day by surprise. Since court participation included Spain, whose two cardinals did not arrive in Rome until the end of April, it also extended this maneuvering to four interminable months. The arrival of the two French cardinals in March only perpetuated this pattern by reinforcing the ranks of the court cardinals and adding to them the court-acquired political acumen of Bernis, who with Orsini was also able to exploit rifts within the zelanti ranks between the Albani contingent and Carlo Rezzonico, who acted as the party's official strategist.[77] For the court party, the days of greatest danger of a successful zelanti coup occurred in mid to late April after Gian Francesco Albani nominated the reputedly philo-Jesuit Gaetano Fantuzzi, whereupon an alarmed conclave learned on 13 April that the Spanish cardinals might not arrive until May. This candidacy was all the more dangerous in that it enjoyed the sympathy of such natural court allies as the Corsini pair. It was in part to the Albani-Rezzonico rivalry that Filippo Maria Pirelli, the conclave's most reliable diarist, attributed Fantuzzi's failure.[78]

It was therefore not before La Cerda and Solis arrived in Rome and entered the conclave at the end of April that things began to happen, the first of which was a sense of alarm at their peremptory instructions and Bernis's successful effort to prompt Choiseul to veto any proposal to exact a written promise from a candidate, much less the whole conclave, to abolish the Society of Jesus. Only at that point did the voting begin in good earnest, at which late date the court cardinals and their unlikely allies were numerous enough to parry every objectionable move. As fast as the nominations flew up they fell down, due not only to Bourbon sharpshooting but also to Austrian indifference to their own eligible cardinal and an ongoing rift between the Albani and Rezzonico clans. By mid-May the conclave had run through all the candidates who might have been acceptable to the Bourbon courts, while the court cardinals did not even dare to put up anybody so notoriously pro-Bourbon as Sersale. The only possible candidate to remain unscathed was Ganganelli, who, the sole monk in the College of Cardinals, had all along held his own on the Bourbon's list of desirables without ever being the most desired. Although early in the conclave Rezzonico had publicly proclaimed that Ganganelli was the last cardinal he would vote for, every poll had produced a few votes for him, while none had taken him out of contention.[79]

The third of four children born to a minor noble family in Sant'Arcangelo near Rimini and Ravenna, Giovanni Vincenzo Antonio Ganganelli saw the light of day on 31 October 1705. His father sent him to study with the Jesuits in Rimini, only to withdraw him and send him for further study with the generally anti-Jesuit Scolopians in Urbino, where at the age of eighteen he decided to enter the Francisan Order under the name of Lorenzo. The success of his studies in theology and philosophy there and elsewhere eventually took him to the elite Franciscan college of Saint Bonaventure in Rome, where he received a doctorate in theology in 1731 and returned as its director in 1741. Throughout these formative years Ganganelli remained on good terms with the Jesuits, and it was with their support and that of the pro-Jesuit cardinal Giuseppe Maria Castelli that Clement XIII raised him to the cardinalate in 1759.

But his unswerving loyalty to the Jesuits did not survive the reverses that began to befall their society that same year, after which Ganganelli began to tack on the isssues that came his way. So although Ganganelli had made it onto Tanucci's ample list of personae non gratae apropos of his vote against Mesenguy's catechism, he also embraced the cause of the canonization of Palafox, in part under the influence of Roda during the Spaniard's sojourn in Rome. As miniser of grace and justice, Roda always ranked Ganganelli very high in his list of *papabili*. In these more polarized circumstances, Ganganelli as cardinal also aquired a reputation of never entirely speaking his mind, of cultivating an aura of mystery rather than a halo of holiness, and of perhaps playing a long political game beneath the guise of humility and timidity.

As the papal conclave of 1769 ran out of options toward mid-May, Gangenelli emerged as a kind of textual claire-obscure into which the conclave's opposing caucuses might read their respective agendas and hope for the best. In conversations with Solis's and then Bernis's assistant conclavists on the last days before the election, Ganganelli gave reason to suppose not only that he was critical of the Jesuits but also that he believed that a pope possessed the right to suppress the Society on his own authority—even that it would be useful to do so—as long as the relevant canonical precepts and standards of justice were not flaunted.[80] At the same time, Castelli himself could not forget that he had reasons enough for having sponsored his elevation to the cardinalate in the first place, and everyone knew that Ganganelli had sided with Clement XIII against Mésenguy's catechism.[81] As Cardinal Pirelli observed, he gave everyone some reason "to believe that he was on his side," while in the conclave itself, as Albani added, he did little more to become pope than "always to stay in his cell."[82]

The decisive development, according to Pirelli, was Albani's success in prying the Spanish away from Orsini and, learning that they wanted Ganganelli, delivering his own party, including Castelli—and minus only Rezzonico—while leaving it to Solis to convert the court cardinals.[83] On the court side one of the last to fall in line was Bernis himself, who until the eleventh hour did not know what to make of Ganganelli.[84] But since Solis had learned from the Spanish envoy Azpuru that Choiseul and the French court thought well enough of him, he had the means to convince Bernis, who in turn converted Orsini. With Orsini's help, Bernis's most important contribution was probably to convince the two Spanish cardinals that, if acted on, their instructions to obtain a formal commitment from either the conclave or a candidate to suppress the Jesuits would be politically fatal as well as simoniacal. In any case, on 19 May forty-six members of the conclave elected Ganganelli by a unanimous vote minus his own, which as a conciliatory gesture he cast for Rezzonico. Assuming in another conciliatory gesture the title of Clement XIV—the namesake of his much maligned predecessor—Ganganelli officially became the new pope with his consecration as a bishop on 28 May and coronation with the Tiara on 4 June. Except among many of the Jesuits, the rejoicing upon his elevation was universal, but nowhere more enthusiastic than in Spain.

By all sober secondary accounts, Cardinal Ganganelli thus emerged from the papal conclave of 1769 without having written or signed any formal promise to abolish the Society of Jesus during his pontificate. At most he expressed himself orally and in general terms to the effect that he deemed it within the papacy's power to suppress such a religious order, and that in this case he was open to doing so. But Clement XIV hardly had time to settle into his new role in the Quirinal Palace before he came under intense pressure to do so promptly from the courts of France, Naples, Spain, and even the Portugal of Carvalho, who similarly made the dissolution of the Jesuits the condition of the restoration of full diplomatic relations. But no one was more insistent than Carlos III, who behaved very much as though the new pope had in fact committed himself to a surgical suppression of the Society without any of his reported conditions.

The first person to feel Spanish impatience was Choiseul, whose idea for a papal suppression had always been more generous than this king's and whose first priority was France's permanent acquisition of Avignon and the Comtat Venaissin. Choiseul in turn deflected that pressure onto Bernis, whom Choiseul had meanwhile persuaded to stay on in Rome and take d'Aubeterre's place as France's ambassador.[85] For his part Bernis had also already found himself the object of intense distrust by Carlos III and Grimaldi, in part because he had dragged his feet on Ganganelli's candidacy, in part because he had opposed the Spanish quest for a written promise from a would-be pope to dissolve the Jesuits, and in part because word had reached Spanish ears that Bernis thought the negotiations in Rome a mere façade for the real diplomatic action going on in secrecy between the new pope and Carlos's confessor.[86]

While these Spanish suspicions about Bernis's speculations were far from unfounded, Choiseul gave both of them short shrift and allowed neither to do any damage so long as he remained in power. Although the Spanish undoubtedly attached more importance to the papal dissolution of the Jesuits than did Choiseul, the architect of the Bourbon Family Pact was not about to endanger it for want of zeal in supporting what had become Spanish policy in Rome. It would only be after the fall of Choiseul from power at the end of 1770 that, in tacit complicity with a new ministry at Versailles, Bernis allowed the spirit if not the letter of French papal policy to drift ever farther from Spain's. Until then, Bernis loyally carried out his official instructions to support Spanish ecclesiastical policy in Rome, sometimes even going beyond the passive support of Spanish policy enjoined on him by his instructions.

The first such occasion presented itself as early as 4 July, when under Spanish pressure Choiseul instructed Bernis to join Azpuru and Orsini in resubmitting copies of their memoirs originally presented to Clement XIII on 16–21 January 1769. What forced Bernis and Choiseul's hand was Clement XIV's pro-forma grant on 12 July to the Jesuits' general Ricci in reply to his request for indulgences for the Society's missionaries, plus the public political use to which the Jesuits immediately put this grant. As the representative of the senior branch of the Bourbon house, Bernis took the initiative in convening a meeting with Azpuru and Orsini and in restating the Bourbon demands in a memoir he presented in one of his first audiences with the new pope, on 22 July.

But well before Bernis had heard back from any of these courts, Choiseul took it upon himself to allay ongoing Spanish impatience by staging a spectacular anticurial as well as anti-Jesuit rant at the expense of the papal nuncio in the presence of the Spanish ambassador, Heredia y Moncayo, conde de Fuentes, in Compiègne on 3 August 1769. Pressing home the point, Choiseul's next dispatches to Bernis gave the pope no more than two months to have done with the Jesuits. Having rightly or wrongly declared war on the Jesuits, Choiseul wrote to Bernis, the Bourbon powers had better win that war, as though finding it intolerable that France and Spain's recent defeats by the English be followed by another by the Jesuits. Choiseul's original idea to use common opposition to the Society to knit the Bourbon Family Pact more tightly now seemed in danger of unraveling it.

In Rome, the papal object of all this pressure was ill prepared to take the helm of Saint Peter's bark, much less brave this storm so early in his voyage. Of modest and unconnected familial pedigree and the only monk in the College of Cardinals, Ganganelli faced the hostility of the largely philo-Jesuit cardinals, having had no time to elevate any of his own. Nor could he even trust his own secretary of state, the former nuncio to Spain Lazzaro Pallavicini, whom Spain all but imposed on him by reason of his being related to Grimaldi, much less the increasingly militant pro-Jesuit secretary of codes, Giuseppe Garampi, whom it took the pope a year or more to "exile" to Poland as nuncio there.[87] Partly for these reasons, Clement XIV had taken to working with a few obscure confidants, such Vincenzo Macedonio, secretary of the Memorials of Rites, and Innocenzo Buontempi, his fellow Franciscan, personal secretary and confessor; for the rest he did as much as possible by himself.[88] His only allies among the cardinals were the Bourbon court cardinals to whom he was most beholden for his election but who had vacated Rome, except for the very cardinals under orders to press him. As Bernis acutely observed a year later, the tendency of Fra Lorenzo under these circumstances was "to promise out of fear and then to postpone making good on [his promises] on account of still other fears, without fully understanding where this conduct [would] lead him."[89]

By that time, alas, this conduct had led the pope to do what he had carefully avoided doing during the conclave: that is, giving written promises to dissolve the Society of Jesus. What led him into this fateful impasse was a flurry of fraught meetings in the months following Bernis's audience of 22 July in the context of Spanish impatience that prompted the pope to look to France for refuge, while Bernis, acutely conscious of Spanish mistrust of his diplomacy, sought to shift the responsibility for the negotiations onto Azpuru and Spain. To be sure, the pope reiterated his need to observe canonical forms and a modicum of justice and to avoid the perception of having obtained the Tiara by promising to destroy the Jesuits. Nor did he fail to remind the ambassadors that, as father of all the faithful, he could not but note that besides Portugal and the Bourbon states no other Catholic states were asking for the dissolution of the Jesuits, to say nothing of Protestant Prussia, whose prince-elector had signaled his opposition to it. Along with real fears of his "enemies" in Rome and of being poisoned by Jesuits or their friends, these reasons for delay became the leitmotifs of Clement XIV's whole anguished pontificate.

But the fears tended to get the better of the reasons and translated into a compensatory need for trust on the part of those powers that had rallied to the candidacy of Ganganelli. So when his repeated oral assurances to Bernis, Orsini, and Azpuru that he meant to keep his promises failed fully to allay Bourbon mistrust, he felt compelled first to write a letter in his own hand to Louis XV on 25 September and then—far more fatefully—another to Carlos III on 29 November. Attributable in part to Bernis's influence, these letters temporarily dissipated Spanish suspicion of Bernis and brought an equally temporary tranquillity to the pope.

What must in part have enabled Clement XIV to commit his promises in writing and regain a modicum of tranquillity is Carlos III's assurance to him that, while renewing his demand to dissolve the Jesuits' society, the king would allow him to "take all the time he need[ed] to settle on the means and take his precautions," unless excessive delays obliged the Bourbon courts to return to the charge. Sent to the pope on 25 July in the midst of this crisis of confidence via Grimaldi and Azpuru—and insufficiently stressed by historians of the papal dissolution—these assurances would later give Carlos cause for chagrin, just as they would fail to make the pope's tranquillity last very long.[90] Carlos would eventually renew his demands, while never releasing the pope from the trap into which his written promises had enclosed him.

In principle, and at Bernis's suggestion, Clement XIV had offered to follow up his written promises with a brief on his own initiative, or *motu proprio*, that would confer retrospective papal approval of the actions that the Bourbon states had already undertaken against the Jesuits and their property.[91] In the end, Spain was the only Bourbon state to take up his offer of such a papal brief, even acceding to his request for a testimony of "national" authority, including the anti-Jesuit testimonies of no fewer than thirty-four—eventually forty-six of sixty—Spanish bishops long mobilized to produce them as part of the Extraordinary Council's strategy of 21 March 1768 and a formal order by Roda on 22 October 1769.[92]

Along the way, however, some accounts by Bernis of his papal audiences forwarded by Azpuru to Grimaldi gave rise to renewed Spanish suspicions of the

French cardinal's intentions because they seemed to assume that Spain had requested the brief rather than accepting a papal offer, that a papal brief was necessary to legitimize Spain's past expulsion instead of helping to dissipate pro-Jesuit "fanaticism" in Spain, and that the brief concerned Spain alone rather than all the Bourbon states.[93] It took a new round of acrimonious exchanges between Madrid and Versailles for Choiseul to calm Spanish qualms and make it clear that Gallican France fully accepted Spain's quite Gallican interpretation of the papal motu proprio. That said, Gallican France was less than ideally positioned to do so, since one of the reasons Louis XV wanted no papal brief was that he wanted no papal approval for what his radically Gallican parlements had done. In contrast to what had transpired in Spain, moreover, his sole consultation of French bishops had produced a resounding endorsement of the Jesuits, minus four or five leftover anti-Molinist Gallicans, and it was highly unlikely that a new consultation would produce a different result.

Carlos III was never to get this brief motu proprio. Throughout the waning months of 1769 and all of 1770 Bernis and Azpuru received assurances from the pope with every other audience that the brief was just about ready, that he had only to add touchups here and there.[94] Still it failed to appear, the reasons varying from one audience to the next. So long as Choiseul remained in power, Bernis too chafed at this delay and continued loyally to press for the official Bourbon demand for a speedy end to the Jesuits. When on 3 December 1769 King José I of Portugal escaped yet another attempted assassination that Carvalho again imputed to the Jesuits, Bernis took it upon himself to represent Portugal as well as the Bourbon courts in a memoir for the pope that, delivered on 22 January, was so "calumnious" in tone as to embarrass one of Bernis's most apologetic biographers.[95] And so peremptory was another such démarche on 9 June 1770 that Choiseul saw fit to remind Bernis that he was only to follow Spain's and Azpuru's lead, not lead himself.[96]

It was only in the wake of this rebuke that a stung Bernis learned from Azpuru that Carlos III had again granted the pope additional time to fulfill his promises. Assuming that Choiseul had known about this exchange of letters, Bernis apologized while acknowledging that it was with reason that the pope had recently told him, "I have informed the king of Spain of the reasons for the delay, and I am authorized by his reply to devote the necessary time to the affair of the Jesuits on which I am working alone."[97] Did Clement XIV ever receive any such dispensation of time in writing from Carlos? He did indeed, according to the historian Danvila y Collado, who, references to the diplomatic archives in Simancas in hand, cites letters giving royal permission to the pope to take the time he needed, first on 25 July 1769 and a year later on 17 July 1770.[98]

Although these minimal exchanges may constitute a direct and "secret" diplomacy of sorts, they apparently represent the full extent of it.

What makes it very difficult to see clearly into this underbrush of unacknowledged correspondence is that, where Bernis is concerned, it is hopelessly tangled with his conviction that the pope was also indirectly in correspondence with the Spanish king via his confessor, Eleta. It is "certain"—so Bernis explained the delay in the papal motu proprio to Choiseul on 18 July—"that the pope maintains a regular relation with the king's . . . confessor, as it is very apparent that it is by this route that His Holiness has secured the tranquillity he enjoys these days and from which, he assures us, he will profit to satisfy the [Bourbon] courts." One of several reasons for Spanish distrust of Bernis from the outset, his belief in the reality of such a secret channel of diplomacy was very real and remained a constant in his correspondence that neither Choiseul nor Bernis's subsequent discovery of a real exchange of letters and a cause for papal delay ever entirely dispelled.[99]

If indeed Clement XIV carried on a confidential correspondence with Eleta about the Jesuits, it has escaped the detection of all historians except for passing on Bernis's references to it without inquiring into their veracity, much less their cumulative effect on French diplomacy. The rumor of such a correspondence seems rather to hearken back to Eleta's acknowledged role in Clement XIV's predecessor's successful attempt to persuade Carlos III to rescind his imposition of the exequatur on papal pronouncements in 1763. The only correspondence Eleta seems to have maintained with Clement XIV concerned Spain's desired canonization of Palafox and María de Ágreda, a seventeenth-century champion of the doctrine of the Immaculate Conception of the Virgin Mary, the mere mention of which exasperated Choiseul's patience.[100]

By the autumn of 1770, however, Choiseul's was not advice that Bernis had to follow for very long, as Choiseul and his "party" fell from power in a spectacular ministerial coup on 29 December 1770. Known as the "Maupeou coup" on account of the rise of the new chancellor, René-Nicolas-Charles-Augustin de Maupeou, this drastic ministerial reshuffling originated in the simultaneous threats of having to go to war against Great Britain on the side of France's Spanish ally in a dispute over the Falkland Islands off Argentina and the Parlement of Paris's ever rising constitutional assertiveness against royal authority, most recently on display in its attempt to try Emmanuel-Armand de Vignerot, the duc d'Aiguillon, for his conduct as the royal governor of the province of Brittany in the 1760s.

Having all too recently suffered an ignominious defeat at the expense of staggering debts at the hands of Great Britain in the Seven Years' War, Louis XV chose war with his parlements instead, in the form of a disciplinary edict that the new chancellor, Maupeou, knew would provoke parlementary resistance. When that resistance materialized, Maupeou used it first to exile the magistrates of the Parlement of Paris, followed by those who imitated them in the provincial parlements, and then to impose a drastic reform on the parlements that took away their right of prior remonstrances while also depriving them of much of their jurisdiction. "Pushed to the limits," as he put it, by his parlements that "went so far as to dispute his sovereign authority held from God alone," Louis XV informed his Spanish "brother and cousin" on 21 December that he had "resolved to make himself obeyed by all means" and that war under these circumstances "would be an atrocious evil for both him and his people."[101]

Since Choiseul's whole system of governance had depended on a modicum of cooperation with the parlements in the pursuit of other goals, Choiseul had to go, as did the rest of his clan at court. On the ashes of Choiseul's pyre arose the "triumvirate" of Maupeou as chancellor, the abbé Joseph-Marie Terray as controller general of finances, and eventually none other than the duc d'Aiguillon as Choiseul's replacement at the helm of foreign affairs. But the antiparlementary aspect of Maupeou's "revolution"—so named by the "patriot" and still partly Jansenist opposition—also carried with it the triumph of the anti-Jansenist and philo-Jesuit parti dévot at the royal court, even though none of the new ministers was particularly "devout" and the whole grouping had to pay court to the king's new mistress, Jeanne Bécu de Cantigny, comtesse du Barry, whose political merit was to have been an agent of Choiseul's fall.

The genuinely devout core of this coterie consisted of the likes of the Antoine de Quélen, duc de La Vauguyon, director of the royal children's education; and the king's pious sisters, or Mesdames de France, led by Madame Louise, who with a great show of rococo devotion took vows at a Carmelite convent in Saint-Denis in 1771. This court "party" enjoyed clerical support from the most anti-Jansenist, pro-*Unigenitus* members of the episcopacy, headed by the archbishop of Paris, Christophe de Beaumont, who tapped his cathedral chapter to designate the clerical councilors in the reformed Maupeou parlement in Paris. In the midst of this mix stood the newly influential papal nuncio, Bernardino Giraud, who immediately began agitating for the return of Avignon and the Comtat Venaissin.

The demise of the old parlements and the rise of the parti dévot inevitably translated into domestic political consequences. The most blatant among these was a royal declaration that ended the exile of all the priests banished from the realm by the old Parlement of Paris during the 1750s for having publicly refused the sacraments to appellants of *Unigenitus* or other suspected Jansenists, most of them under the orders of Christophe de Beaumont.[102] Before the Maupeou coup, this measure in the making had come to the attention of the Parlement's magistrates, at which point the abbé Clément and his Italian friends had entertained the hope that the amnesty might be broadened to include the vastly more numerous Jansenist priests and professors sidelined by the Formula of Alexander VII or the requirement to accept *Unigenitus,* and thereby function as a tacit abrogation of these anti-Jansenist monuments.

But under post-Maupeou circumstances such an irenic turn of this legislation enjoyed no greater chance of realization than the canonization of Jansenius. So the only ecclesiastics to benefit from it were embittered anti-Jansenists, among them a certain number of ex-Jesuits, such as a certain abbé Madier—also the confessor for Mesdames de France—for whom Christophe de Beaumont found Parisian benefices that Madier himself promptly used to find Jansenists to whom he might publicly refuse the sacraments.[103] The pope himself expressed his happiness in reaction to the recall of the exiled priests to Bernis on 10 July, while partisans of the Society read the news of the inclusion of some ex-Jesuits as a hopeful omen for its imminent restitution in France.

The conspicuous appearance and carryings-on of ex-Jesuits in Paris and Avignon did not escape the notice of the conde de Fuentes, Spain's ambassador to Versailles, whose reports prompted Grimaldi to authorize him to complain to d'Aiguillon about the new policy of "introducing Jesuits in France and [even] conferring on them the right to preach, [a policy lending itself] to the belief that France has changed its way of thinking . . . , and that it is no longer interested in the [Society's] extinction."[104] D'Aiguillon's response was to remind the Spanish that, unlike Portugal's and Spain's, France's king had not literally expelled the Jesuits and that, although the Parlement of Paris did so in the wake of the Spanish expulsion in 1767, the royal Edict of November 1764 had allowed them to remain as "particulars" in the realm.

A closely related cause of concern to Spain as well as to Naples and Portugal about the recent turn in French ecclesiastical policy was the Maupeou parlement's registration of royal letters patent of 22 January that seemed to give free entry into France to all papal bulls, briefs, and other "expeditions from the Court of Rome."[105] To France's Spanish ally, these measures appeared to have done nothing short of abrogating the Gallican liberties in France that the other Catholic courts were then busily trying to obtain. This interpretation of the letters patent appeared to be the right one, not only to the Molinist portion of the Parisian clergy but even to Clement XIV, who found himself "touched to the quick" by this manifestation of Louis XV's "piety" and wrote him a letter to this effect while enjoining confidentiality on Bernis, "lest it give umbrage to the Spanish, who have seemed less than content" with the measure.[106]

That lack of contentment is the understatement of the entire year, as Grimaldi and Fuentes all but forced d'Aiguillon to walk those letters patent in reverse and had Maupeou swallow them by means of new letters patent that interpreted those of 22 January as restricted to papal measures that concerned the "for intérieur" or the soul alone in such sacraments as marriage.[107] So it was with great relief that Grimaldi instructed Fuentes on 28 April 1772 to congratulate d'Aiguillon and other "good patriots"—the words are Grimaldi's—in the French ministry for having vanquished the "oppositions and even cabals [in the French court]," behind which Grimaldi spied the influence of the papal nuncio.[108] Together with the chagrin of Carlos III at the fall of Choiseul and pointed criticism of his successor in a letter to Louis XV, the tensions created by France's "devout" and philo-Jesuit turn on the domestic front made for a full-blown crisis in relations between the two Bourbon allies, such that Grimaldi and Fuentes had to defend themselves against accusations of trying to interfere in France's internal affairs.[109]

Meanwhile, in Rome Bernis could not have remained insensitive to these developments and their implications for France's foreign ecclesiastical policies that many drew from them, in Rome as well as France. "Since the changes that the king [of France] has deemed necessary to make in his court," reported Bernis on 16 January 1771, "the partisans of the Jesuits . . . bruit it about that the Society has nothing further to fear," while "just about the whole city of Rome expects the imminent restitution of Avignon."[110] Indeed, no sooner did Louis Phelypeaux de Saint-Florentin, as of 1770 duc de la Vrillière, temporarily take over the helm at the ministry of foreign affairs than Bernis began receiving request upon sanctimonious request from the nuncio in Paris for the restitution of Avignon and the Comtat. When in March it became clear to Bernis that the papal secretary of state, Pallavicini, approved of these requests, he well knew that the impulse came from the pope, whereupon he took it upon himself to plead the case of Rome for restitution. But while the instructions he received from Versailles confirmed that in contrast to Choiseul's policy the new ministry meant to make the matter negotiable, the ministry also subjected it to review by Carlos III, who immediately insisted on making that restitution dependent on the papal suppression of the Jesuits. The king of Spain offered no grounds for supposing that policy had changed in Madrid.

From this much Bernis might have been able to calculate that after France had disappointed Spain by its refusal to stand by its ally in the Falkland Islands crisis, the survival of the alliance with Spain would depend on its allowing its ally to prevail against the Jesuits. And to be sure, Ossun soon received orders from Saint-Florentin via Fuentes reassuring Carlos III that Louis XV meant to keep to his commitments to his royal cousin about the Jesuits, while Bernis conveyed similar reassurance on Saint-Florentin's orders to Azpuru and Orsini in Rome.[111] Yet the spirit behind the letter of these instructions could not but be subverted by addenda to them, such as Saint-Florentin's on 19 March that "although the King [of France] by complaisance for the King his cousin . . . had asked for the suppression of the Jesuits, he has no particular interest in obtaining it."[112] Hints as to Louis's reluctance to follow Spain in pursuing the Jesuits to the point of extinction spoke all the more loudly in that behind Saint-Florentin and until the appointment of d'Aiguillon it was really the king himself who was conducting French foreign policy. This descent from a diplomacy of inertial passivity to that of disloyal lassitude reached bottom with Saint-Florentin's advice that while it was evident that the pope was playing for time on the issue of the Jesuits, France was "disposed to give him the most entire satisfaction on that score, unless the court of Madrid should decide to inject more activity [into that negotiation]."[113]

In Rome, the recipient of such dispatches hardly needed to be a weathercock to know which way the wind was blowing at Versailles or much lubrication to bend with that wind. It was then that Bernis sent packing such "intriguers" as the "Jansenist parlementaire" abbé Clément, who since 1769 had taken up residence in the Corsini Palace in an effort to restore direct communion between the estranged Church of Utrecht and the papacy.[114] Since arriving in Rome he had set up in grand style as the personification of the "grande nation" in the Palazzo di Sciarra, insinuated himself with greater success than the other Bourbon envoys into the confidence of Clement XIV, and had come to sympathize with his reasons for delay.

Nor were such reasons wanting. Although the Austrian empress Maria Theresa had made it clear as of 1769 that her court would not oppose the Bourbon courts' demands, her court no more than any other non-Bourbon or Portuguese Catholic sovereign's was asking for the end of the Jesuits, while in all Catholic countries as well in Asia and the Americas the task of replacing the Jesuits in their colleges, seminaries, and missions loomed as herculean. Although by 1771 the pope had managed to ease such pro-Jesuit cardinals as Garampi out of their employments and Rome itself, the only new cardinal he had elevated whom he could count on was the Augustinian theologian Mario Compagnoni Marefoschi.[115] Given these real reasons for caution, it was hard for Bernis not to be sympathetic. His last critical remarks about the pure fear lurking behind the pope's apparent finesse date back to August 1770; by 1772 we find him calling Clement XIV the "Fabius of popes" and admiring the "prudence and skill with which he is handling the affair of the Jesuits."[116]

Finding it ever harder not to hope that Clement XIV would find a way to wriggle his way out of his promises to Carlos III, but in possession of little evidence that Carlos had changed his mind, Bernis had no better recourse than to revive the supposed secret diplomacy between the pope and that king's confessor. And unlike Choiseul, neither Saint-Florentin nor d'Aiguillon after him was in any position or even disposition to know better. Thus in his report to Saint-Florentin on 24 April 1771 Bernis congratulated himself for having figured out—or at least "not having been wrong"—that the pope's conviction that the king of Spain remained "content" with his conduct was due to the tendency of Carlos to "invest greater trust in his confessor on the affair of the Jesuits than in his ministers."[117] It was therefore "useless to try to speculate in what the pope's correspondence with his Most Catholic Majesty's confessor consists," Bernis speculated a week later, since only its results would "inform us what that monarch will have decided with the Sovereign Pontiff about the Jesuits"— "conjectures" that Saint-Florentin found "very solid" and alone capable of explaining the delays.[118]

For his part, not only did Saint-Florentin find such speculations convincing, he also began openly to express the hope out loud that the king of Spain might imitate France's example and "decide no longer to insist on the fulfillment of [the pope's] promises."[119] From these thoughts it was but a short step to ruminating, as the pro tempore foreign minister did on 19 March, that the only way that the papacy "could . . . solidly fix the status [of the Jesuits] in this realm" was the expedient of a separate vicar rejected by Clement XIII in 1762; or frankly to wishing, as Bernis did in response, that if instead of demanding the entire extinction of the Jesuits the Bourbon courts had "limited themselves to asking for some such reform . . . , they would perhaps have obtained it with the consent of all the other courts."[120] From the Spanish point of view these thoughts were far from loyal, since Clement XIV knew about the failed French edict of reform of March 1762 and had occasionally expressed interest in it.

When d'Aiguillon took over the reins of French foreign affairs in June 1771, it immediately seemed clear to him that the only sense to be made of papal policy was as an attempt to gain time and to "find the means of getting the Spanish Catholic Majesty no longer to insist 'à la rigueur' on an absolute suppression of the society."[121] Besides representing the interests of all the Catholic states that had lodged no complaints against the Jesuits, the pope by then had begun to argue that Spain's desired beatification of Palafox needed to precede the dissolution of the Jesuits, even that Tanucci's attempts to end Naples's feudal dependency on the Papal States distracted him from any other issue.[122] Meanwhile he maintained a steady drumbeat of symbolically punitive gestures against the Jesuits by depriving them of the direction of colleges and seminaries in the Papal States: the Greek College in Rome in 1769, a seminary in Frascati in 1770, and most traumatically of all, an inspection of the Roman and Irish Colleges in Rome by a hostile commission in May 1771 followed by the suspension of the Roman College and reassignment of the Irish College in September 1772. But as time went by, it did not escape the notice of observers, including Bernis and d'Aiguillon, much less of Carlos III, that these measures served just as well as substitutes for the dissolution of the Society as preludes to it.

Yet these developments did nothing to change the tenor of French diplomatic correspondence, in which Bernis continued to attribute the pope's tactics of Fabian delay to a possible change in Spanish policy due to the role of Carlos's confessor, while d'Aiguillon took Saint-Florentin's place in professing to believe him. None of this pro-Jesuit drift in French policy escaped the notice of the royal courts in Madrid, Naples, and Lisbon, which began to accuse Bernis of a fatal "partiality for the Jesuits," behind which the pope himself discerned the further fear that France's king had "changed his system concerning the Jesuits."[123] By November 1771 Bernis was adjusting his sails not only to winds blowing from his own court but also to closer ones emanating from the Duchy of Parma, where a clerical coup aided by the duke's Habsburg wife, Mariá Amelia, sent the anti-Jesuit minister Du Tillot packing, taking Parma momentarily out of the anti-Jesuit coalition and causing Carlos III to dispatch the councilor Pedro de Cevallos in an effort to control the damage. When soon afterward Carlos found it necessary to replace the apoplectically ailing Azpuru with Orsini as Spain's spokesperson in Rome, d'Aiguillon's fear that the pope might be "harder pressed" by a tougher successor gave way to the hope that Orsini's new role would prove to be permanent, and that he would conduct the negotiations with as little "vivacity" as Azpuru had done.[124]

Alas, however, Azpuru may have been down, but he was not yet quite out, and even as d'Aiguillon wrote these lines in January 1772—and in a moment of lucidity that Bernis wrote off as a bout of "senility"—he faulted himself for having allowed the pope to "temporize" while also announcing his composition of a forthcoming memoir for Orsini that would prove that the pope had failed to keep his word to him about the Jesuits on several precise occasions.[125]

That memoir never materialized, but the threat of it was enough to provoke a revealing confession by Bernis to d'Aiguillon of his innermost feelings about the Bourbon project of obtaining the papal dissolution of the Jesuits—and his full distance from the Spanish position.[126] Since in Bernis's reasoning the pope had to act as judge and not solicitor in the affair of the Jesuits, he could hardly ask the many Catholic states that had not demanded the extirpation of the Society that they now do so without irrefutable proof of the jugular premise in the case against them from 1759 onward: namely, that "the rule of the Jesuits is vicious and in no way susceptible to reformation." Since Bernis had constantly been of the opinion that the truth of that premise could never be demonstrated, he had "always regarded the total suppression of the Jesuits as something almost impossible" to obtain, and had come to see the wisdom of Clement's temporiz-ing with a view to the probability that the Spanish might eventually appreciate the advantages of a reform instead of an extinction unwarranted by any "proofs of the total corruption" of the Society.

The reform of the Society that Bernis envisioned was predictably the one proposed by the Parlement's gens du roi in 1761–1762 consisting in a reduction of the power of the general. That reform, Bernis thought, was the pope's "real plan" that would enable the papacy to acquit itself of its promises with "dignity," the Bourbon courts to obtain their promises with "honor," and the Jesuits themselves to emerge from their trials with "utility" as well as "honor." In response, d'Aiguillon not only shared Bernis's "conjectures" but also hoped that if "by complaisance for his cousin and king" Louis XV had supported Spain's policy on the issue, the final "denouement of the affair . . . would take the wise and canonical arrangement" suggested by Bernis.[127]

In fact, that "real plan" was Bernis's and not the pope's. Judging from the few words and many actions of Clement XIV, his plan was gradually to strangle the Jesuits by means of replacing them in their colleges, closing their houses and novitiates, forbidding them to preach and confess penitents, and disempower-ing their general and superiors—Le Paige's first plan of 1761 writ large, and all without a brief or bull that would have formally committed him to suppressing what his predecessors had sanctioned.[128]

As events played out, Carlos III permanently replaced Azpuru not with Ors-ini but with Spain's Neapolitan ambassador, Labaña. But when he too died of an apoplectic attack the king replaced him in turn with none other than José Moñino, Campomanes's fellow fiscal and one of the architects of the expulsion of the Jesuits from Spain. Dated 24 March 1772, Moñino's appointment was soon to puncture the balloon of hopes that the French court had inflated with con-jectures by Bernis, who, getting the news in April, shared with d'Aiguillon his fears that the new minister would be "very heated about the suppression of the Jesuits," and that the "king's confessor would no longer be listened to."[129] Perhaps, he conjectured in a lucid moment self-reckoning, his "conjectures" that the king had given the pope the "liberty to arrange the affairs of the Jesuits as he saw fit had no other foundation than the delays [presumably] granted to His Holiness."[130]

It took until 4 July for Moñino to get to Rome, a week later to have his first audience with the pope, and until 6 September for the moment of clarity to arrive when he presented Clement XIV with a draft proposal to dissolve the Society. But it was less easy to dispel "conjectures" that he had spent years instilling into the French court, all the more so in that as late as 23 August Bernis persisted in hopefully speculating that Moñino's real plan was to have the pope "reduce the Jesuits to a sort of congregation bound by simple vows" on the Oratorian model.[131] A second reckoning with reality was therefore overdue in relations between France and Spain. It was with that aim that d'Aiguillon sent some of Bernis's dispatches of February and March 1772 to Grimaldi via Fuentes even though in the most sensitive of these Bernis had qualified his "conjectures" as such and had enjoined the utmost confidentiality, to which d'Aiguillon had agreed. These dispatches contained an account of the pope's supposed certainty that the Spanish king no longer authorized his ministers to "torment" him about the Jesuits.[132]

Exploding in response in mid-May, Grimaldi attributed his king's supposed assurances to the pope to Bernis's inventiveness, unable as he was to attribute such a "gross artifice" to the pope while being all too well acquainted with the cardinal's "design of disuniting our two courts the better to attain merit in Rome's." So in order to enable Fuentes to convince d'Aiguillon and the French king that his court had never "varied" in its aims, Grimaldi sent him copies of the texts of what purported to be the sum total of the letters exchanged between Carlos III and Clement XIV, accompanied by the order to submit them to inspection by d'Aiguillon and Louis XV. More dangerously, Grimaldi informed Fuentes that, "angrily surprised," the king of Spain had sent Fuentes's dispatch along with Grimaldi's reply to Moñino with orders for him to confront Bernis with these documents in hand on his arrival in Rome.[133]

With another crisis in French and Spanish relations looming and the Bourbon Family Pact again being put to the test, Fuentes lost no time in communicating Grimaldi's dyspeptic dispatch and translated royal letters to d'Aiguillon, nor did d'Aiguillon linger long in sending copies to Louis XV. By 12 June Fuentes could report to Grimaldi that Louis had felt "flattered by . . . the king [of Spain]'s display of trust in him, and that while he had never supposed that the king had ever varied in any way in his just aims," the letters enabled him to see that in fact he never had.[134]

But what most concerned d'Aiguillon at this point was the possibility that, in ordering Moñino to confront Bernis with the evidence of his duplicity, Grimaldi would "compromise" him with Bernis, since any such confrontation would reveal that d'Aiguillon had revealed "conjectures" that Bernis had confided to him "under the seal of the most solemn secrecy." So concerned was d'Aiguillon about this possibility that he reiterated his concerns on three successive occasions, pleading with Fuentes on each to have Grimaldi order Moñino to make no direct use of the evidence with Bernis. Fuentes did as he was asked, as did Grimaldi in turn, with the result that when Moñino received his new instruction in Rome, he made ample use of Bernis's forwarded dispatches in his first conversation with the cardinal without revealing the epistolary evidence in hand.[135]

That much would seem to have ended the matter where the diplomatic understanding between France and Spain was concerned. But not quite. For strange to tell questions of ultimate Spanish intentions lingered in Versailles well into the autumn, further poisoning relations between the two states. It was with no little chagrin that Fernando de Magallón, the secretary of the Spanish embassy who had meanwhile taken Fuentes's place, had to inform Grimaldi on 18 September that d'Aiguillon continued to harbor suspicions of a secret Spanish policy to "moderate" its formal demand for the total suppression of the Society of Jesus by allowing it to be reformed as a "sort of congregation." The occasion for giving voice to these doubts was d'Aiguillon's rendering of the account by Bernis of his and Moñino's successive audiences with the pope, which had gone well enough, the foreign secretary said, except for the "article on the Jesuits." Upon Magallón's protestations that nothing was less true, and that Moñino's instructions had not changed, d'Aiguillon protested that he had never seen these instructions.[136] A flabbergasted Magallón had just enough time to vow to procure those instructions before sitting down to a formal ambassadorial dinner.

Unreproved after dinner and this time in the presence of Vicente Joaquín Osorio Moscoso, the prince de Masserano, Spain's ambassador to England, d'Aiguillon persisted in alleging sources of information to the effect that Spain might approve such a "reform"—an "avis" that Magallón naturally attributed to Bernis. The most worrisome aspect of d'Aiguillon's suspicions for the two Spanish diplomats was the foreign minister's report that France's Most Christian King himself remained in the greatest quandary on the matter, "from which he could not be freed so long as he did not see the most solid . . . proof that what our court demanded was . . . the total extinction of the order, without consenting to a reform or [any other] modifications." In response, d'Aiguillon reported to Grimaldi, it was with the greatest "firmness"—even "anger"—that, taking

Masserano as his witness, Magallón swore to d'Aiguillon that everything he and Fuentes before him had told him was true.

It goes without saying that Magallón lost no time in requesting Grimaldi to send him Moñino's instructions and Labaña's before him, even though d'Aiguillon had meanwhile professed himself convinced of the Spanish king's "firmness and resolve" and promised to reiterate Bernis's instructions to support Spain's lead.[137] By mid-October, however, it was all the easier to convince d'Aiguillon in that meanwhile he had decided to sound out Carlos III himself by suggesting to him via Fuentes that the Spanish king would do well to ask Louis XV to clarify his instructions to Bernis. Aware that the French court was second-guessing his intentions, on 21 September Carlos seized the occasion to ask Louis to renew his orders to Bernis to work with Moñino toward the entire "extinction of the said religious Order," in response to which on 5 October— that is, a week before d'Aiguillon's announced "conversion" to belief in Carlos's sincerity—Louis assured his royal Spanish cousin that Bernis had never had any instructions other than to "concur in my name with all the démarches that your majesty prescribes to his ministers in that matter."[138] That royal reassurance was true in fact if not in spirit. It was left to Grimaldi to drive the point home with a copy of Moñino's instructions together with a blistering dispatch that, after naming each and every corporate part of the Society of Jesus that his court wished to see disappear, asked whether it would take no less than the total "annihilation" rather than the "dispersion" of its former members to convince the French court of the veracity of Spain's demand for the total "extinction" of that order.[139]

After the publication of Clement XIV's brief *Dominus ac Redemptor* dissolving the Society of Jesus on 17 August 1773, the French parti dévot, led by the archbishop of Paris and Madame Louise, all but revolted against its authority and countered with a formal project in December to reestablish the Jesuits in France as a congregation.[140] But that proposal had not arisen immediately from the precedents of the failed reform proposals of 1761–1762; rather it grew from sketches roughed out in the correspondence of d'Aiguillon and Bernis, which by 1772 had found their way into the discursive air that the French and Romans breathed.[141]

That Bernis could meanwhile have imagined as late 23 August 1772 that a transformation into a congregation of secular priests had anything to do with Moñino's plans for the Society of Jesus was due only to his ignorance of those plans maintained by a duly forewarned Moñino, who on that date had his second audience with the pope. Having listened on 6 July to Bernis's assurances that Clement XIV had always meant to honor his promises in the light of Bernis's forwarded correspondence, the new Spanish envoy could not imagine with what purpose Bernis had sworn d'Aiguillon to secrecy about the pope's and Spain's supposed intentions to reform the Jesuits as a secular congregation if not to mislead him and his king or his own court and king.[142] (That Bernis was misleading a royal court that in some sense wanted to be misled is not a hypothesis he could diplomatically entertain.) It was not until the end of August that, having urged Grimaldi to press for Bernis's replacement, Moñino learned that in view of the short leash of Bernis's renewed instructions—and also all the cardinal's many connections in Rome—his court now thought it wiser to retain him.[143]

DOMINUS AC REDEMPTOR

Nor was it until the same time that Moñino began to appreciate the value of a more straightforward Bernis rapport with the pope. For by Moñino's own admission it was in part due to Bernis's suasions that Moñino's obtained his more productive papal audience of 6 September in which he finally persuaded the pope to take his draft proposal and promise to look it over during his scheduled autumn vacation.[144] Entitled *Apunte o nota latina* and sketched out during his enforced leisure after his arrival in Rome, Moñino's plan was nothing less than a draft of a papal brief or bull of total extinction in eighteen articles that sent all Jesuit novices back into the world and allowed all those who had taken "simple" vows to do the same. The only options it permitted to professed fathers and those who did not wish to leave the clerical life were to join another order, to serve as educators or secular priests for those bishops wishing to employ them, or—this provision applied to the poorest and most aged—to remain for a while in their houses, but in secular dress and under the authority of the bishops and their delegates. In addition to a preamble and justificatory reasons and provisions for the Society's property, these articles were to make up the substance of the papal brief *Dominus ac Redemptor.*

The story of the final Spanish phase of the end of the prerevolutionary Society of Jesus is unedifying, even ugly, despite the historian Augustin Theiner's efforts to sanctify it. As it has been adequately told and retold in detail by Theiner, Ludwig Pastor, Enrique Pacheco y de Leyva, and most recently by Enrique Giménes López and Niccolò Guasti, it can be curtailed here.[145]

When after Clement XIV's return from Castel Gandolfo it became clear to Moñino in meetings in early November that Clement had not studied his plan and persisted in his previously alluded to plan for gradual—and always reversible— closures of colleges and novitiates, the Spanish fiscal all but left diplomacy to

Bernis and Orsini and relentlessly pursued his papal quarry by more belligerent means. These means included repeated threats of Portuguese-style schism; the bribery of the papal intimates Buontempi and Macedonia; and the brief's inclusion of Austria's right to dispose of Jesuit property in order to firm up the passive support of Empress Maria Theresa. From the moment of Moñino's arrival in Rome until August 1773, meanwhile, Clement never ceased trying to elude or distract his Spanish pursuer by all the means at hand. These included extended baths and vacations, symbolic measures against Jesuit institutions, inexplicable delays in signing the final brief, and even foot-dragging in naming the papal congregation to oversee its implementation.[146] The final signal of papal capitulation was perhaps the naming of Macedonia as secretary of this congregation. In the end, all the pope had to show for his strategic retreat was *Dominus ac Redemptor*'s form as a brief, more easily reversible than a definitive bull. But that was an issue on which Moñino himself had remained flexible.

Graceless and inglorious to the end, this final phase of the Bourbon campaign against the Jesuits came to its conclusion with the secretary Macedonio's formal presentation of the brief to a still astonished Ricci and his assistants at the Society's headquarters at Al Gesu Church in Rome on the morning of 16 August, the date of the brief's official publication. As of that date in Rome, and by degrees as church and states implemented the papal brief's provisions elsewhere, the once proud Society of Jesus ceased to exist.

The brief's most forthright reason for destroying the Society was the papacy's obligation to see to the "repose and tranquillity of Christendom"—the realization that, in the words of the brief, "it was impossible for the Church to enjoy a true and solid peace so long as that Society subsisted." As a refusal to abolish the Society might well have provoked a schism, the "unity of the church" was indeed at stake. Artfully avoiding the issue of whether the many charges against the Jesuits were true, the brief rather cited them as evidence of the dissentions that the Society had provoked. The capacity of the Society to stir up controversy within Catholicism therefore functioned as a second "real" reason for its abolition.

Predictably prominent among the many other charges mentioned by the brief were doctrines thought to be "totally opposed to orthodox faith" (read "Molinism"); the "usage . . . of maxims that the Holy See has proscribed as scandalous and corrosive of good morals" (read "probabilism"); the "toleration of certain pagan ceremonies" (read "the Chinese rites"); complicity in "certain seditions in Catholic states" (read, "attempted acts of regicide in Portugal and the Esquilache Riots in Spain"); the society's distinction between simple and solemn vows (read: the ability to inherit from members with simple vows as well as the right to dismiss them at will); and last but far from least, the "absolute power of the general." As present in a papal brief, the irony of this charge is that Portugal and the Bourbon monarchies wished the papacy to abolish the Society by virtue of its quite absolute "plenitude of power as vicar of Jesus Christ" and "supreme administrator of Christendom" rather than by means of a congregation of cardinals or a general council, precisely in order to circumvent the opposition that would inevitably have arisen in a more "republican" forum.

Part Three

REFORM CATHOLICISM AND THE ULTRAMONTANIST INTERNATIONAL

6

THE END OF THE JESUITS AND THE
POLARIZATION OF CATHOLIC EUROPE, 1773-1791

Before the arrival of Moñino in Rome, Spain's beneficial agent José Nicolas Azara bitterly speculated to Roda that Bernis had single-handedly prolonged
papal action against the Jesuits by three years. Azara had all along aspired
to take Azpuru's place, and his comments may be taken to mean that Azara
thought that he would have known better how to make Bernis toe the Spanish line.[1]

But no such sour grapes contaminated the lucidity of Andrea Micheli, Oratorian priest and professor at the Chiesa Nuova in Rome, who in a letter to the
abbé Clément in July 1773 gave full vent to his conviction that Chancellor Maupeou's coup had been the final cause of the delay in the end of the Jesuits and
hence also any papal progress in simultaneous negotiations toward Rome's re-
union with the Church of Utrecht. But he also accused Bernis of being the efficient cause. Philo-Jesuit from the start, it was Bernis, Micheli contended, who
as early as October 1770 had warned Clement XIV of the imminent fall of Choiseul, along with the emasculation of the parlements and the likely recall of the
Jesuits in France, in view of which he counseled the pope to wait out these
events and fall back on the sort of reform of the Society proposed by his king in
the abortive edict of March 1762.[2] Lest it be thought impossible for anyone to
have been so prescient so early in Rome, Clément, who was also in Rome at the
time, warned of the probable fall of Choiseul and the attendant danger of the
return of the Jesuits in France—all of this in a letter to Manuel de Roda in September 1770, a few weeks earlier than Bernis's supposed warning.[3] To be sure,
no such speculations appear in Bernis's correspondence, but then again Bernis
would have hardly committed them to writing as a dispatch to Choiseul.

Be all that as it may, the precarious contingency of Clement XIV's Fabian refusal to choose a clear path of action until it was forced upon him points to what was at stake in the choices Clement refused to make, as well as to the consequences of his course of protracted retreat until Spain and Moñino brutally cut it short in the autumn of 1772. Given all the issues for which the Jesuits stood as symbols, the stakes were high and the consequences many. A full fleshing out of them will take the rest of the story into and beyond the French Revolution.

CLEMENT XIV'S UNENVIABLE CHOICES

It seems clear in retrospect that it would have been wiser for Clement XIV either to have acceded to Portugal's and the Bourbon states' demand for the dissolution of the Jesuits soon after his accession, even at the cost of suspicions of simony, or to have firmly refused this demand on the grounds that the combination of the neutrality of the other Catholic states and the lack of proof for the Society's total corruption invalidated the conditions of justice and canonical regularity that he had initially insisted on, even at the risk of schism.

In the first case, compelling circumstantial reasons were not lacking for the papacy to surrender to the demand for the Jesuits' abolition, namely, those invoked in the brief *Dominus ac Redemptor* of July 1773. Given Bourbon intransigence, the "peace" and "unity"—that is, the need to avoid a schism—of Catholic Christendom had indeed come to depend on acceding to the Bourbon monarchies' insistence on total abolition, justice and canonical regularity be damned. Further, the form of a brief would have allowed Clement XIV's successors to reestablish the Society if they desired to, and if conditions permitted it, as Pius VI in fact began to do in 1800. As Micheli had hoped, an early abolition would have allowed Clement XIV to resolve the standoff with Parma and Piacenza, to make a strong case for Rome's reacquisition of the seized papal territories, and to turn his undistracted attention to other items on the state-sponsored reformist agenda. These included a curtailment of the jurisdiction of nuncios' courts, a limitation of the right of sanctuary from secular justice, the beatification and canonization of Palafox, and reconciliation with the estranged Catholic diocese of Utrecht.

As it was, Clement XIV made progress on the first of these items, and above all stopped forever the papacy's ritual and anachronistic annual Maundy Thursday proclamation of the bull *In coena Domini*, which, first fulminated in 1363 and refined for the last time by Urban VIII in 1627, listed twenty some sins that merited automatic excommunication. Since this list included appeals to a general council or from ecclesiastical to secular courts, the prosecution of churchmen in secular courts, the seizure or taxation of church property, and the occupation of any parcel of the papal states, this bull in principle consigned just about all eighteenth-century Catholic sovereigns to a state of excommunication and hence of damnation all of the time, and all the Bourbon sovereigns in particular in the years 1767–1768 alone.

If in the second scenario Clement XIV had chosen to face down Portugal and the Bourbon states and Carlos III in particular and insisted on reforming rather than totally abolishing the Society of Jesus, he might have done better at safeguarding the integrity of the papacy in Roman opinion and avoided the stain of constraint that besmirches the reputation of his pontificate to the present day. But in doing so he would unquestionably have courted a high risk of schism, having heard the threat of it in his audiences with Moñino on more than one occasion.[4] Hate the Jesuits though Tanucci did, his erratic behavior throughout the negotiations gave rise to the suspicion among his allies that the success of those negotiations interested him less than a rupture that would provide him with a pretense for nationalizing the Neapolitan church and ending the kingdom's feudal subordination to the Papal States. That schism would have further solidified the already nine-year-old Portuguese rupture and added Spain, Naples, and the Duchy of Parma to it, perhaps even dragging along already Gallican France as long as Louis XV valued the Bourbon Family Pact. Had such a schism declared itself before the end of 1770, not even the fall of Choiseul in late December 1770 would necessarily have changed this state of affairs.

THE LINEAMENTS OF A POSSIBLE REFORMED
CATHOLIC EUROPE

If the sound of the term "schism" rings too offensively in pious ears, they may substitute the concept of a "withdrawal of obedience" suggested by Hontheim on the model of states that withheld their obedience to one or another of the rival papal claimants during the Great Schism of 1378–1415. In any case, it is arguably profitable if a little unorthodox to indulge in an exercise in counterfactual history and ask what sort of schism it would have been that left Rome in direct communion only with the non-Bourbon Italian states, Austria, Bavaria and the German prince-archbishoprics, and Poland. Further, the German prince-archbishoprics led by Mainz were already chafing at the Roman papal bit by 1770, Poland was about to begin to disappear in 1773, Piedmont-Sardinia began a tilt in a Bourbon direction with the accession of Vittorio Amedeo III the same year, while around 1780 the Habsburg brothers Pietro Leopoldo of

Tuscany and Joseph II of Austria began to go on an anticurial reformist tear that would make Carlos III's Spain look spineless in comparison. The result would have been a magnification to the umpteenth power of the estranged Church of Utrecht's goal of obtaining a state of indirect communion with Rome by soliciting letters of communion with so many Catholic bishops and heads of religious orders across Europe that Rome would appear to be the schismatic exception and those in communion with Utrecht the irenic Catholic rule. Any such state of affairs would have resulted less in a schism than in a differently structured Catholic Church. Those many in Rome who wished to see Clement XIV imitate the intransigence of his predecessor might have well have thought better about what they wished for.

Some indication of what kind of reform those "schismatic" but majoritarian states in that situation might have imposed on the papacy is visible in a manuscript memorandum written in January 1769 by Le Paige at the request of Guillaume Lambert for use by Choiseul.[5] Both of them Jansenist architects of the Parlement of Paris's successful campaign against the Jesuits, Le Paige was a barrister and Lambert a parlementary councilor, while Choiseul would remain at the helm of France's ministry of foreign affairs for another year. Never perhaps did what has here been called Reform Catholicism receive a more programmatic formulation than it did in this memorandum. In Le Paige's opinion, the general outcry in reaction to the Court of Rome's recent actions against Ferdinando of Parma showed that the time was ripe for the states of Catholic Europe to rid themselves "once and for all" of the "usurpations of the Court of Rome" and the "false maxims" that served as their foundation—results, he was convinced, of the medieval "centuries of ignorance," just as they were also causes in turn of the separation from Rome of the Greek Church and the "different classes of Protestants." Like Choiseul for whom the memorandum was intended, Le Paige deemed the needed antidote to the Court of Rome's "false maxims" to be the four Gallican articles promulgated by the Gallican Clergy in 1682. But far from their being unique to France, Le Paige along with Campomanes and Hontheim thought that the four articles constituted nothing less than the "ancient doctrine of all the churches" as well as "incontestable verities established by the words of Jesus Christ himself."

In what he hoped would become the "public law of all the Catholic nations"— indeed, a universal public law—Le Paige summed up these verities as the independence of sovereigns in temporal matters, the recognition of canonical limits to papal power, the fallibility of popes, and the superiority of ecumenical councils. Another law that he might have added, and in effect repeatedly did so later on, was the right of each national Catholic church "to govern itself" by means of its own canonical and liturgical usages, "as indeed each had [done] before the usurpations of Rome." Highest on Le Paige's list of canonical abuses that an international canon law would eliminate figured the infamous annates, or payments to Rome of the equivalent of a year's revenues of a new bishop's diocese; beneficial "preventions" and "resignations," or ways by which the papacy reserved to itself some appointments to French benefices; and above all the papal "reservation" of certain cases dispensing people from the provisions of canon law, most especially in cases of marriage. The annates rendered the spiritual welfare of people hostage to the venal views of a "foreign court," and the "preventions" similarly subjected them to the interests of a "foreign court" at the expense of more meritorious candidates, while the dispensations deprived bishops of what had once had been and still should have been their all but exclusive business. The absence of these "abuses" during the first eight or ten centuries of Christianity had done no damage to the pope's "true rights to primacy," at least in Le Paige's opinion.

Nor did Le Paige think that the elimination of such "usurped rights" would now do any damage to the papacy's rightful honor, since their discovery as "usurpations" and "contraventions" had revealed them as "null and void" by definition. In order to make this wish list a complete one for the cause of Reform Catholicism, Le Paige would only have had to add the readmission of all Augustinian Jansenists, including the clergy of Utrecht, to direct communion with Rome and a legitimate place within Catholicism. The project of an irenic bull known as *Aspicientes* to which he had contributed had no other aim.

The only missing element in this list was the restoration of church councils, especially general councils. Yet general councils found their place in Le Paige's memorandum as the ideal means for implementing his wish list for a common law for Catholic Christendom, a means that, as Le Paige noted, had been an end in itself for the general councils of Constance and Basel. Noting as well, however, that neither those councils nor the Council of Trent had succeeded in reforming many of the abuses he had just enumerated, he also recognized the reality that no general council seemed likely to meet "any time very soon (*sitôt*)." The Jansenist barrister therefore placed his hopes in a kind of congress of European Catholic states that would lay down the Gallican articles as their "common public law" while allowing flexibility for national variations. Meanwhile, the French monarchy in particular should prepare the way by allowing for—even sponsoring—the publication of pro-Gallican treatises, such as those produced in the wake of the first appeal of *Unigenitus* to a general council in 1717.

It is not known whether Lambert sent this memorandum on to Choiseul, and if so what Choiseul made of it. What is known is that in 1769 Choiseul went so far as to suggest to the Portuguese ambassador that his country lay down the four Gallican articles as law in Portugal, requiring all ecclesiastics to swear loyalty to them and universities to teach them. Trying as he then was to end Portugal's diplomatic rupture with Rome, Carvalho did no such thing. Yet that effort did not prevent him from imposing rigid limitations on the church's right to acquire property in an amortization law, from excluding the church entirely from the business of censorship in the newly established Mesa Censoria, endowing the University of Coimbra's canonical and theological curriculum a very long-standing Gallican and philo-Jansenist cast, or from accepting the return of a papal nuncio with only the severest restrictions to his authority—all in 1768–1770. It was also in 1769 that Carvalho sponsored the publication of Pereira's *Demonstração theologica* that justified the consecration of bishops by metropolitan bishops with no need for papal confirmation. That Choiseul rejoiced in 1768 after the papal excommunication of the duke of Parma provoked Carlos III to reimpose the exequatur in Spain, or that with this king's leave the *fiscales* Campomanes and Moñino savored the prospect of a national Spanish Catholic church with "liberties" greater than the church of France—these straws too joined other such indications in the reformist winds of 1768–1769.

Far less moderate than any of these protagonists was Carlos III's weekly correspondent Bernardo Tanucci, who of course wielded real power as the de facto ruler of the Kingdom of the Two Sicilies.[6] Scattered throughout his copious correspondence during the same period are peremptory pronouncements about the pressing need for a reform of the Catholic Church that would end the unholy marriage between Christ's purely spiritual commission to his apostles and the pompous temporal sovereignty wielded by that church and the papacy after their usurpations during the tenebrous centuries since the Isidorian Decretals. What stood in need of drastic reform was a Catholic Church that in Tanucci's estimation had become no less than a "standing crime of lese majesty."[7] Taken together, Tanucci's various proposals for reform would have summarily ended the existence of the Papal States; surgically stripped the papacy and the church of any semblance of coactive jurisdiction; reduced the disciplinary power of the whole canonical hierarchy to a purely spiritual and admonitory role—all this on the grounds that whatever temporal jurisdiction the church had ever or still wielded, it had done so by means of outright usurpation from or by implicit and always revocable delegation from divinely instituted temporal sovereignty. Because in Tanucci's opinion the church's purely spiritual mission was "founded on faith, charity, hope, and humility," its only proper activities consisted in the proclamation of the Gospel, the administration of the sacraments, and the care of the poor. By Tanucci's lights the clergy's only legitimate reason for having anything to do with landed property or its income was to distribute the proceeds to those most in need of them.[8]

Far from leaving the church's spiritual business to the church alone, however, Tanucci had no paucity of equally surgical ideas about how it ought to be administered and redistributed. Since this Neapolitan first minister's "regalism" included the king's duty as "protector and promoter of the veritable ecclesiastical discipline" to see to it that the church abided by its own sacred canons, his ideas were not without consequence.[9] Without doubt the church's sacrament of penance gave it spiritual jurisdiction in the tribunal of the conscience. But because in Catholic states the sentence of excommunication carried with it civil penalties, the state might see to it that at all levels churchmen exercised this jurisdiction collegially with the implicit consent of the whole church and respected all the mandates of the pristine sacred canons. As honorary primate of the whole church, the pope might also legitimately speak in the accents of infallibility, though only if he did so not alone but with the whole church in council assembled, without which he was merely the bishop of Rome. Might he at least speak with the accents of lesser authority as bishop? Surely. But only with the concurrence of the clergy of his own church assembled in synod, thereby setting an example for canonical regularity for his fellow bishops—his only rightful role over the whole church—who like him had received their spiritual authority directly from the church's divine founder in the sacrament of ordination rather than indirectly from the pope.[10]

Further, the church's hierarchy included only bishops and priests and not monks, who without either country or divine institution not only occupied no canonical place in that hierarchy but since the Middle Ages had acted as pope's agents in subverting episcopal authority by getting theirs directly from Rome. Most at fault since the sixteenth century in converting the clergy into a "diabolical profession" were of course the Jesuits.[11] Armed as they were by their mobile morality, a "blind obedience" to a "despotic" regime, and a vow to the aggrandizement of the papacy's spiritual and temporal power, it was above all they in Tanucci's estimation who had subverted the authority of bishops and challenged that of kings, the better to transform the Holy See itself into a total "papal despotism," reserving to themselves alone the exclusive right to disobey it.[12]

Behind Tanucci's thought and action lurked a century-long hinterland of Gallican ecclesiology as radicalized by the Jansenist controversy. For his part, Tanucci could match any Jansenist in point of outrage against the Jesuits for "abolishing the doctrine of Saint Paul, Augustine, and Thomas and substituting for it that of Pelagius, Molina, and Busembaum."[13] The point is to ponder not

Tanucci's putative Jansenism but the degree to which a radicalized Gallican ecclesiology and even a diffuse Augustinianism could find its way into the royal courts and councils of mid- to late eighteenth-century Catholic Europe and from these redoubts and strongholds to exert a formidable reformist influence. Tepid Gallican though he was, even Bernis once expressed to Choiseul his conviction that instead of "defending untenable terrain ad hoc and little by little without perceiving that times and opinions have changed," the papacy would do better to remodel all of its concordats with Catholic states on the model of France's—in effect, to concede all the Gallican liberties while conserving only the "substance of things," whatever he thought that was.[14]

What flowed from the Augustinian wing of Catholic reformism was not only a certain anti-Molinist and probabilistic educational agenda but also a whole program of parochial and liturgical reforms directed against the perceived excesses of "baroque Catholicism" and intended to restore the putatively normative conditions of the early church. So if—to continue this counterfactual experiment—the "schismatic" states of Catholic Europe had ganged up on the papacy in the same way that the Bourbon powers had at the expense of the Jesuits and imposed upon it the radical restructuring that many in positions of power then had in mind, the next wave of reforms would probably have taken this parochial and liturgical form. If so, the reformers would not have had to do battle with a hostile papacy supported by an equally obdurate monastic establishment—the alliance that Tanucci denounced as unholy—as in fact they had to do during the next decade when the Habsburg brothers Pietro Leopoldo and Emperor Joseph II undertook precisely such reforms in ducal Tuscany and in Austria and its possessions. For in this hypothetical scenario conciliar and synodical structures would have limited the papacy's margin for action as well as that of the episcopacy, while much of the monastic clergy would have gone the way of the Jesuits, except for the parish-oriented congregations of secular priests, such as the Oratorians and Scolopians, and "true" and original monks, such as Benedictines.

In clerical education these reforms would have entailed closing down episcopal and monastic seminaries to the benefit of state-supervised ones. In these, qualified priests would have substituted the works of Augustine to those of Thomas Aquinas, Concina's moral theology to anything probabilistic, Mésenguy's catechism to the recently revised Roman one, Sacy's translation of Holy Writ to the Florentine archbishop Antonio Martini's recent one, Nicolas Le Tourneux's meditations for the liturgical year to those by the Jesuit Jean Croisset, and Fleury's ecclesiastical history to Giuseppe Agostino Orsi's—in short, a curriculum weighted toward an Augustinian and Gallican agenda in preference to the Molinist or ultramontanist one. For pastoral education in particular, a favorite on everyone's list was Jan Opstraet's *Pastor bonus.*

With the help of a parish clergy thus educated, these princely reformers would further have aimed to eliminate as many nonpastoral benefices as possible with a view toward creating a one-to-one relation between clerical benefices on the one side and the actual needs of lay parishioners on the other. Even without a monastic establishment to inhibit it, this reform would have entailed a vast harrowing of priests living on endowed Masses for the repose of departed souls, private oratories or chapels in the patronage of laymen, and even the secular canons of cathedral and collegiate churches, all of whom would have been ripe for secular harvest. This reform would have also eliminated the many side chapels and altars and Masses said by beneficeless priests in existing cathedrals and parish churches because a further reformist aim was to cut away the baroque distractions, the better to unite the entire parish around a single altar and to centralize its focus on a single Mass.

The better to convey and prioritize the meaning of Christ's sacrifice in the Mass, yet another array of devotional and liturgical reforms would have sought to educate the lay "faithful," in the first instance by having the priest utter the canon of the Mass in a loud and intelligible voice without the competition of organ music; and in the second by apprizing the laity of the meaning of what was transpiring with the help of explanations in the vernacular, such as the one in Muratori's *Della regolata devozione dei cristiani.* In the longer run, still other likeminded reforms would have taken aim at the laity's ignorance of the rudiments of Christian doctrine by means of catechisms and other manuals, supervised reading of Scripture in the vernacular, and of course by remedial preaching for the many illiterate. Undergirding this effort would have been the neo-Augustinian conviction that ignorance too was a sin—indeed, a consequence of sin—and therefore hardly an excuse for any other.

In order to enable the laity to distinguish between the worship of and faith in Christ alone, a final and most controversial battery of reforms would have launched an all-out assault on "superstitious" but perniciously popular forms of "baroque piety" that in the opinion of reformers diverted the devotion of the lay faithful from Christ and sacramental grace to belief in the miraculous "virtue" of saints, veiled images of saints, and their all too often inauthentic relics, some of them the destination of popular pilgrimages and processions that added the insult of recreational impiety to the insult of misdirected piety. Caught in the reformist crossfire would have been such devotions as to the Sacred Heart of Jesus and Leonardo da Porto Maurizio's newly popular *Via Crucis,* as well as the many parish-affiliated pious confraternities that sponsored them. However remote from Augustinian theology, this program of reform for popular piety was ultimately related to it in its aim to underscore the unique and vertical dependence of sinners on the grace of Christ, in opposition to what in reformist sensibilities seemed earthbound and horizontal "helps" in the motions of devotion.

The top-to-bottom restructuring of the Catholic Church's magisterium, the nationalization of its temporal property, the elimination of the regular clergy, the reeducation and pruning of the secular clergy—none of these hypothetical reforms in ecclesiastical history, much less the "purification' of popular piety, would necessarily have fended off a French-like revolution. An earlier national-ization of the Gallican Church's property would surely have postponed the French monarchy's day of fiscal reckoning, as the abolition of episcopal privi-lege would have begun to loosen the rigidity of its society of orders. But given this "absolute" monarchy's aversion to national consent in any form and its fis-cal dependence on the sale of noble privilege in every form, it is hard to see how it might have staved off a day of revolutionary reckoning forever. Nor is the example of what the Revolution itself did with its windfall of ecclesiastical property very reassuring where the monarchy is concerned.

That much said, the French monarchy's prerevolutionary attempt in 1786–1788 to change the form and distribution of taxation would not have had to face the formidable opposition of the upper clergy as an order, nor would the National Assembly have had very much to reform when it turned its attention to the Gallican Church and its clergy in 1790. Without the clergy as a fiscally privileged "order" to contend with, the National Assembly might have left the clergy with whatever property the monarchy might have endowed it for its maintenance plus the right to assemble in synods and provincial councils vouchsafed by earlier reforms. Even if the National Assembly had chosen to transform the Gallican Church into a salaried department of the state along the radical lines of what it did in 1790, a papacy limited by a Roman synod as well as by councils might not have roundly condemned it.

If—to conclude this experiment—all these post-1770 reforms had left as many of the lay faithful as unhappy as the actually attempted reforms of this sort did, the papacy duly counseled might have taken the occasion of a revolution in France to follow the advice of one of its proto-"conservative" publicists, Nicola Spedalieri, and sided with the people against their princes.[15] In doing so, the papacy would only have been replicating a policy that it had sometimes fol-lowed during the sixteenth-century wars of religion. In that case, however, it is hard to imagine any revolution undoing all the previous reforms and restoring an entire Old Regime, monastic establishment, privileged property, ecclesiastical courts, coactive jurisdiction, and all. In which case the result might have been a precocious separation between the Catholic states and their still quite nationalized Catholic churches, something like free Catholic churches within free states that would at least have accommodated civil toleration of Protestants. Such a state of affairs would not have been unlike the one that the post-Terror constitutional Gallican Church orphaned by the Revolution's hostile Directorial republic briefly if precariously succeeded in creating between 1795 and the Napoleonic concordat of 1801. Had such a situation been the result of the Revolution, much of the nineteenth century's ecclesiastical holding action might have been bypassed, not excluding Pius IX's Syllabus of Errors and the declaration of papal infallibility.

THE RISE AND DEMISE OF DE FACTO REFORM CATHOLICISM, 1759–1789

The point of such a counterfactual experiment is neither wishfully nor warningly to fast-forward European Christendom from the late eighteenth to the present but rather to highlight the obstacles that Reform Catholicism in fact encountered when, after the papal suppression of the Jesuits, several Catholic princes undertook to implement such a reformist agenda in the teeth of an unreformed papal curia and a monastic agenda minus only the Jesuits. So long as the papacy remained unaltered, bishops too depended on it for confirmation and had good reason to think of themselves as such "by the grace of God and the Holy See" rather than as successors in their own right of all the apostles, as represented by Saint Peter. In most places parish priests also remained in the nomination of and dependent on their bishops, monastic establishments, lay patrons, or the papacy.

To encapsulate and recall, late eighteenth-century Reform Catholicism tended toward the nationalization of Catholic churches under the aegis of a weakened papacy redefined as a primus inter episcopal pares on what was thought to be the putative model of the early church. In this model, nationalization meant secularization in the literal sense of the "recovery" of the secular, or temporal, authority of the state from the medieval papacy's putative usurpation of it, along with the "restoration" of the prestige of the secular clergy from the nonapostolic regular clergy. While promising the restoration of the authority of bishops from Rome and sometimes even the rights of parish priests from bishops, this reformist program also entailed the subordination of the entire secular clergy to a state that acknowledged no superior other than God and therefore thought itself divinely authorized to regulate and reform all ecclesiastical and devotional forms and activities surrounding and even impinging on the faith—circa sacram—short of defining the faith or violating the sacramental "interior forum."

That these reforming states opted for Augustinian theology and an inner religious sensibility over Molinist theology and a more tactile religious sensibility was far from circumstantial: in return for its protection of Jansenist theologians and Gallican canonists from papal hostility, these states obtained not only a Catholic theological justification for the extension of their authority but also allies whose inner and purely spiritual conception of the faith gave ample scope for the state's regulation of all external to it. By weaning devotional attention away from saints and relics and vertically refocusing it on Christ and a single altar, Augustinian religious sensibility also hoped to transform the believer's horizontal devotional energy into a neighborly charity that easily took the form of benevolence on the part of subjects in the interest of the state. Hence the reforming states' hostility to religious confraternities and interest in transforming them into charitable associations.

Coming in the wake of Clement XIII's use of the bull in *In coena Domini* in his *Monitorio* against the Duchy of Parma and Piacenza, the first wave of such reforms took the largely symbolic form of state prohibitions of the ritual republication of that bull each Maundy Thursday in all parishes of Catholic realms, as mandated by the bull itself. Endeavoring to hew to its policy of separating the case of the Jesuits from that of Rome, it was with some reluctance that the *Nouvelles ecclésiastiques* turned to the list of these new or renewed prohibitions on 24 and 31 January 1769, by which time it included Parma, Naples, Portugal, Spain, Venice, and Austrian Lombardy, the last at the command of Maria Theresa herself.[16] In a sense, Clement XIV himself tacitly ratified these bans by discreetly omitting the fulmination of the bull in Saint Peter's basilica in Rome in 1770, an omission that proved to be permanent. Only in Lombardy did the Habsburg governor Karl Joseph von Firmian's orders seem to encounter much overt episcopal resistance, although in March 1768 Carlos III complained within Ossun's hearing distance that, "due to the negligence and stupidity that has reigned in this realm," the Holy Thursday just past had in fact prompted the routine republication of the bull in all the parishes in Spain, even the royal chapel.[17] Among these states, only Tanucci's Naples went further and in 1769 abolished the papal Inquisition within its borders.

Like Naples, however, those states that expelled the Jesuits and obtained the dissolution of their society from the papacy did not press the rest of the reformist agenda very noisily after 1773, as though exhausted by that negative effort. Before Clement XIV died in 1774, for example, Spain obtained a reduction in the jurisdiction of the nuncio's office, though neither the beatification of Palafox nor the restoration of communion between Rome and Utrecht, a goal that Roda and Moñino had come to sponsor by 1772. During the long pontificate of Ganganelli's successor, Spain largely contented itself with defanging the Inquisition and minutely and unilaterally regulating and "nationalizing" seminaries and the monastic orders without any wholesale reduction of either. But it was otherwise with some Catholic states that had sat out the campaign against the Jesuits but took advantage of its success to go on an all-out reformist tear. Most spectacular among these were the Habsburg states including the quasi-independent Grand Duchy of Tuscany.

Largely below the papacy's radar until after the pontificate of Clement XIV in 1774, Tuscany's reformist legislation began precociously but modestly with a largely jurisdictional agenda that limited its field of action to freeing state functions from the church. This action began under the regency council that governed the duchy when it came into the Habsburg orbit in 1737 after dynastic reshuffling at the end the War of Polish Succession awarded it to Maria Theresa's future husband and emperor Francis Stephen of Lorraine. Francesco Stefano, as he was known in Tuscany, delegated the duchy's governance to one Marc de Craon aided by the financial officer Emmanuel de Richecourt, who in turn availed themselves of the able Pisan jurists Pompeo de Neri and Giulio Rucellei. Faced with a moribund economy, shriveling revenues, and a tentacular ecclesiastical presence, it was they who reduced the Inquisition to a state of inactivity in 1739, transferred the right of censorship from the Inquisition to state control in 1743, and in 1751 prohibited any further bequests of landed property to a fiscally immune church. This prohibition was the sort of antiamortization law that Carlos III dared not lay down in Spain in 1766 and was among the measures that brought down papal anathemas on Parma in 1768.[18]

In promulgating these reforms, Francesco Stefano's Tuscan regency government benefited from the long and court-friendly pontificate of Benedict XIV, after which the quite contrary-minded Clement XIII found himself too pinned down defending the besieged Jesuits to pay much attention to Tuscany. Similar conditions at first held for Peter Leopold of Habsburg, Francesco Stefano's second son, who assumed the title of Grand Duke of Tuscany upon his father's death in 1765. After seeing out the end of Clement XIII's pontificate, he enjoyed the papal peace afforded by the pontificate of Clement XIV, from which he did not ask for an end to the Jesuits. Known as Pietro Leopoldo in Tuscany, he inherited the help of Neri and Rucellei to whom he eventually added like-minded others, such as Francesco Maria Gianni and Francesco Seratti. He also picked up the generally Muratorian inspiration of their reformism that proposed "public felicity" rather than martial glory as the goal of secular governance while valorizing the greater utility of the secular to the detriment of the regular clergy.

As elsewhere, in Tuscany that reformism bore an Augustinian stamp, in this case due to the influence of Giovanni Lami, editor of the *Novelle letterarie*; the jurist and essayist Antonio Niccolini; and Ceratti, rector of the University of Pisa, as well as the theologian Pier Francesco Foggini—all affiliates of Bottari's and Passionei's Archetto, and in Ceratti's and Niccolini's cases involved in the efforts to obtain a papal "peace" for French appellants and the Church of Utrecht.

With Neri and Rucellei's advice and under Muratorian influence Pietro Leopoldo took advantage of this period of papal slack to complete the defanging of the Inquisitor's office, enlarge the antiamortization law of 1751, and reimpose a long-lapsed royal exequatur requiring state approval for the publication of papal pronouncements.[19] In measures pointing toward future ecclesiastical reforms, he also denied Tuscan nationality to monks who had taken vows elsewhere and discouraged bishops from allowing new monastic admissions without evidence of choice or from ordaining priests without either adequate material means to support them or a parish in need of them. Still, it took until well into the 1770s and the pontificate of Pius VI for the grand duke to begin curbing the temporal power of ecclesiastical courts and the papacy's right to dispense candidates to local benefices from the provisions of canon law. Not until 1779 did he follow other Catholic states in banning the annual reading of the bull *In coena Domini*.[20]

In comparison to his first fifteen years as Tuscany's grand duke, the pace of ecclesiastical reform began to quicken dramatically when Pietro Leopoldo came under the influence of the combination of a harder variant of Augustinianism and Gallicanism in the person of Scipione de' Ricci, whom the grand duke appointed as bishop of Prato and Pistoia in 1780. A youthful habitué of the Archetto while in Rome in the 1750s and in contact with the diocese of Utrecht and the Jansenist International through Clément, it was Ricci more than anyone else who convinced the grand duke that his rights as temporal sovereign included the right of reforming all the external and material aspects of the Tuscan church as outside bishop in Gallican style. It was also he who held the famous diocesan Synod of Pistoia in 1786 and had it proclaim the four Gallican articles of 1682 as no less than indubitable articles of the Catholic faith.[21] Historians differ among themselves about the degree of influence Ricci had on the grand duke, which most certainly waned after their joint reformist project began to unravel in 1787. It was nonetheless sufficient to include Duguet's classic *Institution d'un prince* and an anonymous French Jansenist primer on ecclesiastical reform among Pietro Leopoldo's bed stand favorites, and to have inspired much of the content of the grand duke's own formal program for ecclesiastical reform known as the *Fifty-Seven Points*, published in 1786.[22]

The years between Ricci's promotion as bishop of Prato and Pistoia and the Synod of Pistoia witnessed a hail of peremptory orders and strong recommendations from the grand duke on his own authority, the goal of which was to reassert the right of the state in relation to both papacy and the Tuscan church. Hence such reforms as the abolition of the Roman Inquisition in 1782, the reduction of the papal nuncio's office to an embassy like others, the prohibition of all fees to Rome, the supervision of episcopal reports to Rome, and the exclusion of "foreign" monks as well as any vow of monastic obedience to "foreign" generals. But the scope of other reforms went beyond these jurisdictional limits and took Pietro Leopoldo into neo-Gallican, even Jansenist, territory. For they aimed at nothing less than to loosen the ties between all segments of the clergy with the papacy in an attempt to restore the rights of bishops vis-à-vis Rome; to cut down on the number of regular clergy while reorienting the rest toward service to the parish; to prune the secular clergy of nonparochial benefices the better to enhance the material means and education of parish priests; and to focus the piety of the lay faithful on the parish church and the central mysteries of the Christian faith in lieu of horizontal devotion toward saints, images, and relics.

At the top of the intended beneficiaries of these reforms figured the bishops who as the heads of the canonical ecclesiastical hierarchy stood to regain the right to grant dispensations from canon law heretofore reserved by the papacy, the right to make appointments to many priestly benefices heretofore in the nomination of the curia or monastic houses, and the power with their clergy to act as "judges of the faith" in regularly held diocesan synods. But, consigned by residence, they were to be saddled with the duty of preparing homilies every Sunday and major feast days and also to carry out all the other reforms regarding the clergy and lay piety, whether they agreed with them or not. Equally intended as beneficiaries were the parish priests, who, cast in the role of the main intermediaries between the God and laity, were to profit from enhanced livings obtained by unions of benefices or redirected revenues from mortuary Masses, access to education in new ecclesiastical academies, a role of doctrinal judges in diocesan synods, and preferred access to vacant canonries or even bishoprics.

Left behind or summarily reassigned, however, were secular canons or other "simple" benefices holders without care of souls. Among the most ungrateful of the intended beneficiaries were the lay faithful, who, now the unique objects of the clergy's pastorate, found themselves assailed by catechisms and other instructional material, restricted in their work-free feast days and two-day pilgrimages, and deprived of their confraternities, separate altars, some of their favorite images, relics, and forms of devotion—all dismissed as "superstizione" in the grand duke's thirty-seventh point.[23] The chief target of these reforms were members of a regular clergy now cut off from their superiors elsewhere, diminished by elevated age requirements, reassigned to service in the parish, disbarred from separate chapels and churches, limited to a set number of houses per diocese, and subjected to supervision by both bishops and the state.[24]

Not all of Tuscany's dioceses were equally affected by these reforms, many of which remained proposals only. Most affected were Ricci's diocese of Prato and Pistoia and those governed by like-minded bishops, notably Colle under Nicolas Schiarelli and Chiusi and Pienza under Giuseppe Pannilini. While many of their reforms became casualties of a popular reactionary revolution in the spring and early summer of 1790, by no means all came undone, among them the dissolution of monastic houses and elimination of nonpastoral benefices. Would Pietro Leopoldo's reform of the Tuscan clergy, church, and lay piety have succeeded without the resistance of a still intact papal curia, an entrenched regular clergy, and bishops who had received their investiture from the papacy and remained dependent on it in myriad ways? Perhaps. Sixteenth-century princes and magistrates had often imposed the Reformation's drastic stripping of the altars on populations unreceptive to similar reforms. Yet that similarity tended to damn such reforms by association whenever attempted within Catholicism thereafter.[25] When in 1787 the reformist suffragan bishop Valenti Heimes tried to introduce a vernacular German and therefore Lutheran-like hymnbook in the Rhenish prince-archbishopric of Mainz, the reform provoked one of the biggest peasant uprisings in the prerevolutionary eighteenth-century Empire.[26]

Pietro Leopoldo was unique among eighteenth-century Europe's exemplars of "enlightened absolutism" in his attempts to extend reform to the absolutist mode of governance itself. Although his and his minister Francesco Gianni's plan to limit absolutist rule by means of a constitution on the American model remained on paper except at the local level, it was otherwise in regard to the ecclesiastical domain, where Pietro Leopoldo tried to elicit conciliar consent and collaboration for his fifty-seven-point reform program by means of what was supposed to be a series of diocesan synods leading to a Tuscan national council.

The first diocesan synod to meet was Ricci's in Pistoia on 18 September 1786, which under the influence of Ricci and the Pavian theologian and "promoter" Pietro Tamburini took the opportunity to lay down some hard Augustinian—Jansenist really—articles on divine grace and penitence and the lamentable "obscurity" into which these these truths had fallen, as though they were necessary premises undergirding the grand duke's program of reform.[27] More, this synod went beyond the fifty-seven points to recommend other reforms, including a division between the contractual and sacramental parts of marriage. That distinction would have enabled the state rather than the church to set the legitimate degrees of consanguinity, thereby eliminating a whole segment of the church's "spiritual" jurisdiction and with it papal dispensations from marital canon law, while creating a space for the civil toleration of Protestants.[28]

Correctly judging from the reactions to his fifty-seven points that the synod in Pistoia was unlikely to be followed by very many other bishops as enthusiastic as Ricci about these points, Pietro Leopoldo tried to fast-forward the process by convening, not a council, but an "assembly" of Tuscan bishops and archbishops for 1787 in Florence. There, beginning on 23 September, and in the grand duke's absence, Ricci and his chief allies in Colle and Chiusi and Pienza found themselves outmaneuvered as well as outnumbered by the others, led by the assembly's president, Angiolo Franceschi, archbishop of Pisa, as advised by the "enlightened" conservative Pisan jurist Giovanni Maria Lampredi.

Taking the nuncio's place as the curia's informant, Lampredi at one point enraged the Riccians by suggesting that Augustine was a better rhetorician than theologian; while as president Franceschi skillfully divided the grand duke's various points so as to expose the most important and controversial ones to individual rejection. One by one these provisions went down, either rejected outright or—the same thing—left for implementation to individual episcopal discretion. The only provisions that passed were those that reiterated the mandates of the Council of Trent or were otherwise noncontroversial, such as the extension of ecclesiastical academies. So averse to anything that might displease the papacy was this assembly that Francesco Pio Santi, the bishop of Soana and occasional Riccian ally, could not persuade his colleagues to vote to ban an oath of obedience to the papacy on the occasion of their confirmation after the Riccian bishop Niccolò Sciarelli of Colle turned a discussion about oaths in this anticurial direction.[29]

Meanwhile, worse happened for the reformist cause in Ricci's diocese of Prato, where the assembly had prompted rumors among its parishioners that its purpose was to discipline their unpopular bishop. A visit to Prato's cathedral church by the anti-Riccian bishop of Volterra in the wake of the assembly's discussion of inauthentic relics turned these rumors into the fear that Ricci was about to destroy that church's most venerated relic, the Virgin Mary's *cintola*, or girdle, supposedly left behind by the Virgin during her assumption, later recovered by Saint Thomas and brought to Tuscany from Palestine during the Middle Ages by a returning merchant or crusader. The result was a three-day popular uprising on 18–20 May grouping town day laborers and surrounding peasants. Together they destroyed the bishop's arms and the reformed missals and breviaries while saying rosaries, chanting litanies, reveiling uncovered images and, in the words of Ricci's assistant Reginaldo Tanzini, combining "the most bizarre transports of devotion" and other manifestations of the "religious fanaticism of the seditious" with the aim of restoring "everything as it was" before their bishop's reforms.[30] It was not until Sunday when the uprising spread to Pistoia and the municipal guard intervened that the uprising ran its course.

Less visible actors and motives were undoubtedly at work as well, among them resentments within the bourgeoisie and nobility about the loss of stature in the suppressed confraternities and influence in the familial placements in suppressed benefices and monasteries.[31] But it was not possible to miss the main religious point of the rioting or the damage it had done to the grand duke and his bishop's cause. In the short run, Ricci tried to win back the good will of his parishioners, while Pietro Leopoldo used his "enlightened" authority to impose many of the reforms that the assembly had made optional. But in the late winter of 1790 the grand duke, alas, had to leave Tuscany for Vienna, and in his absence an even more virulent spate of uprisings broke out in Pistoia and Livorno in April 1790, spreading and culminating in Florence itself on 9 June.

This time, moreover, rapidly rising prices of grain and other basic commodities gave additional motives and targets to the rioters, while a weak and unarmed regency government left behind by the grand duke allowed the rioters to wring monumental concessions, nothing less than the compete abrogation of all the ecclesiastical reforms along with the end of the Tuscany's heretofore successful physiocratic experiment in free trade in grain. "I have the sad duty of confirming for you the total overturning of all the wise reforms effected in Tuscany," wrote Giorlamo Astorri, the Austrian—and quite Jansenist—postal agent in Rome to the archbishop of Utrecht's secretary, Jean-Baptiste Mouton, on 20 June 1790. He was not exaggerating, as the concessions proved to be permanent.[32] In real danger of his life, Ricci had meanwhile fled Pistoia for the safety of a family estate in the Chianti, never to return to his diocese.

The reason of state that took Pietro Leopoldo away from Florence and to Vienna was the death on 20 February of his older brother Joseph, whose mantel as ruler of Austria and its possessions and as Holy Roman Emperor now fell upon his shoulders. And no sooner did he arrive in Vienna and assume the title of Emperor Leopold II than he too had to rescind some religious and ecclesiastical reforms similar to the ones he had sponsored in Tuscany. For, as in Tuscany, they had also provoked revolts, especially in the peripheral Austrian possessions in the southern Netherlands. The so-called Brabantine revolt of

1786–1790 would seem to belie any supposition that Pietro Leopoldo might have done better as grand duke in Tuscany if instead of inviting opposition by means of a quest for consent he had ruled dictatorially, as had his brother as emperor. For by 1790 the results had come in, and they were much the same.[33]

One signal difference between the trajectory of like-minded reform in imperial Austria in contrast to that in ducal Tuscany is that whereas in pre-Riccian Tuscany the pace of reform responded mainly to dynastic changes, in Austria it did so in reaction to the shock of the loss of the province of Silesia to Frederican Prussia in the War of Austrian Succession in 1740–1748 and the failure to win it back in the Seven Years' War of 1756–1763. Attempts to match Protestant Prussia's revenue-raising capacities by enhancing the power of the state to the detriment of a baroque church produced a first wave of ecclesiastical reform under Empress Maria Theresa and her chancellor, Wenzel Anton, Prince of Kaunitz-Rietberg.[34] Stretching from 1749 to about 1767, that phase derived its spiritual inspiration from Muratorian circles in the Benedictine University of Salzburg, which already relayed the Archetto's influence by way of theological students who had come into its orbit in Rome; and its political means from Kaunitz's Catholicization of Protestant state cameralism, which had long allowed the "prince" to intervene in ecclesiastical affairs in the interests of the general wellfare. The ecclesiastical reforms undertaken during this phase included the state's assumption of control over the censorship commission, the breaking of the Jesuits' monopoly over both that agency and and theological education in general, and the Augustinian-Thomist reorientation of the University of Vienna's theological faculty in particular. Under the direction of Ambrose Stock, a contingent of largely Italian philo-Jansenist theologians initially took the place of the Jesuits, while the appointment of a Dutch Jansenist, Anton de Haen, as the empress's physician and the substitution of an Austrian Jansenist, Ignaz Müller, for a Jesuit as her confessor opened the Schönbrunn Palace to the influence of the Reform Catholic International.

Although still under the aegis of Maria Theresa and Kaunitz, a second wave of reform from 1767 to 1780 responded to the growing influence of Joseph II, who became coruler in 1770, and the intransigence of Clement XIII, who provoked Kaunitz to abandon any attempt at obtaining Rome's concurrence for church reform. Important as a signal of things to come is Kaunitz's use of the province of Lombardy as a laboratory, where with the help of a new agency called the Giunta economale its governor, von Firmian, imposed a retroactive amortization law on church property, subjected papal pronouncements to the exequatur, assumed control of book censorship, abolished the office of the Inquisition, raised the minimum age for taking monastic vows, and began to suppress underpopulated convents and transfer their wealth to the secular clergy, for whom they established state-supervised "general seminaries." The application of most of these measure to the Austrian provinces waited until Joseph's assumption of sole rule after his mother's death in 1780, although Kaunitz and Joseph prepared the way by replicating the powers of the Giunta in an agency in Vienna called the Consessus in Publico-Ecclesiasticis. By the 1770s also, Joseph and Kaunitz could draw on the ideological support of a cadre of home-grown neo-Gallican, regalist, episcopalist—even theologically Jansenist—professors and churchmen produced by the archbishop of Vienna's establishment of a seminary in the University of Vienna and the reform of that university's theological education in 1759. Prominent among these were Melchior Blarer, Abbot Stephan Rautenstrauch, Johann Baptist de Terme, and the parish priest Anton Wittola.

Yet nothing that even Kaunitz had done quite prepared him, much less Austria and its possessions, for the reformist purification of Catholic institutions and all-out assault on religious culture undertaken by Joseph II in a third stage upon his accession as sole ruler in 1780. The Austrian counterpart to the coming of Ricci to the see of Prato-Pistoia during the same year, Joseph's approach to reform differed from his brother's in its sword-swift and unabashedly top-down style of imposition that overwhelmed the collegial dimension of the reformist conception of the church, thereby earning the separate appellation of "Josephism." The halving by Joseph of monastic establishments' houses and population; his vast transfer of wealth from them to parish clergy and schools; his redefinition of bishops as popes in their own dioceses except in their subjection to him; his substitution of state "general seminaries" for episcopal and monastic ones; his unilateral redrawing of diocesan and parochial boundaries—all this was surgical enough for the ecclesiastical body. Even more so to its soul was the general assault on lay confraternities, feast days, and every form of rococo piety, down to substitution of humble sacks for wooden biers for burials. Yet none of it totally falls outside the overall orbit of Reform Catholicism, however one measures the mix of "enlightened" and reformist Catholic elements that went into the making of the emperor's outlook. That characterization even holds for reforms as radical as those providing for civil toleration of Orthodox, Protestant, and Jewish populations in 1781 and the separation of civil from sacramental marriage in 1783.

After nine years of legislative frenzy Joseph II faced unrest even in the hereditary Austrian provinces and major revolts in Hungary and the Austrian Netherlands. While neither in Hungary nor the other contiguous provinces was his ecclesiastical legislation the first or foremost cause of discontent, it was otherwise in the Austrian Netherlands. To be sure, what put the torch to the tinder of the revolution that overwhelmed Austrian troops in 1789 was Joseph's suppression of Belgium's "Joyous Entry" constitution and the province of Brabant's Estates after these had refused to vote subsidies in protest against Joseph's unilateral reorganization of the judicial system—the sorts of top-down measures of rational institutional centralization the emperor had been imposing everywhere to the detriment of privilege and prescription.

Yet the tinder itself consisted of growing clerical and popular resistance to Joseph's ecclesiastical and devotional reforms, especially the decree on marriage in 1783, the abolition of monasteries, the devotional reforms of the mid-1780s, and most of all the abolition of all episcopal and monastic seminaries and their replacement by a state-supervised "general seminary" at the University of Louvain in 1786. The then Spanish Netherlands may have been Jansen's birthplace and Louvain his university, but Jesuits had been thicker on the ground and Jansenism had never put down popular roots there as it had in parts of France.

Well before Joseph II's judicial reforms and Brabant's refusal of subsidies became issues, revolt took the form of a student uprising at the new seminary shortly after its opening in the fall of 1786, unhappy as the transplanted students were with the beer and unfinished quarters. But they felt even more upset by the anti-ultramontanist bias of some of their new professors and the texts they assigned.[35] Chief among these was the new superior, Ferdinand Stöger, author of an anticurial ecclesiastical history, and Professor Josse Le Plat, who taught canon law by means of one Josef Johann Nepomuk Pehem's *Praelectionum in ius ecclesiasticum universum* (*Introduction to Universal Ecclesiastical Law*), which espoused a very episcopalist, or Febronian, conception of the Catholic Church. Led by one Jan Frans van de Velde, professors sidelined by Joseph's new seminary soon joined the students in disobedience, followed by townsmen—even countrymen—riled up by incendiary sermons in the local churches. Most directly in the crosshairs was Le Plat, of whose "heretical" leanings the students were sure after they found many of the propositions in Pehem's text also singled out for censure in Pius VI's bull in 1786 against Eybel's *Was ist der Papst?* (*What Is the Pope?*) in late 1786.[36]

By 1787 this stream of clerical and religious revolt merged with the one provoked by Joseph II's judicial reforms and fiscal conflicts with the estates of Brabant, obliging the governors-general temporarily to rescind all the emperor's reforms and the targeted professors to flee, Stöger for good. But when in late 1787 the emperor decided to persist in his ecclesiastical reforms and reimpose the seminary in Louvain, he found that he could only do so by dismissing and then exiling all the "orthodox" professors and stationing several battalions to keep order and conduct the "heretical" professors to empty classrooms amid a hostile population. So targeted was the subject of canon law that he had to transfer its teaching—and with it Le Plat—to the relative safety of Brussels in the fall of 1788. Meanwhile, in June 1788, Joseph had rekindled the fiscal and constitutional conflict by suppressing the Estates of Brabant and Hainaut as well as the Joyous Entry after these estates had again withheld their subsidies. By that time Brussels itself had ceased to be safe, as Le Plat and other "imperialists"—the pejorative applied to Joseph's defenders—fled for their lives when revolutionary "patriot" volunteers converged on the city in November 1789 and drove the Austrian troops out of the Flemish provinces entirely.[37]

Throughout his ordeal Le Plat blamed the revolution on the "fanaticism" of the clergy, especially the bishops and monks, who mistook their dedication to ultramontanist maxims for the Catholic faith and who aimed, he said, to establish a "monachal government."[38] Fueling some of the resistance was undoubtedly the clergy's temporal stake in the constitution as Brabant's first estate. But Le Plat rightly insisted that it was only after the emperor's final decision to stand by his ecclesiastical reforms that the revolt turned into a revolution. By far the most targeted "heresiarch" in this conservative revolution and the Flemish counterpart to Ricci in Tuscany, this profusely pamphleteering professor endured insults and threats to his wife and sons as well as the damaging and pillaging of his country house while being burned in effigy. By his own account he only narrowly escaped with his life several times when recognized unguarded, even in the "plat pays" on the occasion of a stop to hear Mass near Tirlemont.[39] Misery seeking company, it was nothing if not appropriate that in 1792 Le Plat struck up a correspondence with Ricci and in 1796 wrote a spirited defense of the Synod of Pistoia against Pius VI's condemnation of it in the bull *Auctorem Fidei* in 1794.[40]

Among the many "men of the church" whose "fanaticism" he held responsible for directing popular anger against the emperor's religious reforms, Le Plat singled out the monks, behind whose ultramontanism he spied the hand of the papacy. With his brief of 1786 against Eybel's primer on the pope, the "court of Rome" in Le Plat's opinion "had come to the aid and succor of these [ultramontanist] fanatics," emboldening them to say that the conception of the papacy propounded in the brief was "dogmatic" and that Le Plat's neo-Gallican view was "heretical."[41] With justification or not, in 1789 Le Plat went so far as to accuse the pope of directly encouraging the bishop of Antwerp's resistance to the emperor's reforms by letter.[42] Reflecting in 1790 in his refuge in Chianti, Ricci similarly discerned monks and the hand of the papacy in the revolt that had just undone Pietro Leopoldo's religious reforms in Tuscany. This "revolution," he told the archbishop of Utrecht, "had been announced in the cafés of Rome well before the event, having also been prophesized by mendicant monks."[43]

In the wake of failure, in sum, it is clear that major proponents of and protagonists in the cause of Reform Catholicism deemed that these reforms would have stood a better chance of success with a reformed papacy and without monks—that is, with the help of two principal preliminary reforms envisioned by Tanucci. Did the absence of these reformist preconditions doom Reform Catholicism to failure? Nothing in history being inevitable except in retrospect, explanations for the reformist failures in Tuscany and the Austrian Netherlands must include such contingencies as the vulnerably Jansenist flank to which Ricci exposed religious reform in Tuscany, Pietro Leopoldo's decision to leave only a weak regency government without a militia after his departure for Vienna in 1790—and above all his brother Joseph II's decision to add institutional injury to religious insult by dictatorially imposing agencies and even the language of central governance at the expense of traditional institutions in all his domains. In the Flemish provinces, it was Joseph's imposition of a centralized and rational judicial structure and his suspension of the Joyous Entry that gave the religious issue constitutional agency and the aspect of a "national" cause.

THE MAKING OF AN ULTRAMONTANIST AND EX-JESUIT INTERNATIONAL

That much said, it must be added that the cause of reformist Catholicism was encountering headwinds that are hard to imagine without the reaction to the total suppression of the Society of Jesus a decade earlier. The most vivid examples at hand of such headwinds are those encountered by the two reformist protagonists Le Plat and Ricci, both of whom mentioned adversaries that might not have been so formidable had papal suppression not turned all Jesuits into ex-Jesuits. Besides the Louvain professor van de Velde, the most mortal personal nemeses Le Plat mentioned were ex-Jesuits, above all François-Xavier de Feller, editor of the biweekly *Journal historique et littéraire* published in Liège and one of the main architects in the use of Pius VI's brief *Super soliditate* to tar Le Plat as a heretic. As for those whom he called "our bishops," Le Plat did not err in detecting Feller's advice in the actions of some of his episcopal enemies, above all Johann Heinrich Franckenberg, archbishop of Mechlin.[44] Although Ricci for his part complained less about ex-Jesuits than about Dominicans and mendicants, his own chief nemesis was a would-have-been Jesuit in the person of Torrigiani's protégé Giovanni Marchetti. It was Marchetti who in a devastating pamphlet entitled *Annotazione pacifiche* (*Pacific Notes*) all but justified the uprising against Ricci's parishioners in Prato in May 1787 and condemned all his "scandalous" devotional and liturgical "innovations" as heretical because undertaken in disobedience based on a heretical Jansenist—and Protestant— conception of papal primacy that stripped it of all jurisdictional authority.[45] As for his fellow bishops, it was Archbishop Antonio Martini of Florence whom Ricci singled out for having "given on every occasion the most terrible examples of schism and rebellion" and on whose support "the Court of Rome had relied during the whole course of its conjuration."[46]

That ex-Jesuits had reason to play a conspicuous role in opposition to neo-Gallican religious reform in the Austrian Netherlands and Tuscany goes without saying. But that bishops and archbishops should have made common cause with them demands explanation, especially in that outside France bishops had generally supported the regalist and anticurial reformist legislation of their Catholic sovereigns, most readily against the Jesuits; and that both Franckenberg and Martini had earlier personified the hopes of reformist Catholics.

When in 1781 Martini obtained Pietro Leopoldo's impromptu nomination for the archbishopric while passing through Florence on his way to Rome for papal consecration as bishop of Bobbio in Piedmont, he must have struck the grand duke as the ideal reformist candidate for Florence, known as he was for his theologically Augustinian and morally rigorist orientation and renowned for his recently published Italian translation of the Bible. Further, his vintage was Muratorian, and his friends and patrons included Lami, Niccolini, and Cardinal Andrea Corsini, who consecrated him in Rome—Muratorian reformers all. Unbeknownst to Pietro Leopoldo, however, a secret catalyst for the growing conservatism of Martini was a pessimistic fear of moral disintegration in an age of "enlightenment" and his conviction of the indispensable spiritual role of the church as a source of order, for which he thought the church's external jurisdiction necessary. If any episode can be pinpointed that tipped Martini's balance from the reformist to the conservative side, it would seem to be the Bourbon powers' brutal response to Clement XIII's *Monitorio* against Ferdinando of Parma and the pan-Catholic offensive against the publication of *In coena Domini* that followed it.[47]

As for Franckenberg, the cause and timing of his conservative "conversion" are less clear, even if his early reformist credentials are just as authentic. These consisted of the reformist circles in which he moved during his education while in Benedict XIV's Rome and his exemplary comportment as confessor and preacher as provost in the collegial church of Altbunzlau in the 1750s. It was for this reputation that Maria Theresa chose him to succeed the Jansenist-scourging Thomas-Philippe d'Alsace de Hénin-Liétard as archbishop of Mechlin in 1759.

Whatever caused his conversion to his predecessor's outlook, it seems to have coincided with Bourbon-imposed papal suppression of the Jesuits and its reformist consequences for the University of Louvain.[48] While in 1762 his recently published mandamus insisting on the importance of scriptural knowledge for the ordination of new clergy gave reason for the *Nouvelles ecclésiastiques* to nourish the most "happy hopes" for his episcopacy's success in dissipating Jesuit-inculcated ignorance, by 1775 the Jansenist weekly was faulting Franckenberg for showing the most "marked predilection" for ex-Jesuits. In what the same journal described as a "tocsin against all the [reformist] bishops of Germany," Franckenberg's Holy Week mandamus of 1783 charged his colleagues across the Rhine with denying the "universal jurisdiction" of the papacy over the church, the divine origin of the monastic clergy, and the veneration due to saints— denials he saw as tantamount to "heresies" heading to "schism," in the weekly's less than neutral account.[49]

Symptomatically similar to Franckenberg's trajectory in Austria was Christoph Bartholomaus Anton von Migazzi's. In a *cursus honorum* similar to Franckenberg's, Migazzi circulated in Muratorian reformist circles while studying theology at the Collegium Germanicum in Rome and later law in Innsbruck, before preceding Franckenberg as the archbishop of Mechlin's coadjutor in 1751 and then graduating to the archbishopric of Vienna on Maria Theresa's nomination in 1757. It was Migazzi who persuaded the Austrian empress to rid herself of the Jesuits as royal confessors and who steered censorship policy and theological education in an anti-Jesuit, pro-Augustinian, and Thomist direction. For the University of Vienna that direction displaced Jesuits to the benefit of the Jansenist Simon Ambros Stock, who as director of the theological faculty appointed Augustinians and Dominicans, such as Pietro Maria Gazzaniga. Throughout the late 1750s and early 1760s Migazzi's name circulated as the hope and mainstay of the Augustinian cause in the correspondence of the Jansenist International.

But, as with Franckenberg, a sort of conservative conversion overtook Migazzi, in his case in 1767 around the time of the Jansenist Müller's replacement of a Jesuit as the empress's confessor and the controversy over François Richer's *De l'autorité du clergé et du magistrat politique*. As these illustrate, the decisive factors seem to have been the maturation of an indigenous Jansenist presence and the unilateral anticurial turn in Austrian ecclesiastical policy, both in reaction to the growing rigidity of Clement XIII's pontificate amid the Bourbon and Portuguese offensive against the Jesuits. Thereafter Migazzi's name seldom surfaced in Jansenist correspondence without the adjective "traitorous" accompanying it. Such was his evolution to the "right" that when Pius VI visited Vienna in 1782, he did so in part in order in order to forestall the politically explosive possibility of Migazzi's publicly refusing Easter Communion to Joseph II.

One factor that may have gone into the making of Migazzi's growing ultramontanism was his cardinal's hat, which he obtained on Maria Theresa's nomination in 1761. But promotion to the cardinalate in 1778 only reinforced the direction of Franckenberg's evolution, while exerting even less effect on the spectacular "conversions" of two other cardinals: namely, the Piedmontese Carlo Vittorio Amedeo Ignazio delle Lanze, whom Benedict XIV elevated to the cardinalate in 1747 well before any such conversion, and the Modenese Giuseppe Garampi, whose elevation by Pius VI waited until 1785.

The most dramatic turnabout of the two was that of Delle Lanze, who picked up his philo-Jansenism as a canon regular at the Sainte-Geneviève Abbey in Paris and maintained it as royal chaplain in his native Piedmont with help from a Port-Royalist library and correspondence with Bottari and Clément. This turnaround became apparent in 1759–1760 with his reaction to the brutality and secrecy of the Portuguese court in expelling its Jesuits and breaking with Rome, and it culminated when his Jansenist vicar-general, Gaspare Nizzia, reluctantly reported to the Châtelet councilor Marolde du Coudray that the cardinal had committed his Port-Royalist library to flames, especially books either condemned by Rome or against the Jesuits.[50]

More influential although less incendiary was the slower evolution of Cardinal Giuseppe Antonio Francesco Baldassare Garampi, who, without Delle Lanze's youthful Jansenist sins to atone for, nonethesse began his career by casting his spiritual and moral net to the Muratorian and Concinian side of the bark after renouncing a scientific career for an ecclesiastical one in the late 1740s. Garampi even fell in with Cardinal Passionei's Archetto while studying law and theology and taking orders in Benedict XIV's Rome, numbering such Jansenist figures as Giovanni Cristofano Amaduzzi and Parma's educational reformer Paciàudi among his friends and correspondents.[51] Most decisive in his subsequent ultramontanist turnaround were several diplomatic missions in the 1760s as Vatican archivist to settle jurisdictional disputes on Rome's behalf in the Catholic German Rhineland, where he encountered the anticurial winds that Choiseul and Bernis took note of in 1770, along with Febronius's *De statu Ecclesiae*, which he read with consternation in 1764.[52]

By 1770 his newfound sympathy for the Jesuits as was well enough known in Rome for Bernis and the Bourbon courts to put pressure on Clement XIV to send Garampi packing as nuncio to Poland. In his next post in Austria his already militant ultramontanism increased in proportion to the pace and scope of Thersesian and Josephist ecclesiastical reform. Beginning with his attempt to choreograph refutations of and a recantation by Febronius, Garampi thereafter devoted ever more of his energies to organizing a sort of ultramontanist epistolary, journalistic, and book-publishing international to meet the Jansenist International on its own terms. By the eve of the French Revolution this network had outposts in all quarters of Catholic Europe that he had visited and where he had recruited correspondents. The most telling of these proved to be Brussels, Louvain, Vienna, and even Paris, where he made the acquaintance of the anti-philosophe Catholic apologist Jean Pey.[53] By the time Pius VI made Garampi a cardinal in 1785, promotion to the purple had become a means to add clout and luster to an ultramontanist international that had become Garampi's main achievement and claim to fame.[54]

Besides their contact with each other, what all of these figures have in common is to have experienced a "rightward" antireformist and ultramontanist politicization during the 1760s, if not directly in reaction to the international campaign against the Jesuits, then to the brutal assertion of secular state power against the papacy that accompanied it. Yet such was the pressure that the Bourbon states had to put on the papacy to obtain the dissolution of the Jesuits that, as events played out, it proved impossible to separate these things. While Choiseul's policy sought to minimize embarrassment to the papacy with a softer secularization of the Society and Spain's policy was to hide its ulterior anti-ultramontane objectives behind the case against it, the combination of Clement XIII's *Monitorio* against the Bourbon duchy of Parma and Piacenza in 1768 and Clement XIV's tactic of postponing the promised dissolution of the Society *sine die* made it necessary for the Bourbon states to train their heaviest artillery directly against the Court of Rome.

Lest all the blame for the polarization of Catholic Europe be laid on the Bourbon states and the enemies of Jesuits, many of the cardinals who voted for Ganganelli in the conclave of 1769 did so because they too thought that Clement XIII and Torrigiani's anachronistic recourse to *In coena Domini*'s anathemas against the Lilliputian duchy had done more harm than good to the curial cause. By the time Moñino got to Rome in July 1772, even Bernis had come to think that Clement XIV would have done better either promptly to dissolve the Society after promising in writing to do so or to have flatly refused to promise more than a canonical reform. In lieu of either scenario, however, the prolonged agony of the papal phase of the dissolution made for a Roman spectacle of the martyrization of the proverbial janissaries of the papacy as well as of two popes of opposite orientation, the first of whom died shortly after refusing Bourbon demands to dissolve the Society and the second after not doing so rapidly enough. It was as though two pontiffs and their elite guards had figured as the vanquished victims of a classic Roman triumph, all but ending in the colosseum.

The antireformist and ultramontanist reaction that was soon to make its force felt in all of Catholic Europe did so in Rome immediately after the promulgation of the papal brief of suppression. Writing from Rome in December 1773 in reply to Clément's inquiry about a new "peace" initiative by Utrecht's agent in Rome, the Corsini theologian Foggini replied that he could not imagine what universe this agent inhabited. Far from accepting as orthodox the Utrecht clergy's *Acts* of 1763, any new edition of these *Acts* would probably result in a more anathema-bristling condemnation by Rome, even while the recent publication of the French clergy's condemnation of those *Acts* by its assembly in 1765 circulated freely in Rome precisely "with the object of preventing any such accommodation." As Foggini described it, the post-Jesuit Rome of December 1773 was undergoing the rapid "multiplication of the sect of Jesuitism," while "Augustinians [such as himself and Cardinal Marefoschi] found themselves neglected on all sides." The Jesuits might well no longer have formed a "legal corps," he further reported, "but disguised as priests they were still the same," with the addition of "a thousand adulators and devotees" in their train—all this from a "friend" who had always advised the clergy of Utrecht that peace with Rome would have to wait until after the papal dissolution of the Jesuits![55]

The news only got worse after 15 February 1775 when the papal conclave elected Giovanni Angelo Braschi, who took the name of Pius VI. After a year or so of testing the waters, what remained of the Archetto warned the clergy of Utrecht to put its hopes of reconciliation indefinitely on hold because the new pope had let himself be "governed by the likes of [the cardinals] Castelli and Torrigiani" and manifested "no zeal except against the supposed Jansenists, vaunting his desire to exterminate this chimerical sect."[56] Already diminished by the death of Bottari in 1775, the Archetto was one of Pius VI's first targets when in April 1776 the pope attempted to oust and exile reputed "Jansenists" in the Scolopian church and seminary in the Chiesa Nuova, among them Utrecht's advocate Micheli. A vigorous intervention by the Augustinian general Vásquez in defense of his order's cause prevented the worst from then happening.[57] But Pius VI's relentless hostility to Rome's Augustinian effectives sent the theologian Gianbattista Molinelli from the Scolopian Collegio Nazareno to the Republic of Genoa in 1777, and the heavyweight theologians Tamburini and Zola from the formerly Jesuit English and Irish Colleges to the University of Pavia in Habsburg Lombardy two years later.[58] There, they metamorphosed into genuine Jansenists and in collaboration with secular authorities and Ricci and other theologians took a hand in reformist legislation in Genoa and Habsburg Italy.[59]

Redeemed by martyrdom, ex-Jesuits thererfore came to cut conspicuous figures as allies of erstwhile reformist but newly converted bishops in the Ultramontanist International against the reformist one. Behind Franckenberg in Mechlin stood Feller in Liège; taking Martini's side in Florence was Marchetti in Rome; and backing up Migazzi in Vienna was Johann Heinrich von Kerens, formerly the director of the Jesuit-run Collegium Theresianum but now bishop of Wiener-Neustadt. More conspicuous still was the role of ex-Jesuits in the formation of an international ultramontanist press, in which capacity they proved far more lethal as editorial loose cannons than mere Jesuits would have been. For every Jansenist periodical modeled on the *Nouvelles ecclésiastiques* there came to correspond an ex-Jesuit one: in 1778 Feller took on the *Nouvelles* with his *Journal*, just as in 1782 Hermann Goldhagen directed his *Religions-Journal* against both Franz Scheidel's *Monatsschrift* in Mainz and Wittola's *Kirchenzeitung* in Vienna. In Rome itself ex-Jesuit Zaccaria's *Giornale ecclesiastico* took on Follini's *Annali ecclesiastici* in Florence. When the French Revolution broke over Europe, the Augustin Barruel was in France to man the barricades against the *Nouvelles ecclésiastiques* as well as the *Annales de la religion*, the mouthpiece of the post-Terror constitutional church.[60]

No longer having a privileged order against which to unite, moreover, the Dominicans broke with the Augustinians, prying Thomas Aquinas's doctrine of grace from Augustine's and adding more recruits to the anti-Jansenist cause. "It is only too true," the Augustinian general Vásquez responded on 28 May 1775 to Dupac de Bellegarde's query about this schism.[61] Whether the quarrel was principally about theology or part of the wider reaction against the rough handling of the papacy by Catholic states is open to question, as even the Augustinian Luigi Cuccagni drifted into the ultramontanist orbit after breaking with Tamburini over the issue of secular authority. Whatever the cause of the split, Dominicans rallied more naturally to the papal cause, among them such formidable polemicists as Tommaso Maria Mamachi, who like Cuccagni reinforced the ex-Jesuits on the editorial staff of the *Giornale ecclesiastico* in 1782. Both subsidized and monitored by Pius VI himself, this periodical became the propagandistic medium whereby such ex-Jesuit polemicists as Giovan Vincenzo Bolgeni and Zaccaria could demonstrate that they were indeed the papacy's best defenders, while the papacy rewarded them with a leading role in articulating its message.[62]

Ex-Jesuits aided by Mamachi and others also supplemented their journalistic activity with monumental tomes that confronted and "refuted" the neo-Gallican conciliar, episcopalist, and statist ecclesiology of Hontheim alias Febronius and Pereira and, behind them, the whole Gallican corpus, from Gerson to van

Espen. Reversing the Gallican interpretation of Saint Cyprian's ecclesiology defining unity as each bishop's right to act for the whole, these ex-Jesuit polemicists in one way or another factored Petrine primacy into their conception of episcopal collegiality, whether like Bolgeni by mediating the bishops' universal jurisdiction via a papacy that alone received it directly from Christ or like the early Zaccaria by demoting bishops to the status of mere delegates and intermediaries between the pope and the lay faithful. The result in either case was to reconceive the Catholic polity as an absolute monarchy rather than an episcopal "aristocracy," much less as a Richerist democracy, by translating papal primacy into a universal jurisdiction over the whole church as well as each part of it.

Another result of the rise of the "Roman school" of militant ultramontanist thought from the 1770s into the French Revolution is the subjection of Gallican ecclesiology to condemnation as a heresy the likes of which it had never sustained before.[63] That this was so and that the enemies of Le Plat in Louvain were not wrong in thinking that his teaching deviated from papal dogma became apparent with Pius VI's fulmination in the brief *Super Soliditate* against Eybel's pamphlet. For that brief enunciated many of the Roman school's chief theses in adamantly unadorned form. The bishop of Rome was Peter's only successor and sole vicar of Christ, the Roman see the only truly apostolic one. Far from being the merely honorific first among episcopal equals as in Eybel's ecclesiology, the pope was the only universal bishop, as Christ's vicar the only unique bishop, and the sole pastor of the entire church, including all the other pastors, who received their jurisdictions only by ecclesiastical law as applied by him. Far from deriving his authority from church councils, his authority preceded the tenure of any councils, the decrees of which were binding after papal approval alone. Given such principles, it followed that the Roman see alone possessed the authority to confirm—or infirm—episcopal consecrations, without which they were schismatic. Last but not least, all of these tenets belonged to the domain of dogma rather than of ecclesiastical law alone. Thus did the brief also implicitly condemn the Gallican tenets of the Acts of the Synod of Pistoia in retrospect, not to mention the provisions of the French Revolution's reform of the Gallican Church as though by anticipation.[64]

THE FRENCH EXCEPTION, 1771–1789

In France, meanwhile, nothing in comparison to reformism in Habsburg Europe seemed to presage anything so surgical as that reform, better known as the Civil Constitution of the Clergy, passed and promulgated by the revolutionary National Assembly in 1790. As for the other Bourbon states, the philo-Roman moderation displayed by Louis XV's France in comparison to Carlos III's Spain or Ferdinando IV's Naples in the diplomatic phase of the suppression of the Jesuits finds its counterpart in domestic ecclesiastical policy, even apart from the "devout" turn that it took between the fall of Choiseul and the death of Louis XV in 1774. Alone among monarchies until then to produce no "enlightened despot," France hardly changed course toward that model after the long reign of Louis the Well-Beloved gave way to that of the virtuous Louis XVI. Louis XVI's continuation of his predecessor's post-1757 policy of putting the issues of the hundred-plus years of Jansenist wars out of sight and mind left little room for bold reformist initiatives, none of which could be perceived as already striking out in either a philo-Jansenist or an ultramontanist direction.

Comparable to the antimonastic measures undertaken by Pietro Leopoldo and Joseph II, the French monarchy's most daring such action was its establishment of a royal Commission des réguliers under the presidency of the archbishop Loménie de Brienne in 1766, with the goal of eliminating or reforming superfluous and morally lax religious orders or houses within orders. But after fourteen years of labor, the commission succeeded only in raising the minimum age for vows from sixteen to eighteen for women and twenty-one for men and reducing the monastic population in the amount of ten small orders, along with a comparably modest reduction of houses and monks within the retained orders—nothing remotely comparable to Joseph II's *raz-de-marée* of thousands.[65] Hardly bolder were Louis XVI's minor adjustments to the diocesan map, consisting only in the breakup of the diocese of Toul into three and that of Grenoble into two, while adding the dioceses of Moulins and Lille plus five more in the newly annexed island of Corsica.[66]

On the surface of things, then, France would seem to have successfully exorcised its Jansenist-related political and religious divisions by exporting them to the rest of Catholic Europe via the international suppression of the Jesuits, the better to rest in the peace of an autumnal "Catholic enlightenment" that had passed France by when in full orb earlier elsewhere. Except at a surface level, however, nothing could have been further from the truth. While on the one hand Louis XVI continued his predecessor's post-1757 policy of ridding the episcopacy of rabid pro-*Unigenitus* zealots—Christophe de Beaumont breathed his last in 1781—of the sort that were beginning to find counterparts elsewhere in Catholic states, that slow action left a remnant of them in place in 1789, together with parish priests still at liberty to refuse the sacraments to reputed opponents to the anti-Jansenist Formula and bulls, which in principle remained in force. After the outbreak of the Revolution, it would take little time for a clerical "religious right" to reconstitute itself on the model of the one at mid-century and comparable to the ones that had come to exist in Catholic Europe. Although the monarchy got the chastened postexilic parlements to shy away from the Jansenist issue after their restoration by Louis XVI in 1774—even to eschew the terms "citizen" and "despotism" in their remonstrances until 1787—the "patriotic" political ideology that had formed in the course of the Jansenist conflict still festered close to the surface and remained capable of fastening on adjacent issues.

Of largely French origin, elements of patriotic ideology had in various degrees informed the case against the Jesuits, not only in France but in exported form in every other state that had acted against them. That case, to repeat, consisted in four premises: first, that the Society's structural combination of despotic authority on top and blind obedience everywhere below made it objectionable by any account; second, that these traits in combination with the Society's additional aim of universal monarchy made it incompatible with and in a condition of conspiracy against the laws of any state that harbored it; third, that its adopted morality of probabilism not only reduced immorality to a system but also functioned as an essential means toward the Society's political ends; and fourth, that among these political applications, none was more criminal than the justification and practice of regicide or tyrannicide with a view toward advancing the Society's interests.

But while elsewhere in Catholic Europe this largely imported case found limited applicability beyond the campaign against the Jesuits, in France itself it had already long directed its ire against the alleged despotism of the bishops and even of the monarchy, or at least its ministers, because there—again in sharp contrast with the rest of Catholic Europe—the monarchy and an episcopacy chosen for this reason had long cooperated in upholding the authority of the Formulary and *Unigenitus* against Jansenists defined by opposition to these measures. The result was that whereas elsewhere in Catholic Europe it was the newly absolute monarchs and their regalist ministers allied with most of their bishops who used elements of Gallican and Jansenist ideology to indict the Jesuits, in France the parlements used that same ideology not only against Jesuits but also to indict absolute monarchy as despotic and the Gallican bishops as ultramontanist. The guilt of the Jesuits, contended one Jansenist pamphleteer in 1762, lay not only in their own "despotism" but also in their aim "to place an iron scepter in the hands of the Bourbons" by equating their constitution with the French monarchy's.[67]

That the French monarchy's conception of its monarchical constitution was far closer to the Society of Jesus's supposedly despotic constitutions than to the parlements' quasi-representative consitution became glaringly apparent in 1771 when Louis XV disgraced Choiseul and let Chancellor Maupeou engineer a "coup" against the parlements and their pretensions. Calculated to provoke the Parlement of Paris's resistance, which would in turn justify such measures against it, the occasional cause of this set-to was the Edict of December that condemned the very constitutional tenets with which the Parlement of Paris in particular had justified its resistance to the monarchy during the Jansenist controversy: for example, that the Parlement of Paris together with France's provincial parlements made up the various "classes" of a single Parlement, that these parlements legitimately "represented" the French "nation" vis-à-vis the king, or again that this "representative" capacity entitled them to refuse their consent, or "registration," to royal declarations and edicts—including the Edict of December.

At the royal court of Versailles, the result of this coup, as has been noted, was the rise of a philo-Jesuit parti dévot and with it the reorientation of the spirit if not the letter of France's papal diplomacy in the same direction. This "devout" turn at Versailles in 1771 would have its counterparts elsewhere in Catholic Europe, in Parma and Piacenza as early as the summer of 1771. But what simultaneously took place in Paris and some other parts of France occupied a category by itself, at least until much later.[68] For what happened then and there between 1771 and 1774 was the formation of what called itself a "patriot" protest against Maupeou's "despotic" destruction of France's "constitution" that, besides a judicial strike by the order of barristers and a boycott of Versailles by the princes and peers, produced about five hundred anonymously written and clandestinely printed books and pamphlets, including reprints of official judgments and remonstrances by the various parlements.

Comparable to the anonymous production of *pasquins* against the governance of Carlos III in the wake of the Eschilache Riots in late March 1766, it differed radically in that it was implicitly for the kind of antiecclesiastical reformism against which the Spanish pasquins protested. What further distinguished the French patriot protest was that Jansenist participation was obvious enough for the philosophical publicist Mathieu-François Pidansat de Mairobert to comment that "Jansenism, having . . . made its most valuable contribution in the suppression of the Jesuits . . . , has transformed itself into the party of patriotism," a metamorphosis he took to mean that Jansenism had now redirected its adversarial energy from papal to "political despotism."[69] French Jansenists did not for all that abandon their theological, moral, liturgical, or ecclesiastical concerns, although they did indeed yield the lead in the theological defense of their signature doctrines to their Italian coreligionists at the University of Pavia. In order for the protest against the Maupeou coup to have been

perceived as continuous with the Jansenist campaign against the Jesuits, it sufficed that many anti-Maupeou "patriots," including Mairobert himself, saw ex-
Jesuits as the real authors of that coup.

It is nonetheless true that many French and specifically Parisian Jansenists
threw themselves body and soul into the pamphlet defense of the parlements that
had long protected them and recently suppressed the Jesuits, even though the
constitutional issues raised by the Edict of December engaged none of the religious or ecclesiastical concerns in defense of which Jansenist canonists and
parlementary magistrates had helped forge these constitutional justifications for
parlementary resistance in the first place. In terms of sheer numbers, Jansenists
of one description or another contributed at least half of a sampling of about
eighty of the roughly five hundred books and pamphlets written and printed
against Maupeou, while constituting at least a third of the people arrested and
imprisoned in the Bastille for printing and distributing them.

As for the books and pamphlets, a sampling of eighty includes those most
commented upon by these books and pamphlets themselves as well as by such
contemporary newssheets as Mairobert's *Journal historique*.[70] As for those caught
and "embastilled" in the Maupeou ministry's all-out dragnet, they consisted exclusively in small fry in the judicial, printing, and bookselling trades and in
such professions as colporters, clerks, and attorneys, and those related to bigger
fish in these trades in yet other ways, plus a few apprentices in unnamed trades.
In comparison, members of the clergy constitute a distinct minority.[71] However
disappointing this social catch might have been from Maupeou's point of view,
its very low-level nature indicates that antidespotic patriotism could mobilize a
popular lay constituency quite foreign to anti-Jesuit reformism elsewhere in
Catholic Europe, as indeed the parlementary campaign against the Society had
been able to do in France as well.

That the Jansenist flank of the anti-Maupeou patriotic front was more than
willing to redeploy its constitutionalist weaponry forged during a half century's
defensive battle against *Unigenitus* and Jesuits in a political cause that had nothing overtly to do with these issues became equally clear in its signature pamphlets after 1771. Given an impressive semblance of erudite "proof" by Le Paige
in his *Lettres historiques* in the context of the refusal of sacraments conflict, the
thesis that the Parlement of Paris's constitutional pedigree derived at once from
the Merovingian "royal court" and the general assemblies of the Frankish
"nation" continued to do duty in support of the patriotic protest against Maupeou's despotic "revolution," just as it had for Jansenist resistance to the royal as
well as the papal will during the *Unigenitus*-related conflicts since the 1720s.[72]
For patriots as for Jansenists that historical lineage made the Parlement an inte-

gral part of that constitution, and as such entitled both to represent the king so long as his will was legal, but also passively to defend the constitution's "fundamental laws" against the king in the name of the nation when, as exercised by Maupeou, the royal will became unlawful and therefore despotic. In many of the patriotic pamphlets this parlementary constitutionalism continued to convey the figuratist tonality that Le Paige and others had given it, by casting the Parlement in the role of a faithful remnant whose lot was passively to "witness" to these pristine constitutional "truths" while suffering the blows of "despotism" during periods of constitutional apostasy, much as Jansenists themselves had long "witnessed" to the pristine truths condemned by *Unigenitus* while suffering periodic persecution during an ongoing period of doctrinal "obscurity" and oppression.[73]

Yet even this figuratist version of parlementary constitutionalism underwent a degree of radicalization under the unprecedented pressure of Maupeou's coup, giving the Parlement an active "role in legislation" as "representative of the nation" in contrast to the hitherto uniquely passive role in resisting legislative expressions of the king's unconstitutional will.[74] Another pamphlet in this patriotic genre nonetheless addressed its "petition" for national reform to the king in the name, not of the Parlement, but rather of the Estates General, an institution hitherto shunned in statements of parlementary constitutionalism that had not met in more than 150 years.[75] In contrast, the Estates General had played no role in the post-Frondish Parlement's version of its constitutional pedigree, having petitioned the king only at his behest and on bended knee.

So it was of the greatest importance that this protest against Maupeou's coup produced a competitive strain of Jansenist constitutionalism that, reflecting the weakened state of the post-1771 parlements, challenged the Parlement's right to "represent" the nation where taxes were concerned and called instead for a more direct representation of the French nation in a revival of the Estates General. Earlier anticipated here and there in books and pamphlets produced by the Jansenist conflict, this variety of constitutionalism achieved its most telling exposition in the same authors' *Maximes du droit public françois* (*Maxims of French Public Law*) published in 1772, most especially in a brief pungent *Dissertation sur le droit de convoquer les États-généraux* (*Dissertation on the Right to Convoke the Estates General*) appended to the first volume of the 1775 edition.[76]

In the place of a dubious lineage from Frankish general assemblies, this constitutionalism vested the right of the Estates General to convene itself by virtue of divinely created natural law whereby, wholes being superior to their parts, "nations" in possession of public power could never do more than to delegate its "exercise" to this or that part and might always reclaim and reassign it when circumstances warranted. What put a Gallican stamp on this kind of constitutionalism was its appeal to the analogy of the Gallican conception of the church, which had long and similarly argued that only the whole church possessed the spiritual power symbolized by the Petrine keys while delegating its "usage" to the clergy, just as the whole church assembled in general councils was superior to its papal head. As noted earlier, Jacques Almain and John Major had precociously used this conciliar analogy to subordinate the king to the nation as early as the sixteenth century. What in 1772 also put a Jansenist stamp on this kind of argument for the nation's legislative sovereignty was that after 1713 Jansenists had all but come to monopolize the articulation of the Gallican tradition.[77]

Parlementary barristers all, the authors of the *Maximes* professed gratitude to the parlements for their antidespotic holding action in church and state despite taking partial leave of them in favor of a more direct form of national representation. Yet the same cannot be said for the authors of all the most read patriot pamphlets, who also did not always follow the *Maximes* in explicitly grounding the pertinent dictates of natural law in the divine origin of all sovereignty. Among these pamphlets figured Jean-Baptiste Target's *Lettre d'un homme à un autre homme (Letter from One Man to Another)*, in the opinion of whose fictive correspondents the parlements had never compensated for the loss of the Estates General, and Jacques-Matthieu Augéard's novelistic *Extrait de la correspondance secrète et familière (Secret and Familiar Correspondence)*, which called the Parlement's arrogation of the right to consent to taxes a "felony" and "usurpation."[78]

The anti-Maupeou patriot movement also proved the occasion for the politicization of France's self-consciously "enlightened" philosophical movement that, grouped around Denis Diderot's *Encyclopédie*, had held aloof from the century's earlier political conflicts about the Jesuits, the status of *Unigenitus* or the refusal of sacraments to Jansenists except to wish a pox on all their parties. Although they did not enter the fray very publicly much less as a "party," members of this philosophical flank found in this patriotic protest ample grist for thinking about France's "constitution." Like Jansenists, most of its members such as Claude-Adrien Helvétius or Diderot himself sided against Maupeou and therefore more or less on the side of the parlements. In contrast, however, their thoughts about how France ought to be "represented" and the monarchy contained tended to stretch the Old Regime's repertory of existing institutions to the breaking point, not excluding the traditional Estates General.[79]

All that said, it remains remarkable to what extent by his testimony Le Paige and his Jansenist parlementary cohorts were able to control "patriotic" discourse in France between 1771 and 1774. Reflecting in 1788 as his familiar world collapsed around him, Le Paige thought it a pity that the production of pamphlets was deviating from the example of 1771, when "everything [was] reviewed by the same pair of eyes"—his own—"in order to ensure the unity and veracity of principles."[80] In France, and France alone, Gallican, Jansenist, and parlementary "patriotism" also spelled "Reform Catholicism" as applied to an apparently secular subject. Although its success was ephemeral in the sense that, as so applied, it did not long continue to dominate discursive field, Reform Catholicism nonetheless succeeded in sanctifying the principle of national sovereignty in terms so indigenous to the French Old Regime that it could not disavow them. In so doing it prepared the ground for the eventual acceptance of far more audacious formulations, notably those able to conceive of the political nation as composed of propertied individuals rather than diversely privileged corps and corporations.

Aside from hints here and there—Campomanes's *Juicio imparcial* and Pietro Leopoldo's project of a representative constitution for Tuscany—the application of the reformist Catholic case against papal and Jesuitical despotism to a state's constitutional makeup remained confined to Gallican France until the era of the Revolution.[81] The apparent exception of the Austrian Netherlands in the 1780s serves only to prove the rule. For the sort of constitutionalism invoked in opposition to Emperor Joseph II's "despotism" emanated from the pens of ultramontanist churchmen and professors against nearly a half century's accumulation of Gallican and Jansenist-like reformism, culminating in the ecclesiastical legislation imposed by the emperor on his Flemish and Walloon provinces.

A POSSIBLE FRENCH REVOLUTION—AND THE REAL ONE

A 125-year royally sponsored campaign against Jansenism that eventually positioned the monarchy on the ultramontanist and anti-Gallican side of one of France's defining traditions, a Gallican episcopacy so chosen for its anti-Jansenism as also ironically to put it in an anti-Gallican posture, a "patriot" movement of still visibly religious origin with deep popular support that aspired to put nationally willed constitutional shackles on a heretofore "absolute" monarchy: these traits distinguished the political direction of reformist Catholicism in contrast to its counterparts in Catholic Europe and already pointed France in a revolutionary direction. Had the monarchy not avoided its fiscal cul-de-sac in

1771 by perpetrating a partial bankruptcy instead of convening the Estates General as in 1788, some kind of revolution would probably have occurred in France in 1771, even if more "managed" and moderate than the one in 1789.[82] The structural skeleton of any argument for the French Revolution's having had "religious origins," the features that point France in that direction are more salient in comparative perspective than when considered alone.[83]

Given this probability, it may again be helpful to indulge in a counterfactual exercise—this one for France alone, and assuming that events elsewhere had played out as they did—and imagine what might have been the lineaments of an ecclesiastical reform if in 1771 an Estates General had not only de-absolutized the monarchy but also, while still preserving the distinction between orders, produced a clergy as democratically elected as that elected in 1789 to implement a reformist Catholic agenda such as it stood in 1771.

The implications of French Reform Catholicism would at that point have been at once more and less radical than the ones imposed by "enlightened" absolute monarchs elsewhere in Catholic Europe. Like the programs of Pietro Leopoldo and especially Joseph II, a royally empowered French reform program would most certainly have moved further to diminish the jurisdiction of the papacy, redefining the bearer of the Tiara as the bishop of Rome with only supervisory oversight of the Catholic Church. The papacy would thereby have found itself divested of any role in the appointment to benefices in France, being limited to acknowledging the expressions of "communion" by bishops chosen otherwise and confirmed by their colleagues, while losing all control over the parish clergy and monastic abbacies.

But while in Austria or Tuscany such a reform would have left the appointment to major benefices to the monarchy, in France a constitutional monarchy might have relinquished an exclusive role in the choice of bishops or abbots in favor choosing among candidates nominated by an electoral process involving clerical assemblies with some form of popular concurrence. What such reforms would have entailed was the unilateral abrogation of the Concordat of Bologna of 1516 and an updating of the Pragmatic Sanction of Bourges in 1438, which had institutionalized the canons of the Councils of Constance and Basel. The reinstituted vigor of these canons would in principle have allowed for the regular meeting of provincial and national councils. It is these that would have reformed the mode of beneficial appointments as well as canonical, liturgical, and still other reforms, giving the Gallican Church a modicum of independence not only from the papacy but also from the monarchy except for taxes, to which the clergy would have been subjected far more directly and equitably than before. The conciliar aspect of these reforms would have distinguished French Reform

Catholicism from Reform Catholicism in most other parts of Catholic Europe, except perhaps the Rhineland's prince-bishoprics, which in 1786 went in quest of their long-lost Germanic liberties.[84]

If in the provincial and national councils the reformers had got their way, they would not only have broken the aristocratic hold on the episcopacy but also pursued the Richerist goal of liberating the parish clergy from the "despotism" of their bishops, perhaps even subjecting bishops to the advice and consent of elected curés. In France, the most spectacular change in the criteria for eligibility for a benefice would have been the abolition of any obligation to sign the Formulary of Alexander VII or to accept *Unigenitus*. Radically Richerist in comparison with reformist agenda elsewhere though such councils were, they would probably have been more moderate in their reform of the regular clergy, since in France a number of these orders contained many more Jansenists and Jansenist sympathizers than elsewhere. These councils would nonetheless have also redirected the tithe away from monastic houses and cathedral canons to the parish clergy exclusively, while further integrating most members of the religious orders into the parish ministry. It goes without saying that France would have followed the Austrian and Tuscan examples in separating the clergy from any "foreign" subjection while imitating Spain in ridding France of any remaining ex-Jesuits.

Finally, there is no reason to suppose that reformist Gallican councils would not also have rationalized and nationalized the contours of diocesan boundaries more rapidly than the Old Regime monarchy was already doing, although not as surgically as Joseph II did. Nor would they have been less hard on confraternities or austere in their reforms of popular devotions, particularly the devotion to the Sacred Heart. As for other confessional communities, French reformist opinion was ready by 1771 to institute a policy of civil toleration for the Reformed members of the Protestant population but was unlikely to have imitated Joseph II's Toleration Patent in favor of the Jews, much less grant Protestants the right of public worship as in 1791.[85]

Now, that this French revolution did not happen has to be the understatement of the entire eighteenth century, perhaps the nineteenth as well. This hypothetical scenario ignores the reality check that, even in 1771, the monarchy's fiscal dependence on indirectly borrowing from the public through privileged corps and corporations propped up by means of the royal sale of nobility-conferring offices meant that it could never be totally serious about its episodic attempts to eliminate tax-exempting privileges for the purpose of widening the tax base. That much held even for the abbé Joseph-Marie Terray, the supposedly reforming controller general whom the Maupeou coup had catapulted into that position in 1771. Although he made a great show of eliminating venal offices at the level of the adversarial parlements, he expanded—even created—new privilege-bearing offices everywhere else, all the way down to the guild of wig makers and shoemakers.[86]

Eventually the monarchy's juggling act of secretly propping up with one hand what, in the long run, it had to eliminate with the other was bound to catch up with it and the whole realm, which is what happened with the fiscal crisis and the convocation of the Estates General in 1787–1789. At that point the state in some form would have had to strike out against the whole privilege of principle, and therefore also against the nobility and the clergy, all but precluding any merely reformist or political-constitutional outcome. The form of the state that did so turned out to be the Estates General that a revolutionary Third Estate transformed into a National Assembly without distinction of estates or orders.[87] Indeed, so tarnished in opinion had corps and corporations emerged from the monarchy's exploitation of them for fiscal purposes that the Revolution had done with them, noble or not, leaving nothing in principle between equally entitled individuals on the one hand and the state on the other.

Unique in its extent in all of Old Regime Europe, the monarchy's system of propping up privileged corps for fiscal purposes played a role in the making of another feature unique to the French Old Regime: namely, the eighteenth century's most virulent and obdurate religious controversy in the form of the Jansenist conflict. For that conflict could not have gone on with such usurious effect without the institutional support of the periodic General Assembly of the Gallican Clergy, which with the king upheld the authority of the bull *Unigenitus*; and the Parlement of Paris, which protected its Jansenist opponents. It was the monarchy's need to maintain the Gallican Clergy's corporate presence in order to borrow money that made this clergy the most politically powerful one in all the major states of Europe, Protestant as well as Catholic; while the monarchy's dependence on a body of already venal magistrates in order to obtain some semblance of national consent for taxes and international loans likewise gave the parlements political power that had no counterpart in any other Catholic state. Only in France could the monarchy feel obliged to convene an extraordinary assembly of the clergy for its opinion about the Jesuits; only in France could an institution such as the parlements take the initiative against the Jesuits despite the opposition of the monarchy fortified by episcopal opinion.

In combination, the political strength of the Gallican Clergy, the Parlement of Paris, and the longevity and virulence of the Jansenist controversy also took a hand in the making of singularly radical anti-Catholic, even anti-Christian, enlightenment—yet another feature that made France unique in eighteenth-century Europe. That this conflict embroiled church and state and went on as long as it did was cause enough for the growth of philosophical unbelief. While elsewhere the Reformation-vintage wars of religion were a mercifully receding memory, in France they flourished in verbal form under the high noon of the Enlightenment, putting wind in the sails of those who equated revealed religion with the enthusiasm and fanaticism thought to be among the chief sources of civil disorder in the past.

But when in the early 1750s the Parlement of Paris animated by Jansenists became embroiled with the archbishop of Paris encouraged by the Jesuits over their complicity in a Lockian thesis defended at the Sorbonne by a contributor to Diderot's fledgling *Encyclopédie*—the famous *affaire* of the abbé de Prades—a pattern developed whereby the two institutionally fortified sides of the religious conflict took to blaming each other for the growing encyclopedic, or philosophical, "unbelief" in France.[88] Unique as well to France, the result was the separating out of a very self-consciously antireligious group of "enlightened" men of letters and the emergence of a tripartite pattern of Jesuit, Jansenist, and philosophic "parties." In 1777, to be sure, Mairobert conceptualized the appearance of the anti-Maupeou "patriotism," including its Jansenist contingent, as the third and last stage of a "philosophical" movement that had begun with the "encyclopedists," who had "perfected metaphysics," and had continued with the "economists," or "physiocrats," who had discovered the economic laws of the natural order.[89] The province of "patriotism," he thought, was to "[demonstrate] the reciprocity of obligations of subjects and sovereigns" and fathom the "depths of history."

But although on the one hand this conflation and telescoping of France's intellectual developments since mid-century forgot that Jansenists had peopled the "patriotic" province long before 1771, it also ignores that Jansenists figured prominently among the *fauteurs* of "fanaticism" and "enthusiasm" targeted by the encyclopedic phalanx of what Mairobert called the "philosophical" movement, the Jesuits of course being the others. And while the physiocrats, from François Quesnay and Victor de Riqueti, marquis de Mirabeau, to Anne-Robert Turgot or André Morellet, were duly deist and far from antireligious, it was otherwise with the encylopedic contingent of Diderot, Helvétius, and d'Holbach, whose monist, materialist, and atheistic metaphysics excluded the possibility of any and all revealed religion. Unlike proponents of constitutionalist patriotisms, both camps came down hard against the Old Regime's corporations, as did Jean-Jacques Rousseau's even more radical constitutionalism in *Du contrat social*, which, bursting on the scene in 1762, also cut the notion of national sovereignty loose from any moorings in a putatively historic constitution.

A further retrospective telescoping of quite distinct currents took place in Mairobert's identification of the "destruction of the Jesuits" as the "point at which the philosophical movement broke out." What demonstrates the divisions between segments of Mairbobert's unified movement is that only in France could the trial of the Jesuits have produced a pamphlet by someone, like d'Alembert, who claimed that "philosophy" was the real victor in this trial in which Jansenist barristers and magistrates had played the role of unwitting "solicitors."[90] If again the patriotic protest against the Maupeou coup had issued in a meeting of the Estates General in 1771, such parlementary barristers and magistrates, including numerous Jansenist ones, would have surfaced in force in that meeting, both in the Third and Second Estates, not to mention more Jansenist priests in the First Estate. Among barristers who might already have shown up in 1771 who did in fact play important roles in the Estates General in 1789, a Bertrand Barère from Toulouse or a Jean-Baptiste Target from Paris would not yet have been the Barère or the Target of 1789, leaving an Armand-Gaston Camus to have remained the same.

But by breaking the self-recruiting capacity of the barristers' order, Maupeou opened the floodgates of barristers more attuned to century's newer philosophical currents and adept at taking their cases directly to the public by way of print.[91] Meanwhile the restored but much chastened judges in the post-1774 Parlement of Paris gradually took themselves out of political contention as the voices of the "nation" by registering the monarchy's every request for new loans, siding with the prince and peers in defense of noble privilege, and mending their fences with an exclusively noble episcopacy in defense of "property."[92] At the political if not the social level, a kind of "aristocratic" reaction undoubtedly took place.[93]

To be sure, the fiscal crisis of the Old Regime in 1787–1789 lent renewed relevance to the Parlement of Paris when it refused to register the monarchy's fiscal measures just rejected by an Assembly of Notables and appealed instead to the "nation" as assembled in the long-defunct Estates General. In the ensuing set-to between the monarchy and the parlements, antidespotic "patriotic" ideology reentered the discursive field in pamphlet force and until September 1788 all but defined the political situation. But all that changed dramatically when after obtaining the convocation of the Estates General from a bankrupt monarchy the Parlement of Paris stipulated that this archaic institution should meet as it last had in 1614, whatever the magistrates may have meant by these forms.[94] That if literally so constituted the newly convoked Estates General would have given the privileged clerical and noble estates the right to veto any measures proposed by the delegates of the meanwhile vastly increased numbers of the lay and commoner Third Estate enabled the Parlement's royal ministry's publicists to accuse the magistrates of concealing "aristocratic" and antinational aims behind the façade of their "patriotic" and antidespotic rhetoric. While a similar tactic by the Maupeou ministry failed to gain any purchase in 1771, in 1788 this counterattack worked, bringing into the debate a contingent of more philosophical publicists critical of corporate privilege, who in the next three months managed to redefine "patriotism" to mean the cause of civic equality and the "nation" as all but excluding "aristocracy."

It was the cause of "patriotism" thus redefined that prevailed in June 1789 when, taking advantage of the monarchy's passivity, the delegates of the Third Estate acted on its claim to constitute the "nation," with or without the clergy or the nobility. But when on 23 June the king belatedly intervened on the side of the two "privileged" orders and undo what the Third Estate had done, even heretofore mainly antiaristocratic patriots, such as Honoré-Gabriel Riqueti, comte de Mirabeau, had no choice but to act on the older anti-"despotic" meaning of "patriotism," take the Parlement's place in challenging royal authority, and subordinate the king's legislative will to that of the sovereign "nation." The principles of both national sovereignty and civic equality thus found their place in the Declaration of the Rights of Man and the Citizen, the credo promulgated by the National Assembly after the Parisian uprising of 12–14 July apparently saved it from another royal attempt to undo it.[95]

When combined with the notion of natural rights with which the National Assembly's Declaration of the Rights of Man and the Citizen justified both public and individual liberty as well as social equality, these political "heresies" were perhaps reasons enough to provoke a condemnation by a papacy that, for all its recent set-tos with divine-right Catholic kings, still believed in the divine origin of all political authority. Dated 10 March 1791, the papacy's first brief in reaction to the revolutionary legislation indeed condemned the concept of "rights in society," including "absolute liberty," a principle the brief attributed to the National Assembly's usurpation of not only temporal but also spiritual power. For what really brought Pius VI's anathemas down on the French Revolution was the National Assembly's unilateral attempt to bring the organization of the Gallican Church into conformity with the principles of the Revolution by means of the legislation known as the Civil Constitution of the Clergy. Combined with the inevitable papal condemnation of 1791, it was that ecclesiastical legislation and the French and European Catholic reaction to both that would ring the death knell of Reform Catholicism.

As the irony of this history would have it, Cardinal Bernis still represented France in Rome when revolutionary France's foreign minister, Armand Marc, comte de Montmorin, requested him to persuade Pius VI provisionally to "bless" the chief features of the Civil Constitution in order to head off a schism. If the Civil Constitution stood any such chance, Bernis scuttled it by urging the pope to begin by condemning the principles that underpinned it.[96] While under Clement XIV he had conspired with the French court against Spain to postpone sine die the suppression of the Jesuits, on this occasion he conspired with the Spanish envoy, José Nicolas Azara, against his country's revolution and its ecclesiastical legislation.[97] Not to be outdone in point of reversals, as Spain's beneficial agent in Rome after 1765 the same Azara had faulted Bernis for betraying Spanish policy by helping Clement XIV delay the suppression of the Jesuits.[98]

AFTERWORD AS FAST-FORWARD

Passed by the National Assembly in July 1790, the Civil Constitution of the Clergy implemented many of the mixed Gallican-Jansenist reforms that would have come out of any such legislative opportunity in 1771.[1] These included the abolition of anti-Jansenist oaths, the nonpapal collegial confirmation of bishops, the narrowing of the material and even moral differences between bishops and their curés, the pruning of the nonpastoral clergy, the abolition of contemplative monastic orders, and even a role for the people in the election of the clergy. But by 1789 reformist Catholicism was far from the National Assembly's only source of ideological direction, and competing with it were strong Rousseauvian and physiocratic, or enlightened "economic," biases against all privileged corporate or "intermediary" bodies. For physiocrats, such corporate bodies interfered with the workings of economic natural law; for Roussseauvians, they stood between the desired communication between the newly sovereign nation and equally entitled citizens; and for all sympathetic to the Revolution thus far the privileges conferred on these bodies constituted an affront to the principle of equality for which the Revolution stood. Yet the effect of the provisions inspired by these strains in the French Enlightenment was to deprive the Gallican Church of all corporate independence, including the right to own any property, to play a role in the election of its own clergy, or even to assemble for any reason, if only to lend the National Assembly's reform a semblance of independent "spiritual" concurrence. As a consequence, the National Assembly promulgated its ecclesiastical legislation on its own uniquely secular authority, ironically leaving any such concurrence to the discretion of the papacy.

Although the resultant subordination of the church to the national state made a certain contact with the regalist tenet of the Gallican liberties, the surgical reduction of the church to the status of a department of state went far beyond anything the Gallican tradition could have accommodated and immediately split the reformist Gallican and Jansenist constituency, alienating those for whom the independence and deliberative freedom of the Gallican Church— the conciliar tenets of the Gallican liberties—were just as important as its independence from the papacy. For their part, the physiocratic and Rousseauvian deputies did not represent anything like the most "radical" or antireligious strains in the French Enlightenment, nor did the Civil Constitution in part shaped by them fail to embody the regalist tenets of the Gallican liberties. But the total shape of the Civil Constitution did not bode well for the future of the Gallican Church in the newly "regenerated" national state, especially when combined with the National Assembly's declaration of religious liberty for Protestants, enfranchisement of Jews, and repeated refusals to grant Catholicism the status of official religion of that state.

One result was to make those reformist Catholics who had collaborated in the making of the Civil Constitution vulnerable to the accusation of complicity with heresy and philosophical unbelief. Particularly prone to see the National Assembly's ecclesiastical legislation as nothing less than a combined Jansenist, Protestant, and philosophic updating of the original Bourgfontaine plot against Catholicism was the French clerical contingent of what had become the Ultramontanist International. In relative abeyance in France since the pacification of the directly Jansenist-related political conflicts since 1770, that clergy and its constituents found in this legislation a renewed reason for existence and casus belli against "unbelief" on revolutionary stilts. At least a year before Pius VI's condemnations of the Civil Constitution, that legislation had already produced something like a Religious Right while alienating a good part of its "natural" reformist Catholic constituency.

When the successive papal briefs of condemnation came in March and April 1791, their effect was therefore only to formalize a schism already in the making within the Gallican Church, between those for whom loyalty to the papal head of the church prevailed over ecclesiastical implications of the revolutionary principles and those reformist Catholics who in good conscience thought that they could swear an oath of loyalty to the constitution imposed by the National Assembly on the benefice-seeking clergy in November 1790. Since the "refractory" clergy that refused that oath included almost the entire blue-blooded noble episcopacy, the birth of the pro-revolutionary, or "constitutional," church hung on the thin thread of those few bishops willing to sign the oath and assure the semblance of apostolic succession continuity by consecrating new bishops from among the constitutional priesthood, as in fact the diocese of Utrecht had done in 1723. It goes without saying, however, that in principle this new schism also separated the constitutional church from the rest of the Catholic Church, and therefore also its reformist Augustinian and Gallican correspondents and communicants elsewhere in Catholic Europe.

The papacy's formalization of this schism also completed a process whereby the religious issue comingled with the diverse aristocratic and monarchical reasons for opposition to the Revolution and elevated them into a Counter-Revolution endowed with an ideology and a holy cause. But it also, alas, added the Catholic clergy as a whole to the aristocracy as a symbol of Counter-Revolution, thereby making it into a target for increasingly anticlerical revolutionary ire. That the constitutional clergy was already the bête noire of members of the refractory clergy and their former parishioners did not therefore spare it from the fallout from the ever more anticlerical revolutionary side. Nothing if not pious, the "Most Christian" King Louis XVI hardly helped when he let his own qualms about having signed the Civil Constitution figure as a factor in his abortive attempt at flight from France in June 1791, and then passive aggressively let his resistance to the Legislative Assembly's legislation against refractory priests as well as émigré nobles maneuver him into an increasingly untenable posture as a still constitutional king vis-à-vis a distrustful Legislative Assembly. That assembly's declaration of war in 1792 against the very Habsburg Austria to which Louis XVI had tried in vain to flee completed his and the assembly's process of reciprocal alienation, while the war in turn made religiously motivated opposition to the Revolution an act of treason. As the Legislative Assembly began to exile refractory priests, an ever more suspiciously treasonous king fell victim first to an arrest after Parisians stormed his palace, and then to a trial, conviction, and execution at the hands of a newly elected National Convention.

With the fall of the monarchy and the Convention's proclamation of the Republic, the situation of the constitutional clergy rapidly deteriorated from difficult to impossible, after which an infernal cycle of mutual action and reaction took hold.[2] At the Revolution's Parisian center, the religious vacuum created by the schism sucked into it the most anti-Christian Voltairian and atheistic Holbachian strains of a French Enlightenment that itself had taken shape in reaction to decades of uniquely French religious conflict. Under its sway, the quasi-autonomous commune of Paris, followed by the Jacobin-dominated Convention, launched a campaign of radical "dechristianization" that totally secularized citizenship, redefined marriage as a revocable contract, replaced the Christian with a neopagan calendar, effaced Christian place names, destroyed or defaced Christian art and architecture, and by 1794 closed all the churches in France. The campaign fell most heavily on the forty-some thousand constitutional priests and bishops, all of whom ceased their public functions and at least half of whom renounced their vocations under pressure and with varying degrees of finality. Not even the end of the Terror in August 1794 and the formal separation of church from state in 1795 ended the anticlerical persecution, which the Directorial Republic continued sporadically until Napoleon Bonaparte's coup of 9–10 November 1799 brought both to an end.

What the French Revolution did was therefore not so much to create a new religious schism ex nihilo as to relay while refracting a very old one that by 1789 had come to pit reformist against ultramontanist Catholics. For France itself, the long-term effect of the revolutionary ordeal would be a once-and-for-all transformation of the terms of the religious division from one dividing ultramontanist and absolutist from Gallican and politically constitutionalist Catholics into one dividing newly christened "conservative" ultramontanist and absolutist Catholics, but now from militantly secular political "liberals" and and anti-Catholic republicans. Apparently vindicated by the Revolution's excesses, "conservative" Catholics came gradually to monopolize the religious space previously shared by Gallicans and Jansenists, who held onto a steadily shrinking presence until the Revolution of 1848 or of 1870 at the latest. Attempts by the priest Hughes-Félicité de Lamennais in around 1830 to "liberalize" Catholicism and by a number of neo-Cartesian republicans a half centuy later to "spiritualize" the Third Republic's republicanism fell on ever-stonier ground. As early as under Napoleon, émigré bishops began to return with baggage carrying not only mandatory retractions of the recent oath to the Civil Constution but also acceptances of the Formula of Pope Alexander VII and the bull *Unigenitus*— even renunciations of the Gallican Declaration of 1682. At ground level in the parishes, and despite official policy to leave them in peace, formerly constitutional priests fought a losing rearguard action against such bishops.

To be sure, after the Terror and during the brief separation of church from state from 1795 to 1801, what remained of the constitutional church renamed itself the Gallican Church, and under the leadership of the abbé Henri Grégoire and the indomitable abbé Clément it undertook a heroic and largely successful attempt to fill the empty parishes and bishoprics. More Gallican and Jansenist than the constitutional church had ever been, it produced a Gallican liturgy, experimented with the vernacular administration of the sacraments, accepted its status as a church in a non-Catholic republic, restructured the church along deliberative lines, held two national councils, and appealed against the papacy's antirevolutionary briefs to a general council. It even took a page from Utrecht's book and began an aggressive campaign to solicit letters of communion from reformist priests and bishops elsewhere in Catholic Europe, most successfully in Italy. But Napoleon Bonaparte's concordat with Pius VII and the restoration of the French Catholic Church to a state status smothered in its infancy that experiment of a free Catholic church in a free state.

By then, however, reformist Catholics elsewhere in Europe found themselves almost as much on the defensive against temporal powers and principalities as did French ones. None of the Catholic princes and potentates who had expelled the Jesuits or had taken antipapal reformist advantage of their suppression waited for the Terror or dechristianization to react to the French Revolution. Although the Revolution had done little more to nationalize the Gallican Church than Joseph II had done to nationalize the church in his domains, no more than Pius VI did Joseph and his princely peers or successors welcome such reforms enacted from below at the expense of the absolute authority of any of their royal own. Among them only Joseph's brother Peter Leopold had dabbled with councils and representative assemblies as grand duke in Tuscany, but he behaved no differently from Joseph when he succeeded him as Emperor Leopold II in 1790. At that point and only then did they seem to grasp that the Gallican or reformist case against the "despotic" structure of the Society of Jesus and the papacy and the Catholic Church themselves might be part of a larger case against "despotic" power of any sort, including their own.

Himself a believer in the updated edition of the version of the supposed Jansenist Bourgfontaine plot to destroy Catholicism, the pro-papal publicist Nicola Spedalieri voiced what had already become a common "conservative" theme when in 1791 he warned all sovereigns that their own complicity in aiding reformist attempts to "denude bishops of their tiara" was but a necessary preliminary to a plan to "knock crowns from the heads of kings."[3] The lesson was clear: papal altar and Catholic thrones stood or fell together. Nor was Spedalieri's lesson lost on the ears of Catholic Europe's princes, who everywhere—in Italy, Spain, Portugal, Austria, and the German prince-bishoprics—had begun to retreat from the advanced positions of "enlightened" ecclesiastical reformism, sometimes, as in Brabant and Tuscany, under the pressure of popular anger stirred up by these very reformist ventures. The alliance between papal infallibility within the church and popular piety against the "enlightened" classes was also to be the hallmark of the postrevolutionary Catholic Church, culminating in the pontificate of Pius VI, the Syllabus of Errors, and Vatican I's declaration of papal infallibility.

But this royal retreat from reformism in 1790 was not to spare Catholic Europe from the secularization of ecclesiastical property and forms of anticlericalism and dechristianization, because the revolutionary and Napoleonic wars and French armies directly brought them with them wherever they went, first in their most virulent form by French revolutionary armies from 1792 to 1797, and then in more attenuated form by Napoleonic armies from 1801 until 1814. As in France, the effect was to tar the cause of religious and ecclesiastical reform with the brush of complicity with—even the cause of—atheistic unbelief as well as the whole. Revolution and its worst excesses, against which absolute throne and infallible papal altar were thought to have to reunite and stand together. This association was all the easier to make for the inhabitants of places like Habsburg Brabant, Lombardy, and Tuscany, in that for many Revolution's iconoclasm was sometimes hard to tell from earlier reformist attempts to purify their piety. When the French front briefly collapsed in the face of the armies of the Second Coalition in Italy in 1798, the restored authorities arrested—in Naples literally massacred—Jansenists and Jacobins indiscriminately, having been assured by no few "conservative" publicists that Giansenisti and Giacobini were the same things. These associations would stick; for France, Spain, and Portugal, much of the nineteenth century would consist in conservative restorations punctuated by anticlerical revolutionary episodes. Having already imposed its religious divisions on Europe via the campaign against the Jesuits, France now all too successfully superimposed its new ones as well.

Reacting to France's brief imposition of a republic on Rome in 1798 after abducting Pope Pius VI in 1796, the Mainz professor Franz Scheidel precociously if prejudicially summed up his elegiac line of thought to Jean-Baptiste Mouton, Dupac de Bellegarde's successor and editor of the *Nouvelles ecclésiastiques* in Utrecht. The "affliction" from which the Roman Church itself was now suffering, he thought, was the just "punishment for its misguided politics, . . . especially during the revolution in France when it could have prevented many misfortunes had it chosen to put the common good ahead of its [mundane] interests." In the best of worlds, he ventured, "now would be the ideal time to reform the worst of [the church's] abuses had only kings and prelates alike not permitted the fear of revolution to change their principles and to flee from the very lights that they had so eagerly sought until recently." As reform-minded Catholics, he confided to Mouton, "we find ourselves in just about the same situation as did those following the so-called Reformation of the sixteenth century . . . , [a revolution] that long prevented the reform of theology and the church begun earlier by enlightened men and the [late medieval] councils. The French revolution," he concluded, "will have had the about the same effect by casting the suspicion of having favored it on all those who from now on [dare to broach the subject] of the reforms that the passage of time has made [so very] necessary."[4]

As for the ex-Jesuits, some of them figured prominently as polemicists in the antireformist Ultramontanist International, most notably Barruel, Feller,

Goldhagen, Pey, Zaccaria, and Giovanni Vincenzo Bolgeni, until he lost courage and accepted the Roman Republic in 1798! Most minded their business as best they could when in exile in other pedagogical, sacerdotal, literary, or learned ways, as did the eminent Croation scientist Rudjer Josip Boskovi'c, or Boscovich. Beginning in the mid-1790s, moreover, some began to reaffiliate as de facto Jesuits in Amsterdam, Parma and Piacenza, and elsewhere under various labels in advance of being able to do so officially by affiliating with the restored Society in Russia, where Pius VII allowed Catherine the Great to retain it by virtue of the papal brief *Catholicae fidei* promulgated in 1801. So synonymous, however, had the Society of Jesus become with the principles of papal and absolute royal authority that when the restoration of both triumphed after the collapse of the Napoleonic Empire in 1814, it was all but a foregone conclusion that Pius VII would resurrect it in Rome and everywhere in its previous form with the bull *Sollicitudo omnium ecclesiarum* on 7 August the same year.[5]

The price was steep, however, because the circumstances of its restoration locked the postrestoration Society, if not all its members, into the role of bulwark against revolution in defense of allied thrones and altars in Catholic Europe for the rest of the nineteenth century and well into the twentieth. A good part of the logic of the Society's restoration was that because the beginning of the expulsions had preceded the Revolution by a quarter of a century, the total suppression of the Society had removed a crucial barrier to that revolution, and that its restoration would prevent further such revolutions. But compelling as it may have seemed, that dubious logic and the ideologically rearguard role it assigned to the restored Society also condemned it to a future of repeated—almost innumerable—expulsions and returns each time a new revolution breached the walls of the ever more fragile restoration order. It would not be until the era of Vatican II that the Society would begin to recover the daring and capacities for innovation that had been its hallmarks throughout most of its prerevolutionary history.[6]

NOTES

INTRODUCTION

1. Works on the Jesuits are numberless, but this short characterization is dependent on John O'Malley, *The First Jesuits* (Cambridge, MA: Harvard University Press, 1993);

Willliam V. Bangert, *A History of the Jesuits*, 2nd ed. (St. Louis: Institute of Jesuit Resources, 1986); and James Broderick, *The Origin of the Jesuits* (Garden City, NY: Doubleday, 1940).

2. Ignatius Loyola, *The Spiritual Exercises*, trans. Elisabeth Meier Tetlow (Lanham, MD: University Press of America, 1987). The secondary description I have found most helpful is René Füulop-Miller, *The Jesuits: A History of the Society of Jesus*, trans. F. S. Flint and D. F. Tait (New York: Capricorn, 1956), 3–18.

1. FROM THE CATHOLIC ENLIGHTENMENT
TO REFORM CATHOLICISM

1. Jean Le Rond d'Alembert, *Sur la destruction des jésuites en France, par un auteur désintéresé* (N.p., 1765), 78–79.

2. Ludwig von Pastor, *History of the Popes*, trans. E. F. Peeler, vols. 36–38 (London: Routledge and Keegan Paul, 1950–1952), 36:247–93.

3. Marcel Gauchet, *Le désenchantement du monde: Une histoire politique de la religion* (Paris: Gallimard, 1985).

4. On the origins of Gallicanism, Victor Martin's *Les origines du gallicanisme*, 2 vols. (Paris: Bloud and Gay, 1939), remains essential.

5. See Francis Oakley, *The Conciliarist Tradition: Constitutionalism in the Catholic Church, 1300–1870* (Oxford: Oxford University Press, 2003), which argues in favor of a modicum of continuity in reformist Gallicanism through the early modern period; and Jotham Parsons, *The Church in the Republic: Gallicanism and Political Ideology in Renaissance France* (Washington, DC: Catholic University of America Press, 2004), which argues for a radical reshaping it by erudite humanists after the Concordat of Bologna. Between the two, this thumbnail account tends toward Oakley's side.

6. Parsons, *The Church in the Republic*, 33–51.

7. On the thought of Almain and Major, see Quentin Skinner, *The Age of the Reformation*, vol. 2 of *The Foundations of Modern Political Thought* (Cambridge: Cambridge University Press, 1982), 113–34.

8. This account of the absolutist addition to the royal tenet of the Gallican liberties is dependent on Victor Martin, *Le gallicanisme politique et le clergé de France* (Paris: Picard, 1929).

9. Parsons, *The Church in the Republic*, 137–84.

10. Aimé-Georges Martimort, *Le gallicanisme de Bossuet* (Paris: Éditions du Cerf, 1953). In his *Assemblées du clergé de 1670 à 1693* (Rome: Università Gregoriana Editrice, 1972), Pierre Blet nuances Martimort's emphasis on the royal initiative in the Declaration of 1682 by showing that the Gallican bishops did not declare anything they did not believe.

11. This thesis is spelled out in Dale K. Van Kley, *The Religious Origins of the French Revolution: From Calvin to the Civil Constitution of the Clergy, 1560–1791* (New Haven: Yale University Press, 1996), 15–74.

12. Pierre Pithou, *Traitez des droits et des libertez de l'Église gallicane-preuves des libertez de l'Église gallicane* (N.p., 1651); Pierre Dupuy, *Commentaire sur le traité des libertez de l'Église gallicane* (Paris: Musier, 1715); Noël Alexandre, *Selecta historiae ecclesiasticae capita, et in loca ejusdem insignia dissertationes historicae, chronologicae, criticae, dogmaticae*, 26 vols. (Paris: Dezalier, 1676–1686); Claude Fleury, *Histoire ecclésiastique*, 20 vols. (Paris, 1720); and Jacques-Bénigne Bossuet, *Defensio declarationis conventus cleri gallicani an. 1682: De ecclesiastica potestate* (Amsterdam: Sumpt. Societatis, 1745), which appeared in French the same year as *Défense de la déclaration de l'Assemblée du clergé de France de 1682: Touchant la puissance ecclésiastique*.

13. For an overview of the history of the Parlement, see J. H. Shennan, *The Parlement of Paris* (Ithaca, NY: Cornell University Press, 1968).

14. On the Fronde as a parlementary revolt, see Lloyd Moote, *The Revolt of the Judges: The Parlement of Paris and the Fronde* (Princeton: Princeton University Press, 1971).

15. Hubert Carrier, *La presse de la Fronde, 1648–1653: Les mazarinades*, 2 vols. (Geneva: Droz, 1989–1991); and Hubert Carrier, ed., *La Fronde: Contestation démocratique et misère paysanne: 52 mazarinades* (Paris: EDHIS, 1982).

16. On the Jansenism of the Order of Barristers, see David A. Bell, *Lawyers and Citizens: The Making of Political Elite in Old Regime France* (Oxford: Oxford University Press, 1994). The best example of the reworking a Frondish pamphlet for parlementary use in the eighteenth century is the *Judicium Francorum* in 1732, an updating of [Louis Machon,] *Les véritables maxims du gouvernement de la France, justifiés par l'ordre des temps, depuis l'établissement de la monarchie jusqu'à présent*, originally published in Paris in 1652. For examples of the application of Gallican theory to the nation, see Van Kley, *The Religious Origins of the French Revolution*, 77–81, 203–10, 254–62, 312–16.

17. Justus Febronius [Johann Nikolaus von Hontheim], *Justini Febronii JCti De statu Ecclesiae et legitima potestate romani pontificis: Liber singularis, ad reuniendos dissidentes in religione Christianos compositus* (Bouillon: Guillaume Evrardi, 1763). I cite this treatise in French translation as *Traité du gouvernement de l'église, et de la puissance du pape, par rapport à ce gouvernement*, 3 vols. (Venice: Pierre Ramundi, 1767), 1:92–93.

18. Hontheim, *Traité du gouvernement de l'église et de la puissance du pape*, 2:71, 166–67.

19. Matthias Höhler, "Vorvart," in Heinrich Aloys Arnoldi, *Tagebuch über die zu Ems gehaltene Zuzammenkunft der vier Erzbischoflichen deutschen Herrn Deputierten*, ed. Höhler (Mainz: von Kirchheim, 1915), 25–46.

20. Hontheim, *Traité du gouvernement de l'église et de la puissance du pape*, 3:454

21. Ibid., 166–67.

22. Ibid., 2:589; 3:323. See also 3:46, 48–49, 114, 307, 315–18, 323–30, 412.

23. Because France produced many variations on the Gallican theme, I take issue with Ulrich Lehner's "Johann Nikolaus von Hontheim's Febronius: A Censored Bishop and His Ecclesiology," *Church History and Religious Culture* 88/2 (2008): 207, which distinguishes Hontheim's thought in *De statu Ecclesiae* from "pure Gallicanism."

24. Dale K. Van Kley, "Civic Humanism in Ecclesiastical Garb: Gallican Memories of the Early Church and the Project of Primitivist Reform," *Past and Present* 200 (August 2008): 96–106.

25. Hontheim, *Traité du gouvernement de l'église et de la puissance du pape*, 1:139; and Giuseppe Agostino Orsi, *Storia ecclesiastica*, 20 vols. (Rome, 1747–1761).

26. Claude Fleury, *Discours sur l'histoire ecclésiastique* (Paris: Emery et al., 1720); and Louis Thomassin, *Ancienne et nouvelle discipline de l'église* (Paris: F. Muguet, 1679–1681).

27. Hontheim seldom indicates these sources with precision, but both Barthel and Zall-wein were prolific contemporary authors of commentaries on German concordats and canon law.

28. The relevant work is Cyprian's *De catholicae ecclesiae unitate*. On Cyprian's con-ceptions of the church and the episcopacy, see J. Patout Burns Jr., *Cyprian the Bishop* (London: Routledge, 2002), 78–99, 151–65.

29. Pierre de Marca, *Dissertationum de concordia sacerdotii et imperii, seu de libertati-bus ecclesiae Gallicanae, libri octo* (Roboreto, 1742); Claude Fleury, *Institution au droit ecclésiastique* (Paris: Emery et al., 1721); Edmond Richer, *Apologia pro Joanne Gersonio, pro suprema Ecclesiae et Concilii generalis auctoritate atque independentia regiae potestatis ab alio quam a solo Deo* . . . (Louvain: Paulus Moriaen, 1676). It is not clear if Hontheim actually cited Richer's most notorious work, *De la puissance ecclésiastique et politique* (Paris: N.p., 1612).

30. Hontheim, *Traité du gouvernement de l'église et de la puissance du pape*, 1:134–35. Edmond Richer's edition of works by Gerson and other conciliarists is entitled *Ioannis Gersonii, Doctoris et Cancellarii Parisiensis, Opera* . . . (N.p., 1606); and Louis-Ellies Dupin, *Opera Omnia,* . . . *quibus accessêre Henrici de Hassia, Petri de Alliaco, Joan-nis Brevicoxæ, Joannis de Varenis scriptorum coætaneorum, ac insuper Jacobi Almaïni & Joannis Majoris tractatus*, 5 vols. (Antwerp: Assumptibus Societatis, 1706–1728).

31. Other relevant verses are John 14:16 and 16:13.

32. Hontheim, *Traité du gouvernement de l'église et de la puissance du pape*, 2:391–92.

33. Ibid., 2:590–91.

34. On the supposed absence of the *recursus ad principem* from *De statu Ecclesiae*, see E. Preclin and E. Jarry, *Les lutes politiques et doctrinales aux XVIIIe et XVIII siècles*, in *Histoire de l'église depuis les origines jusqu'à nos jours* (N.p.: Bloud and Gay, 1955–1956), 773.

35. On Pereira, see most recently Evergton Sales Souza, *Jansénisme et réforme de l'église dans l'empire portugais* (Lisbon: Fundação Calouste Gulbenkian, Centre culturel Calouste Gulbenkian, 2004).

36. António Pereira de Figueiredo, *Doctrinam veteris Ecclesiae de suprema regum etiam clericos potestate* . . . (Lisbon: Miguel Francisco Rodríguez, 1766), lauded in *Nouvelles ecclésiastiques, ou Mémoires pour server à l'histoire de la constitution Unigenitus* (henceforth *NE*), 3rd ed. (Utrecht, 1728–1803), 23 January 1766, 18–19.

37. *Tentativa theologica: Em que se pretende mostrar, que impedido o recorso á Sé apos-tolica se devolve aos senhores bispos a faculdade de dispensar nos impedimentos publi-

cos do matrimonio, e de prover espiritualmente em todos os mais cazos reservados ao papa (Lisbon: Miguel Rodrigues, 1766). I cite the *Tentativa* in Pierre Olivier Pinault's French translation as *Traité du pouvoir des évêques* ([Paris,] 1782).

38. Pereira de Figueiredo, *Traité du pouvoir des évêques*, 284–85.

39. *Ibid.*, 235–37.

40. Ibid., 211.

41. Among those cited were Andrès de Escobar and Dias Andrès de Lisboa, both Dominicans and bishops of Megara; Juan de Segovia, archdeacon of Oveido, Alfonso Tostado, bishop of Avila; and the theologians Diego de Payva d'Andrada, Doctor Navarro don Martín de Azpilcueta, Antonio de Cordova, Domingo de Soto, and Francisco de Victoria, 172–74, 205–7, 221–29.

42. Ibid., 92, 288–89.

43. Ibid., 33, 38, 51.

44. Het Utrechts Archief (henceforth HUA), Pièces d'archives françaises se rapportant à l'abbaye de Port-Royal des Champs et son cercle et à la résistance contre la bulle *Unigenitus* et à l'appel, 215 (henceforth 215), Ms. 2460, Pereira de Figureiedo to Dupac de Bellegarde, 1769.

45. Hontheim, *Traité du gouvernement de l'église et de la puissance du pape*, 2:406–09.

46. Ibid., 368–406.

47. Although definitions and characterizations of Jansenism are innumerable, several recent short syntheses in English are helpful, among then William Doyle, *Catholic Resistance to Authority from the Reformation to the French Revolution* (London: Palgrave Macmillan, 2000); and Leszec Kolakowski, *God Owes Us Nothing* (Chicago: University of Chicago Press, reprint ed. 1998). In French, older ones such as Louis Cognet's *Le jansénisme* (Paris: PUF, 1964) are still useful.

48. Henri Bremond, *Histoire littéraire du sentiment religieux en France: Les mystiques français du grand siècle*, ed. Jean Duchesne and Emile Poulat (Paris: Presses de la Renaissance, 2008), 182.

49. The reference is to the Jesuit Pierre Le Moyne's treatise *La dévotion aisée* (N.p., 1652).

50. Cornelius Jansenius, *Augustinus, seu doctrina S. Augustini de humanae naturae sanitate, aegritudine, medicina adversus Pelagianos et Massilienses*, 3 vols. (Louvain: Jacobi Segreri, 1640).

51. On these differences, no treatment is clearer than Jean La Porte, *La doctrine de Port-Royal*, 2 vols. (Paris: J. Vrin, 1923–1951). For a recent comparison between the Protestant and Jansenist experiences, see *Port-Royal et les protestants*, *Chroniques de Port-Royal* 47 (Paris: Bibliothèque Mazarine, 1998).

52. François Pinthereau, *Naissance du jansénisme découverte à Mgr le chancelier, par le sieur Préville* (Louvain: Jacques Gravius, 1644). On early Jesuit caricatures of "Jansenism," see Marie-José Michel, *Jansénisme et Paris, 1640–1730* (Paris: Klincksieck, 2000), 25–70.

53. D. Ludovico Molina, *De Concordia Liberi arbitrii cum grati donis, divina praescientia, providentia praedestinatione et reprobatione* (Olyssipone: Riberius, 1588).

54. Although this account of Jansenism's origins privileges the issue of penitential theology and practice over the issues of efficacious grace and predestination, I persist in the view that "Jansenism" did not become the divisive force it did until the publication of Jansen's book and Arnauld's defense of it exposed the predestinarian underpinnings of Saint-Cyran's penitential practice. I therefore take issue with Anthony D. Wright's revisionist version of this matter in *The Divisions of French Catholicism, 1629–1645* (Burlington, VT: Ashgate, 2011). On these origins, I remain dependent on such classics as Nigel Abercrombie, *The Origins of Jansenism* (Oxford: Clarendon Press, 1936), and Jean Orcibal, *Jean Duvergier de Hauranne, abbé de Saint-Cyran et son temps* (Louvain: J. Vrin, 1948).

55. Antoine Arnauld, *De la fréquente communion; ou le sentiment des pères, des papes, et des conciles, touchant l'usage des sacremens de la pénitence et de l'Eucharistie, sont fidèlement exposés: Pour servir d'adresse aux personnes qui pensent sérieusement à se convertir à Dieu; et aux pasteurs et confesseurs zélés pour le conduite des âmes* (Paris: Antoine Vitré, 1643).

56. Arnauld's apology of Jansen's book appeared soon after his book on frequent communion, and already in response to Habert's sermons against Jansen and his new "sect." See *Apologie de M. Jansénius, évesque d'Ipre, et de la doctrine de S. Augustin, expliquée dans son livre intitulé, Augustinus, contre trois sermons de Monsieur Habert, théologal de Paris* (N.p., 1644).

57. Jacques Sirmond, *Praedestinatus praedestinatorum haeresis et libri S. Augustino temere adscripti refutatio* (Paris: Sébastien Cromoisy, 1643).

58. Richard M. Golden, *The Godly Rebellion: Parisian Curés and the Religious Fronde, 1652–1662* (Chapel Hill: University of North Carolina Press, 1981).

59. Monique Cottret, "Edmond Richer, 1539–1631: La politique et le sacré," in Henri Méchoulan, ed., *L'état baroque: Regards sur la pensée politique de la France du premier XVIIe siècle* (Paris: J. Vrin, 1985), 62–77.

60. Hubert Carrier, "Port-Royal et la Fronde: Deux mazarinades inconnues d'Arnauld d'Andilly," *Revue d'histoire littéraire de la France* 75 (1975): 3–29,

61. On the condemnation of the five propositions, see Lucien Ceyssens's somewhat pro-Jansenist "Les cinq propositions de Jansénius à Rome," *Revue d'histoire ecclésiastique* (1971): 449–501; and Bruno Neveu's more pro-papal *L'erreur et son juge: Remarques sur les censures doctrinales à l'époque moderne* (Naples: Bibliopolis, 1993), 480–613. On Mazarin's religious policy, see P. Jansen, *Le cardinal Mazarin et le jansénisme, 1653–1659* (Paris: J. Vrin, 1967), 45–53.

62. P. Dieudonné, *La paix clémentine: Défaite et victoire du premier jansénisme français sous le pontificat de Clément XI (1667–1669)* (Louvain: Peeters, 2003).

63. Antoine Arnauld and Claude Lancelot, *Grammaire générale et raisonnée contenant les fondemens de l'art de parler, expliquée d'une manière claire et naturelle* (Paris: Le Petit, 1660).

64. Pierre Nicole, *Essais de morale, contenus en divers traitez sur plusieurs devoirs importans* (Paris: (Desprez, 1769); Antoine Arnauld and Pierre Nicole, *La logique ou l'art de penser* (Paris: Savreux, 1662); and *La perpetuité de la foy de l'Église catholique touchant l'Eucharistie, déffendue contre le livre du sieur Claude*, 3 vols. (Paris: Sav-

reur, 1669–1674); Isaac-Louis Le Maître de Sacy, *La sainte Bible en latin et en fran-çois avec des explications du sens littéral et du sens spirituel*, 32 vols. (Paris: L. Roulland and Guillaume Desprez, 1682–1700); Blaise Pascal, *Pensées de M. Pascal sur la religion et sur quelques autres sujets, qui ont esté trouvées après sa mort parmy ses papiers*, 2nd ed. (Paris: Guillaume Desprez, 1670).

65. Blaise Pascal, *Les provinciales ou les lettres écrites par Louis de Montalte, à un pro-vincial de ses amis, et aux RR. PP. Jésuites: Sur le sujet de la morale et de la politique de ses pères* (Cologne: Pierre de la Vallée, 1757).

66. Albert Hamscher, *The Parlement of Paris after the Fronde* (Pittsburgh: University of Pittsburgh Press, 1976), 110–17, 148–51.

67. The bibliography on eighteenth-century Jansenism is also overwhelming. As they become relevant, some will be cited in this chapter and those following. For an excellent recent overview, see John McManners, *Church and Society in Eighteenth-Century France*, 2 vols. (Oxford: Clarendon, 1998), 2:343–559, 661–78.

68. On the context and making of this bull, see Louis Ceyssens, and J. A. G. Tans, *Autour de l'Unigenitus: Recherches sur la Constitution* (Louvain: Peeters, 1987).

69. Pasquier Quesnel, *Le Nouveau Testament en françois: Avec des réflexions morales sur chaque verset, pour en rendre la lecture plus utile, & la méditation plus aisée* (Brussels: E. H. Fricx, 1700–1702).

70. Dale Van Kley, "Church, State, and the Ideological Origins of the French Revolu-tion: The Debate over the General Assembly of the Gallican Clergy in 1765," *Journal of Modern History* 52/4 (December 1979): 652–62.

71. NE. On the extent of Jansenism's lay constituency within the Parisian bourgeoisie, see David Garrioch, *The Formation of the Parisian Bourgeoisie, 1690–1830* (Cambridge, MA: Harvard University Press, 1997), and more recently Nicolas LyonCaen, *La boîte à Perette: Le jansénisme parisien au XVIIIe siècle* (Paris: Michel Albin, 2010).

72. Catherine-Laurence Maire, *Les convulsionnaires de Saint-Médard: Miracles, con-vulsions, et prophéties à Paris au XVIIIe siècle* (Paris: Gallimard-Julliard, 1985); and *La cause de Dieu à la cause de la nation: Le jansénisme au XVIIIe siècle* (Paris: Gal-limard, 1998), 241–326; B. Robert Kreiser, *Miracles, Convulsions, and Ecclesiastical Politics in Eighteenth-Century Paris* (Princeton: Princeton University Press, 1978).

73. On the valorization by "Richerism" of the rights of priests as directly commissioned by Christ, see Edmond Préclin's indispensable *Les jansénistes du XVIIIe siècle et la Constitution civile du clergé: Le développment du richerisme, sa propagation dans le bas clergé, 1713–1791* (Paris: Librarie Universitaire J. Gamber, 1929). The movement called Richerism got its name from the Sorbonne's syndic Edmond Richer and his work *De la puissane ecclésiastique et politique*.

74. Georges Hardy, *Le cardinal de Fleury et le mouvement janséniste* (Paris: Champion, 1925).

75. Van Kley, *The Religious Origins of the French Revolution*, 75–190.

76. Catherine M. Northeast, *The Parisian Jesuits and the Enlightenment* (Oxford: Vol-taire Foundation, 1991); and Monique Cottret, *La Bastille à prendre: Histoire et mythe de la forteresse royale* (Paris: PUF, 1986).

77. Mario Rosa, *Riformatori e ribelli nel '700 religioso italiano* (Bari: Dedalo, 1969).

78. Bernardo Tanucci, *Epistolario* 10 (1761–1762), ed. M. G. Maiorini (Rome: Istituto Poligrafico e Zecca dello Stato, 1988), Tanucci to Carraciolo, 5 September 1761, 83.

79. On the history of this church, see B. A. van Kleef, *Geschiedenis van de oud-katholieke kerk van Nederland* (Assen: Gorkum, 1953).

80. *Actes et décrets du IIe Concile provincial d'Utrecht, tenu le 13 septembre MDCCLXIII dans la chapelle de l'église paroissiale de Sainte-Gertrude, à Utrecht* (Utrecht: P. G. Simon, 1764).

81. On this phenomenon, see Marina Caffiero, *Lettere da Roma alla chiesa di Utrecht* (Rome: Edizioni dell' Ateneo, 1971); Ciro Cannarozzi, "L'adesione dei giansenisti italiani alla chiesa scismatica di Utrecht," *Archivio storico italiano* 100/383-84 (1942): 3-52; and Dale K. Van Kley, "Civic Humanism in Clerical Guise: Gallican Memories of the Early Church and the Project of Primitivist Reform, 1719–1791," *Past and Present* 200 (August 2008), 90–96.

82. HUA, OKN Aartsbisschoppen Utrecht, R86-1 (henceforth OKN, R86-1), Ms. 108, Daguesseau to Meindaerts, 15 January 1765.

83. Ibid., Ms. 110, Charles Bardon to Meindaerts, December 1765.

84. Ibid., Ms. 107, 18 February, 1765, letter in French accompanied by one in Latin signed by Bouchaud, Sauvage, Jouan, Destrriere, Hulot, Drouot, Hardouin, Lorry, Merlin, the syndic Crassoud, and Thomassin for the dean.

85. For example, one Foucher of the Académie roialle des inscriptions et belles letters in Tours to Meindaerts, in ibid., Ms. 108, 10 August 1764.

86. Gabriel Dupac de Bellegarde, *Nouveaux témoignages en faveur des évêques et du clergé catholique de la métropole d'Utrecht, tirés des lettres, et d'autres écrits authentiques, d'auteurs célèbres, donnés depuis peu au public* (Utrecht: Guillaume vander Weide, 1769), 1–2, in Bibliothèque de Port-Royal, Collection Le Paige, Ms. 407, fol. 10b.

87. Signatures are here distinguished from letters because many of the letters were collective, some of them bearing twenty or more signatures. Since most of these came from France, the foreign provenance after 1765 would be even greater if letters rather than signatures were counted.

88. This information comes from an unpublished list of epistolary communicants with the diocese of Utrecht, compiled by me, that is based on two collections held by HUA, OKN, which contains most of these letters; and the letters to the archbishop's secretary, Gabriel Dupac de Bellegarde, in the Port-Royal Collection, or 215. In view of a publication that never occurred, Dupac collected all the letters that might be construed as expressions of communion from both these sources and still others, counting from 12 August 1764 until 8 November 1790 (R86-1, Mss. 193–94). Since these archives are now in an accessible database, this information may be verified according to date.

89. Ibid., R86-1, Mss. 193–94. In case of multiple letters, I have counted only the augural letter: Blarer, 1772ff.; Haen, 1766ff.; 1772; Lopez, 1767; Palmieri, 1788ff.; Pannilini, 1778ff.; Simioli, 1769; Wittola, 1787.

90. For Pereira de Figueredo, ibid., 1769; Roda, 1771; Vázquez, 1764ff.

91. For Georgi, ibid., 1775; Marefoschi, 1775.
92. For Colloredo, ibid., 1787; Arellano, 1769; Caissotti, 1774; Sanseverino, 1775; and Taglialatela, 1765. On Utrecht's friends among the Neapolitan bishops, see Domenico Ambrasi, "Conseni di Napoli ai dissidenti di Utrecht," *Riformatori e ribelli a Napoli nella seconda metà del settecento* (Naples: Regina, 1979), 114–71.
93. HUA, OKN, R86-1, Ms. 163, 1769.
94. Enrico Dammig, *Il movimento giansenista a Roma nella seconda meta del secolo XVIII* (Rome: Biblioteca Apostolica vaticana, 1945), 260–69; and R. Polozzi, "Mons. Giovanni Bottari e il circolo dei giansenisti romani," *Annali della Scuola Normale Superiore di Pisa,*" 10 (1941): 70–90. On Italian Jansenism in general, see most recently Mario Rosa, *Il giansenismo nell'Italia del settecento: Dalla riforma della Chiesa all democrazia rivoluzionaria* (Rome: Carocci, 2014).
95. HUA, 215, Ms. 1631, "Résultat de la conférence tenue à Vienne le 27 décembre 1767 fête de Saint-Jean." In addition to Anton de Haen and Ignaz Müller, the "conference" included the theologians Anton Berhand Gürtler, Pietro Maria Gazzaniga, and Ambros Simon Stock, and the abbé Gionvanni Giuseppe Rammaggini. On the Viennese *Abendsgesellschaft,* see Peter Hersche, *Der Spätjansenismus in Österreich* (Vienna: Österreichischen Akademie der Wissenschaften, 1977), 128–29.
96. Lyon-Caen, *La boîte à Perette,* 40–68, 85–142, 251–59. On the international distribution of the books and the NE, see Douglas Bradford Palmer, "The Republic of Grace: International Jansenism in the Age of Enlightenment and Revolution" (Ph.D. dissertation, Ohio State University, 2004), 58–60; and Willem Frijhoff, "Les ventes de la vérité: La diffusion des *Nouvelles ecclésiastiques* d'après les comptes de l'abbé Mouton, agent janséniste à Utrecht," *Bijdragen tot de geschiedenis* 84 (2001): 97–107. For Dupac's correspondence with Besson, see HUA, 215, Ms. 2071.
97. HUA, 215, Ms. 2076, Blarer to Dupac, 4 March 1775; and Ms. 2044, Baldovinetti to Dupac, 21 December 1778.
98. These soundings sample the geographical coverage on the estimate of 150 centimeters of printed space per issue, yielding the results of 0 percent of "foreign" coverage in 1750, 6 percent in 1755, 12 percent in 1760, 21 percent in 1765, 19 percent in 1770, 17 percent in 1775, 44 percent in 1780, and 35 percent in 1785. Given the subsequent crescendo of reformist activity in Austria and Tuscany, these percentages would probably rise in the years between 1785 and 1789. These soundings match the findings displayed in pie charts by Olivier Andurand and Maxime Hermant in Monique Cottret and Valérie Guittienne-Mürger, eds., *Les Nouvelles ecclésiastiques: Une aventure de presse clandestine au siècle des Lumières (1713–1803)* (Paris: Bibliothèque Beauchesne, 2016), appendix III, 351–62.
99. For evidence for Bottari and Wittola, respectively, Emmanuel Lecam, "Au fondement de d'une approche renouvelée de la presse janséniste . . ."; and Juliette Guilbaud, "Un pale avatar des *Nouvelles ecclésiastiques?* Les *Wienerischen Zeitungen,*" in ibid., 76–83, 181–88.
100. The full titles are *Annali ecclesiastici di Firenze, Mainzer Monatsschrift von geistlichen Sachen,* and *Wienerische Kirchenzeitung.*

101. Sebastian Merkle, *Die katholische Beurteilung des Aufklärungszeitalters* (Berlin: K. Curtius, 1909). For recent literature on the subject, see Jeffrey D. Burson and Ulrich Lehner, eds., *Enlightenment and Catholicism: A Transnational History* (Notre Dame: Notre Dame University Press, 2014), especially Burson's introduction, 1–37; Harm Kleuting, Norbert Hinske, and Karl Hengst, *Katholische Aufklärung: Aufklärung in katholischen Deutschland* (Hamburg: Felix Meiner, 1993); and Ulrich Lehner and Michael Printy, eds., *A Companion to the Catholic Enlightenment in Europe* (Leiden: Brill, 2010), especially Lehner's introduction, "The Many Faces of Catholic Enlightenment," 1–61.

102. Another pioneering essay that uses these terms synonymously is the introductory chapter, entitled "The Catholic Enlightenment," in Samuel J. Miller, *Portugal and Rome, c. 1748–1830: An Aspect of Catholic Enlightenment* (Rome: Università Gregoriana Editrice, 1978), 1–27.

103. Bernard Plongeron, "Recherches sur l' 'Aufklärung' catholique en Europe occidental, 1770–1830," *Revue d'histoire moderne et contemporaine* 16 (1969): 555–605.

104. Eric Cochrane, *Florence in the Forgotten Centuries* (Chicago: University of Chicago Press, 1973), 374.

105. Robert R. Palmer, *Catholics and Unbelievers in Eighteenth-Century France* (Princeton: Princeton University Press, 1939). On more recent scholarship, see Catherine M. Northeast, *The Parisian Jesuits and the Enlightenment*; Jeffrey D. Burson, *The Rise and Fall of Theological Enlightenment: Jean-Martin de Prades and Ideological Polarization in Eighteenth-Century France* (Notre Dame: Notre Dame University Press, 2012); and Daniel Watkins, "Enlightenment, Catholicism, and Conservatism: The Isaac-Joseph Berruyer Affair and the Culture of Orthodoxy in France, ca. 1700–1830" (Ph.D. dissertation, Ohio State University, 2014).

106. Ulrich L. Lehner, *The Catholic Enlightenment: The Forgotten History of a Global Movement* (Oxford: Oxford University Press), 104–24. More recently on the same subject, Jeffrey D. Burson, "Between Power and Enlightenment: The Cultural and Intellectual Context for the Jesuit Suppression in France," in Jeffrey D. Burson and Jonathan Wright, eds., *The Jesuit Suppression in Global Context* (Cambridge: Cambridge University Press, 2015), 41–52; and Guy G. Stroumsa, *A New Science: The Discovery of Religion in the Age of Reason* (Cambridge, MA: Harvard University Press, 2010).

107. Dale K. Van Kley, "The Varieties of Enlightened Experience," in William Bulman and Robert Ingram, eds., *God in the Enlightenment* (Oxford: Oxford University Press, 2016), 278–316.

108. On this subject, I am quite indebted to Kors's discussion of seventeenth- and early eighteenth-century Jesuits' investment in Aristotelian epistemology in *Atheism in France*, 297–302 and in general 297–322.

109. On this subject, see the works of Burson, Palmer, Northeast, and Watkins cited in note 105 above.

110. For bibliography on this subject, see chapter 2.

111. The first attempt to argue this point was in "Catholic Conciliar Reform in an Age of Anti-Catholic Revolution," in James E. Bradley and Dale K. Van Kley, eds., *Reli-*

gion and Politics in Enlightenment Europe (Notre Dame: Notre Dame University Press, 2001), 78–80.

112. Peter Hanns Reill, *The German Enlightenment and the Rise of Historicism* (Berkeley: University of California Press, 1975), 100–89; and Germaine de Staël-Holstein, *De l'Allemagne* (Paris: Charpentier and Fasquelle, n.d.), 410–44.

113. Saint Augustine, *Of True Religion* (Chicago: Gateway, 1968), 64; See in general ibid., nos. 52–75, 49–75; and the *Confessions*, trans. P. Pine-Coffin (London: Penguin, 1961), book 10, 211–32.

114. J. G. A. Pocock, *Barbarism and Religion*, vol. 1, *The Enlightenments of Edward Gibbon, 1737–1764* (Cambridge: Cambridge University Press, 1999), 1–9, 50–71; and Van Kley, "The Varieties of Enlightened Experience."

115. Parsons, *The Church in the Republic*.

116. Some canonical books on civic humanism or classical republicanism are Bernard Bailyn, *The Ideological Origins of the American Revolution* (Cambridge, MA: Harvard University Press, 1967); J. G. A. Pocock, *The Machiavellian Moment: Florentine Political Thought and the Atlantic Republican Tradition* (Princeton: Princeton University Press, 1975); and Gordon Wood, *The Creation of the American Republic, 1776–1787* (New York: Norton, 1969).

117. On classical republicanism in France, see Johnston Kent Wright, *A Classical Republican in Eighteenth-Century France: The Political Thought of Mably* (Stanford: Stanford University Press, 1997).

118. Van Kley, "Civic Humanism in Clerical Guise."

119. Reginaldo Tanzini, "Prefazione," in *Opere di Machiavelli*, 6 vols. (Florence, 1782–1783), liv–lvi. That Tanzini "retracted" his "prefazione" in a letter to Pius VII in 1800 is hardly to the point, since he was undoubtedly under tremendous pressure to do so during the anti-Jansenist reaction under Austrian auspices after the collapse of French presence in Italy in 1799. See Mario Rosa, *Dispotismo e libertà nel Settecento: Interpretazioni "repubblicane" di Machiavelli* (Pisa: Edizioni della Normale, 2005), 57–61.

120. Jacques-Joseph Duguet, *Institution d'un prince: Ou traité des qualités, vertus et des devoirs d'un souverain*, 4 vols. (London, 1750), 2:253, 256.

121. On Peter Leopold's relation to Duguet's *Institution du prince*, see Mario Rosa, "Il 'cuore del re,'" in *Settecento religioso: Politica della ragione e religione del cuore* (Venice: Marsilio, 1999), 75–109. See also Antonella Alimento, "Un gioco di scacchi?" *Rivisiti Storia Italiana* 110/2 (1998): 529–71.

122. [Claude Mey and Gabriel-Nicolas Maultrot,] *Apologie de tous les jugemens rendus par les tribunaux séculiers en France contre le schisme*, 2 vols. ("En France," 1752). On the diffusion of Mey and Maultrot's treatise, see D. Carroll Joynes, "The *Gazette de Leyde*: The Opposition Press and French Politics, 1750–1757," in Jeremy Popkin and Jack Censer, eds., *Press and Politics in Pre-Revolutionary France* (Berkeley: University of California Press, 1987), 133–69.

123. On this subject, see Michael Printy, *The Enlightenment and the Creation of German Catholicism* (Cambridge: Cambridge University Press, 2009), esp. 101–21. The

best and subsequently most cited edition of Zeger Bernhard van Espen's work came out in 1763 as *Jus ecclesiasticum universum antiquae et recentiori disciplinae praesertim Belgii, Galliae, Germaniae, & vicinarum Provinciarum accommodatum . . .*, 4 vols. (Louvain, 1753).

124. François Richer, *De l'autorité du clergé et du pouvoir du magistrat sur l'exercise des fonctions du ministère ecclésiastique*, 2 vols. (Amsterdam, 1766).

125. Van Kley, "Church, State, and the Ideological Origins of the French Revolution," 646–52.

126. Reginald Ward, "Late Jansenism and the Habsburgs," in Bradley and Van Kley, eds., *Religion and Politics in Enlightenment Europe*, 170–72.

127. On this development, see Michaeil Stolleis, *Histoire du droit public en Allemagne: Droit public impérial et science de la police, 1600–1800*, trans. Michel Senellart (Paris: PUF, 1998).

128. Taddeo von Trautmansdorf [Pietro Tamburini and Giuseppe Zola], *Trattato della tolleranza ecclesiastica e civile* (Modena: Societa Tipografica, 1785). Heavily dependent on Louis-Adrien Le Paige's *Lettres pacifiques au sujet des contestations présentes* (N.p., 1753), this treatise underwent translation back into French in 1796 as *De la tolérance ecclésiastique et civile, ouvrage composé en Latin par Thadée de Trautmansdorff . . . , traduit par le citoyen P. S. S.* (Paris: L'Imprimerie-Librairie Chrétienne, 1796), when it functioned as a justification for the position of the post-Terror Gallican Church. I have referred to this treatise in this French translation.

129. *De la tolérance ecclésiastique et civile*, on the state's basis in natural law, 145, for spiritual means, 162; on felicity and tranquillity, 90, 137, 151–53; and praise of Joseph II, 129–30, 153, 163. Tamburini and Zola of course expected to reserve the rights of public worship for the "public and dominant religion," as stated on 144.

130. On Tamburini and his in Italian "patriotism," see Dale K. Van Kley, "From the Catholic Enlightenment to the Risorgimento: The Exchange between Nicola Spedalieri and Pietro Tamburini, 1791–1797," *Past and Present* 223/2 (August 2014): 108–60.

131. Hontheim, *Traité du gouvernement de l'église et de la puissance du pape*, 3:277, 280, 288.

132. [Tamburini and Zola,] *De la tolérance ecclésiastique et civile*, 90, 129–37, 151–53, 162–62.

133. Van Kley, *The Religious Origins of the French Revolution*, 254–68, 309–16, 423–45.

2. THE GENESIS AND TRAJECTORY OF ANTI-JESUITISM

1. Although this work seems to have appeared in 1614, the earliest edition I can find is [Hieronim Zahorowski], *Monita privata societatis Jesu edita M.DC.LVII.* (N.p., [1752]). As early as 1616 a refutation appeared under the names of Jan Ostroróg, Jan Wielewicki, and Andrzej Kanski, entitled *Ad filios admonitoria epistola: Contra fraudulentiam scripti editi sub titulo: Monita privata Societatis Jesu* (Lviv: Malachiowicz, 1615). The edition I have used is the *Instructions secrètes des jésuites suivant*

l'original (Cologne: Ignace Le Sincère, 1704), in Bibliothèque de Port-Royal (henceforth BPR), Fonds Le Paige (henceforth FLP), Ms. 15M=3 (or 1511). On this work, see Sabina Pavone, *Le astuzie dei gesuiti: Le false "Istruzioni segrete" della Compagnia di Gesù e la polemica antigesuitica nel secoli XVII e XVIII* (Rome: Sallerno Eitric, 2000).

2. [Giovanni Bernardino Capriata,] "*Monita Secreta Societatis Jesu*," in *I lupi smascherati nella confutazione, e traduzione del libro intiulato . . .* (Ortignano: Tancredi et al., 1761), cxv–cxci; and "Les instructions secrètes des jésuites, traduites de leurs *Secreta Monita*," in [Louis-Adrien Le Paige and Christophe Coudrette,] *Histoire générale de la naissance et des origines et des progrès de la Compagnie de Jésus, avec l'analyse de ses constitutions et privilèges*, 4 vols. (N.p., 1761), 4:197–228.

3. Juan de Ribas y Carrasquilla, *Teatro jesuitíco: Apologetico discurso, con saludables y seguras dotrinas, necessarias a los principes y señores de la tierra* (Coïmbra: Guillermo Cendrat, 1654). See René François Wladimir Guettée, *Histoire des jésuites composée sur documents authentiques en partie inédits* (Paris: Lécrivain and Toubon, 1858–1859), 206; and François-Xavier de Feller, *Biographie universelle ou dictionnaire des hommes qui se sont fait un nom par leur génie, leurs talents, leurs vertus, leurs erreurs ou leurs crimes*, 13 vols. (Paris: Gaulthier, 1833–1838), 10:261.

4. Sébastien-Joseph du Cambout de Pontchâteau, *La morale pratique des jésuites, représentée en plusieurs histoires arrivées dans toutes les parties du monde* (Cologne: Gervinus Quentel, 1669), 8–31, 188–287. Cambout de Pontchâteau is thought to be the sole or at least main author of this and the following volume.

5. José Edouardo Franco, *O mito dos Jesuítas em Portugal, no Brasil e no Oriente (Séculos XVI a XIX)*, 2 vols. Vol. 1, *Das Origens ao Marqués de Pombal* (São Paulo: Gradiva, 2006), 118–20 and note 279. It seems as though he wrote a manuscript, "Apologia contra la economia jesuitica por el Insigne Doctor Benedito Arías Montano del Aucto de Santiago, cononigo de Sam Marcos de Leon, Capellan de Honor de S. Majestad Católica Don Phelipe II. . . ." (1571), now in the Biblioteca Nacional de Madrid, Sección de manuscritos, cód. 10129, fols. 1v–2.

6. "Avertissement sur la lettre qu'on donne ici au public, et sur celui qui en est l'auteur, " in [Antoine Arnauld,] *Lettre du célèbre docteur Arias Montano, chevalier de l'ordre de Saint-Jacques, bibliothécaire de S[a] M[ajesté] [C]atholique, au roi d'Espagne Philippe II, touchant la conduit que le gouverneur des Pays-Bas pour S. M. devoit garder envers les jésuites.* (N.p., 1701), 2–3; and "Lettre du docteur Arias Montano au roi d'Espagne Philippe II touchant les jésuites," in *ibid.*, 4–7.

7. Fernando Caballero, *Vida del Illmo. Sel D. Fray Melchor Cano, del orden de San Domingo* (Madrid: Imprenta del Colegio Nacional de Sordo-Mudos T. de Ciegos, 1871), 347–68.

8. John W. O'Malley, *The First Jesuits* (Cambridge, MA: Harvard University Press, 1993), 292–94.

9. Ibid., 317–20, 372–74. See also Terence O'Reilly, "Melchor Cano and the Spirituality of St. Ignatius Loyola," in Juan Plazaola, ed., *Ignacio de Loyola y su tiempo: Con-*

greso Internacional de Historia (9–13 setiembre 1991) (Bilbao: Ediciones Mensajero, 1992), 369–80.

10. Alain Tallon, *La France et le concile de Trente (1518–1563)* (Rome: École française de Rome, 1997), 715–24, 770–85.

11. "Causes d'opposition fournies par Eustache du Bellay " and "Conclusion de la faculté de théologie de Paris, et son jugement sur ledit Institut," 1554, in [Jean-Antoine Gazaignes, alias Emmanuel-Robert Philibert,] *Annales de la société des soi-disans jésuites; ou Recueil historique-chronologiques de tous les actes, écrits, dénonciations, avis doctrinaux . . . [c]ontre la doctrine, l'enseignement, les enterprises et les forfaits des soi-disans jésuites, depuis 1552, époque de leur naissance en France, jusqu'en 1763*, 5 vols. (Paris, 1764–1771), 1:4–8.

12. "Conclusion de la Faculté de théologie de Paris, et son jugement sur ledit Institut," 1 December 1554, in ibid., 8.

13. Ibid., "Interrogation subi par les soi-disans jésuites devant l'université," 18–23; "Consentement donnée par l'évesque de Paris à l'établissement des soi-disans jésuites," 9–10; "Avis et résolution de messieurs du clergé de France, assemblés à Poissy le 15 septembre 1561, sur la cause des soi-disans jésuites," 13–16; and "Arrest du parlement de Paris, qui ordonne l'enregistrement et approbation fait à l'Assemblée tenue à Poissy [au] 13 février 1561," 16–17.

14. "Consultation de Me. Charles Dumoulin . . . ancien avocat au parlement de Paris, sur l'utilité ou les inconvéniens de la nouvelle secte," in ibid., 23–28.

15. Étienne Pasquier, "Plaidoyer de l'Université de Paris, encontre les jésuites," in *Les recherches de la France*, ed. Maris-Luce Demonet et al. (Paris: H. Champion, 1996), 3:834 and in general 807–52.

16. See A. Lynn Martin, *Henry III and the Jesuit Politicians* (Geneva: Droz, 1973).

17. [Antoine Arnuaud, père,] *La fleur de lys: Qui est un discours d'un François retenu à Paris, sur les impiétés et déguisemens contenus au manifeste de l'Espagne, publié au moye de janvier 1593*, 17. See also *Copie de deux lettres au Roy, l'une envoyée à messieurs du maire, échevins, et habitans de la ville de Dijon. L'autre au sieur de Franchese, commandant au château de ladite ville.* (Lyons: Gichard et al., 1594), 6–7.

18. [Étienne Pasquier,] *Histoire prodigieuse d'un détestable parricide entrepris en la personne du roy par Pierre Barrière, dit La Barre . . .* (N.p., 1594).

19. The reference is to the book of Judges 3:12–30.

20. Echoes of these events are quite audible in Étienne Pasquier's, *Catéchisme des jésuites*, ed. Claude Sutto (Sherbrook, Quebec: Éditions de l'Université de Sherbrook, 1982), book 3, chapters 1, 2, 3, and 15, pp. 319–31, 365–67.

21. Antoine Arnauld, *Plaidoyer de M. Antoine Arnauld, avocat en parlement de Paris, pour l'université de Paris demanderesse. Contre les jésuites défendeurs, des 12 et 13 juillet 1594*, in *Les plaidoyers de M. Antoine Arnauld, avocat en parlement, contre les jésuites . . .* (N.p., 1716), 53–54, 61–64, 78. Arnauld's plaidoyer of 1594 saw its first publication in Lyon, by Thibaud Ancelin and Guichard Jullieron, in 1594

22. Ibid., quotations from 13–14, 49, 55, 58, 71, 86, 91.

23. The relevant documents are printed in ibid., among them the *Interrogatoires de Jean Chastel*, 27 décembre 1594, 581–83, 581–83; *Arrest du parlement de Paris contre Jean*

Chastel et les jésuites, 29 décembre 1594, 583–84; *Arrest du parlement de Paris contre le P. Gueret, jésuite, et Chastel, père [du] 7 décembre 1595*, 585; *Extraits des écrits trouvés dans la chambre de Jean Guignard, jésuite*, 599–600; and *Arrest du parlement de Paris, contre Jean Guignard, attaint & convaincu du crime de lèze-majesté. Du 7 janvier 1595*, 600.

24. *Ibid., Procédure faite contre Jean Chastel, écolier éudiant au collège des jésuites de Paris, pour le parricide par lui attenté sur la personne du roi très-chrétien Henri IV. roi de France & de Navarre; par le cour de parlement de Paris, ensemble les arrêts donnés contre le parricide & contre les jésuites*, 576–600; and *Edit du roi Henri IV. portant expulsion des jésuites des états et royaume de France, . . . ensemble les arrêts d'enregistrement dudit édit ès cours de parlement séant à Rouen, à Dijon & à Rennes. Du 7 janvier 1595, 21 janvier, 11 février, et 16 février*, 603–6.

25. Roland Mousnier, *L'assassinat d'Henri IV* (Paris: Gallimard, 1964), 84–85.

26. Although hardly an unbiased source, the section on lese-majesty and regicide in the Parlement of Paris's *Extrait des assertions dangereuses et pernicieuses en tout genre, que les soi-disans jésuites ont, dans tous les temps et perséverément soutenus, enseignés et publiés dans leurs livres, avec approbation de leurs supérieurs et généraux . . .*, 4 vols. (Paris: P.-G. Simon, 1762), 4:90–393, is a reasonably good guide to the timing of such publications.

27. *Lettres patentes du roi Henri IV, pour le rétablissement des jésuites ès villes de Toulouse, Auch, . . . et permission de demeurer à la Flèche; en septembre 1603, sous plusieurs charges et conditions, entr'autres, de n'entreprendre ne faire aucune chose, tant au spirituel qu'au temporel, au préjudice des universités, des évêques, ni des autres religieux, et de se conformer au droit commun*, in [Gazaignes,] *Annales de la Société des soi-disans jésuites*, 2:14–15.

28. [Achilles de Harlay,] *Remontrances de la cour de parlement*, 24 December 1603, in ibid., 2:26–29.

29. Antoine Arnauld, père, *Le franc et véritable discours au roi, sur le rétablissement qui lui est demandé pour les jésuites* (N.p., 1762).

30. [Louis Richéome, alias François des Montaignes,] *La vérité défendue pour la religion catholique: En la cause des jésuites: Contre le plaidoyer d'Antoine Arnauld* (Liège: Henry Hostius, 1596), 55–65.

31. Antoine Arnauld, père, *Le franc et véritable discours au roi*, 47, 52. On the theory of regicide in particular, see 27–39.

32. Pasquier, *Catéchisme des jésuites*, book 1, chapters 14–15, 187–206.

33. Ibid., 232, but in general book 2, chapter 1, 222–32.

34. Ibid., book 3, chapters 12, 25–26, 358–60, 427–44.

35. On this subject, Erik Nelson, *The Jesuits and the Monarchy: Catholic Reform and Political Authority in France (1590–1615)* (Farnham, U.K.: 2005), 147–71.

36. Quotations from [Jacques Gillet,] *Le Caton françois, au roy* (N.p. 1614), 34; and *Le recontre du Caton et le Diogène françois, réunis dans l'autre monde. Sur le sujet des Etats tenus à Paris en l'année 1615* (N.p., n.d.), 36–37.

37. [Fancan,] *Le Miroir du temps passé, à l'image du présent, à tous bons pères religieux et vrais catholiques non passionez* (N.p., n.d.), 55.

38. *Le rencontre du Caton et le Diogène françois*, 42–43.

39. "Censure de la faculté de théologie de Louvain, sur quelques points de l'Écriture sainte, de la Grace, et de la prédestination, enseignés à Louvain en l'année 1586 par Lessius et Hamelius, Jésuites"; and "Censure de la faculté de théologie de Douai, sur quelques propositions . . . 20 janvier 1588," both in *Annales de la Société des soi-disans jésuites*, 5:163–275.

40. The pertinent sources on the *De auxilliis* controversy are printed in *Annales de la société des soi-disans jésuites*, 1:720–823.

41. *Projet de la bulle de Paul V contre Molina*, in ibid., 1:823–48. For a recent treatment of the *De auxilliis* controversy, see Paolo Broggio, *La teologia e la politica: Controversia dottrinale, Curia romana e monarquia spagnola tra cinque e seicento* (Florence: Olschki, 2009).

42. *Somme théologique des vérités capitals de la religion chrétienne, par le R. P. Garasse, théologien de la Compagnie de Jésus*, 4 vols. (Paris: Sébastien Chappelet, 1625), 1:649; and *Propositions extraites de la Somme théologique du père Garasse jésuite, et dénoncées à la faculté de théologie . . . 1 & 16 septembre 1626*; and *Conclusion et censure de la faculté de théologie de Paris, portant condemnation de la Somme théologique des vérités capitals de la religion chrétienne, par le P. Garasse jésuite*, in ibid., 3:335–42.

43. Jean Orcibal, *Jean Duvergier de Hauranne, abbé de Saint-Cyran et son temps (1581–1638)* (Paris: J. Vrin, 1948), 88–93.

44. Anthony F. Allison, "A Question of Jurisdiction, Richard Smith, Bishop of Chalcedon, and the Catholic Laity, 1625–31," *Recusant History* 16 (October 1982): 111–45. On the political background of Smith's appointment, see also Allison, "Richard Smith, Richelieu, and the French Marriage: The Political Context of Smith's Appointment as Bishop for England in 1624," in *Recusant History* 7 (1964): 148–211.

45. Allison, "Richard Smith's Gallican Backers and Jesuit Opponents: Some of the Issues Raised by Kellison's *Treatise of the Hierarchie*, 1629, Part I," *Recusant History* 18 (October 1987): 329–59.

46. Ibid., 361–73.

47. On the controversy about the propositions, see ibid., 373–93. For the propositions themselves, *Censure des propositions presentées à la faculté de théologie de Paris . . .* ; and *Censures des propositions continues dans un livre écrit en anglois et traduit fidèlement en Latin, qui a pour titre: Modeste et courte discussion de quelques propositions enseignées par le docteur Kellisson, en son Traité de la hiérarchie ecclésiastique, par Nicolas Smith, c'est-à-dire Matthias Wilson, jésuite anglois*, all in *Annales de la Société des soi-disans jésuites*, 3:487–520.

48. All the relevant propositions by English and Irish Jesuits and the censures and qualifications by Gallican bishops and the Sorbonne are conveniently at hand in ibid., 3:482–87, 457–75, and 475–81.

49. Although embedded in the notes of this anti-Jesuit compilation, a good summary of the positions in the debate pitting Leomelius against "Petrus Aurelius" is in ibid., 448–74.

50. Godefroy Hermant, *Apologie pour l'Université de Paris, contre le discours d'un Jésuite: Par une personne affectionnée au bien public*, 2nd ed. (N.p., 1643), in Fonds Le Paige (henceforth FLP), Ms. 1511=2, fols. 7–8, 58.

51. *Observations importantes publiées par ordre de l'université, sur la requête des jésuites* (1643), in *Annales de la Société des soi-disans jésuites*, 3:753–54.

52. Jean Lesaulnier, "La fréquente communion d'Antoine Arnauld: Genèse d'une oeuvre," in *Antoine Arnauld (1612–1694): Philosophe, écrivain, théologien, Chroniques de Port-Royal* 44 (Paris: Bibliothèque Mazarine, 1994), 61–68. See also Hervé Savon, "L'argument patristique dans la querelle de la Fréquente communion," in ibid., 83–95; and Michel Le Guerm, "Arnauld et les jésuites," ibid., 221–27.

53. On the portrait of the Jesuit father, see Anne Régent-Susini, "Les provincials, une comédie," in *La champagne des Provinciales, Chroniques de Port-Royal* 58 (Paris: Bibliothèque Mazarine, 2008).

54. Blaise Pascal, *Les provincials*, in *Oeuvres complètes*, ed. Louis Lafuma (Paris: Éditions du Seuil, 1963). For invincible ignorance, see the "quatrième lettre," 383; for probabilism, the "sixième lettre," 393; for direction of intention, the "septième lettre," 397.

55. Pavie de Fourquevaux's *Catéchisme historique et dogmatique sur les contestations qui divisent l'église: Où l'on montre l'origine et le progrès des disputes présentes: Et où l'on fait des réflexions qui mettent en état de discerner de quel côté est la vérité*, 2 vols. (The Hague: Aux dépens de la société, 1729–1733), 2:4.

56. Daniele Concina, *Della storia del probabilismo e del rigorismo: Dissertazioni teologiche, morali, e critiche* (Venice: Simon Occhi, 1748); and *Lettere teologico-morali in continuazione della difesa della storia del probabilismo e rigorismo, ecc. del P. Daniele Concina: Overro confutazione della riposte pubblicato dal M. R. P. B. della compagnia [di Jesù]*, 6 vols. (Trent [Venice]: [Simone Occhi], 1751–1754).

57. [Antoine Arnauld and/or Pierre Nicole,] *Les pernicieuses conséquences de la nouvelle hérésie des jésuites contre le roy et contre l'état, par un avocat au parlement* (Lille: 1683), 6–8, 15–18, 26–28. Originally published in 1664, the pamphlet refers to a thesis defended in the Jesuit College of Clermont on 12 December 1661 in support of the papal bull *Ad sanctam* declaring the recently condemned five propositions to be in Jansen's *Augustinus*.

58. Sarah Caroline Wegener, "Popery, Publics, and Plots: Public Use of Reason and History in the Controversy over the 'Popish Plot' in Late Seventeenth-Century England" (M.A. thesis, Ohio State University, 2005), 17–56.

59. Antoine Arnauld and Sébastien-Joseph du Cambout de Pontchâteau, *La morale pratique des jésuites*, 8 vols. (N.p., 1683–1695), vol. 4.

60. Ibid., 1:1. The Jesuit publication is J. Bollandus and J. Tollenare, *Imago primi saecvli Societatis Iesu a Provincia Flandro-Belgica eiusdem Societatis repraesentata* (Antwerp: Officina Plantiniana, 1640).

61. Arnauld, *La morale pratique des jésuites*, vols. 1 and 8, passim.

62. On the subject of Palafox, see Cayetana Alvarez de Toledo, *Politics and Reform in Spain and Viceregal Mexico: The Life and Thought of Juan de Palafox, 1600–1659*

(Oxford: Clarendon Press, 2004). The following account is based largely on Alvarez de Toledo's account, supplemented by Palafox's three public letters to Innocent X and Philip IV referred to below.

63. "Lettre de Dom Juan de Palafox, évêque d'Angelopolis, au pape Innocent X, sur les différents qu'il avoit avec les jésuites," 25 May 1647; and "Lettre de Jean de Palafox, évêque d'Angélopolis . . . au roi d'Espagne," 12 September 1647, printed successively in *Annales de la Société des soi-disans jésuites*, 3:1034–46, 1046–55.

64. These details are contained in Palafox's third letter, 8 January 1649, in ibid., 4:70–106.

65. "Lettre de Dom Jean de Palafox . . . au pape Innocent X," 25 May 1647, in ibid., 3:1036.

66. "Lettre de Dom Jean de Palafox . . . au pape Innocent X, contenant diverses plaints de ce saint prélat contre. . . . leur manière peu évangélique de prêcher l'Évangile dans les Indes occidentale," 8 January 1649, in ibid., 4:106–49.

67. Ibid., 3:83.

68. Erik Zürcher, "Jesuit Accommodation and the Chinese Cultural Imperative," in D. E. Mungello, ed., *The Chinese Rites Controversy in History and Meaning* (Nettelal, Germany: Steyler, 1994), 56–57. On belief guardian angels in late antiquity, see Peter Brown, *The Cult of Saints: Its Rise and Function in Latin Christianity* (Chicago: University of Chicago Press, 1981).

69. Liam Matthew Brockey, *Journey to the East: The Jesuit Mission to China, 1579–1724* (Cambridge, MA: Harvard University Press, 2007), 137.

70. John Willis Jr., "From Manila to Fuan: Asian Contexts of Dominican Mission Policy," in Mungello, ed., *The Chinese Rites Controversy*, 123–24.

71. "Décret de la Congrégation de Propaganda Fide, tenue le 12 septembre 1645," in *Annales de la Société des soi-disans jésuites*, 3:841. The decree came in response to a series of *Doutes ou difficultés concernant les nouvaux chrétiens de la Chine; proposés par la Congrégation de Propaganda Fide au S. Office*, while the seventeen "questions" resolved by the congregation were unquestioningly those formulated by Juan Batista de Morales, as is clear from the *Requête ou supplique présentée à la congrégation de Propaganda Fide par le P. Moralés, religieux dominicain et missionnaire de la Chine*," all in ibid., 828–41.

72. Brockey, *Journey to the East*, 119–22.

73. Fernández Domingo Navarrete, *Tratados historicos, politicos, ethicos, y religiosos de la monarchia de China*, 2 vols. (Madrid, 1676).

74. Claudia von Collani, "Charles Maigrot's Role in the Chinese Rites Controversy," in Mungello, *The Chinese Rites Controversy*, 180. Longobardi's refections are entitled "Respuesta breve, sobre las controversias de el Xang Ti, Tien Xin, y Lin Hoen . . . y otros nombres, y terminus Chinicos," and appeared for the first time in Navarrete's *Tratados*, 1:246–89.

75. Antoine Arnauld and Sébastien-Joseph du Cambout de Pontchâteau, *Histoire des différens entre les missionaries jésuites d'une part et ceux des ordres de St. Dominique et de St. François de l'autre, touchant les cultes que les Chinois rendent à leur maître Confusius, à leurs ancestres et à l'Idole Chin-hôam*, in *Morale pratique*, 6:48–49.

76. On this point, see Catherine M. Northeast, *The Parisian Jesuits and the Enlightenment* (Oxford: Voltaire Foundation, 1991), 157–61. Since Pontchàteau died in 1690, it may safely be assumed that Arnauld alone wrote this and subsequent volumes.

77. Charles Alan Kors, *Atheism in France, 1650–1729* (Princeton: Princeton University Press, 1990), 159–77.

78. Arnold H. Rowbothan, *Missionary and Mandarin: The Jesuits at the Court of China* (Berkeley: University of California Press, 1942), 141–45.

79. On Maigrot's decree, see Collani, "Charles Maigrot's Role," 163–67 and 151–58; Edward Malateta, "A Fatal Clash of Wills: The Condemnation of the Chinese Rites by the Papal Legate Carlo Tomasso Maillard de Tournon," in Mungello, ed., *The Chinese Rites Controversy*, 212–15.

80. On the confrontation between Kangxi and Maigrot, see Collani, "Charles Maigrot's Role," 163–67.

81. These ironies emerge from the geopolitical lay of the land in Brockey's *Journey to the East*, 164–203.

82. Michel Le Tellier, *Défense des nouveaux et des missionnaires de la Chine, du Japon, & des Indes: Contre deux livres intitulez, La morale pratique des jésuites, et L'esprit de M. Arnauld*, 2 vols. (Paris: Estienne Michallet, 1687–1690).

83. [Nicolas Petitpied, Pasquier Quesnel et al.,] *Recueil de pièces touchant l'Histoire de la Compagnie de Jésus composé par le père Jouvenci Jésuite: Et supprimé par arrêt du parlement de Paris du 24 mars 1713*, 2nd ed. (Liège, 1713), 495–509. The target was Joseph Jouvency, *Historia Societatis Jesu parte quinta, tome posterie ab anno Christi 1591, ad anno 1616, autore Josephio Juvencio, Societais ejusdem sacerdote*, vol. 2. (Rome: Georgio Plachi, 1710).

84. Ibid., 491–93.

85. "Parallèle de la conduit du P, Q. & des théologiens de la Société, sur l'obéissance due aux rois," in [Pasquier Quesnel,] *Hexaples ou les six colonnes sur la constitution Unigenitus*, 2nd ed. (N.p., 1715), 568–82.

86. [Pasquier Quesnel,] *Histoire des religieux de la Compagnie de Jésus, contenant ce qui s'est passé dans ordre depuis son établissement jusqu'à présent*, 4 vols. (Utrecht: Aux dépens de la compagnie, 1741).

87. On this subject, Catherine L. Maire, *De la cause de Dieu à la cause de la nation: Le jansénisme au XVIIIe siècle* (Paris: Gallimard, 1998).

88. [Pavie de Fouquevaux,] *Catéchisme historique et dogmatique sur les contestations qui divisent maintenant l'Église*, 1:76–84.

89. Ibid., 1:34–79.

90. Ibid., 2:14–15, 24–101.

91. *Mémoire pour MM. les plénipotentiaires du Congrès de Soissons* (N.p., 1728); and republished under the title and attributed to Pierre Boyer as *Juste idée que l'on doit se former des jésuites et leur vrai caractère: Avec un Recueil de pièces concernant leur bannissement du Royaume, pour avoir enseigné et fait mettre en pratique, qu'on peut tuer les Rois, &c.* (Utrecht: Aux dépens de la compagnie, 1755), consulted in BPR, FLP, Ms. 2359–10, iv, 9–12, 34.

92. Antoine Arnauld, *Le franc et véritable discours* (N.p., 1735), consulted in BPR, Salle Port-Royal (henceforth SPR). Ms. 265=6, no. 677; and [Antoine Arnauld,] *Anti-Coton, ou Réfutation de la lettre déclaratoire du P. Coton: Livre où est prouvé que les jésuites sont coupables et auteurs du parricide exécrable commis en la personne du Roy Très-Chrestien Henry IV. d'heureuse mémoire* (N.p., 1736), consulted in BPR, SPR, Ms. 265=7, no. 678.

93. *Mémoire pour MM. les plénipotentiaires du Congrès de Soissons*, 42, 48–50.

94. See, for example, an assertion to this effect in *NE*, 18 July 1732, 144.

95. Bibliothèque de l'Arsenal (henceforth BA), Archives de la Bastille (henceforth AB), Ms. 10189, fol. 250, 15 July 1729.

96. This account is massively indebted to Mita Choudhury, *The Wanton Jesuit and the Wayward Saint: A Tale of Sex, Religion, and Politics in Eighteenth-Century France* (University Park: Pennsylvania State University Press, 2015), 69–151, and on the role of the Quietist accusation in particular, 61, 91–94, 98–99, 103–4, 134–35.

97. For the year 1731 alone, the *NE* serialized its coverage of the affair in issues on 6 February, 20 March, 25 April, 28 May, 16 June, and 19 July, and in special forty-page issue on 3 December. On the affair's wider spillover into the satirical press, see also Stephane Lamotte, "Le P. Girard et la Cadière dans la tourmente des pieces sat-iriques," *Dix-Huitième Siecle*, 39/1 (2007): 431–53; and Choudhury, *The Wanton Jesuit and the Wayward Priest*, 127–51.

98. Choudhury, *The Wanton Jesuit and the Wayward Saint*, 105, 161–69.

99. Jean Pichon, *L'esprit de Jésus-Christ et de l'église sur la fréquente communion* (Paris: Guerin, 1745).

100. *NE*, table, 1:707–11.

101. Norbert [de Bar-Le-Duc], *Mémoires historiques sur les missions des Malabares . . .* 2 vols. (Rome, 1744); and reviewed in *NE*, 20–27 February 1745, 29–36.

102. *NE*, table, 1:681.

103. Ibid., 1:689.

104. René-Louis Voyer de Paulmy, marquis d'Argenson, *Journal et mémoires du marquis d'Argenson*, ed. E. J. B. Rathery, 9 vols. (Paris: Renouard, 1859–1867), 13–14 April 1752, 7:184. See also 204 and April 1755, 8:483.

105. *NE*, 2 January 1752, 4.

106. Another early accusation of "despotism" equated with "absolute" power leveled against the structure of the Society of Jesus can be found in [Louis-Adrien Le Paige,] *Annales pour servir d'étrennes aux amis de la vérité* (N. p., [1733]), 2–3, 38.

107. *NE*, 2 January 1755, 4.

108. Ibid., 2 January 1758, 2–5.

109. Ibid., 10 April 1754, 57.

110. Ibid., 18 June 1756, 101–2.

111. Ibid., 19 November 1757. The pamphlet is *Lettre écrite de Paris à un ami de province sur l'éducation des jeunes gens dans les collèges des jésuites, par un homme de qualité* (N.p., n.d.).

112. Ibid., 7 August 1753, p. 126; and in general 31 July and 7 August, 121–27.

113. [Pierre Boyer,] *Juste idée que l'on doit se former des jésuites.* For the documents, see 54–96.

114. *NE*, 2 January 1756, 4.

115. *Pièces originales et procédure du procès fait à Robert-François Damiens, tant en le prévôté de l'Hôtel qu'en la cour du parlement* (Paris: P.-G. Simon, 1757). For a pro-Jesuit treatment of Damiens's trial, see *Histoire de Robert-François Damiens, contenant les particularités de son parricide et de son supplice* (Amsterdam: Jacques Le Caze, 1757).

116. *Réflexions*, 13–14; and *Lettre d'un patriote*, 27–28.

117. *Les jésuites criminels de lèze-majesté, dans la théorie et dans la pratique* (The Hague: Vaillant, 1758); and reviewed in *NE*, 21 August 1758, 139, 188. This pamphlet went through three editions in 1758 alone.

118. *Arrest de la cour de parlement de Toulouse, qui condamne au feu le livre intitulé R. P. Herm. Busembaum, societatis Jesu, . . . Coloniae, sumpt. Fratrum de Tournes, 1757* (Toulouse: Bernard Pijon, 1757); and *NE*, 9–16 October 1757, 165–70; 6 November, 181–82; 23 December, 208.

119. Hermann Busenbaum, *Theologia moralis, antehac ex probatis auctoribus breviter concinnata a R. P.Herm. Busenbaum, nunc pluribus partibus aucta a R. P. Claudio La Croix, . . . Editio altera . . . —Index locupletissimus resolutionum omnium quae continentur tam in "Medulla" R. P. Hermanni Busenbaum, . . . quam in omnibus ad illam a . . . P. Claudio La Croix, . . . factis additamentis secundum ordinem alphabeti digestus a R. P.*, 2 vols. (Cologne: S. Noethen, 1729–1739). I have been unable to find any evidence for an edition in Toulouse in 1757, the chronologically closest being in Venice in 1755 and Ferrara in 1756.

120. *NE*, 23 February 1729, 36.

121. Ibid., 3 April 1758, 60.

122. Ibid., 2 January 1758, 7.

123. Isaac-Joseph Berruyer, *Histoire du peuple de Dieu, depuis son origine jusqu'à la naissance du Messie, tirée des seuls livres saints, ou le texte sacré des livres de l'ancien Testament, réduit en un corps d'histoire*, 10 vols. (Paris: Durand, 1753), 1:16–17. On Berruyer, see Daniel Watkins, "Enlightenment, Catholicism, and Conservatism: The Isaac-Joseph Berruyer Affair and the Culture of Orthodoxy in France, ca. 1700–1830" (Ph.D. dissertation, Ohio State University, 2014).

124. For example, *NE*, 19 March 1760, 49–64, which pages were really devoted to a thorough review of the bishop of Soissons's pastoral instruction against Berruyer and his master Hardouin's whole corpus. This pastoral instruction was in turn largely the work of the bishop's Jansenist theologian Étienne Gourlin.

125. On the literal depiction of Jesuits in contemporary engravings that corresponds to the description that follows in this chapter, see Christine Gouzi, *L'art et le jansénisme au XVIIIe siècle* (Paris: Nolin, 2007), 99–104, 138–44; Christine Vogel, *Der Untergang des Gesellschaft Jesu als europäisches Medienereignis (1758–1773)* (Mainz: Philipp von Zabern, 2006), 75–91, 110–18, 133–40, 253–73, and passim; and Pierre

Wachenheim, "De la physiognomonie à la tératologie: Les jésuites portraiturés ou les visages de l'antijésuitisme," in Pierre-Antoine Fabre and Catherine Maire, eds., *Les antijésuites: Discours, figures et lieux de l'antijésuitisme a l'époque moderne* (Rennes: Presses Universitaires de Rennes, 2010), 13–52.

126. *NE*, 9 January 1755, 7–8.
127. *Ibid.*, 2 January 1759, 2, 6.
128. Ibid., 6.
129. Ibid., 4.
130. Ibid.
131. Ibid., 6–7.
132. [Le Paige and Coudrette,] *Histoire générale de la naissance et des origines et des progrès de la Compagnie de Jésus*, 3:371–72, 395.
133. Ibid., 3:223.
134. Ibid., 4:123–24.

3. THE CASE OF FRANCE

1. Since the subject of this chapter retells in summary form a story first recounted in Dale Van Kley, *The Jansenists and the Expulsion of the Jesuits in France, 1767–1765* (New Haven: Yale University Press, 1975), fuller documentation for some of what follows may be found there. But because subsequent research in adjacent areas has corrected some assertions in that book while expanding the purview of the whole, complete documentation is provided here for what is new or corrective.

2. On this correspondence, see Dale K. Van Kley, "Catholic Conciliar Reform in an Age of Anti-Catholic Revolution: France, Italy, and the Netherlands, 1758–1801," in James E. Bradley and Dale K. Van Kley, eds., *Religion and Politics in Enlightenment Europe* (Notre Dame: Notre Dame University Press, 2001), 46–118.

3. BA, Ms. 11,883, fol. 112, Bottari to Clément, 15 November 1757.

4. BPR, FLP, Ms. 547, fol. 312, "extrait d'une lettre de Pise," a letter by Cerati to either Clément or Marold du Coudray, a councilor in the Paris court called the Châtelet.

5. Benedict XIV. *Bref de N. S. P. le pape contre le père Berruyer: Condamnation et prohibition d'un ouvrage qui a pour titre: Histoire du peuple de Dieu, depuis la naissance du Messie jusqu'à la fin du Synagogue, seconde partie* (Rome: Typographia Reverendae Camerendae Apostolicae, 1757) in BPR, FLP, Ms. 547, fol. 271. This brief was the strongest of all papal pronouncements against this book, using the qualifications of "favoring heresy and even approximating it." According to Bottari (BA, Ms. 11,883, Bottari to Clément, 21 February 1758), Benedict shied away from the unqualified adjective of "heresy" only because of opposition by cardinals in the Congregation of the Index.

6. F. Henrico De Noris, *Historia Pelagiana et dissertatio de Synodo V. Oecumenica in qua origenis ac Theodori Mopsuesteni Pelagiani erroris auctorum justa damnatio exponitur . . .* , (Padua: Typis Petri Mariae Frambotti, 1673).

7. BPR, FLP, Ms. 312, "extrait d'une lettre de Pise."

8. Ibid., Ms. 321, fragments of Le Paige's manuscript diary on the subject. What First President Molé told the abbé Bernis is therefore based on Le Paige's testimony.

9. Ibid.

10. Ibid.

11. Ibid., Ms. 551, fol. 16, Clément to Clément de Feillet, Rome, 5 July 1558.

12. Ibid., fol. 25, Clément to Clément de Feillet, August 1758.

13. Ibid., fol. 16, Clément to Le Paige, 5 August 1758. The nuncio was Ludovico Gualterio De' Gualtieri.

14. Ibid., fol. 27, Clément to Le Paige, 9 September 1758.

15. Ibid., fol. 27, Christophe Coudrette (although unsigned) to Le Paige, 11 September 1758.

16. Ibid., fol. 27, Clément to Le Paige, Naples, 19 September 1758.

17. Ibid., fol. 27, "extrait d'une letter de Pise," 1 November 1758.

18. BA, Ms. 11, 883, fol. 137, Bottari to Clément, 22 March 1758.

19. BA, Ms. 12, 883, Bottari to Clément, Rome, 20 December 1758.

20. BPR, FLP, Ms. 549, fol. 30, "lettre de Rome du 20 décembre de M. le comte de Gross." I have not been able to find the original of this letter either in Clément's correspondence or in the Bibliothèque de l'Arsenal at Saint-Sulpice. But letters from Carlo di Grosso with the same advice to the abbé Clément are abundant enough at the Bibliothèque de Saint-Sulpice (henceforth BSS) in the Fonds Clément (henceforth FC), for example, Ms. 1293, fol. 23, 2 January 1759; and Ms. 1294, fol. 23, 16 January 1759. Expressed in these letters, di Gosso's belief in the obligation "di riferire le nostre azione a Dio" and hope for the return of the prophet Elijah, it would seem as though the count's "Jansenism" consisted in more than anti-Jesuitism only.

21. BSS, FC, Ms. 1293, fol. 23, Di Grosso to Clément, 2 January 1759.

22. BSS, FC, Ms. 1294, fol. 23, Di Grosso to Clément, 16 January 1759. This translation is the best sense I can make of a run-on sentence, the relevant fragment of which reads as follows: ". . . una gloria deve essere questa del Parlemento, il quala ha per dovere di vegliare alla custodia del Re, e de vantagii, e tranquilito della stato di farli caricare, ne' sperino ne pace, ne bene sino che non si fa questo colpo."

23. *Ibid.*, fol. 40, Clément to no one named, January 1759. Clément took the trouble to include the Italian original in his translation of the possible French role in a return of the Jesuits: "Verra tempo che la Corta stessa di Francia gli rimettera in questa di Spagna, di Portugallo.

24. BPR, FLP, Ms. 547, fol. 321.

25. BSS, FC, Ms. 1293, fol. 43, "réflexions faites en France," 10 January 1759.

26. BSS, FC, Ms. 1293, Coudrette to Clément in Auxerre, 29 January 1759.

27. [Louis-Adrien Le Paige,] *La légitimité et nécessité de la loi du silence* (Paris, Aux dépens de la Companie, 1759).

28. BSS. FC, Ms. 1294. fols. 11–12. Clément was probably the author of the article on this subject in *NE*, 15 May 1759, 82.

29. HUA, 215, Ms. 2672, Clément to La Rivière [d'Etemare], 31 January 1760.

30. Catherine-Laurence Maire, *De la cause de Dieu à la cause de la nation: Le jansé-nisme au XVIIIe siècle* (Paris: Gallimard, 1998), 85–114.

31. BPR, FC, Ms. 547, fol. 336. This document is Le Paige's translation of the Latin.

32. Ibid., Ms. 551, fol. 18, Clément to Clément de Feillet and like-minded colleagues.

33. BSS, FC, Ms. 1294, fol. 23, Di Grosso to Clément, 16 January 1759.

34. Étienne-François, duc de Choiseul, "Anecdote particulière à la cour de Louis XV," in *Mémoires du duc de Choiseul*, ed. F. Calmettes (Paris: Plon-Nourrit, 1904), 180–85.

35. BA, Ms. 4987, fol. 64, Delle Lanze to Clément, 6 February 1760. The intended foil in this argument against Choiseul's indispensable agency is Julian Swann in *Politics and the Parlement of Paris under Louis XV, 1754–1774* (Cambridge: Cambridge University Press, 1995), 208–13.

36. [Joseph Adrien Lelarge de Lignac,] *Avis paternels d'un militaire à son fils, jésuite, ou Lettres dans lesquelles on développe les vices de la constitution de la Compagnie de Jésus, qui la rendent également pernicieuse à l'église & à l'état, & fournissent les motifs & les moyens de la détruire* (N.p., 1760). For Bottari's reaction, see BA, Ms. 11, 883, fol. 227, Bottari to Clément, 22 July 1760.

37. BA, Ms. 1281, fol. 48, Passionei to Du Coudray, 17 December 1760.

38. Ibid., fol. 27, Passionei to Du Coudray, 17 September 1760.

39. On this subject generally, D. G. Thompson, "The Lavalette Affair and the Jesuit Superiors," *French History* 10/2 (June 1996): 206–39; and Ludwig von Pastor, *History of the Popes*, trans. E. F. Peeler, vols. 36–38 (London: Routledge and Kegan Paul, 1950–1952), 36:386–406.

40. *Extrait des registres des juges et consuls de marchands, établi par le Roi notre Sire, à Paris*, in *Sentences des juges et consuls de Paris, du 30 janvier 1760, qui condamne tous les jésuites de France solidairement, à payer la somme de trente mille livres . . .* (N.p., [1760]), 6–16.

41. Ibid., 1–6.

42. Charlemagne Lalourcé, *Mémoire à consulter pour Jean Lioncy, créancier, et syndic de la masse de la raison de commerce, établie à Marceille [sic] sous le nom de Lioncy frères, et Gouffre, contre le corps et Société des pp. jésuites* (Paris: P. Alex Le Prieur, 1761).

43. Thompson, "The Lavalette Affair and the Jesuit Superiors," esp. 227–29; and D. G. Thompson, "The French Jesuit Leaders and the Destruction of the Jesuit Order in France, 1756–62," *French History* 2/3 (September 1988): 254–60.

44. Gabriel Sénac de Meilhan, "Morceaux historiques," in *Mémoires de Madame Du Hausset, femme de chambre de Madame de Pompadour, avec des notes et éclaircisse-ments historiques*, ed. J. Tastu (Paris: Baudoin, 1824), in *Collection des mémoires relatifs à la Révolution française*, 36, 249–50. It may also be, as D. G. Thompson has suggested, that Frey calculated that if the Jesuits lost their case, the verdict would at least oblige the four other French Jesuit provinces to shoulder the financial burden with that of France. See "General Ricci and the Suppression of the Jesuit Order in France," *Journal of Ecclesiastical History*, 37/3 (July 1986): 228.

45. This vote is recorded in until recently a typed copy of the manuscript "Mémoires" of the Jansenist councilor Robert de Saint-Vincent, but now happily edited by Monique Cottret, Valerie Guittienne-Mürger, and Nicolas Lyon-Caen as *Un magistrat janséniste du siècle des lumières à l'émigration, Pierre-Augustin Robert de Saint-Vincent*, and henceforth cited as such (Bordeaux: Presses Universitaires de Bordeaux, 2012), 204.

46. This was precisely Cardinal Passionei's prophetic calculation in as early as September 1760, as is evident in his letter to Marold du Coudray in BSS, FC, Ms. 1281, fol. 27, 17 September 1760.

47. Edmond-Jean-François Barbier, *Chronique de la Régence et du règne de Louis XV, 1718–1763, ou Journal historique et anecdotique*, 8 vols. (Paris: Charpentier, 1866), 7:352; and *NE*, 4 September 1761, 141–43.

48. Among the barristers who pleaded the case of the prosecution—Lalourcé did not— the relevant judicial memoirs are Rouhette and Guy-Jean-Baptiste Target, *Mémoire sur les demandes formulées contre le général et la société des jésuites, au sujet des engagements qu'elles a contractés par le ministère du père de la Valette* (Paris, 1761); and Jean-Baptiste Legouvé, *Plaidoyer pour le syndic des créanciers des sieurs Lioncy frères et Gouffre, négociants à Marseille, contre le général et la Société des jésuites* (N.p., 1761). On Gerbier, see *NE*, 13 December 1759, 197; and René Cerveau, *Nécrologe des plus célèbres défenseurs et confesseurs de la vérité du dix-huitième siècle*, 2 vols. (N.p., 1760), 2:425.

49. BPR, FLP, Ms. 582, fol. 44, Lalourcé to Le Paige, 11 March 1760.

50. Charlemagne Lalourcé, *Mémoire à consulter pour Jean Lioncy, créancier, et syndic de la masse de la raison de commerce, établie à Marceille [sic] sous le nom de Lioncy frères, et Gouffre, contre le corps et Société des pp. jésuites* (Paris: P. Alex Le Prieur, 1761), 64–66, 137–41, 154–59, 252–53, 286–92.

51. Ibid., 165.

52. The relevant memoirs on the part of the defense are Gillet, Lherminier, Mallard, et al., *Mémoire à consulter et consultation pour les jésuites de France* (Paris, 1761); Laget-Bardelin, *Mémoire pour les jésuites des provinces de Champagne, Guyenne, Toulouse et Lyon . . .* (Paris, 1761); and Claude-François Thevenot d'Essaules, *Plaidoyer pour les jésuites de France* (Paris, 1761).

53. [Henri-Philippe Chauvelin,] *Discours d'un de messieurs des enquestes du parlement, toutes les chambres assemblées, sur les constitutions des jésuites: Du dix-sept avril, mille sept cents soixant-un* (N.p., n.d.): on his identity as citizen, 4; and on all the others, 4–39.

54. Ibid.: on Chinese rites, 38–39, on Palafox, 41–44, and on "despotism," 18, 26, 41.

55. On Frey's possible motives and the king's reaction, see Thompson, "The French Jesuit Leaders and the Destruction of the Jesuit Order in France," 254–55.

56. BPR, FLP, Ms. 582, fol. 90, Le Febvre de Saint-Hilaire to Le Paige, n.d.; Ms. 91, Lambert to Le Paige, 30 May 1761; and *NE*, 13 November 1761, 183.

57. The term is most prominent in the memoirs of the anti-Jansenist barrister Barbier in his *Chronique de la Régence et du règne de Louis XV*, especially from 1750 forward.

58. On the composition of such a "party," see Van Kley, *The Jansenists and the Expulsion of the Jesuits*, 37–61, plus names subsequently gleaned from the identity of magistrates who sent letters of communion to Utrecht in HUA, 215; and, in the same archive, OKN, R86-1.

59. It is true that Durey de Meinières's entente with the "parti janséniste" occurred after his marriage to one Madame Belot, the widow of a Jansenist barrister.

60. Jean Omer Joly de Fleury, *Compte rendu des constitutions des jésuites, par MM. les gens du roi, M. Omer Joly de Fleury, avocat dudit seigneur roi portant la parole, les 3, 4, 6, et 7 juillet 1761, en exécution de l'arrêt de la cour du 17 avril précédent, et de son arrêté du deux juin audit an* (N.p., [1761].

61. Ibid., 138–39, 157, 161, 165–67.

62. [Chauvelin,] *Discours d'un de messieurs . . . du huit juillet*, 7–8.

63. On invincible ignorance and probabilism, ibid., 6; and on role of Jean Simon, NE, 22 May 1789, 80.

64. [Chauvelin,] *Discours d'un de messieurs . . . du huit juillet*: for Berruyer and Hardouin, 2–3; for Pichon, 29, 34; for regicide, 2, 10.

65. BPR, FLP, Ms. 582, fol. 95.

66. NE, 20 November 1761.

67. BPR, FLP, Ms. 582, fol. 96, "esquisse d'un plan général," July 1761.

68. Ibid., fol. 97, unsigned letter to Le Paige, 10 July 1761. Careful examination of signed letters elsewhere makes it possible to identify the handwriting as that of Meinières.

69. Ibid., fol. 98, July 1761.

70. Bibliothèque nationale de France (henceforth BnF), Fonds Joly de Fleury (henceforth FJF), Ms. 1612, fol. 332.

71. Ibid., "projet de déclaration," fols. 318–32.

72. The University of Paris's legal challenge to the Jesuits' right to teach anything at all at the College of Clermont had been "appointed" and was still technically pending in the Parlement of Paris because the royal council had "evoked" the case and highhandedly given the Society the right to offer classes in 1618. As Jean-Omer well knew, the most that the University or the Parlement would have allowed the Society of Jesus to teach was the subject of theology to their own members, on the model of the arrangement worked out between the university and the four mendicant orders. Never would either have allowed the Jesuits to teach every subject to all comers, as Louis XIII and the queen regent allowed them to do in 1618.

73. René-Louis Voyer de Paulmy, marquis d'Argenson, *Journal et mémoires du marquis d'Argenson*, ed. E. J. B. Rathery, 9 vols. (Paris: Renouard, 1859–1867), 6:454; 7:179–80; 8:448, 9:196–97.

74. Archives nationales (henceforth AN), Archives privées (henceforth AP), 162 mi. (Archives du marquis de Rosanbo).

75. Paul-Alexandre, comte Gibert de Voisins, ed., *Procédure contre l'Institut et les constitutions des jésuites* (Paris: Ponthieu, 1823), 37.

76. BnF, FJF, Ms 1609, fol. 101. A remarkably personal document in an otherwise impersonal set of papers, this folio contains Omer Joly de Fleury's recollections of what transpired during the critical days from 2 to 6 August 1761.

77. Cottret, Guittienne-Mürger, and Lyon-Caen, eds., *Un magistrat janséniste du siècle des lumières*, 214.

78. Gibert de Voisins, ed., *Procédure contre l'Institut et les constitutions des jésuites*, 37–51.

79. *NE*, 11 December 1761, 210.

80. AN, AP, 162 mi, carton 1, dossier 6, fol. 17, dauphin to Lamoignon, 7 August 1761; and Cottret, Guittienne-Mürger, and Lyon-Caen, eds., *Un magistrat janséniste du siècle des lumières*, 215.

81. AN, O1, Ms. 604, fol. 268. Based on a letter dated 8 August 1761, this information comes from one "Brunet, maître des requestes honoraire," who is probably Brunet d'Evry, a member the Bureau pour les Affaires concernant les Unions des Bénéfices aux Maisons des Jésuites," according to the *Almanach royale* (Paris: Imprimerie royale, 1761), 149, 156.

82. AN, AP, 162 mi, carton 1, dossier 6, fol. 37, "Réflections sur l'arrest de l'enregistrement de la déclaration du 2 aoust 1761."

83. Gibert de Voisins, *Procédure contre l'Institut et les constitutions des jésuites*, 81–122.

84. AN, Ms 241, fol. 4, unnumbered piece, 1761, in the hand of Gilbert de Voisins.

85. For example, the Parlement's *Extraits des assertions dangéreuses et pernicieuses en tout genre, que les soi-disans jésuites ont, dans tous les temps et persévérément, soutenues, enseignées et publiées dans leurs livres, avec approbation de leurs supérieurs et généraux*, 4 vols. (Paris: P. G. Simon, 1762), 4:356–93.

86. Pastor, *History of the Popes*, 36:419 and in general 415–31.

87. The following account is largely based on a manuscript entitled "Relation exacte de tout ce qui s'est passé relativement au décret interprétif de celuy d'Acquaviva de 1610: Envoyé à Rome et refusé par le Général ainsy qu'à la déclaration que le Général a pareillement refusée d'approuver." The author of the account, hereafter called the Flesselles manuscript, seems to be Jacques de Flesselles, one of the members of the special royal commission, and later prévôt des marchands de Paris. This manuscript originally emanated from the papers of Rolland d'Erceville, president of the third Chambre des requêtes, and contains a note in the hand of this magistrate specifying "Le manuscrit par lequel celuy cy a été copié m'a été prêté par M. de Flesselles en avril 1764," indicating, it seems, that Flesselles was the author and narrator. After no little pleading in 1967, the archivist, Père Joseph Dehergne, allowed me to consult it and make a handwritten copy of large parts of it. At that time, the manuscript bore a call number of 1445. Since then these archives have been moved to Vanves, where I have no idea under what *cote* it may be found. But what alerted me to its existence was its publication in Auguste Carayon, ed., *Mémoires du président d'Eguilles sur le parlement d'Aix et les jésuites, addressés à S. M. Louis XV* (Paris: L'Écureux, 1867), 293–303.

88. Gustave-Xavier de la Croix de Ravignan's *Clément XIII et Clément XIV*, 2 vols. (Paris: Lanier, 1856), 2:204–5, La Croix to Flesselles, 30 September 1761; and 211–12, "projet de déclaration concernant les quatre articles."

88. Flesselles manuscript, fols. 2–3.

90. Archives des Affaires étrangères (henceforth AAE), Correspondance politique (henceforth CP), Rome, Ms. 831, fol. 63, Ricci to king, 13 May 1761; fol. 64, Ricci to chancellor, 13 May 1761; and fols. 259, 262–63, 266–67, 325, Ricci's pleas during September and October to the king, the dauphine, the queen, and Choiseul, respectively.

91. Thompson, "The French Jesuit Leaders and the Destruction of the Jesuit Order in France," 256–60; "General Ricci and the Suppression of the Jesuit Order in France, 1760–64, esp. 432; and Pastor, *History of the Popes*, 36:407–31.

92. Claudio Acquaviva, *Le décret dv Révérend Père Clavde Acqvaviva, général de la Compagnie de Jésus: Contre le pernicieuse doctrine d'attenter aux sacrées personnes des royes* (Paris: Claude Chappelet, 1614).

93. Flesselles manuscript, fol. 4.

94. Traces of this "council" are visible in AN, AP, Ms. 162 mi., carton 1, dossier 5, fol. 86, Louis XV to Lamoignon, 2 January 1762.

95. For Le Paige's reaction, BPR, FLP, Ms. 582, fol. 11, "du janvier 1762." See also the account in the *NE* probably written by Le Paige, 12 October 1762, 161–62.

96. Maison de Saint-Louis, Flesselles manuscript, Ms. 1445.

97. BPR, FLP, Ms. 582, fol. 6, Murard to Le Paige, 4 January 1762. The letter closes with the instructions, "Je vous prie de Brùler ma lettre."

98. AAE, CP, Ms. 832, fol. 4, Choiseul to Rochechouart, 5 January 1762. Choiseul took the occasion to deliver the following profession of Gallican faith: "Quelle que puisse être à Rome la façon de penser sur nos maximes et sur nos libertés, nous continuerons de les soutenir avec la plus grande fermeté et la persevérance la plus invariable. Les Papes feront toujours des tentatives imprudentes et pour le moins inutiles, lorsqu'ils entreprendront de donner quelque atteinte à des principes aussi enciens [*sic*] que notre monarchie."

99. AN, M, Ms. 241, Ricci to Louis XV, 28 October 1761; and published by Ravignan, *Clément XIII et Clément XIV*, 2:214–15.

100. These justifications are set forth in Choiseul's dispatch to Cardinal Rochechouart, 16 January, in AAE, CP, Ms. 832, fol. 20.

101. AN, M, Ms. 241, fol. 4, a piece entitled "articles commun aux deux projets."

102. Ibid., unnumbered piece by Gilbert de Voisins entitled "Au Conseil des dépêches du vendredi 4 janvier 1762 où fût rapporté et approuvé le plan des commissaires, et [où] la rédaction en fut ordonné par le Roi."

103. AN, AP, Ms. 162 mi., carton 1, dossier 5, fol. 84, Desmarets to Louis XV, 5 December 1761; and Claude Frey, *Observations sur l'institut de la Société des jésuites* (Avignon: Alexandre Giroud, 1761), 61–62.

104. Choiseul's extensive instructions to Cardinal Rochechouart are in the AAE, CP, Ms. 832, fol. 20, Choiseul to Rochechouart, 16 January 1762.

105. Thompson, "General Ricci and the Suppression of the Jesuit Order in France," 434; and, in general, Pastor, *History of the Popes*, 36:431–48.

106. For Clement XIII's reply of 28 January, see Ravignan, *Clément III et Clément XIV*, 1:87–90; and for Ricci's reply, Augustin Theiner, *Histoire du pontificat de Clément*

XIV d'après des documents inédits des archives secrètes du Vatican, 2 vols. (Paris: Firmin Didot, 1852), 1:46.

107. AN, AP, Ms. 162 mi., carton 1, dossier 6, fol.48, Lamoignon to dauphin, 17 February 1762.

108. *NE*, 12 October 1762, 162.

109. BPR, FLP, Ms. 582, fol. 11, "Extraits des letres [*sic*] d'une dame de Paris à une de ses amis de province, au sujet de l'assemblée des Évêques au mois de décembre 1762 à Paris, et de leur avis sur les jésuites. Du 8 février 1762."

110. For fuller documentation on the role of the provincial parlements and *conseils supérieurs*, see Jean Egret, "Le procès des jésuites devant les parlements de France, 1761–1770," *Revue Historique* 204 (July–December 1950): 1–27, supplemented in selective detail in Van Kley, *The Jansenists and the Expulsion of the Jesuits*, 163–207.

111. BPR, FLP, Ms. 582, fol. 11, "Extrait de letres [*sic*] d'une dame de Paris a une de ses amies de province. . . . Du 14 février 1762." For Le Paige's preceding correspondence with Thomas du Fossé, see ibid., fols. 161, 175.

112. Ibid., Ms. 583, fol. 3; and Ms. 582, fol. 21.

113. AN, AP, Ms. 162 mi., carton 1, dossier 5, fol.97, Lamoignon to dauphin, 1 May 1762; and BPR, FLP, Ms. 583, fol. 3, "Réponse du Roy à Monsieur le Chancelier," undated.

114. *Extraits des assertions dangéreuse et pernicieuses en tout genres, que les soi-disans jésuites ont, dans tous les temps et persévéramment soutenues, enseignées et publiées dans leurs livres, avec l'approbation de leurs supérieurs et généraux . . .* (Paris: P.-G. Simon, 1762).

115. That this was the purpose is made clear in a note from Chancellor Lamoignon to the dauphin in AN, AP, Ms. mi. 162, carton 1, dossier 6, fol. 47, chancellor to dauphin, 29 November 1761.

116. "Procès-verbal de l'assemblée extraordinaire des évêques en 1761," in AN, K, Ms. 1361, fol. 1a.

117. On the Gallican articles and the subjection of the Jesuits to the bishops, see ibid., fols. 14–16.

118. The letter from Texier convoking his confreres to a meeting about how to counter the favorable episcopal evaluation of the Jesuits is in BPR, FLP, Ms. 582, fol. 137, Texier to Le Paige, 29 November 1761. That Roussel de la Tour was among the redactors is clear from a letter to Le Paige in ibid., Ms. 583, fol. 33; that Murard was also involved is evident from the letters on the subject in his handwriting in ibid., fol. 35, 3 April 1762; fol. 54, 2 March 1762. Robert de Saint-Vincent spelled out his role as well as that of the others in the redaction of the *Extraits* in his memoirs, in Cottret, Guittienne-Mürger, and Lyon-Caen, eds., *Un magistrat janséniste du siècle des lumières*, 221–24.

119. Michel-Joseph-Pierre Picot, *Mémoires pour servir à l'histoire ecclésiastique pendant le XVIIIe siècle*, 2nd ed., 4 vols. (Paris, 1815–16), 2:408–9.

120. For such reactions by bishops, see BnF, Manuscrits Français (henceforth Mss. Fr.), FJF, Ms. 1615.

121. Assemblée Générale du Clergé de France, "Remontrances du clergé concernant les vœux des jésuites que plusieurs parlements ont entrepris d'annuler," in AN, K, 1361, Ms. 3, fols. 2, 11, 12–13.

122. Christophe de Beaumont du Repaire, *Instruction pastorale de monseigneur l'archévêque de Paris sur les atteintes données à l'autorité des tribunaux séculiers dans l'affaire des jésuites* (N.p., 23 October 1763). On this pastoral instruction, Thomas Worcester, "Friends as Liabilities: Christophe de Beaumont's Defence of the Jesuits," in Jeffrey D. Burson and Jonathan Wright, eds., *The Jesuit Suppression in Global Contex: Causes, Events, and Consequences* (Cambridge: Cambridge University Press, 2015), 65–79.

123. *Edit du roi portant règlement pour les collèges qui ne dépendent pas des universités, donné à Versailles au mois de février 1763* (Paris, 1763); *Lettres patentes du roi, concernant l'administration d'une portion des biens de la Compagnie et Société des jésuites: Données à Versailles le 2 février 1763* (Paris, 1763); and *Lettres patentes du roi, pour l'abréviation des procédures et la diminution des frais dans la discussion des biens des jésuites: Données à Versailles, le 2 février 1763* (Paris, 1763), all in *Actes royaux*, F21167.

124. *Edit du roi, concernant la Société des jésuites. Ddonné à Versailles, au mois de novembre 1764* (Lyon: Valfrey, imprimeur du roi, 1764).

125. Maison de Saint-Louis, Flesselles manuscript, Ms. 1445, fol. 3.

126. BnF, FJF, Ms. 1612, fol. 334, a draft in the hand of the procureur-général, Guillaume-François Joly de Fleury.

127. AAE, FC, Ms. 831, fol. 312, Rochechouart to Choiseul, 3 November 1761.

128. *Damnatio, et prohibition, versionis Italicae operis Gallicae scripti hoc titulo: Exposition de la doctrine chrétienne, ou Introductions sur les principales vérités de la Religion, editae quinque voluminibus* . . . (Rome: Typographica Apostolicae, 1761).

129. For Di Grosso's opinion, BSS, FC, Ms. 1281, fol. 77, Di Grosso to Coudray, 27 May 1761; on Rochechouart, AAE, CP, Ms. 831, fol. 69, Rochechouart to Choiseul, 19 May 1761; fol. 71, Rochechouart to Berryer, 20 May 1761; and fols. 159–60, Berryer to Rochechouart, 7 July 1761

130. AAE, CP, Ms. 831, fols. 178–79, Rochechouart to Choiseul, 22 July 1761.

131. Ibid., CP, Ms. 831, fol. 127, P. Lamballe to Choiseul, 17 June 1761; and BSS, FC, Ms. 1281, fol. 79, Di Grosso to Coudray, 3 June 1761. According to Di Grosso, the six votes against the condemnation were cast by the cardinals Corsini, Galli, Orsi, Passionei, Spinelli, and Tamburini; the seven votes by Castelli, Cavalchini, Elsi, Feroni, Ganganelli, Torrigiani, and of course Rezzonico.

132. Ibid., fol. 128, Rochechouart to Choiseul, 17 July 1761

133. BPR, FLP, Ms. 555, fol. 116, "Mémoire sur le bref que le pape vient de donner malgré la France et Naples, contre le livre de M. Mésengui," 4 July 1761; and fol. 116 bis, Murard to Le Paige, 6 July 1761.

134. AAE, CP, Ms. 831, fols. 159–60, Berryer to Rochechouart, 2 July 1761.

135. *Epistola encyclica ad patriarchos primatos, archipiscopos, et episcopos universae catholicae* (Rome: Typographica Apostolicae, 1761).

136. AAE, CP, Ms. 831, fols. 69–70, someone to Berryer, 27 May 1761.

137. Ibid., Ms. 831, fol. 352, Choiseul to Rochechouart, 24 November 1761.

138. Ibid., fol. 377, Flesselles to Rochechouart, 30 November 1761.

139. Ibid., fol. 380, Rochechourart to Versailles, fol. 380, 1 December 1761; and fol. 404, December 1761.

140. BPR, FLP, Ms. 583, fol. 76, Le Paige to himself, 28 April 1762.

141. Keith Michael Baker, *Inventing the French Revolution: Essays on French Political Culture in the Eighteenth Century* (Stanford: Stanford University Press, 1990), 170.

142. Jean-Antoine Joachim Cerutti's *Apologie générale de l'Institut des jésuites* (Geneva: Grasset, 1763); For a discussion of this defense and the others, see Van Kley, *The Jansenists and the Expulsion of the Jesuits*, 137–62.

4. PORTUGAL AND SPAIN

1. Archives de la Bastille (henceforth AB) in the Bibliothèque de l'Arsenal (henceforth BA), Ms. 11883, fol. 205, Bottari to Clément, 5 March 1760.

2. On Carvalho's collaborators, see Dauril Alden, "The Gang of Four and the Campaign against the Jesuits in Eighteenth-Century Brazil," in John O'Malley, S. J., Gauvin Alexander Bailey, Steven J. Harris, and T. Frank Kennedy, S. J., eds., *The Jesuits II: Cultures, Sciences, and the Arts, 1540–1773* (Toronto: University of Toronto Press, 2006), 707–24. From Alden's list I have subtracted Gomes Freire de Andrade, governor of Rio de Janeiro, and to it have added Almeida e Mendonça.

3. Samuel J. Miller, *Portugal and Rome, c. 1748–1830: An Aspect of the Catholic Enlightenment* (Rome: Università Gregorianna Editrice, 1978), 32–35.

4. For a recent account of Carvalho's campaign against the Jesuits from its beginnings until the expulsion, see José Eduardo Franco, *O Mito dos Jesuítas em Portugal, no Brasil e no Oriente (Séculos XVI a XX)*, 2 vols. (Sao Paulo: Gradiva, 2006), 1 (*Das Origens ao Marqués de Pombal*), 411–53.

5. Kenneth Maxwell, *Pombal: Paradox of the Enlightenment* (Cambridge: Cambridge University Press, 1995), 51–68.

6. Alden, "The Gang of Four," 716–17.

7. On this treaty and its consequences, see Guilleremo Kratz, *El Tratado hispano-portugués de Límites de 1750 y sus consecuencias: Estudio sobre la abolición de la Compañía de Jesús* (Rome: Institutum Historicum S. I., 1964), esp. 45–72, 163–213.

8. On the subject of this "myth," see Girolamo Imbruglia, *L'invenzione del Paraguay: Studio dell'idea di comunità tra seicento e settecento* (Naples: Bibliopolis, 1983); and José Eduardo Franco, *O mito dos Jesuítas: Em Portugal, no Brasil e no Oriente (séculos XVI a XX)* (Lisbon: Gradiva, 2006), vol. 1.

9. Maxwell, *Pombal: Paradox of the Enlightenment*, 69–83.

10. *Accordam os consehlo, e desembargo de Elrey Nosso Henhor, &c.*, in, 43–67; translated into French as *Jugement du Conseil souverain, chargé par Sa Majesté tres-fidèle d'instruire le procès au sujet de l'attentat commis sur sa Personne Sacrée . . . Du douze janvier 1759*, 3–42, consulted in BPR, FLP, Ms. 1972=4. Without dates or

places of publication, these printed documents are parts of a collection of such occasional pieces bound together by Le Paige.

11. *Edit d'expulsion des jésuites de tous les états de la couronne de Portugal* (signed by the "king" and "comte d'Oeyras" and registered in the Secretariat of the Affairs of the Realm in the department of Royal Letters, Ordinances, and Patents, fol. 52, at Notre Dame d'Ayuda, 4 September 1759, but not published until 3 October 1759).

12. On this theory, see Franco, *O Mito dos Jesuítas em Portugal,* 1:327.

13. António Pereira de Figueiredo, *Doctrinam veteris Ecclesiae de suprema regium etiam clericos potestate ex Sacris Litteris, Sanctis Patribus, Incorruptique priorum saeculorum Monumentis depromptam* (Lisbon: Miguel Francisco Rodríguez, 1766); and reviewed in *NE,* 23 January 1766, 19–20; and Pereira's regalist works in general, Franco, *O Mito dos Jesuítas em Portugal,* 1:337–44.

14. António Pereira de Figueiredo, *O Novo Testamento de Jesu Christo: Traduzido em portuguez segundo a Vulgata Segunda impressão, mais correcta no texto, e accrescentada nas notas,* 6 vols. (Lisbon: Na Regia Officina Typografica, 1781). The definitive version of his translation of the entire Bible appeared in installments as *Bíblia Sagrada: Traduzida em portuguez segundo a vulgata latina. . . . Edição nova pelo texto latino . . . ,* 7 vols. (Lisbon: Simaõ Thaddeo Ferreir[ra], Officina da Academia Real das Sciencias, 1794–1819).

15. Evergton Sales Souza, *Jansénisme et réforme de l'église dans l'empire portugais* (Lisbon: Fundação Calouste Gulbenkian, Centre culturel Calouste Gulbenkian, 2004), 433–50.

16. HUA, OKN, R86-1, Ms. 163, 1770. On the catechism, see Miller, *Portugal and Rome,* 121–22. The catechism in question is Pierre-Curel Parisot, *La foi des catholiques: Ouvrage tendant à instruire et confirmer les catholiques dans leur croyance . . . : Dédié à Monseigneur le comte d'Oeyras, premier ministre d'État* (Lisbon: d'Antoine Rodrigues Galhardo, 1763). On his anti-Jesuit pamphlets for Portugal, see Christine Vogel, *Der Untergang des Gesellschaft Jesu als europäisches Medienereignis (1758–1773)* (Mainz: Philipp von Zabern, 2006), 107–8, nn. 212–15.

17. Sales Souza, *Jansénisme et réforme de l'église dans l'empire portugais,* 344–81.

18. Ibid., 145–67.

19. *NE,* 22 July 1767, 117–19.

20. Miller, *Portugal and Rome,* 51.

21. Mar García Arenas, *Portugal y España: Las monarquías ibéricos y la Compañia de Jesús (1755–1773)* (Madrid: Centro de Estudios Políticos y Constitucionales, 2014), 60–94.

22. AB, BA, Ms. 11,883, Bottari to Clément, 6 February 1754.

23. Quoted in Miller, *Portugal and Rome,* 48–49.

24. [Sebastião José de Carvalho e Melo,] *Relação abreviada da república que os religiosos das províncias de Portugal e Hespanha, estabelecerão nos dominios ultramarinos das duas monarchias, e da guerra, que neles tem movido, e sustentado contra os exercitos hespanholes, e portuguezes; e por outros documentos authenticos* (Lisbon: N.p., 1757). On this and the following pamphlets, see also Claude-Henri Frêches, "Pombal

et la compagnie de Jésus: La campagne des pamplets," in *Revista da Historia das Ideias* 4/1 (1982): 299–337; José Eduardo Franco, "Os catecismos antijesuitícos pombalinos: As obras fundatoras do antijesitismo do marquês de Pombal," in *Revista Lusófono de Ciécia das Religiões* 4/7–8 (2005): 247–68; and José Eduardo Franco and Christine Vogel, "Um acontecimento mediático na Europa das Luzes: A propaganda antijesuítica pombalina em Portugal e na Europa: Obras fundadoras," *Bróteria* 169/2–3 (2009): 349–506.

25. [Carvalho,] *Relação abreviada*, in *Collacção dos negocios de Roma no reinado de el-rey dom José I: Ministério de el-rey Dom José I, ministério de marquez de Pombal, pontificos de Benedicto XIV e Clemente XIII, 1758–1760* (Lisbon: Impressor Nacional, 1874), no. 4, 22–41, 22–23, 27–28.

26. Ibid., 27–28.

27. "Capítulos de Gabriel Soares de Sousa contra os Padres de Companhía de Jesus, que reside in Brasil," in Leita Serafim, ed., *Anais da Biblioteca nacionale de Rio de Janeiro*, vol. 62 (1941), 379.

28. Franco, *O Mito dos Jesuítas em Portugal*, 1:161–66.

29. *Histoire de la persécution de deux saints évêques par les jésuites: L'un Dom Bernardin de Cárdenas, évêque du Paraguai dans l'Amérique méridionale . . .* , in Antoine Arnauld, *Morale pratique des jésuites*, vol. 5 (N.p., 1691), in particular Juan de San Diego e Villalón, "Mémorial présenté au Roi d'Espagne le 26 de novembre 1652, par un religieux de Saint-François, pour la défense . . . de la personne . . . Dom Bernardin de Cardenas évêque de Paraguai," part 1, 21–129, esp. 117, 126; and the *Procès-verbal* by Cárdenas defending his expulsion of the Jesuits from the city of Asunción, part 5, 131–75, esp. 147. Comparable to the simultaneous conflict between Palafox and the Jesuits in New Spain, this one pitted the Jesuits not only against the secular authority of a bishop but also, since Cárdenas was a Franciscan, against the Franciscan Order at a time when the Portuguese revolt against Spain in 1640 rendered the authority of either colonial state exceptionally uncertain and fluid in South America.

30. Although she draws no hard connection such as argued here, it was Christine Vogel in *Der Untergang des Gesellschaft Jesu als europäisches Medienereignis*, 144–46, who alerted me to the existence of this earlier pamphlet in relation to the *Relação abreviada*.

31. *Mémoire touchant l'etablissement des pères jésuites dans les Indes d'Espagne, envoyés à Monseigneur de Pont-Chartrain, Ministre d'État*, said to have been published in Paris in 1710, although the earliest edition I can find is from 1712. But it is on no evidence that Fleche ("Pombal et la Compagnie de Jésus," 323) dates its publication only in 1758. On "despotism" and "absolute power," 26; on "slaves and deprivation of liberty," 11–12, 41, 43; on obedience, 8–9; on independence from and disobedience to Spain, 40, 43; on commerce, 11–12, 22–24; on military force, 27–32; on Guaraní language and quarantine from Spanish, 30–32.

32. Ibid.: on obedience, 8–9, 22; on mines, 7, 34–38.

33. Arnauld and du Cambout de Pontchâteau, *La morale pratique des jésuites*, 2nd ed., vol. 5: *Histoire de la persécution de deux saints évêques par les jésuites: L'un Dom*

Bernardin de Cárdenas, l'évêque du Paraguay dans l'Amérique merdionale; l'autre Dom Philippe Pardo, l'archévêque de Manille métropolitaine des Iles Philippines dans les Indes orientales (N.p., 1717), 502–17, esp. 510, 516.

34. *NE*, 2 January 1756, 4; and "Avertissement," *Mémoires touchant l'établissement des pères jésuites dans les Indes d'Espagne envoyés à Monseigneur de Pont-Chartrain, ministre d'état* (N.p., 1758).

35. The translated pamphlet appeared as *Relation abregée concernant la république que les religieux nommés jésuites, des provinces de Portugal & d'Espagne, ont établie dans les pays & domaines d'outremer de ces deux monarchies, & de la guerre qu'ils y ont excitée & soutenue contre les armées espagnoles & portugaises . . .* (Amsterdam: Aux dépens de la compagnie, 1758), in BPR, FLP, Ms. 1972=1.

36. Niccolò Guasti, "Niccolò Pagliarini, stampatore e traduttore al servizio del marchese di Pombal," *Cromohs* 12 (2007): 1–12.

37. [Joseph de Scabra de Silva,] *Deducção chronológica e analytica . . . na qual se manifesta, pela successive serie de cada um dos reinados da Monarchia Portugueza que decorrêrão desde o governo do Senhor rei D. João III, até o presente . . .* (Lisbon, 1767); part 1; and part 2: *Na qual se manifesta o que successivamente passou nas differentes epocas da Igreja sobre a censura, prohibição e impressão dos livros . . .* (Lisbon: Miguel Manescal da Costa, 1768). Like Carvalho's *Relação abreviada*, however, this history was not as indigenous as it might seem, even on such Portuguese terrain as that kingdom's sixty-year loss of independence to the Spain of Felip II and his successors after the heirless King Sebastião's disastrous and fatal decision to do battle against the Moors in Morocco in 1578. For the role of royal Jesuit confessors in Sebastião's North African crusade and his uncle Henriques's decision to favor Felip's claims of succession first took form as an incriminatory narrative in the barrister Antoine Arnauld's anti-Jesuit harangue in 1594 (*Plaidoyé . . . , en parlement, pour l'Université de Paris demanderesse: Contre les jésuites défendeurs, des 12 et 13 juillet 1594, in Les plaidoyers de M. Antoine Arnauld, avocat en parlement, contre les jésuites . . .* [N.p., 1716], 68–71), whereupon it received immediate amplification in Jacques-Auguste de Thou's widely read *Histoire universelle* (11 vols. [The Hague: Henri Schuleer, 1740, first published in 1604–1608], vol. 8; book 110, 475), as well as Arnauld's own often reprinted *Franc et véritable discours* in 1602 (*Le franc et véritable discours au roi, sur le rétablissement qui lui demandé pour les jésuites* [N.p., 1762, but published in this version in 1610], 77–78). This narrative subsequently hardened as a commonplace in French Gallican and Jansenist historiography until reappearing in Christophe Coudrette and Louis-Adrien Le Paige, *Histoire générale de la naissance et des progrès de la Compagnie de Jésus, avec analyse de ses constitutions et privilèges,* 4 vols. (N.p., 1761), 1:54–56, 138–44), in 1761. What Seabra de Silva did was to put on a great display of indigenous erudition in support of this narrative on the basis of source material and Portuguese histories of either the Jesuits or Portugal that, even when these histories made contact with each other, did not villainize the Jesuits. Listed in its "Introducção Previa" (ii–v), the *Deducção* does indeed acknowledge both Arnauld's *Plaidoyer* and de Thou's *Histoire* as well as Bonaventure Racine's ecclesiastical history and François Eudes de Mézeray's history of France.

38. Notably, *Lettre de l'abbé Platel, ci-devant le père Norbert, à un évêque de France, au sujet de l'exécution de Gabriel Malagrida* (N.p., [1761]; and *Lettre de l'abbé Platel à un de ses amis à Paris, contenant une relation exacte et circonstsaciée du P. Malagrida, jésuite* (N.p., [1761].

39. Christine Vogel, *Der Untergang des Gesellschaft Jesu als europäisches Medienereignis*, 54–55, 69–73, 93–100, 131–40.

40. *Nouvelles intéressantes au sujet de l'attentat commis le 3 septembre 1758 sur la personne sacrée de Sa Majesté très fidèle, le roi de Portugal* (N.p., 1759–1760), and reviewed in *NE*, 1759:6, 23 February, 25–26, 32; 6 March, 41–43; 3, 10, 17 April, 59–60, 61–63, 65–66; 1, 8 May, 73–77; 17 July, 117–18; 11 September, 149–152; 13 November, 185–88; 22 December, 201–3; and 1760:13 February, 32–33; 12 March, 45–48; 16 April, 80; 25 June, 118–20; 9 July, 127–28; 20 August, 50–52 ; 22 October, 187–88; 19 November, 201–2; 10 December, 215–16.

41. [Sebastião José de Carvalho e Melo,] *Erros impios e sediciosos, que os religiosos da Companhia de Jesus insinarão aos reos, que forão justiçados, e pertenderão espalhar nos povos destes reynos* (Lisbon: Miguel Rodrigues, n.d.). I have located a French translation of this document under the title of *Manifeste du roi de Portugal, contenant les erreurs impies et séditiceuses que les religieux de la Compagnie de Jésus ont enseignées aux criminels qui ont été punis, et qu'ils se sont efforcés de répandre parmi les peuples de ce royaume: Traduit du Portuguais: Avec d'autres pièces intéressantes sur le même sujet* (Lisbon : Miguel Rodriguez, Imprimerie de son Éminence Monseigneur le Cardinal Patriarche, n.d.), in BPR, FLP, Ms. 1972=5.

42. Ibid., 2, 7–9.

43. Ibid., 6, 13, 19–20, 29–31.

44. Attention to moral, theological, and regicidal issues occupies only five pages of 316 in Franco's section on pre-Pombalian Portuguese anti-Jesuitism in *O Mito dos Jesuítas em Portugal, no Brasil e no Oriente*, 1:287–92. I must therefore take exception to Franco's claim that Carvalho was the sole author of this coherent anti-Jesuitism, as spelled out in this book and stated in summary form in "L'antijésuitisme: Composition, fonctioinalités, et signification du mythe des Jésuites (De Pombal à la 1er République)," in Pierre Favre and Catherine Maire, eds., *Les antijésuites: Discours, figures et lieux de l'antijésuitisme à l'époque moderne* (Rennes: Presses Universitaires de Rennes, 2010), 353–81.

45. Étienne Pasquier, *Catéchisme des jésuites*, ed. Claude Souto (Sherbrooke, Quebec: University of Sherbrooke, 1982). "Que l'on ne peut excuser qu'il n'y ait de l'hérésie et du Machiavéllisme au vœu simple des Jésuites, " book 2, chapter 9.

46. BA, AB, Ms. 11,883, fols. 257–58, Bottari to Clément, 3 and 17 July 1761.

47. The most recent estimates, these numbers come from José Antonio Ferrer Benimeli, *Expulsión y extinción de los jesuitas (1759–1773)* (Bilbao: Ediciones Mensajero, 2013), 55–56, 93.

48. On the Concordat of 1753, Rávago's role in negotiating it, and its immediate and changing consequences both for the Spanish Jesuits and for Spain's relation to the papacy, see Rafael Olaechea, *Las relaciones hispano-romanas en la segunda mitad*

del siglo XVIII: La Agencia de Preces, 2 vols. (Saragossa: Talleres Editoriales "El Noticiero," 1965), 1:105–57.

49. On this tectonic shift, see Andrea Smidt, "'*Luces por la Fe*': The Cause of Catholic Enlightenment in 18th-Century Spain," in Ulrich Lehner and Michael Printy, eds., *A Companion to the Catholic Enlightenment in Europe* (Leiden: Brill, 2010), 425–28.

50. On Rávago and the Jesuit rebellion in Paraguay, see J. F. Alcaraz Gómez, *Jesuitas y Reformismo: El padre Francisco de Rávago (1747–1755)* (Valencia, Facultad de Teología San Vicente Ferrer, 1995).

51. Niccolò Guasti, *Lotta politica e riforme all'inizio del regno di Carlos III: Campomanes e l'espulsione dei gesuiti dalla monarchia spagnola (1759–1768)* (Florence: Alinea, 2006), 32–41.

52. Kratz, *El Tratado hispano-portugués de Límites de 1750 y sus consecuencias*, 179–213, esp. 197–205; and García Arenas, *Portugal y España: Las monarquías ibéricos y la Compañía de Jesús*, 139–51.

53. Arenas, *Portugal y España: Las monarquías ibéricos y la Compañía de Jesús*, 151–83; Kratz, *El Tratado hispano-portugués de Límites de 1750 y sus consecuencias*, 183–215.

54. Isidoro Pinedo Iparraguirre, *Manuel de Roda: Su pensiemento regalista* (Saragossa: Institucion Ferdinande el Catholico, 1983), 75, 118–21.

55. Ibid., 17–58.

56. Ibid., 71–78, 118, 127–32; on Vázquez, Ludwig von Pastor, *History of the Popes*, trans. E. F. Peeler, vols. 36–38 (London: Routledge and Kegan Paul, 1950–1952), 37:41–43, 88–90; and on Roda's stay in Rome, see also Olaechea, *Las relaciones hispano-romanas en la segunda mitad del siglo XVIII*, 1:273–308.

57. The preceding account is largely dependent on Guasti, *Lotta politica e riforme*, esp. 42–69, 84–85, 126, 199–201.

58. Bibliothèque de Saint-Sulpice, Correspondance Clément, Ms. 1289, fol. 99. Jean-François Le Blanc de Castillon to Clément, 29 July 1768, with a copy of a letter by Le Blanc de Castillon to Campomanes, undated.

59. Helpful introductory works on Spanish Jansenism are Émile Appolis, *Les Jansénistes espagnols* (Bordeaux: Sobodi, 1966); Joël Saugnieux, *Le jansénisme espagnol du XVIIIe siècle: Ses composantes et ses sources* (Oveido: Cátedra Feijoo, 1975); Maria G. Tomsich, *El giansenismo en España: Estudio sobre ideas religiosas en las segunda mitad del siglo XVIII* (Madrid: Siglo Veintiuno, 1972).

60. [Francois-Philippe Mésenguy,] *Esposizione sulla dottrina christiana*, 5 vols. (Naples: Simoniana, 1760).

61. Zeger-Berhard van Espen, *Commentariua in Canones juris veteris ac novi, & in Jus novissimum: Opus posthumum hactenus ineditum*, vols. 3 and 4 of *Jus ecclesiasticum universum antiquae et recentiori disciplinae praesertim Belgii, Galliae, Germaniae, & vicinarum provinciarum accommodatum*, . . . (Louvain, 1753); and Johann Nikolaus von Hontheim [Febronius], *De statu Ecclesiae et legitima potestate romani pontificis: Liber singularis, ad reuniendos dissidentes in religione christianos compositus* (Frankfurt am Main, 1765).

62. José Francisco de Isla, *Historia del famoso predicador Gerundio de Campazas alias Zotes* (Madrid, 1758).

63. On this tectonic shift, see Smidt, "'*Luces por la Fe*,'" 425–28.

64. Rafael Olaechea, "El anticolegialismo de gobiermo de Carlos III," in *Cuadernos de investigación: Geofrafia e Historia* 2/2 (1976): 53–90; María del Carmen Irles Vicente, "Tomismo y jesuitismo en los tribunals españoles en vísperas de la expulsion de la Compañia," in Enrique Giménez López, ed., *Expulsión y exilio de los jesuitas españoles* (Alicante: Universidad de Alicante, 1997), 41–63; and Guasti, *Lotta politica e riforme*, 63.

65. John Lynch, *Bourbon Spain, 1700–1808* (Oxford: Basil Blackwell, 1989), 281–82.

66. Pedro Rodríguez Campomanes, *Tratado de la regalia de amortización, en el qual se demuestra por la série de las varias edades, desde el nacimiento de la iglesia en todos los siglos y países católicos, el uso constante de la autoridad civil, para impedir las ilimitadas enagenaciones de bienes raíces en iglesias, comunidades, y otras manos-muertas* (Madrid: Imprenta de la Gazeta, 1765).

67. Guasti, *Lotta politica e riforme*, 91–127.

68. José Andrés-Gallego, *Por qué los Jesuitas: Razon y sinrazón de una decisión capital* (Madrid: Fundación Larramendi, 2005), 99–109.

69. Ibid., 109–12.

70. For a comprehensive account, S. M. Corona Gonzalez, *Un debate previo: Los dictámenes fiscales de Lope de Sierra y Campomanes sobre la admisión de jesuitas expulsos de Francia (1764)* (Madrid: Editorial Complutense, 1994).

71. Guasti, *Lotta politica e riforme*, 76–86; and Antonio Mestre Sanchis, "Reacciónes en España ante la Expulsión de los Jesuitas de Francia," in Giménez López, ed., *Expulsion y exilio de los jesuitas españoles*, 30–37.

72. Guasti, *Lotta politica e riforme*, 86–90.

73. Ibid., 138–43, 201–8. At issue was the clergy's nonpayment of that tax on land acquired by the church since the concordat of 1737.

74. José Andrés-Gallego, *El motín de Esquillace, America Europa* (Madrid: Fundacíon Mapfre-CSIC); and Pierre Vilar, *Hidalgos, amotinados y guerrilleros: Pueblo y poderes en la historia de España* (Barcelona: Critica Editorial, 1982), 93–140; and Laura Rodriguez, "The Spanish Riots of 1766," *Past and Present* 59 (May 1973): 117–46.

75. The preceding account is again dependent on Guasti, *Lotta politica e riforme all'inizio del regno di Carlos III*, esp. 129–80.

76. Andrés-Gallego, *Por qué los Jesuitas*, 43–45, 279–80; and Modesta Lafluenta, *Historia general de España, Edad moderna*, vol. 20 (Madrid: Establecimeto Typicgrafio de Méllardo, 1858), 214–19.

77. Aranda's initial assessment is reproduced in the appendix of Pastor, *History of the Popes*. 37:439–40.

78. Guasti, *Lotta politica e riforme all'inizio del regno di Carlos III*, 181–82.

79. Pinedo, *Manuel de Roda*, 87–96. For a strong case for Roda's largely hidden yet preponderant role in the framing the Jesuits as the authors of the riot, see in general 79–108, 132–49.

80. On the composition, nature, and work of this council, see Teófanes Egido and Isidoro Pinedo, *Las causas "gravísimas" y secretas de la expulsión de los jesuitas por*

Carlos III (Madrid: Fundación Universitaria Española, 1994), 36–37; Guasti, *Lotta politica e riforme*, 182–85; and Olaechea, *Las relaciones hispano-romanas en la segunda mitad del siglo XVIII*, 1:316–17.

81. Bernardo Tanucci, *Epistolario 17 (1766)*, ed. Maria Grazia Maiorini (Naples: Società Napoletana di Storia Patria, 2003), Tanucci to Losada, 9 September 1766, 440.

82. Egido and Pinedo, *Las causas "gravísimas" y secretas*, 34, 56. Instead of Eleta, whose role Guasti tends to emphasize, Egido and Pinedo (57, 61) place epistolary influence on Tanucci. That Eleta shared with the Jesuits an advocacy for the still contested doctrine of the Immaculate Conception suggests that his hostility toward the Society consisted in little more than his rivalry with it as a Francisan and his veneration of Palafox. On Eleta, see M. García García, "Fray Joachín de Eleta, oxomense, confessor real," *Celtiberia* 13 (2003): 123–36.

83. For example, Tanucci, *Epistolario 17 (1761–1762)*, Tannucci to Carlos, 22 April 1766, 140; to Losada, 29 April, 155; to Centomani, 10 May, 178; to Losada and Carlos, 24 June, 171–72; and to Losada, 26 August, 409.

84. Ibid., Tanucci to Centomani, 16 August 1766, 385.

85. Guasti, *Lotta politica e riforme*, 186–87, 196–97.

86. *Real cedula de su Magestad, en que declara nulo, de ningun valor, ni efecto el Decreto de Transacción expedido en el año de 1750, en el playto de diezmos con los colegios, y casas de la Compania de Jesus . . .* (Madrid: Impreste Real de la Gazeta, 4 December 1766).

87. Guasti, *Lotta politica e riforme*, 207; and Teófanes Egido López, "La expulsión de los jesuitas de España," in Ricardo Garcia-Villoslada, ed., *Historia de la Iglesia en España*, vol. 4, La *Iglesia en la España de los siglos XVII y XVIII* (Madrid: La Editorial Catolica, 1979), 772–76.

88. Guasti, *Lotta politica e riforme*, 202.

89. Andrés-Gallego, *Por qué los Jesuitas*, 54, 58, 139–40

90. Ibid., 40.

91. Egido López, "La expulsión de los jesuitas de España," 4:771; and Andrés-Gallego, *Por qué los Jesuitas*, 47. As transcribed by Gallego, the whole squib reads as follows: "[¿]Por qué lloras tan triste, Monarquía? / Con razón me lamento, [¡]oh suerte estraña! [*sic*] / porque veo a mi amada Compañía / con furor perseguida, encono y saña; / porque veo se aumenta la herejía / por Osma introducida en nuestra España; / y miro en el Señor Carloss Tercero, / un rey ateísta, un rey frailero. / . . . / . . . / De un intruso Monarca, y sin talento, / de un Osma sin conciencia, y un Roda tirano, / de un Esquilache injusto y avariento, / de un tributo anual napolitano, / de un Campomanes, [¡]oh fiscal cruento!, / [¿]cómo a España no libra excelsa mano; / Si España registrara sus anales, / con veneno quitara tantos males. / Cuando se ve la Iglesia perseguida, / o alguna de sus ramas despreciada, / es opinión de doctos muy seguida / si no basta prudencia moderada, / se puede con cautela prevenida / matar por una causa tan sagrada, / pues matar al tirano no es locura, / que es opinión probable, y muy segura."

92. Tanucci, *Epistolario 17 (1766)*, Tanucci to Losada, 15 July 1766, 320.

93. Andrés-Gallego, *Por qué los Jesuitas*, 124–25.

94. Guasti, *Lotta politica e riforme*, 214–15.

95. Egido and Pinedo, *Las causas "gravísimas" y secretas*, 70.

96. The following account is dependent on Andrés-Gallego, *Por qué los jesuitas*, 126–29, 139–40.

97. Ibid., 121, 140; and Enrique Gimenez López, "El antijesuitismo en la España de mediados del siglo XVIII," in Pablo Fernandez Albaladejo, ed., *Fenix de España: Moderdad y cultura propria en la España del siglo XVIII (1737–1766)* (Madrid: Marcial Pons, Ediciones de Historia, 2006), 311.

98. Egido and Pinedo, *Las causas "gravísimas" y secretas*, 68–69.

99. Tanucci, *Epistolario* 17 (1766), Tanuccci to Azara, 6 September 1766, 432. Tanucci's doubts lasted into October, as evident in his letter to Centomani, 4 October 482.

100. Pastor, *History of the Popes*, 37:74–85.

101. Guasti, *Lotta politica e riforme*, 216–20. For the full text of the *alegación*, see D. Manuel Danvila y Collado, *Reinado de Carlos III*, 6 vols. (Madrid: El Progresso Editorial, 1890–1895), 3:128–32.

102. Pedro Rodríguez Campomanes, *Dictamen fiscal de expulsión de los Jesuitas de España (1766–1767)*, ed. Jorge Cejudo López and Teófanes Egido López (Madrid: Fundación Universitaria Española, 1977. On the circumstances of the discovery and publication of the *Dictamen*, see the "Introduccion," 6–7; and Teófanes Egido and Isidoro Pinedo, *Las causas "gravissimus" y secretas*, 22–23.

103. Egido López, "La expulsión de los jesuitas de España," 4:762.

104. Egido and Pinedo, *Las causas "gravísimas" y secretas*, 24–25.

105. Guasti, *Lotta politica e riforme*, 84–85.

106. Campomanes, *Dictamen fiscal de expulsión de los Jesuitas de España*, 86, 109, 155, 168.

107. Ibid., 142

108. Ibid., 60, 155

109. Egido López, "La expulsión de los jesuitas de España," 4:765–67, 788.

110. Egido and Pinedo, *Las causas "gravísimas" y secretas*, 37–63.

111. José Antonio Ferrer Benimeli, *Expulsión y extinctión de los jesuitas (1759–1773)* (Bilbao: Mensajero, 2013), 68–70; and Egido and Pinedo, *Las causas "gravísimas" y secretas*, 37–63.

112. *Pragmatica sanción de Su Magestad en fuerza de Ley para el estrãnamiento de estos reynos á los regulares de la Compañia, ocupación de sus temporalidades, y prohibición de su restablecimiento in tiempo alguno, con las demás precauciones que expresa* (Madrid: Impreste Real de la Gazeta, 1767). On the dates of signing and execution, see Egido López, "La expulsion de los jesuitas de España," 750–51; Ferrer Benimeli, *Expulsión y extinctión de los jesuitas (1759–1773)*, 68–69.

113. Egido López, "La expulsión de los jesuitas de España," 4:755; Ferrer Benimeli, *Expulsión y extinción de los jesuitas (1759–1773)*, 93–94.

114. Egido López ("La expulsión de los jesuitas de España," 4:764–65) tends to minimize the religious content of the stated motivation for the expulsion. The point

stressed here is that the clinching argument mobilized to justify the need for expelling the whole society from Spain bore an incontestably ecclesiastical and religious pedigree, and was essential to the Spanish case.

115. AAE, CP, France, Ms. 448, fols. 321–22, Ossun to Choiseul, 13 April 1767.

116. Ibid., Ms. 438, Ossun to Choiseul in diplomatic code, 21 May 1767.

117. Ibid., Ms. 347, Choiseul to Ossun, 21 April 1767.

118. Ibid., Choiseul to Ossun, 21 April 1767.

119. Gordon Wood, "'Conspiracy and the Paranoid Style: Causality and Deceit in the Eighteenth Century," *William and Mary Quarterly*, 3rd series, 39/3 (July 1982), 401–41.

120. AAE, CP, France, Ms. 549, fols. 296–300, 433, Ossun to Choiseul, St. Ildefonse, 31 August and 28 September 1767.

121. *Rapport judiciaire du procès criminel instruit à la poursuite et diligence de l'Illustrissime Seigneur D. Pedro Rodriguez Campomanes, procureur général du Conseil de Castille, en exécution de l'arrêt du 21 décembre 1766* (Madrid: Joachin de Ibarra, 1768; et se trouve à Paris, chez P.-G. Simon, Imprimeur du Parlememt, rue de la Harpe), in BPR, FLP, 1136=14. Based on this publicized procedure, coverage of this case also found space in the *NE*, 6–13 June 1768, 89–96. See also AAE, CP, France, Ms. 550, fols. 161ff., Ossun to Choiseul, Escurial, 26 October 1767.

122. Christophe de Beaumot du Repaire, *Instruction pastorale . . . sur les atteintes données à l'autorité de l'église par les jugemens des tribunaux séculiers dans l'affaire des jésuites* (Paris: N.p., 1763).

123. *Rapport judiciaire*, 76–79.

124. *Consulta del Consejo extraorinario de Castilla, al Rey en vista del breve del papa con fecha de 30 abril 1767* (Madrid: N.p., 1767). For the purposes of this chapter, I am consulting a copy with an accompanying French translation (making it easy to check the accuracy of the translation), in *Ve suite des pièces concernant les jésuites d'Espagne* (Madrid, et se trouve à Paris: Antoine Boudet, 1767), in BPR, FLP 1136, fol. 11. The French translation is entitled *Rapport du Conseil extraordinaire de Castille, pour le roi, sur la lettre du pape à Sa Majesté*. For Clement XIII's letter to the king, see *NE*, 22 June 1767, 101–2.

125. *Rapport du Conseil extraordinaire de Castille*, 30–34.

126. Ibid., 6–11; Campomanes, *Dictamen fiscal de expulsión de los jesuitas de España*, 159. On Roda, Egido and Pinedo, *Las causas "gravísimas" y secretas*, 62.

127. BPR, FLP, Ms. 1136=2, p. 20: "On a répandu dans le public une traduction de cette sanction pragmatique imprimée sans permission et sans nom d'imprimeur, et contre le privilège de la Gazette de France. Cette traduction est désastreuse en plusieurs endroits, et paraît avoir été imprimée sur une copie très incertaine. On a réformé celle-ci sur celle de la Gazette."

128. Jean-Charles Augustin Clément du Tremblay, *Journal de correspondances et voyages d'Italie et d'Espagne pour la paix de l'Église en 1758, 1768 et 1769 par M. Clément, alors trésorier de l'église d'Auxerre, et depuis évêque de Versailles*, 3 vols. (Paris: Languet, 1802), vol. 2.

5. NAPLES, PARMA, AND THE BOURBON FAMILY PACT

1. Bibliothèque de l'Arsenal (henceforth BA), Ms. 11,883, fol. 164, Bottari to Clément, 21 March 1759.
2. Ibid., Ms. 11,882, fol. 192, Bottari to Clément, 29 [April] 1767. The month of April has been arrived at on internal textual evidence, by the location of this letter vis-à-vis the others, and by eliminating all other alternatives.
3. *Discours d'un de messieurs de grand' chambre au parlement, toutes les chambres assemblées. Du mecredi 29 avril 1767*, in Gilbert de Voisins, ed., *Nouvelles pièces pour servir de complément à la procédure contre les jésuites* (Paris: Librairie française et étrangère, 1824), 32, 50.
4. Ibid., 52, and further reported in NE, 1 June 1767, 89.
5. *Arrêt de la cour du parlement du Paris, du 9 mai 1767* (Paris: P.-G. Simon, 1767).
6. AAE, CP, Spain, Ms. 548, fols. 404–7, Choiseul to the marquis d'Ossun, Marly, 11 May 1767. For Chauvelin's speech of 29 April and the text of the Parlement of Paris's *arrêt* of 9 May, BnF, Collection Joly de Fleury, Ms. 1611, fols. 111–14, 148–53; and NE, 18 May 1767, 84.
7. BA, Ms. 11,882, fol. 200, Lambert to Clément, 12 May 1767.
8. AAE, CP, Spain, Ms. 548, fols. 404–5, Choiseul to d'Ossun, 11 May 1767.
9. Ibid., fols. 404–7, Choiseul to d'Ossun, Marly, 11 May 1767.
10. Ibid., Ms. 549, fol. 203, 4 July 1767.
11. Ibid., fol. 120, d'Ossun to Choiseul, Madrid, 7 July 1767. See Enrique Giménez López, "La expulsión de los jesuitas como problema de estado," *Anales de la Real Sociedad Económica de Amigos del País* (1997–1998), 251, n. 9; Mar García Arenas, *Portugal y España contra los jesuitas: Las monarquias ibéricas y la Compañía de Jesús* (Madrid: Centro de Estudios politícos y constitucionales, 2014), 328–42, 355–62.
12. AAE, CP, Spain, Ms. 548, fols. 404–07, Choiseul to d'Ossun, Marly, 11 May 1767; and Ms. 549, fols. 21–22, same to same, 8 June 1767.
13. Ibid., 449: on the tactic of waiting for a new pontificate, fols. 59–61, Choiseul to d'Ossun, 16 June 1767; and on waiting for Carlos III to order the expulsion in Naples and Parma, ibid., fols. 443–45, d'Ossun to Choiseul, 28 September 1767.
14. Ludwig von Pastor, *History of the Popes*, trans. E. F. Peeler, vols. 36–38 (London: Routledge and Kegan Paul, 1950–1952), 37:320–21.
15. Enrique Giménez López, "'La extirpación de la mala doctrina': Los inicios del proceso de extinción de la compañia de Jesús (1767–1769)," in Enrique Giménez López, ed., *Expulsión y exilio de los jesuitas españoles* (Alicante: Universidad de Alicante, 1997), 234–42.
16. Ibid., 242–45.
17. The full text may be found in D. Manuel Danvila y Collado, *Reinado de Carlos III*, 6 vols. (Madrid: El Progresso editorial, 1890–1895), 3:appendix, doc. 7, 638–65.
18. Teófanes Egido and Isidoro Pinedo, *Las causas "gravísimas" y secretas de la expulsión de los jesuitas por Carlos III* (Madrid: Fundación Universitaria Española, 1994), 100–102, 122, 154.

19. Giménez López, "'La extirpación de la mala doctrina,'" 245–50.

20. AAE, CP, Spain, Ms. 549, fols. 21–22, Choiseul to d'Ossun, 8 June 1767; and fols. 396–97; d'Ossun to Choiseul, St. Ildefonse, 21 September 1767.

21. Domenico Ambrasi, "Aspetti della vita sociale e religiose di Napoli tra il 1759 e il 1776 attraverso le lettere di Bernardo Tanucci a Carlo III," in *Riformatori e ribelli a Napoli nella seconda metà del settecento* (Naples: Regina, 1979), 16–17.

22. Ambrasi, "L'expulsione dei gesuiti dal regno di Napoli nelle lettere di Bernardo Tanucci," in ibid., 65–75.

23. Ambrasi, "Conseni di Napoli ai dissidenti di Utrecht," in ibid., 125–27, 151–52.

24. Francesco Renda, *L'espulsione dei gesuiti dalle Due Sicilie* (Palermo: Sellerio, 1993), 50–63.

25. Ambrasi, "L'expulsione dei gesuiti dal regno di Napoli," 70–72, 74.

26. Ibid.

27. Ibid., 75–77. In his *History of the Popes* (37:231, 236), Pastor insists that the assenting churchmen were not formally members of the Giunta but rather were later prevailed upon for their assent to its decision with the aim of calming the young Ferdinand's remaining qualms.

28. Tanucci's text may be found in Danvila y Collado, *Reinado de Carlos III*, 3:120–21. See also José Antonio Ferrer Benimeli, *Expulsión y extinción de los jesuitas, 1759–1773* (Bilbao: Mensajero, 2013), 111–12.

29. Ferrer Benimeli, *Expulsión y extinción de los jesuitas*, 111–12.

30. Ambrasi, "L'expulsione dei gesuiti dal regno di Napoli," 80–84.

31. Ibid., 84–85. I wish here to acknowledge the help of Niccolo Guasti in sorting through and reconciling the apparently contradictory information in the works heretofore cited by Ambrasi, Renda, and Pastor.

32. Pastor, *History of the Popes*, 37:226–31; and AAE, CP, Spain, Ms. 550, fols. 417, 435, Choiseul to d'Ossun, 8 December 1767; and d'Ossun to Choiseul, 21 December 1767.

33. Renda, *L'espulsione dei gesuiti dalle Due Sicilie*, 80.

34. Pastor, *History of the Popes*, 37:259–64.

35. Giovanni Gonzi, *L'espulsione dei gesuiti dal ducato parmensi (Febraio, 1768)* (Parma: Edizione di "Avrea Parma," 1967), 29–30; and Paciàudi to Francesco Berta, 17 November 1767, in Pietro Stella, ed., *Il giansenismo in Italia: collezione di documenti. Piemonte*, vol. 1 in 3 parts (Zürich: PAS-Verlag, 1966–1974), 1/2 (1970):63–64.

36. Ibid., 12–16, 45–49, and for quotation, "appendice," 105–7. On Paciaudi's connections with the Archetto, see the review of Leonardo Farinelli, ed., *Paciaudi e i suoi corrispondenti* (Parma: Biblioteca Palatina, 1985), in *Rassegna storica del Risorgimento*, 74 (1987): 229–30, which asserts that while in Rome, Pacciaudi "aveva frequentato assiduamente il circolo filogiansenista del Bottari e del card. Passionei." It is true that in his "La mente del P. Paciaudi, collaboratore di un ministro nell'età delle Riforme" (*Miscellanea di studi storici in onore di Giovanni Sforza* [Lucca: Baroni, 1920]), 425–58, Umberto Benassi pares down Pacciaudi's "philo-Jansenism" to an anti-Jesuitical Thomism. But aside from the consideration that even *Unigenitus*—rejecting French Jansenists—took cover under Thomistic orthodoxy, some of Benassi's evidence (451–58) comes from utterances after the proto-consevative reaction in

Parma that sent Du Tillot into exile and put Pacciaudi on the defensive against accusations of the "heresies" Lutheranism, Huguenotism, and of course Jansenism.
Umberto Benassi, "La mente del P. Paciaudi, collaboratore di un ministro nell'età
delle Riforme," in *Miscellanea di studi storici in onore di Giovanni Sforza* (Lucca:
Baroni, 1920), 425–58.

37. For texts, see George Frederic de Martens, ed., *Recueil des principaux traités
d'alliance de paix, de trêve, de neutralité, de commerce, de limites, d'échange . . .* , 6
vols. (Göttingen: Dieterich, 1791–1801), 6:84–104.

38. For the texts of this and previous measures, ibid., 6:84–104.

39. AAE, CP, Spain, Ms. 551, fols. 199–201, "copie d'une lettre de M. le duc de Choiseul
à M. le marquis de Grimaldi," Versailles, 19 February 1768; and fol. 230–31, Choiseul to d'Ossun, 23 February 1768.

40. Ibid., Ms. 553, fol. 62, Choiseul to d'Ossun, 19 July 1768.

41. *Real provision, de los señores del Consejo de Su Magestad, para recoger a mano real
todes los exemplares impressos o manuscritos de cierto Monitorio, que parece haberse
expedito en 30 de enero de este año en la Corta Romana contra el ministerio de
Parma . . .* (Madrid: Don Antonio Sanz, Impressor del Rey, 1768) in AAE, CP, Spain,
Ms. 551, fols. 382–88.

42. The two measures are the *Real cedula de Su Magestad, y señores del Consejo, to-
canta à la forma que se debe observer en quanto à las prohibiciones de libros, publi-
cación de edictos de la Inquisicióon, y execucion de bulas, concernientes al Santo
oficio . . .* (Madrid: Sanz, 1768); and *Pragmatica sanción, par la qual S. M. restablece
la diez y ocho de enero de mil setecientos sesenta, y dos, en punto a la pevia precent-
ación de bulas, breves, y despachos de la corta de Roma en el Consejo . . .* (Madrid:
Sanz, 1768), both in AAE, CP, Spain, Ms. 552, fols. 353–60.

43. AAE, CP, Spain, Ms. 552, fols. 400–401, d'Ossun to Choiseul, 22 June 1768; and
Choiseul to d'Ossun, Ms. 553, fols. 23–24, 5 July 1768.

44. Egido and Pinedo, *Las causas "gravísimas" y secretas*, 122.

45. AAE, CP, Spain, Ms. 552, fols. 335–36, d'Ossun to Choiseul, 13 June 1768; and fol.
422, Choiseul to d'Ossun, 27 June 1768.

46. Ibid., Ms. 553, fols. 63–64, Choiseul to d'Ossun, 19 July 1768.

47. Ibid., Ms. 552, Choiseul to d'Ossun, 21 June 1768, fol. 395; and d'Ossun to Choiseul,
27 June 1768, fol. 414. See also Egido and Pinedo, *Las causas "gravísimas" y secretas*,
117–18.

48. AAE, CP, Spain, Ms. 553, fols. 103–4, 112–14, 119, d'Ossun to Choiseul, 1 August
1768.

49. Ibid., Choiseul to d'Ossun, 29 August 1768, fol. 400.

50. For full text, see Danvila y Collado, *Reinado de Carlos III*, 3: appendix, doc. 8,
666–72.

51. Giménez López, "'La extirpación de la mala doctrina,'" 251–55.

52. Ibid., 251.

53. The five were J. J. Rodríguez de Arellano, archbishop of Burgos; J. Sáenz de Buru-
aga, archbishop of Saragossa; J. Molina Larios, bishop of Albarracín; J. Tormo, bishop
of Orihuela; and J. Laplana, bishop of Tarazona.

54. AAE, CP, Spain, Ms. 554, fols. 186–89; and "Copie d'une lettre du 5 décembre [1768] de M. du marquis de Grimaldi à M. le comte de Fuentes, " 5 December 1768, ibid., fols. 204–5.

55. Antonio Ferrer Del Rio, *Historia del reinado de Carlos III en España*, 6 vols. (Madrid: Matuta, 1856), 2:250–52.

56. AAE, CP, Spain, Ms. 554, fols. 270–71, Choiseul to d'Ossun, 27 December 1768.

57. Ibid.

58. Pastor, *History of the Popes*, 36:350–55; and Augustin Theiner, *Histoire du pontificat de Clément XIV d'après des documents inédits des archives secrètes du Vatican*, 2 vols. (Paris: Firmin Didot, 1852), 1:140–47.

59. AAE, CP, Spain, Ms. 551, fols. 362–63, d'Ossun to Choiseul, 16 March 1768.

60. Suplemento à la *Gázeta de Madrid* del martes 15 diciembre de 1767, in AAE, CP, Spain, Ms. 551, fols. 440–41.

61. Pedro Rodriguez Campomanes, *Juicio imparcial sobre las letras en forma de breve, que ha publicado la curia romana, en que se intentan derogar ciertos edictos del serenísimo señor infante duque de Parma, y disputarle la soberanía temporal con este pretexto* (Madrid: Joachin de Ibarra, 1769). Even the historian Teófanes Egido López, who has denied the "myth" that "enlightened" regalism under Carlos III marked any sharp departure from Old Regime Spanish regalism, concedes that this treatise puts Campomanes in a category by himself that displays "foreign" and specifically French influence. See his "El regalismo y relaciones Iglesia-Estado en el siglo XVIII," in Ricardo Garcia-Villoslada, ed., *Historia de la Iglesia en España*, vol. 4, *La Iglesia en la España de los siglos XVII y XVIII* (Madrid: La Editorial Catolica, 1979), 126–41, 153–58.

    The citations that follow are from a French translation published in two volumes the following year entitled *Jugement impartial des lettres en forme de bref, que publie la curie Romaine . . .* trans. Nicolas-Gabriel Vaquette d'Hermilly, 2 vols. (Madrid, 1770). I have used the French translation for the sake of convenience, but not without checking it against the Spanish.

62. Based on the fact that the Spanish edition contains an "advertencia" about the treatise's subjection to censorship, while the French edition does not, the hope that the French edition represented a translation of the first uncensored Spanish edition did not survive a careful comparison between the French and Spanish versions of the treatise's most controversial utterances. Claiming to have seen the censored edition, however, the *NE*'s reviewer of the *Jucio imparcial* (NE, 27 March 1781, 51–52) deemed the differences between the censored and uncensored editions to be minor.

63. *Jugement impartial*, 1:378.

64. Ibid., 1:22–23, 66–74; 2:64–65. On the eighteenth-century Spanish quest for the lost Visigothic church councils and constitution, see Antonio Mestre Sanchis, "La imagen de la iglesia visigoda en la mentalidad de los ilustrados españoles: El caso de Mayans y Compomanes," in *Homenaje al Dr. Antonio Bethencourt Massieu* (Las Palmas: Cabildo Insular de Gran Canaria, 1995), 586–745n.; and Richard Herr, *The Eighteenth-Century Revolution in Spain* (Princeton: Princeton University Press, 1958), 414–34.

65. *Jugement impartial*, 2:76–77.

66. Ibid., on infallibility, 1:383–85; on Constance and Basel, 1:82–83, 103–4; on Richer and Febronius, 1:17; on superiority of the universal church, 1:16–27, 103–5, 368, 383–85; on church as assembly of the faithful, 1:211; on role of faithful in the collation of benefices, 1:313.

67. Ibid., on "aristocratic" constitution of the church, 1:10; on condemnation of papal "despotism" and absolute power, 1:293, 314; on need of laws for universal consent, 1:230; 2:23–24, 26–29; and on assemblies of the nation, 1:69–72.

68. Ibid., on Jesuits, 2:66 and in general 65–69; and on Torrigiani, 2:12.

69. Frédéric Masson, *Le cardinal de Bernis depuis son ministère, 1758–1794* (Paris: Plon, Nourrit, 1884), 88, n. 2.

70. Egido and Pinedo, *Las causas "gravísimas" y secretas*, 125–26.

71. Andrea J. Smidt, "Fiestas and Fervor: Religious Life and Catholic Enlightenment in the Diocese of Barcelona, 1766–177," Ph.D. dissertation, Ohio State University, 2006, 94–130.

72. BSS, FC, Ms. 1289, October 1768, fol. 54.

73. Ferrer Benimeli, *Expulsión y extinción de los jesuitas*, 250–52.

74. Bernardo Tanucci, *Epistolario 10 (1761–1762)*, ed. M. G. Maioini (Rome: Istituto Poligrafico e Zecca dello Stato, 1988), Tanucci to Bottari, 24 October 1761, 238–39.

75. Theiner, *Histoire du pontificat de Clément XIV*, 1:197.

76. Garcia Arenas, *Portugal y España contra los jesuitas*, 399–400.

77. Ibid., 194, 233–35. Although few historians have followed Theiner in emphasizing the Albanni-Rezzonico rivalry to anything like the same degree, no one has invalided his basic observation either.

78. Luigi Berra, "Il diario del conclave di Clemente XIV del cardinal Filippo Maria Pirelli," in *Archivio della Società Romani di Storia Patria*, vols. 85–86, 3rd series, 16–17 (Rome: Società alla biblioteca Vallicellina, 1962–1963), 69–73, 177–225.

79. Theiner, *Histoire du pontificat de Clément XIV*, 1:191.

80. Ibid., 78; Pastor, *History of the Popes*, 38:69, 71, 78–80.

81. In spite of Filippo Corali's assertion to the contrary, Pirelli's diary contains no evidence that Ganganelli ever told anyone that he was voting against Stoppani because Stoppani would suppress the Jesuits. See Filippo Coralli, "La vita del P. Lorenzo Ricci generale della Compagnia di Gesù: Biografia inedita del P. Tomasso Termanini S.J. Transcritione e note di F. Coralli," in *Archivium Storicae Pontificae*, 44 (2006), 79.

82. Berra, "Il diario del . . . cardinal Filippo Maria Pirelli," 303, 315.

83. Egido and Pinedo, *Las causas "gravísimas" y secretas*, 131–47.

84. Masson, *Le cardinal de Bernis depuis son ministère*, 106. But most of the evidence belies the claim by Bernis, echoed by Masson (108–11), that his was the decisive role in the election of Ganganelli, since Choiseul never opposed his candidacy.

85. Ibid., 114–16.

86. AAE, CP, Spain, Ms. 557, fols. 158–59, d'Ossun to Choiseul, 27 July 1769; and fol. 210, Fuentes to Choiseul, 1 August 1769.

87. Bernis began complaining about these influences in a dispatch to Choiseul dated 4 July 1770 and thereafter (ibid., Rome, Ms. 853, fols. 17–19).

88. Pastor, *History of the Popes*, 38:95–101.

89. Ibid., 169; and AAE, CP, Rome, Ms. 853, fols. 204–5, Bernis to Choiseul, 5 September 1770.

90. Danvila y Collado, *Reinado de Carlos III*, 3:363; and Ferrer Del Rio, *Historia del reinado de Carlos III en España*, 2:304–5. Danvilly y Collado's reference is to "Carta de Grimaldi a Azpuru," 25 July 1769, Archivio General de Simancas, Estado, Legajo 5.036.

91. Masson, *Le cardinal de Bernis depuis son ministère, 1758–1794*, 154.

92. Danvila y Collado, *Reinado de Carlos III*, 3:428–31. See also Ferrer Benimeli, *Expulsión y extinción de los jesuitas*, 274–79. On Roda's order, see ibid., 164; Pastor, *History of the Popes*, 38 :165, 174–75; and Theiner, *Histoire du pontificat de Clément XIV*, 545–47.

93. AAE, CP, Spain, Ms. 558, fols. 81–83, d'Ossun to Choiseul, undated.

94. Masson, *Le cardinal de Bernis depuis son ministère*, 162–63; Pastor, *History of the Popes*, 38:169, 175–181.

95. Theiner, *Histoire du pontificat de Clément XIV*, 1:543. For the text of Bernis's memoir, see Ferrer Benimeli, *Expulsión y extinción de los jesuitas*, 284–86.

96. AAE, CP, Rome, Ms. 853, fol. 8, Choiseul to Bernis, 3 July 1770; and fol. 204, Bernis to Choiseul, 5 September 1770. See also Theiner, *Histoire du pontificat de Clément XIV*, 1:549–50.

97. AAE, CP, Rome, Ms. 853, fols. 179–83, Bernis to Choiseul, 29 August 1770.

98. Danvila y Collado, *Reinado de Carlos III*, 3:421–22. The references are to "Carta de Clement XIV a Carlos III," 28 June 1770, Archivio General de Simancas, Estado, Legajo, 5.037; and "Carta de Carlos III á Clement XIV," 17 July 1770, ibid.

99. Theiner, *Histoire du pontificat de Clément XIV*, 1:356. On Choiseul's attempt to stamp out Bernis's fixation on secret negotiations, Masson, *Le cardinal de Bernis depuis son ministère*, 156.

100. Masson, *Le cardinal de Bernis depuis son ministère*, 156; and Theiner, *Histoire du pontificat de Clément XIV*, 1:338–39.

101. Masson, *Le cardinal de Bernis depuis son ministère*, 174–75.

102. *Déclaration du roi, portant rappel des prêtres décrétés ou bannis. Donné à Marly le 15 juin 1771. Registré au Parlement le 19 juin 1771*, in BPR, CLP, Ms. 570, fol. 262. See also Mathieu-François Pidansat de Mairobert, *Journal historique de la révolution operée dans la constitution de la monarchie françoise, par M. de Maupeou, chancelier de France* (London, 1775), 27 June 1771, 1:373; and Hardy, "Mes loisirs," BnF, Mss. Fr., Ms. 6681, 6 September 1772, 94.

103. On the subject of the sacrament-refusing behavior of these priests in Paris, including Madier, see Dale K. Van Kley, "The Religious Origins of the Patriot and Ministerial Parties in Pre-Revolutionary France," in Thomas Kselman, ed., *Belief in History: Innovative Approaches to European and American Religion* (Notre Dame: University of Notre Dame Press, 1991), 203–10.

104. AAE, CP, Spain, Ms. 565, fol. 281, "Extrait d'une lettre de M. de Grimaldi à M. le comte de Fuentes," 29 July 1771. See also ibid., fols, 292–93, Grimaldi to Fuentes, 21 October 1771.

105. *Lettres patentes du roi, portant qu'il sera sursis à l'exécution de l'arrêt du Parlement de Paris, du 26 février 1768, concernant les bulles, brefs et autres expéditions de la cour de Rome. Donné à Versailles le 18 janvier 1772. Registré en parlement le 22 Janvier 1772* (Paris: P.-G. Simon, 1772), in BnF, Anisson-Duperron 41, Mss. Fr. 22101, fols. 166–67.

106. On Molinist clerical opinion, see [Pidansat de Mairobert,] *Journal historique*, 5 February 1772, 3:302–3. On Clement XIV, AAE, CP, Rome, Ms. 854, fols. 122–24, Bernis to d'Aiguillon, 19 February 1772.

107. *Déclaration du Roi, concernant les bulles, brefs, rescrits et autres expéditions venant de la cour de Rome. Données à Versailles le 8 mars 1772. Registrées en parlement le 30 dédits mois et an* (Paris: Imprimerie royale, 1772), in BnF, Anisson-Duperron, Mss. Fr. 22101, fols. 171–72.

108. AAE, CP, Spain, Ms. 565, fols. 356–58, "Extrait d'une lettre de M. de Grimaldi à M. le comte de Fuentes," 28 April 1772.

109. For example, ibid., fols. 301–1, Fuentes to Grimaldi, 11 September 1771; fols. 302–5, Fuentes to Grimaldi, 11 November 1771; and fols. 309–10, Grimaldi to Fuentes, 23 November 1771.

110. Masson, *Le cardinal de Bernis depuis son ministère*, 176; and AAE, CP, Rome, 5 February 1771, Ms. 854, fol. 47, Bernis to Saint-Florentin, 5 February 1771.

111. Masson, *Le cardinal de Bernis depuis son ministère*, 177; and AAE, CP, Rome, Ms. 854, fol. 35, "Copie du billet de M. le cardinal de Bernis à M. le cardinal d'Orsini et à M. de Valence."

112. AAE, CP, Rome, Ms. 854, fol. 132, Saint-Florentin to Bernis, 19 March 1771.

113. Ibid., fols. 137–38, Saint-Florentin, 26 March 1771.

114. Ibid., Ms. 855, fol. 87, Bernis to Saint-Florentin, 29 May 1771.

115. Ibid., Ms. 856, fols. 83–84, Bernis to d'Aiguillon, 7 August 1771; and Masson, *Le cardinal de Bernis depuis son ministère*, 193–95.

116. Ibid., Ms. 857, fols. 162–63, Bernis to d'Aiguillon, 14 December 1771.

117. Ibid., Ms. 854, fol. 193, Bernis to Saint Florentin, 24 April 1771.

118. Ibid., Ms. 855, fol. 11, Bernis to Saint-Florentin, 1 May 1771; and Ms. 855, fol. 34, Saint-Florentin to Bernis, 11 May.

119. Ibid., Ms. 854, fols. 85–86, Saint-Florentin to Bernis, 26 February 1771.

120. Ibid., Ms. 854, fol. 133, Saint-Florentin to Bernis, 19 March 1771; and fols. 197–98, Bernis to Saint-Florentin, 24 April 1771.

121. Ibid., Ms. 856, fol. 50, d'Aiguillon to Bernis, 19 August 1771.

122. Ibid., Ms. 858, fols. 103–5, Bernis to d'Aiguillon, 12 February 1772.

123. Ibid., Ms. 857, fol. 59, Bernis to d'Aiguillon, 13 November 1771; and fols. 107–8, Bernis to d'Aiguillon, 27 November 1771.

124. Ibid., fols. 198–200, Bernis to d'Aiguillon, 25 December 1771; Ms. 858, fol. 4, Bernis to d'Aiguillon, 1 January 1772; fols. 45–46, d'Aiguillon to Bernis, 21 January 1772; and fols. 79–80, same to same, 4 February 1772.

125. Ibid., Ms. 858, fols. 90–93, Bernis to d'Aiguillon, 5 February 1772.

126. Ibid., Bernis to d'Aiguillon, 12 February 1772.

127. Ibid., fols. 169–70, d'Aiguillon to Bernis, 10 March 1772.
128. That this was in fact the pope's plan is strongly suggested by Clement XIV's words to José Moñino as recorded by Moñino in his account to Grimaldi of his most recent audience with the pope in late September 1772. "Ainsi," reportedly said the pope, "on les dépouillera (toujours en parlant des Jésuites) aujourd'hui d'une chose, demain d'un autre et par dégrés nous viendrons à la conclusion." See ibid., Spain, Ms 567, fol. 245, translation of a letter from Moñino to Grimaldi, 24 September 1772.
129. Ibid., Ms. 858, CP, Rome, fol. 313, Bernis to d'Aiguillon, 15 April 1772.
130. Ibid., fol. 346, Bernis to d'Aiguillon, 29 April 1772.
131. Theiner, *Histoire du pontificat de Clément XIV*, 2:235.
132. According to Bernis (AAE, CP, Rome, Ms. 858, fols. 221–24, Bernis to d'Aiguillon, 25 March 1772), "Le pape m'a confié sous le secret que dans une des dernières lettres qu'il a reçues du Roi d'Espagne, Sa Majesté Catholique assuroit la Sainte Père qu'il n'autorisera plus ses ministres à la tourmenter par des instances trop pressantes sur l'affaire de l'extinction de la société. Cela revient parfaitement aux conjectures que vous formiez à cet égard dans une de vos dernières lettres."
133. AAE, CP, Spain, Ms. 565, fols. 374–76, "Traduction d'une lettre à Grimaldi a Fuentes," 18 May 1772. The copies of Carlos III's exchanges with the pope are contained in fols. 358–72. The copies of Carlos III's exchanges with the pope in the AAE do not contain anything about the king's plans for the Jesuits, but it is possible that d'Aiguillon removed these from the rest for Louis XV's perusal and never reunited them with the others.
134. Ibid., fols. 400, 405–6, translations of letters from Fuentes to Grimaldi, 6 and 12 June 1772.
135. Ibid., fol. 410, translation of a letter from Grimaldi to Fuentes, 22 June 1772; in Conde de Floridablanca, *Cartas desde Roma para la extinción de los jesuitas: Correspondencia julio 1772–septiembre 1774*, ed. Enrique Giménez López (Alicante: Universidad de Alicante, 2009), Moñino to Grimaldi, Rome, 9 July 1772, 79–89.
136. AAE, CP, Spain, Ms. 565, fols. 445–45, Magallón to Grimaldi, 18 September 1772.
137. Ibid., fol. 446–58, Magallón to Grimaldi, 12 October 1772.
138. Ibid., Ms. 567, fols. 198–200, Carlos III to Louis XV, San Ildefonso, 21 September 1772; and fol. 286, Louis XV to Carlos III, Versailles, 3 October 1772. See also Danvila y Collado, *Reinado de Carlos III*, 3:476, 482, 485. For portions of the texts of the two letters, see Masson, *Le cardinal de Bernis depuis son ministère*, 210.
139. AAE, CP, Spain, Ms. 565, fols. 467–68, Grimaldi to Magallón, 26 October 1772,
140. Masson, *Le cardinal de Bernis depuis son ministère*, 251–52, n. 2.
141. Ibid., in general, 258–62. In his introduction to the volume of Moñino's diplomatic correspondence (*Cartas desde Roma para la extinción de los jesuitas*, 12–13), Enrique Giménez López curiously glides over Moñino's own lucid analysis of the evidence of Bernis's past duplicity, as does every other historian of this diplomacy.
142. Moñino to Grimaldi, Rome, 6 July 1772, in Floridablanca, *Cartas desde Roma para la extinción de los jesuitas*, 79–89.
143. Moñino to Grimaldi, Rome, 23 July 1772, in ibid., 102–7, 110.

144. Moñino to Grimaldi, Rome, 27 August, 3, 10 September 1772, in ibid., 149–50, 163, 171–73.

145. Ibid., 175–201; Pastor, *History of the Popes*, 38:217–92; Enrique Pacheco de Leyva, "La intervención de Floridablanca en la redacción del breve para la supresión de los jesuitas (1772–1773)," *Escuela española de arquelogía e historia en Roma: Cuadernos de trabajos 3* (1915): 37–198 ; Theiner, *Histoire du pontificat de Clément XIV*, 2:199–268, 322–79; Rafael Olaechea, *Las relaciones hispano-romanas en la segunda mitad del XVIII.: La agencia de preces* (Saragossa: El Noticiero, 1965); Enrique Giménez López, *Floridablanca y la extinción de los Jesuitas* (Murcia: Universidad de Murcia, 2008) ; Niccolò Guasti, "Clemente XIV e la diplomazia Borbonica: La Genese del breve di soppressione della compagnia de Gesù," in Mario Rosa and Marina Colonna, eds., *L'età di papa Clemente XIV: Religione, politica, cultura* (Rome: Bulzioni, 2010), 29–77.

146. The cardinal members were Marefoschi as president, plus Antonio Casali, Carafa, Andrea Corsini, and Zelada.

6. THE END OF THE JESUITS AND THE POLARIZATION OF CATHOLIC EUROPE

1. Rafael Olaechea, *Las relaciones hispano-romanas en la segunda mitad dell XVIII*, 2 vols. (Saragossa: Institución "Fernando el Catolico" and Asociación Española de Historia Moderna, 1999), 1:237–336, 363–96. Also, "la influencia de Febronio," 1:363–80.

2. Ibid., Ms 1291, fol. 373, Micheli to Clément, 5 May 1773.

3. Ibid., Ms 1290, fol. 126, Clément to Roda, 22 September 1770.

4. For example, on 3 September 1772. See Conde de Floridablanca, *Cartas desde Roma para la extinctión de los jesuitas: Correspondencia julio 1772–septiembre 1774*, ed. Enrique Giménez Lopez (Alicante: Universidad de Alicante, 2009), Moñino to Grimaldi, 162–63.

5. Ibid., fols. 132–36, "Mémoire pour le M. le duc de Choiseul en janvier 1769, demandé par M. Lambert."

6. On the subject of Tanucci's ecclesiastical thought, see José Andres-Gallego, *Por qué los Jesuitas: Razon y sinrazón de una decisión capital* (Madrid: Fundación Larramendi, 2005), 59–70; and Mario Rosa, "Religione e politica ecclesiastica attraverso l'epistolario di Bernardo Tanucci," in *Bernardo Tanucci e la Toscana: Tre giornata di studio: Pisa-Stia 28–30 settembre 1983* (Florence: Olschki, 1986), 31–54.

7. Bernardo Tanucci, *Epistolario 10 (1761–1762)*, ed. M. G. Maiorini (Rome: Istituto Poligrafico e Zecca dello Stato, 1988), Tanucci to Galiani, 27 February 1762, 572.

8. Ibid, Tanucci to Wall, 5 January 1762, 429.

9. Ibid., Tanucci to Caracciola, 5 September 1761, 83.

10. Ibid., *Epistolario 9 (1760–1761)*, ed. M. G. Maiorini (Rome: Edizioni di storia e letteratura, 1985). Tanucci to Bottari, 9 May 1761, 633.

11. Tanucci, *Epistolario 10 (1761–1762)*, Tanucci to Wall, 13 October 1761, 205–6.

12. On papal "despotism," ibid., Tanucci to Caraccioli, 31 December 1761, 253; on "blind obedience," to Pignatelli, 29 September 1761, 161. .

13. Ibid., Tanucci to Centomani, 19 December 1761, 378.

14. AAE, CP, Rome, Ms. 853, fol. 360, Bernis to Choiseul, 14 November 1770.

15. Dale K. Van Kley, "From the Catholic Enlightenment to the Risorgimento: The Exchange between Nicola Spedalieri and Pietro Tamburini, 1791–1797," *Past and Present* 223/2 (August 2014): 121–33, 149–51.

16. NE, 24–31 January 1769, 13–20.

17. AAE, CP, Spain, Ms 551, fols. 321–33, Ossun to Choiseul, 14 March 1768.

18. Eric Cochrane, *Florence in the Forgotten Centuries 1527–1800: A History of Florence and the Florentines in the Age of the Grand Dukes* (Chicago: University of Chicago Press, 1973), 354–67.

19. Dino Carponetto and Giuseppe Ricuperati, *Italy in the Age of Reason, 1685–1789*, trans. Caroline Higgitt (London: Longman, 1987), 218.

20. Reginaldo Tanzini, "Prefazione," in *Istoria dell'assemblea degli arcivescovi e vescovi della Toscana* (Lugano: Agnelli, 1793), 25–26, 29, 30, 37. In *Atti dell'assemblea degli arcivescovi e vescovi della Toscana tenuta in Firenze nell' anno 1787*, 7 vols. in 12 (Lugano: Agnelli, 1787–1793), consulted in the Bodleian Library, University of Oxford, Soc. 1190. e. 77. This preface contains a convenient summary of all of the grand duke's reformist orders and recommendations before 1787.

21. On Ricci's contacts with Bottari and the Archeto, see Scipione de' Ricci, *Memorie di Scipione de' Ricci, vescovo di Prato e Pistoia, scritte da lui medesimo, e pubblicate con documenti*, ed. Agenore Gelli, 2 vols. (Florence: Felice Le Monnier, 1863–65), 1:7–8; and on the Synod of Pistoia's proclamation of the four Gallican articles, "Decreto delle fede e della chiesa," in *Atti e decreti del concilio diocesano di Pistoia dell'anno 1786*, ed. Pietro Stella, 2 vols. (Florence: Olschki, 1986), 2:81–83.

22. *Punti ecclesiastici compilati e trasmessi da S.A.R. a tutti gli arcivescovi e vescovi della Toscana e loro respettive risposte*, 2nd ed. (Lugano: Agnelli, 1791), part 1, 54, 24, in *Atti dell' assemblea degli arcivescovi e vescovi della Toscana tenuta in Firenze nell' anno 1787*.

23. Ibid., no. 39, 20; and no. 33, 17.

24. Ibid., no. 57, 25–27.

25. The reference is to Eamon Duffy, *The Stripping of the Altars: Traditional Religion in England, c. 1400–c. 1580* (New Haven: Yale University Press, 2005).

26. Timothy C. W. Blanning, *Reform and Revolution in Mainz, 1743–1803* (Cambridge: Cambridge University Press, 1974), 176, 207–9.

27. *Atti e decreti del concilio diocesano di Pistoia dell' anno 1786*, ed. Pietro Stella, ristampa dell'edizione Bracali, 3 vols. (Florence: Olschki, 1986), sessione 3, "Decreto della fede e della Chiesa" and "Decreto della grazia, della predestinazione, e dei fondamenti della morale," and sessione 4, "Decreto della penitenzia," 2:75–83, 84–96, 141–57.

28. Ibid., sessione 6, "Supplica da umiliarsi a Sua Altezza Reale," and " Promemoria relativa agli sponsali, agl' impedimenti matrimoniali &c.," 2:221–24.

29. *Protocollo delle deliberazioni fatte degli arcivescovi e vescovi della Toscana sui diversi articoli preposti da S. A. R. Reale al loro esame* (Lugano: Agnelli, 1789), sessione 18, 30 May 1787, 180; in *Atti dell'assemblea degli arcivescovi e vescovi della Toscana*.

30. Tanzini, *Istoria dell'assemblea degli arcivescovi e vescovi della Toscana*, 284–88, in *Atti dell'assemblea degli arcivescovi e vescovi della Toscana*.

31. For a nuanced treatment of all the protagonists and motives at work, see Carlo Fantappie, *Riforme ecclesiastiche e resistenze sociali* (Bologna: Molino, 1986).

32. HUA, 215, Ms. 3394, Astorri to Mouton, 20 June 1790.

33. The German bibliography on Austrian absolutism, Jansenism, and Josephism is staggering and cannot be cited here, except for Peter Hersche's authoritation *Der Spätjansenismus in Österreich* (Vienna: Österreichischen Akademie der Wissenschaften, 1977). Suffice it to say that in English I have most heavily relied on Derek Beales, *Joseph II*, 2 vols. (Cambridge: Cambridge University Press, 1987–2009); T. C. W. Blanning, *Joseph II* (London: Longman, 1994); David Sorkin, *The Religious Enlightenment: Protestants, Jews, and Catholics from London to Vienna* (Princeton: Princeton University Press, 2008), 217–59; Franz A. Szabo, *Kaunitz and Enlightened Absolutism, 1753–1780* (Cambridge: Cambridge University Press, 1994); and Reginald Ward, "Late Jansenism and the Habsburgs," in James E. Bradley and Dale K. Van Kley, *Religion and Politics in Enlightenment Europe* (Notre Dame: Notre Dame University Press, 2001), 154–86

34. Although indebted to Hersche's *Der Spätjansenismus in Österreich* (45–101, 243–338), the periodization here is different from Hersche's in that it concerns the tempo of Catholic reform rather than the Jansenist movement in particular.

35. HUA, 215, Ms. 2344-2, Le Plat to Dupac de Bellegarde, 10 December 1786.

36. Samuel J. Miller, "A Belated Conversion from Jurisdictionalism to Jansenism, Josse Le Plat, 1732–1810," *Proceedings of the American Philosophical Society*, 4/131 (1987): 412. See also Pius VI, *Super Soliditate*, dated 28 November 1786, in Gérard Pelletier, ed., "Recueil des principaux brefs du pape Pie VI," "La théologie et la politique du Saint-Siège devant la Rèvolution française (1789–99)," (Université de Paris, Sorbonne IV and Institut Catholique de Paris: thèse de doctorat, December 2000), 3:789–96.

37. Jan Roegiers, "Un janséniste devant la Révolution: les avatars de Josse Le Plat de 1787 â 1803," in F. Stevens and E. Van den Auweele, eds., *Houd voet bij stuk : Xenia jurishistoriae G. van Dievoet oblate* (Louvain: KU Leuven Kulak, 1990), 75–103.

38. HUA, 215, Ms. 2344-2, Le Plat to Dupac de Bellegarde, 31 June and 10 August 1787, 22 December 1788.

39. Ibid., 22 June and 25 July 1787; 2, 18 August 1788.

40. Roegiers, "Un janséniste devant la Révolution," 95. Le Plat's defense of the Acts of the Synod of Pistoia is entitled *Lettres d'un théologien canoniste à N. S. P. le pape Pie VI.: Au sujet de la bulle Auctorem Fidei*, 2 vols. (Brussels: Hayez, 1796).

41. HUA, 215, Ms. 2344-2, Le Plat to Dupac de Bellegarde, 10 August 1787. See also ibid., Le Plat to Dupac, 30 June 1787.

42. On the bishop of Antwerp, see ibid., Le Plat to Dupac, Brussels, 30 March 1789.

43. HUA, OKN, R86-1, Ms. 166, Ricci to the archbishop of Utrecht, 7 October 1790. Several months later Ricci similarly wrote to Mouton in Utrecht, "[L']insubordination, le libertinage, et le défaut de l'instruction sont les fruits amers d'une révolution que Rome a ou excitée ou au moins fomentée," see ibid., 215, Ms. 3553, Ricci to Mouton, 10 May 1791.

44. HUA, 215, Ms. 2344-2: on ex-Jesuits and Feller, see ibid., Ms. 2344-2, Le Plat to Dupac de Bellegarde, 25 July, 5 September, 29 October, 17 November, 7 December 1787; 2 August, 22 December 1788. On bishops, ibid., same to same, 12 November 1786, 18 February and, 9 April 1787; 27 January 1788, 2 February 1789; and on Franckenberg in particular, 19 November 1786, 20 October 1788, 2, 30 March, 13 April 1789. On Franckenberg's pastoral instruction, see "Révolte du clergé belge contre Joseph II et motifs donnés au pape (mars 1790)," in Bernard Plongeron, *Théologie et politique* (Geneva: Droz, 1975), "documents, " 336–37.

45. Giovanni Marchetti, *Annotazione pacifiche di un paroco cartholico à monsignor vescovo di Prato e Pistoia sopra la sua lettera pastorale de' 5 ottobre 1787 al clero, e populo della città e diocesi di Prato*, new ed. (N.p., 1788), 19, 60–62, 72–76, 102. The phrase "innovazione scandalose" is on p. 84. For Ricci's immediate reaction to Marchetti's pamphlet, see HUA, 215, Ms. 2489, fol. 227, Ricci to Dupac de Bellegarde, 6 June 1787.

46. HUA, OKN, R86-1, Ms. 166, Ricci to the archbishop of Utrecht, 7 October 1790.

47. Pietro Domenico Giovannoni, "Gli orientamenti culturali e politici di Antonio Martini tra il 1750 ed il 1769 nelle lettere ad Antonio Niccolini," in Daniele Menozzi, *Antonio Baldovinetti e il reformismo religioso Toscano del settecento: Atti dei seminario di marti, 30 settembre 2000* (Rome: Edizioni di Storia e Letteratura, 2002), 39–80, esp. 49–55.

48. Elisabeth Kovács, *Ultramontanismus und Staatskirchtum im theresianisch-josephinischen Staat* (Vienna: Wiener Dom, 1975), 23–25, 139–42.

49. NE, 2 August 1762, 123–24; 5 September 1774, 144, and 11 December 1775, 200; and 24 April 1783, 68.

50. On Portugal and the Jesuits, BA, Ms. 4987, fol. 60, Della Lanze to Clément, 31 August 1759; and Pietro Stella, *Il giansenismo in Italia: collezione di documenti, Piemonte*, vol. 1 in 3 parts (Zürich: PAS-Verlag, 1966–1974), 1/1 (1966):242, 247–48, Delle Lanze to Bottari, 2 January and 6 February 1760; and on Delle Lanze's conversion, ibid., 509, Gaspare Nizzia to Marolde du Coudray, Turin, 30 May 1767.

51. Dries Vanysacker, *Ca rdinal Giuseppe Garampi (1725–1792): An Enlightened Ultramontane* (Brussels: Institut Historique de Rome, 1995), 54–76.

52. Ibid., 77–136.

53. Ibid., 109–10, 152, 159, 161–62, 165–69, 188.

54. Ibid., 149.

55. BSS, FC, Ms. 1291, fol. 115, Foggini to Clément, 15 December 1773.

56. HUA, 215, Ms. 2375, Giacomo Massa to Dupac de Bellegarde, 18 April 1776.

57. Ibid., Ms. 3435, Dupac to Jean-Baptiste Mouton, 17 April and 12 May 1776.

58. Ibid., Ms. 2207-2, Clément to Dupac, 23 October 1776.

59. On the transformation in general, see Maria Rosa, *Riformatori e ribelli nel '700 religioso italiano* (Bari: Dedalo, 1969).

60. Full ultramontanist titles are the *Giornale ecclesiastico di Roma* and *Religions-Journal, oder Auszüge aus den letzten alten und neuen Schriftstellern und Vertheidigern der Christlichen Religionen mit Anmerkungen.*

61. *Ibid.*, Ms. 2556, Francisco Vásquez to Dupac, 28 May 1775.

62. Giuseppe Pignatelli, *Aspetti della propaganda cattolica a Roma da Pio VI a Leone XII* (Rome: Ist. per la storia del Risorgimento italiano, 1974).

63. Gérard Pelletier, *Rome et la Révolution française: La théologie et la politique du Saint-Siège devant la Révolution française (1789–1799)* (Rome: École française de Rome, 2004), 334–72.

64. Pius VI, *Super Soliditate*, in Gérard Pelletier, ed., "Recueil des principaux brefs du pape Pie VI," 789–96.

65. John McManners, *Church and Society in Eighteenth-Century France*, 2 vols. (Oxford: Clarendon, 1998), vol. 1: *The Clerical Establishment and Its Social Ramifications*, 607–14; Bernard Plongeron, *La vie quotidienne du clergé français au XVIIIe siècle* (Paris: Hachette, 1974), 157–62; and in general Pierre Chevalier, *Loménie de Brienne et l'ordre monastique, 1766–1789*, 2 vols. (Paris: J. Vrin, 1959–1960).

66. Plongeron, *La vie quotidienne du clergé français*, 16.

67. [Henri-Philippe de Chauvelin,] *Réplique aux apologies des jésuites*, 3 vols. in 1 (N.p., 1761–1762), 3:52.

68. Claudio Maddalena, *Le regole del príncipe: Fisco, clero, riforme a Parma e Piacenza (1756–1771)* (Milan: Franco Angeli, 2008).

69. Mathieu-François Pidansat de Mairobert, *Journal historique sur la révolution opérée dans la constitution de la monarchie française, par M. de Maupeou, chancelier de France*, 7 vols. (London, 1774–1776), "du 20 janvier 1772," 2:288–89.

70. Dale K. Van Kley, "The Religious Origins of the Patriot and Ministerial Parties in Pre-Revolutionary France," in Thomas Kselman, ed., *Belief in History: Innovative Approaches to European and American Religion* (Notre Dame: Notre Dame University Press, 1991), 189–95.

71. *Ibid.*, 195–203.

72. [Louis-Adrien Le Paige,] *Lettres historiques sur les fonctions essentielles du parlememt, sur le droit des pairs, et sur les loix fondamentales du royaume*, 2 vols. (Amsterdam, 1753–1754).

73. *Ibid.*, 178–89.

74. The phrase comes from a pamphlet entitled *Lettre de Monsieur Xxx, conseiller au parlement, à M. le comte de Xxx* (N.p., 1771), 11–12. All textual and extratextual indications point to Le Paige's authorship of this pamphlet.

75. *Requête des États-généraux de France au roi* (London, 1772). All indications again point to the authorship of Le Paige.

76. *Maximes du droit public françois, tirées des capitulaires, des ordonnances du royaume, et des autres monumens de l'histoire de France* (Amsterdam: Rey, 1772 and 1775), most especially "Dissertation sur le droit de convoquer des États-généraux," appended to the end of the first volume of the 1775 edition of the *Maximes*, particularly 17–18. On what might be called "conciliar constitutionalism," see Dale Van Kley, "The Estates General as Ecumenical Council: The Constitutionalism of Corporate Consensus and the *Parlement*'s Ruling of September 25, 1788," *Journal of Modern History* 61/1 (March 1989): 1–52.

77. Besides Mey and Maultrot, the authors of the *Maximes* are thought to be Gaston-Armand Camus and Pierre Olivier Pinault—parlementary barristers, Gallicans, and Jansenists all. For another discussion of this work, see Dale Van Kley, "The Jansenist Legacy in the French Prerevolution, 1750–1789," in *Historical Refections/ Réflexions historiques* 13/2–3 (Fall–Summer 1986): 436–38.

78. [Jean-Baptiste Target,] *Lettre d'un homme à un autre homme* (N.p., n.d.); [Jacques-Matthieu Augéard,] *Correspondance secrète et familière de M. de Maupeou avec M. de Sorhouet, conseiller au nouveau parlement*, in *Les efforts de la liberté et du patrio-tisme contre le despotisme du Sr de Maupeou, chancelier de France, ou Recueil des écrits patriotiques publiés pour maintenir l'ancien gouvernement françois*, 6 vols. (London, 1775), 2:32, 62–63, 95–96; and Mairobert, *Journal historique*, 17 June 1771, 1:280–81.

79. On the subject of this "third" party, see Durand Echeverria, *The Maupeou Revolu-tion: A Study in the History of Liberarianism* (Baton Rouge: Louisiana State Univer-sity Press, 1985). My only quibble with the book's thesis is that this third political option did not yet constitute a "party" comparable either to the "patriots" or to Mau-poeu's hired pamphleteers, consisting as it did of mainly uncoordinated reflections of scattered individuals.

80. BPR, FLP, Ms. 928, fol. 6, handwritten reaction of Le Paige to an assertion in his copy of the second part of Pierre-Jean Agier's *Le jurisconsulte national*.

81. Giulio M. Manetti, "Una costituzione liberale (Il projetto costituzionale di Pietro Leopoldo)," in *Rassegna Storico Toscana* 30/2 (July–December 1984): 149–63.

82. On the concept of a "managed" revolution, see Keith M. Baker, "A Script for a French Revolution: The Political Consciousness of the Abbé Mably," in *Inventing the French Revolution: Essays on French Political Culture in the Eighteenth Century* (Cambridge: Cambridge University Press, 1990), 86–106.

83. Dale K. Van Kley, *The Religious Origins of the French Revolution: From Calvin to the Civil Constitution of the Clergy* (New Haven: Yale University Press, 1996).

84. T. C. W. Blanning, *Reform and Revolution in Mainz, 1743–1803* (Cambridge: Cam-bridge University Press, 1974), 177–78, 220–28, 236–40; and Heinrich Aloys Arnoldi, *Tagbuch über die zu Ems gehaltene Zuzammenkunft der vier Erzbischoflichen deutschen Deputirten die Beschwerde des deutschen Nazion gegen des römishchen Stuhl und sonstige geistliche betr. 1786*, ed. Matthias Höhler (Mainz: von Kirch-heim, 1915).

85. On Jansenists and civil toleration of Protestants, see Jeffrey Merrick, *The Desacral-ization of the French Monarchy in the Eighteenth Century* (Baton Rouge: Louisiana State University Press, 1990), 135–64; and articles of Charles H. O'Brien, "Jansenists on Civil Toleration in Mid-Eighteenth-Century France," *Theologische Zeitschrift* 37 (1981): 71–93; "Jansenists on Civil Toleration of Protestants in France, 1775–1778: Lepaige, Guidi, and Robert de Saint-Vincent," in Roland Crahay, ed., *La tolérance civile: Colloque internationale* (Brussels: Editions de l'Université de Bruxelles, 1982); "The Jansenist Campaign for Toleration of Protestants in Eighteenth-Century France: Sacred or Secular?" *Journal of the History of Ideas* 46 (1985): 523–38: and "New Light on the Mouton-Natoire Case ((1786): Freedom of Conscience and the Role of the Jansenists," *Journal of Church and State* 27 (1985): 65–82.

86. David Bien, "Every Shoemaker an *Officier:* Terray as Reformer," in Rafe Blaufarb, Michael S. Christopherson, and Darrin McMahon, eds., *Interpreting the Ancien Régime* (Oxford: Voltaire Foundation, 2014), 135–42.

87. David Bien, "Offices, Corps, and a System of State Credit: The Uses of Privilege under the Ancien Regime," in Keith Baker, ed., *The Political Culture of the Old Regime* (Oxford: Pergamon Press, 1987), 87–114.

88. Jeffrey Burson, *The Rise and Fall of Theological Enlightenment: Jean-Martin de Prades and the Ideological Polarization of Eighteenth-Century France* (Notre Dame: Notre Dame University Press, 2010), 239–309.

89. Louis Petit de Bachaumont, *Mémoires secrets pour server à l'histoire de la république des lettres en France, depuis MDCCLXII jusqu'à nos jours, ou journal d'un observateur . . .* , 36 vols. (London: John Adamson, 1781–1789), 1:3–4.

90. Jean Le Rond d'Alembert, *Sur la destruction des jésuites en France, par un auteur désintéressé* (N.p., 1765), 192.

91. David Avrom Bell, *Lawyers and Citizens: The Making of a Politial Elite in Old Regime France* (Oxford: Oxford University Press, 1994); and Sarah Maza, *Private Lives and Public Affairs: The Causes Célèbres of Prerevolutionary France* (Berkeley: University of California Press, 1993); Nicolas Lyon-Caen, *La boîte à Perette: Le jansénisme parisien au XVIIIe siècle* (Paris: Albin Michel, 2010), 508–24.

92. Van Kley, *The Religious Origins of the French Revolution*, 290–302.

93. Dale K. Van Kley, "Pure Politics in Absolute Space: The English Angle in the Political History of Prerevolutionary France," *Journal of Modern History* 69/4 (December 1997): 773, 783.

94. On what the Parlement meant by the forms of 1614, see Van Kley, "The Estates General as Ecumenical Council."

95. For an account of these events, I persist in a dialectical version, as in Dale Van Kley, "From the Lessons of French History to Truths for Times and Places: The Historical Origins of an Anti-Historical Declaration," in Van Kley, ed., *The French Idea of Freedom: The Old Regime and the Declaration of Rights of 1789* (Stanford: Stanford University Press, 1994), 72–113.

96. Dale K. Van Kley, "The Ancien Régime, Catholic Europe, and the Revolution's Religious Schism, 1789–1801," in Peter McPhee, ed., *The Wiley-Blackwell Companion to the French Revolution* (Oxford: Blackwell, 2013), 138–39.

97. Albert Mathiez, *Rome et le clergé français sous la Constituente: La Constitution civile du clergé, l'affaire d'Avignon* (Paris: Armand Colin, 1911), 428–33, 483–94.

98. José Nicolás de Azara, *El espiritu de D. José Nicolás de Azara, describierto en su correspondencia epistolar con Don Manuel de Roda*, 3 vols. (Madrid: J. Martin Alegria, 1846), 2:4 June 1772, 305–6; 24 December 1772, 367–68; 11 February 1773, 384–85.

AFTERWORD AS FAST-FORWARD

1. For a full statement of the argument that follows, see Dale K. Van Kley, "The Ancien Régime, Catholic Europe, and the Revolution's Religious Schism, 1789–1801," in Peter McPhee, ed., *The Wiley-Blackwell Companion to the French Revolution* (Oxford: Blackwell, 2013), 123–44.

2. And for a fuller statement of the following argument, Dale K. Van Kley, "Christianity as Casualty and Chrysalis of Modernity: The Problem of Dechristianization in the French Revolution," in *American Historical Review* 108/4 (October 2003): 1081–1104.

3. Nicola Spedialieri Siciliano, *De' diritti dell' uomo libri VI, ne' quali si dimonstra, che la più custode de' medisimi nella società civile e la religione cristiana; e che però l'unico progetto utile alle presenti circonstanze e di far riforire essa religione* (Assisi: Con licenza de' superiori, 1791), 420.

4. HUA, 215, Ms. 3569, F. Scheidel to Jean-Baptiste Mouton, 18 June 1798.

5. On the Society's restorations, see most recently Robert A. Markys and Jonathan Wright, eds., *Jesuit Survival and Restoration: A Global History, 1773–1900* (Leiden: Brill, 2015), and Jeffrey D. Burson and Jonathan Wright, eds., *The Jesuit Suppression in Global Context: Causes, Events, and Consequences* (Cambridge: Cambridge University Press, 2015), 248–77.

6. On this subject, see Gary Wills, "Jesuits Admirable and Execrable," a review of recent scholarly literature in the *New York Review of Books* 64/2 (9 February 2017): 39–41.